D0502091

RIPPER

THE SECRET LIFE OF WALTER SICKERT

ALSO BY PATRICIA CORNWELL

RIPPER

THE SECRET LIFE OF WALTER SICKERT

PATRICIA CORNWELL

THOMAS & MERCER

Published by Thomas & Mercer, Seattle

www.apub.com

Amazon, the Amazon logo, and Thomas & Mercer are trademarks of Amazon.com, Inc.,
or its affiliates.

ISBN-13: 9781503936874
ISBN-10: 1503936872

Jacket design by Jason Blackburn
Cover design by Tyler Freidenrich

Printed in the United States of America

First edition

To my partner, Staci Gruber—

whose earliest images of glorious England

thanks to me are Kew.

CONTENTS

There was a general panic, a great many excitable people declaring that the evil one was revisiting the earth.

—*H.M., anonymous East End missionary, 1888*

1

MR. NOBODY

MONDAY, AUGUST 6, 1888, was a bank holiday, and London was a carnival of wondrous things to do for as little as pennies if one could spare a few. The bells of Windsor's Parish Church and St. George's Chapel rang all day. Ships were dressed in flags. Royal salutes boomed from cannons to celebrate the Duke of Edinburgh's forty-fourth birthday. The Crystal Palace dazzled with every entertainment imaginable.

There were organ recitals, military band concerts, a monster display of fireworks, a grand fairy ballet, ventriloquists, world-famous minstrel performances, and horse and cattle shows. Madame Tussaud's titillated with a special wax model of Frederick II lying in state and of course the ever-popular Chamber of Horrors. *Dr. Jekyll and Mr. Hyde* was playing to sold-out houses, and the famous American actor Richard Mansfield was brilliant in the starring dual role at Henry Irving's Lyceum Theatre. The Opera Comique also had its version, a scandalous one because Robert Louis Stevenson's novella had been adapted without permission.

Bazaars in Covent Garden overflowed with Sheffield Plate, gold, jewelry, and a vast variety of weapons and used clothing including military uniforms. If one wanted to pretend to be a soldier on this festive day, he could do so with little expense and no questions asked. That just might have appealed to a gifted impersonator like Walter Richard Sickert, a former actor whose stage name was Mr. Nemo. *Nemo* is Latin for "nobody."

Twenty-eight-year-old Sickert had given up the theater for art and was a student of the American master James McNeill Whistler. At this time in Sickert's life he was an apprentice struggling for independence and his own place in the art world. He couldn't make a living. He'd been married three years, and his wife supported him as women always would. He was known for his striking good looks.

James McNeill Whistler was an American-born artist and proponent of "art for art's sake." Sickert was a student of and assistant to the master until 1888.

Walter Sickert at almost twenty years old. During this time, he was likely touring as an actor.

During what by now is a fifteen-year investigation into the Jack the Ripper case, I've been able to find few early photographs of Sickert. But one taken when he was twenty shows a chiseled face with a perfectly angled nose and jaw, and thick wavy hair. He was blond with penetrating blue eyes, his features flawless and sensual except for his mouth. People who knew him described it as cruel.

He was slender, with a strong upper body from swimming, and considered a little above average in height. In those days that was about five foot seven for a man. Several pairs of his painting coveralls donated to the Tate Archive in the 1980s suggest he could have been as tall as five foot eight or nine. But it depends on whether he wore his pant legs short or long. That could make the difference of an inch or two. A caricature or doodle Whistler apparently dashed off of him in 1885 depicts Sickert as rail thin, long legged, slouching, loudly and cheaply dressed and predominantly right-handed.

Such details would become important when witnesses described men last seen with Jack the Ripper's victims. But as I will explain later, the women he murdered were seen with many men on streets that had very poor lighting, and the Ripper was resourceful. I believe he was a chameleon. He could change his appearance including the color of his hair, his height and weight when he wanted to blend with his environment. That's what disguises are for, and Sickert was fond of them onstage and off.

He was a master of greasepaint and wardrobe. As a child he was capable of completely transforming himself into someone else, usually a

A quick sketch of Sickert apparently made by Whistler in 1885 shows Sickert as a tall, thin man, slouching and possibly right-handed.

decrepit elderly man. In a letter Sickert wrote in 1880 to historian and biographer T. E. Pemberton, he described playing an "old man" in *Henry V* while on tour in Birmingham: "It is the part I like best of all." He constantly changed his appearance with a variety of beards and mustaches. He was known for his bizarre hairstyles and clothing that in some instances were so outlandish they looked like costumes.

When the mood struck, he might shave his head or change his name. Onstage he was Mr. Nemo. In published articles and letters and in signatures on his art he was An Enthusiast, A Whistlerite, Your Art Critic, An Outsider, Walter Sickert, Sickert, Walter R. Sickert, Richard Sickert, W. R. Sickert, W.S., R.S., S., D., Dick, W. St., Rd. Sickert LL.D., R.St.W., R.St. A.R.A., and RdSt A.R.A.

He was a "Proteus," wrote French artist and friend Jacques-Émile Blanche. Sickert's "genius for camouflage in dress, in the fashion of wearing his hair, and in his manner of speaking rival Fregoli's." Sickert was described as having a great range of voice. He was proficient if not fluent in German, English, French and Italian. He knew Latin well enough to teach it to friends, and he was adept at Danish and Greek and possibly knew Portuguese and Spanish.

Such details were of interest when a team of scientists and I examined the only physical evidence that remains in the Ripper case, the hundreds of mockingly violent letters locked in the vaults of The National Archives and the London Metropolitan Archives. Not all of the letters the Ripper allegedly wrote to the media and the police are in English. They are rife with artistic media and drawings. The handwriting wildly varies. Much of it is obviously disguised.

Sickert was a skilled draftsman. He could write his name backward in cursive. He could write in perfect copperplate script or calligraphy or illegibly or any way he wanted. He may have been ambidextrous. It's said that he liked to read the classics in their original languages, but he didn't always finish a book once he started it. Usually there were dozens of them scattered about, opened to the last page that had caught his interest. Not much did unless it somehow affected him. Walter Sickert was center stage of his own drama. He never hesitated to admit he was pathologically selfish.

Today he would be diagnosed a psychopath, a narcissist. Typical of people with personality disorders, he had compulsions, and the media was one of them. He was addicted to newspapers, tabloids and journals. Throughout his life his studios looked like a recycling center for just about every bit of newsprint to roll off the European presses. If it struck his fancy he might dabble with newspapers from the United States or as far away as Australia.

He was a graphomaniac, firing off so many articles for newspapers and journals that he would apologize to whomever he submitted them to. It's likely he sent anonymous letters to the editor, using pseudonyms including his former stage name, Nemo. His correspondence with acquaintances and friends was compulsive but not warm or hinting of any genuine interest in their lives or well-being. He was charming and witty but attention-seeking, snide, nosy, gossipy and a voyeur. He didn't seem to have a habit of saving letters from anyone including his family, his wives or his mentors such as Whistler. But it's hard to say. So much has vanished. It's impossible to know what might have been destroyed by the people who have protected him.

What is clear after going through the many archival repositories that contain letters Sickert wrote to others is that he liked knowing what people were doing, especially in the privacy of their not-always-so-tidy Victorian lives. "Write, write, write!" he would beg his friends. "Tell me in detail all *sorts* of things, things that have amused you and *how* and *when* and *where*, and all sorts of gossip about every one."

He despised the upper class and authoritative figures such as religious leaders and the police. But given the chance he didn't hesitate to circulate with major celebrities of the day. He would seek them out. He might spy on them or disregard and disrespect them later if they were vulnerable, as Oscar Wilde was after he got out of jail. The stars in Sickert's constellation are astonishing and include Henry Irving, Ellen Terry, Aubrey Beardsley, Henry James, Bram Stoker, Max Beerbohm, Degas, Monet, Renoir, Pissarro, Rodin, André Gide, Édouard Dujardin, Proust and Members of Parliament.

He moved in high circles that ironically included the creator of Sherlock Holmes, Sir Arthur Conan Doyle, and in later life he would give painting lessons to Winston Churchill. Sickert hobnobbed with plenty of important people, almost anybody who was a *somebody* in Victorian England and Europe. But he didn't necessarily know many of these luminaries well, if at all, and no one famous or otherwise really knew him. Not even his first wife, Ellen, who would turn forty in less than two weeks. On this bank holiday in the late summer of 1888 he may not have given much thought to his wife's birthday. But it was extremely unlikely he'd forgotten it.

Sickert was admired for his amazing memory. He loved to entrance dinner guests by performing long passages of musicals and plays, dressed for the parts, his recitations flawless. He wouldn't have forgotten that Ellen's birthday was August 18 and a very easy occasion to ruin. Maybe he'd make her think he forgot. Maybe he would vanish into one of his secret rented hovels that he called studios. Or he might take her to a romantic café and leave her alone at the table while he dashed off and stayed out the rest of the night. Ellen loved Sickert all her sad, lonely life despite his cold heart, his pathological lying, his self-centeredness and his habit of disappearing for days or weeks without warning or explanation.

He was comfortable in any environment he placed himself in, logical, coolly calculating, fearless and disciplined. For the most part he abstained from alcohol, until the end of his life when he began to abuse it. But during the Ripper time for however long it went on, possibly decades, he rarely touched a drop. Staying in control is crucial if a psychopath is to be successful and not caught. Sickert didn't write his memoirs. As far as I know he didn't keep a diary or a calendar. He didn't date most of his letters, paintings, drawings or etchings. One of many frustrations in this investigation is having very little evidence of where he was or what he was doing during any given day, week, month or year.

I don't think it's a coincidence that he left almost no trail. He was cunning enough to be careful about his whereabouts, and I could find no record of his activities on August 6, 1888. But there's good reason to suspect he was in London, based on notes he scribbled on music hall sketches, what I will continue to refer to as depictions and souvenirs of what he was experiencing, thinking and feeling.

He carried small pieces of cheap paper and pencils so he could capture a moment, a movement, a theme. These remnants of his outings and observations are some of the most important Sickert documents in the Jack the Ripper case. In them he made perhaps his only mistake. He eroded the alibi that his apologists continue to flaunt today. Sickert couldn't have murdered anyone in London if he were someplace else, specifically France. It's said that's where he was in the summer and fall of 1888 when the Ripper began his bloody crimes. But it isn't true.

Had Sickert not dated his hasty, rough drawings it would be impossible to prove he was in England. But he was. He was there on August 4, 5 and 12, possibly attending shows at Gatti's Hungerford Palace of Varieties, the Paragon Theatre of Varieties, the Temple of Varieties and the Royal Cambridge Hall of Varieties. Art historians and Sickert experts Professor Anna Gruetzner Robins and Wendy Baron say that when he was particularly interested in a certain performer such as the handsome brunette singer Emily Lyndale, he might follow her from music hall to music hall.

Since these mobbed variety shows rarely let out before midnight, it would be reasonable to entertain the idea that Sickert was in London on August 6. Perhaps he was enjoying the bank holiday, taking in plays and musical performances or simply watching the crowds. In the very early morning hours the Ripper would strike possibly for the first time. I say *possibly* because we can't know for sure when he began his shocking murderous spree. But it's a fact that in the late summer/early fall of 1888 Jack the Ripper would introduce the world to his stage name. Assuming his first bloody performance was in early August, one has to ask why now? What transitions, frustrations and stressors might have been a catalyst for sexually violent fantasies to become realized?

It's obvious, perhaps even a cliché, to say that indifference, dismissal, jealousy and abandonment could have set Sickert off. They would for most people, and he had just learned that Whistler had gotten engaged quite suddenly. He would be getting married in London on August 11 and planned to honeymoon and travel with his new bride for the rest of the year in France, where they hoped to reside permanently. The famous painter had fallen madly in love with the beautiful Beatrice Godwin. She was to occupy the most prominent position in his life and entirely change the course of it.

Likewise, Whistler occupied the most prominent position in Sickert's life. He had entirely changed the course of it and not necessarily in a good way. Their relationship was unequal and dysfunctional. Whistler must have pushed his apprentice's buttons in a way that few people could, belittling him, bossing him around, making him feel untalented and like a failure. Sickert's wife Ellen didn't help matters much. The daughter of the famous politician Richard Cobden, she was the head of the Sickert house. She supported him in every way. She was his caretaker. Today she would be called an enabler, as were all of his women.

There's no evidence of anything romantic between Ellen and Sickert and in fact there might not have been. A portrait Whistler painted of her possibly not long after she and Sickert married in 1885 depicts a dark-haired, fine-featured woman who is beginning to show her age. She looks prim and proper, almost regal, possibly a bit humorless and no-nonsense. Ellen was a feminist. But first and foremost she was a Cobden.

Well-bred and well connected, she helped her fledgling artist husband by getting him portrait work, often with political figures and social activists she knew because of her father. Sickert painted upper class and prominent people even if he secretly despised them. It seemed he had little control over his life. He may have felt small and unimportant at times. It wouldn't be surprising if he seethed inside.

"Nice boy, Walter," Whistler used to say to him. "Manage the letting of the Cheyne Walk nicely for me Walter—right off—like a good fellow," he writes Sickert on July 9 (possibly 1892). Some of Whistler's condescension and ire were dished

Ellen Cobden, the wealthy daughter of famous politician Richard Cobden, was married to Walter Sickert from 1885 to 1899.

out behind his young apprentice's back. In a letter to Edith Emma Marzetti (1883 or 1884) Whistler writes, "Entirely Walter Sickert's fault—as usual!" Around this same time Sickert fired off a letter to Ms. Marzetti stating, "This message of Mr. Whistler is a base libel. Don't believe a word of it."

In another letter Whistler wrote, this time to his pupil Mortimer Menpes in 1885 or 1886, Whistler complains, "Walter Sickert has behaved in the most shockingly I might say brutally graceless way—and after deliberately leaving this morning to follow out his own ambition I am not surprised to hear that he passed the afternoon in absolute idleness and drivel—".

Five months later in May of 1887 Whistler makes the angry, cryptic comment "The Harvest Moon rises over Hampstead and the cocks of Chelsea crow." Sickert was living at 54 Broadhurst Gardens in South Hampstead. He had just written a review for the *New York Herald* praising artist Frederic Leighton's painting *Summer Moon*. The demanding, egocentric Whistler was outraged. He felt betrayed.

Around this same time Sickert complains that Whistler owed him money: "If you remember, my rent fell due & I had lent you the money with which I should have paid it." He goes on to say, "You know perfectly well that whenever I do take up any branch of your affairs I push on unremittingly with a certain enthusiasm to its conclusion." Apparently Sickert was referring to a fit Whistler pitched over etchings sold by the Fine Art Society without his permission. Throughout it all, the apprentice Sickert continued to know his place in the pecking order. "Always & entirely Grateful & devoted," he would sign his letters to his master.

A search through Whistler's correspondence, now online at the University of Glasgow, paints a portrait of a relationship that at times was volatile, with Sickert swinging from sycophantic to offended and defensive. Whistler's regard for him ranged from gracious to mocking and enraged. They would have cordial exchanges and visits, and then go long periods with little or no contact. This escalated with time, and the relationship would finally end acrimoniously and litigiously in 1897 when Whistler publicly dismissed Sickert as rather much a nobody.

When one reads Sickert and Whistler biographies and the correspondence between and about them, it's impossible not to imagine that Sickert must have grown resentful of being criticized and ridiculed. Often he was treated as nothing more than a personal assistant or errand boy. In late 1886, Ellen was sitting for her portrait by Whistler, and on December 2 she assured him, "I will drive Walter down (as I should always come dressed) and he will be able during the sittings [to] attend to any affairs in which he can be useful to you—"

By the spring of 1888 the relationship seemed even more strained, with Whistler depicted as moody and difficult. "You have written to me in a fit of blues," Sickert writes to him. "Indifference you know perfectly well I have never shown towards anything that concerned you. . . . And o master 'be not as a lion within thy house nor frantick [sic] among thy pupils!' For they mean very well." In this same letter Sickert also asserts, "Painting must be for me a profession & not a pastime, or else I must give it up & take to something practical." Would he write such a thing if Whistler were encouraging or respectful of him?

By the time of Whistler's marriage and departure for France in August of 1888, his relationship with Sickert was distant and rapidly falling apart. In a November 18 letter regarding a business trip, Whistler clearly was back in London, but there's no sense he had any dealings with his former pupil. By December the distance between the two of them bordered on estrangement. In a letter to Whistler's new wife, Sickert explains that he wrote to her instead of him because "Jimmy might not read."

The summer of 1888 must have been a time of great stress for Sickert. He couldn't have been prepared for Whistler's abrupt marriage and move away from England. For all practical purposes Sickert had been fired. It must have felt like a complete abandonment by the megalomaniacal master he idolized, faithfully served, envied and despised.

Added to this was bitter fighting within the prestigious New English Art Club (NEAC) that was in full tilt by the spring and summer of 1888. The impressionists were in high gear in their attempt to take it over. At the vanguard of this insurgency or "Whistler gang" was Sickert. He was being savaged by many of his detractors. Critics were trashing his controversial painting *Gatti's Hungerford Palace of Varieties—Second Turn of Katie Lawrence*, exhibited at the NEAC in 1888.

Founding member of the adversarial Newlyn school of painters Stanhope Forbes said of it, "I'm sure you will be quite pained with Sickert's picture. It is really perfectly astonishing & I only hope it is not in any way a true reflection of the painter's mind. Tawdry vulgarity & the sentiment of the lowest music hall. I am bewildered by it. What Mrs. Sickert must think of it I can't guess but it is a pity her good influence is not brought to bear." In May of 1888 the *Artist* referred to Sickert as "the best abused man in London."

While the bad press and controversy were bringing him attention, the open hostility and severe criticisms couldn't have been easy to stomach especially when he was striving to stand on his own and escape the label of an apprentice and a Whistlerite. But no matter how much Sickert might claim his independence as an artist and a man, he would always be haunted by his former master. Sickert would vacillate from revering him to trying to destroy him. Much later in Sickert's life he was said to emulate him in personality and elegance. On occasion he went so far as to wear Whistler's signature monocle and black ribbon tie.

In August 1888, Whistler's wedding may have been disconcerting to Sickert at a deeply personal level for another reason. One of his many roles was the irresistible womanizer but behind the scenes it's doubtful he was anything of the sort. Sickert needed women and loathed them. They were intellectually inferior. They were useless except as caretakers or objects to manipulate for art or money. Women were a dangerous reminder of an infuriating and humiliating secret he carried not only to the grave but beyond it, because cremated bodies reveal no tales of the flesh.

Sickert was born with a deformity that continues to be the subject of much debate. At the beginning of my work on this case I was told by John Lessore, the nephew of Sickert's third wife, Thérèse Lessore, that Sickert was born with a fistula of his penis. John Lessore's comment was witnessed and I wrote it down in my journal at the time.

I will go into more detail about Sickert's deformity later. But it's almost certain that surgeries he required when he was a young child would have traumatized him and likely left him disfigured if not mutilated. He may have been incapable of an erection. He may not have had enough of a penis left for penetration. He may have had to squat like a woman to urinate.

In the Ripper letters there are multiple phallic allusions in words and in drawings. Not all of these mocking missives were signed "Jack the Ripper." He used different names, and I believe some of the letters supposedly from concerned citizens are actually from him. An example of this is a letter dated October 4, 1888. The writer speculates, "My theory of the crimes is that the criminal has been badly disfigured—*possibly had his privy member destroyed*—& he is now revenging himself on the sex by these atrocities." The letter is written in purple pencil and signed "Scotus," which could be the Latin for "Scotsman." *Scotus* can mean "a shallow incision" or "to cut." November 11, 1888, the Ripper writes, "I have caught the pox and cannot piss."

In boyhood sketches Sickert depicted women being abducted, terrorized and attacked. One of them is tied up in a chair and being stabbed to death. His violent fantasies weren't new. Why he acted on them when he did will always be up for debate. But I believe Whistler and his universe are hugely important in the mix. His passion for a woman and subsequent abandonment of Sickert may have been part of the alchemy that created the most notorious killer in history.

Of course there are no facile explanations or infallible sequences of cause and effect, but there are layers. Perhaps one of them was the sensuously beautiful Ellen Terry, one of the most famous actresses of the Victorian era, the Elizabeth Taylor or Angelina Jolie of the day. As a teenage actor, Sickert had stalked her. Now Whistler had a connection to her. His wife-to-be was the widow of architect and archaeologist Edward Godwin, who had lived with Ellen Terry and fathered her children. Sickert might have felt jealous. He played no part in his master's joyous drama. He wasn't invited to any of the festivities. He must have felt left out and unimportant. He might have felt impotent.

Five days before the wedding, Jack the Ripper may have slipped out of the wings for the first time. I reiterate that we can't know conclusively when he began and ended his crimes or whom he killed or how many. But it's a sad fact that contrary to popular belief the Ripper's violent spree didn't end as abruptly as it began. It's recycled as indisputable that he struck five times out of nowhere and vanished three months after he started. But that's just one more claim that simply isn't true. He left far more victims in his wake than the "canonical five," as the murders are often referred to in Ripper lore.

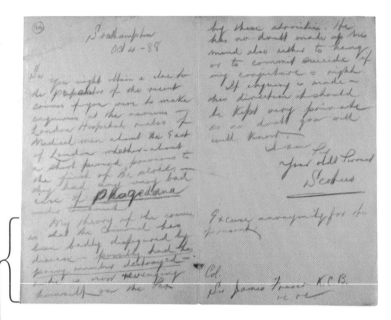

A letter supposedly from a concerned citizen reads, "My theory . . . is that the criminal has been badly disfigured—*possibly had his privy member destroyed*—& he is now revenging himself on the sex by these atrocities." The letter is signed "Scotus," a Latin word which may mean either "Scotsman" or "a shallow incision."

He killed only prostitutes, the experts say, and that's untrue too. I intend to show that it's highly likely his modus operandi or MO also included murdering and mutilating children, primarily young boys.

With rare exception the MO of violent sexual psychopaths evolves. The Ripper was no exception. His violence escalated. He moved around to other cities, and he may have killed in other countries. His victimology wasn't always the same. It was convenient for Scotland Yard, Queen Victoria and everyone else to believe this demon from hell was gone for good. In an asylum. Better yet, dead. Any similar murders were the work of some other lunatic. Any additional Ripper letters were from crackpots and simply filed with the "others."

Decades passed, then fifty years, then a hundred, now more than a hundred and twenty-five, and his bloody sexual crimes have become anemic. Most people don't feel the horror or intuit the terror and suffering that preceded the deaths. The Ripper crimes are puzzles, mystery weekends, games and "Ripper Walks" that end with pints in a local pub.

Saucy Jack, as the Ripper sometimes called himself, has starred in moody movies featuring famous actors and special effects and spates of what the Ripper said he craved: "blood, blood, blood." His butcheries no longer inspire fright, rage or even pity as his victims molder quietly, some of them in unmarked graves.

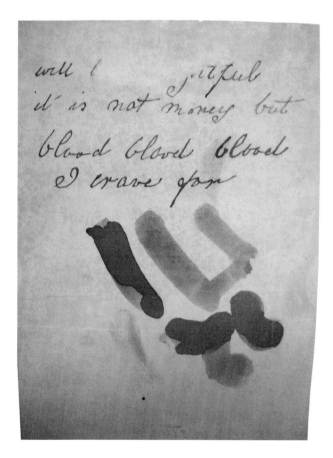

An infamous and chilling letter from Jack the Ripper reads, "It is not money but blood blood blood I crave for."

2

THE UNFORTUNATES

WALTER SICKERT WAS IN LONDON the first week of August, according to his dated music hall sketches. It's hard to imagine he didn't engage in the festive activities of the holiday on the sixth. For the art lover on a budget a penny would buy admission into all sorts of exhibits in the squalid East End. For the better off a shilling would pay for a peek at the masterpieces of Corot, Diaz and Rousseau in the high-priced galleries on New Bond Street.

There were cheap fares to Whitechapel, the crowded clothing district. In this impoverished part of the Great Metropolis costermongers, merchants and money changers hawked their goods and services seven days a week. Children prowled the filthy streets for food and a chance to trick a stranger out of a coin. Whitechapel was home to "the people of the dustbin," as many good Victorians called the desperate wretches who lived there. For a few farthings a visitor could watch street acrobatics, performing dogs and freak shows. One could get drunk or solicit sex from a prostitute, an "unfortunate," and there were thousands to choose from.

One of them was Martha Tabram. She was about forty and separated from a furniture warehouse packer named Henry Samuel Tabram. He'd walked out of her life because of her heavy drinking but was decent enough to give her a weekly allowance of twelve shillings. That stopped when he

In impoverished parts of London, it was not uncommon to see children roaming the streets, seeking food or money.

heard she was living with another man, a carpenter named Henry Turner. He too lost patience with Martha's drinking habits. He'd left her two or three weeks earlier. The last time he saw her alive was two nights before on Saturday, August 4, the same night Sickert was making sketches at Gatti's music hall near the Strand. Turner handed Martha a few coins and she spent them on drink.

For centuries many people believed women turned to prostitution because they suffered from a genetic defect that caused them to enjoy sex for the sake of sex. There were several types of immoral or wanton women, some worse than others. Concubines, mistresses and good wenches were trash but the greatest sinner was the whore. A whore was a whore by choice. She wasn't about to retire from her "wicked and abominable course of life," Thomas Heywood laments in his 1624 *Nine Books of Various History Concerning Women*. "I am altogether discouraged when I remember the position of one of the most notorious in the trade, who said, 'For once a whore and ever a whore, I know it by my self.'"

Sexual activity was to be confined to the institution of marriage and had been ordained by God for the sole purpose of the continuation of

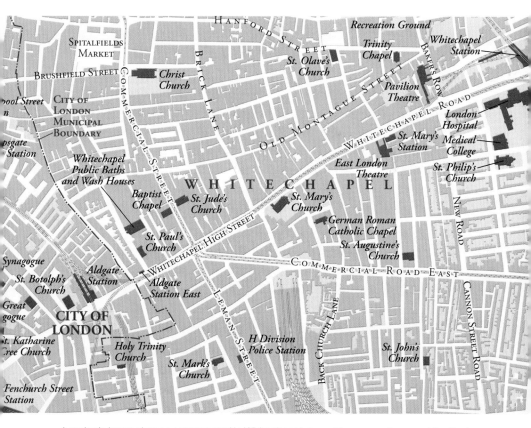

London's lower classes congregated in Whitechapel, one of the poorest areas of the East End. It offered cheap lodging, low-priced gin, and underpaid prostitutes.

the species. The solar center of a woman's universe was her uterus, and monthly menstrual cycles precipitated great storms of throbbing lust, hysteria and insanity. Women were a lower order. They were incapable of rational abstract thinking, a view Sickert held. He was quite eager to assert that women had no understanding of art. They were interested in it only when it "ministers to their vanity" or elevates them "in those social classifications they study so anxiously." Women of genius, the rare few there were, Sickert said, "count as men."

His beliefs weren't unusual for the era. Women were a different "race." Contraception was a blasphemy against God and society, and poverty flourished as women gave birth at an alarming rate. Sex was to be enjoyed by women for the sole reason that physiologically an orgasm was thought to be essential for the secretion of the fluids necessary for conception. To experience the "thrill" while unmarried or through masturbation was perverse. It was a serious threat to sanity, salvation and health. Some nineteenth-century English physicians cured masturbation with clitorectomies. The "thrill" for the sake of the "thrill" was socially abhorrent. It was wicked. It was barbaric.

Christian men and women had heard the stories. In the ancient world of Herodotus, Egyptian females were so aberrant and blasphemous they dared to mock God by giving themselves up to raging lust and flaunting the pleasures of the flesh. In those heathen days paying to satisfy lust was desirable, not shameful. A voracious sexual appetite was good, not evil. When a beautiful young woman died there was nothing wrong with enjoying her body until it was getting a bit ripe and ready for the embalmer. *How appalling* would have been the protest during Sickert's day when sex served a sacred purpose and the Bible hadn't a single good word to say about strumpets.

The notion that only guiltless people cast the first stone was forgotten. That was plain enough when crowds swelled to watch a public beheading or hanging. Somewhere along the way the belief that the sins of the father will be visited on the children got translated into the mother. Thomas Heywood wrote that a woman's "virtue once violated brings infamy and dishonour." The poisons of the offending woman's sin, Heywood promised, will extend to the "posteritie which shall arise from so corrupt a seed, generated from unlawful and adulterate copulation."

Some two hundred and fifty years later, the English language was a bit easier to understand but Victorian beliefs about women and immorality were the same. Sexual intercourse was for the purpose of procreation, and the "thrill" was the catalyst to conception. Quackery perpetuated by physicians claimed the "thrill" was essential to a woman's becoming pregnant. If a raped woman got pregnant then she must have experienced an orgasm during the sexual encounter. Intercourse couldn't have been against her will. If she didn't become pregnant, obviously she'd had no orgasm. Her claims of violation might be true.

Men of the nineteenth century were very much preoccupied with the female orgasm. The "thrill" was so important one has to wonder how often it was faked. That would be a good trick to learn. Then barrenness could be blamed on the male. If a woman couldn't have an orgasm her condition might be diagnosed as female impotence. A thorough examination by a doctor was needed. A digital manipulation of the breasts and clitoris was often sufficient in determining whether the patient was impotent. If the nipples hardened during the examination, the prognosis was promising. If the patient experienced the "thrill," the husband would be most pleased to know that his wife was healthy.

London's unfortunates didn't drift along the cold, dirty, dark streets in search of the "thrill." They didn't choose a life of prostitution because of their insatiable sexual appetites. Giving up their evil ways and turning to God wouldn't result in food and shelter, contrary to what the Salvation Army preached when its female volunteers braved the East End slums and handed out little cakes and promises from the Lord. Unfortunates such as Martha Tabram would gratefully take the cake and then take to the streets.

Without a man's support, a woman had scant means of keeping herself or her children alive. Employment, assuming a woman could find it, meant working six twelve-hour days making coats in sweatshops for the equivalent of twenty-five cents a week. If she was lucky she might earn seventy-five cents a week working seven fourteen-hour days gluing together matchboxes. Most of the wages went to greedy slumlords, leaving mothers and children to search the streets for food or to pick through garbage.

Sailors from foreign ships anchored at the nearby docks, and military men and upper-class ones clandestinely on the prowl made it all too easy for a desperate woman to rent out her body for a few coins until it became as dilapidated as the vermin-infested ruins where the people of the East End lived. Malnutrition, alcoholism and physical abuse reduced a woman to shambles quickly. The worse an unfortunate looked, the lower she slid in the pecking order. She was relegated to seeking out the darkest, most remote streets, stairwells and courtyards, she and her client probably falling-down drunk.

Alcohol was the easiest way not to be present, to medicate one's miseries. A disproportionate number of people of "the Abyss," as writer Jack London called the East End, were alcoholics. Probably the vast majority of unfortunates were. These pitiful women were diseased and old beyond their years, cast out by their families and a society ill equipped or unwilling to address the "immorality" of alcoholism. Made desperate by addiction, women were driven into prostitution, haunting the public houses (pubs) and asking men to treat them to drinks. Business usually followed.

No matter the weather, unfortunates haunted the night like nocturnal animals. They lay in wait for any man who might be enticed into parting with pennies for pleasure. Preferably sex was performed standing up, the prostitute gathering her many layers of clothing and lifting them out of the way, her back to her client. If all went according to plan, he was too drunk to know that his penis was being inserted between her thighs and not into any orifice.

Martha Tabram fell behind on the rent after Henry Turner walked out on her. Her whereabouts after that aren't clear but one might guess she was in and out of common lodging houses. If the choice was between a bed and a drink, she most likely took the drink and dozed in doorways, in parks and on the street, continually chased off by the police. Martha spent the nights of August 4 and 5 in a common lodging house on Dorset Street just south of a music hall on Commercial Street.

DORSET STREET

A lodging house on Dorset Street, 1895. Martha Tabram spent the nights of August 4 and 5, 1888, in a common lodging house on Dorset Street much like this one, just south of a music hall on Commercial Street.

The next night at ten o'clock she met up with Mary Ann Connolly, who went by the alias of Pearly Poll. The weather had been unpleasant all day, overcast and rainy as the temperature continued to drop to an unseasonable fifty-two degrees. The two women, like other unfortunates, had a habit of walking about wearing everything they owned. If one didn't have a permanent residence there was no place to leave belongings.

The late hour on this bank holiday was lively and alcohol flowed freely as Londoners stretched out what was left of their day off from labor. Most plays and musicals had begun at 8:15 and would have let out by now. Many theatergoers and other adventurers in horse-drawn taxis and on foot braved the rainy streets in search of refreshment and other entertainment. Visibility in the East End was poor under the best conditions. Gaslights, few and spaced far apart, gave out smudges of illumination, the shadows impenetrable. The world of the unfortunate was a continuum of petty labor, sleep and drink before venturing out into another numbing night of sordid and dangerous employment.

The events leading to Martha Tabram's murder are well documented and considered reliable unless one is inclined to feel as I do that the recollections of a hard-drinking prostitute named Pearly Poll might lack a certain clarity and veracity. When she was interviewed by the police and later testified at the coroner's inquest, she may have outright lied. Or she may have been confused or suffering from alcohol-induced amnesia. Pearly Poll was frightened. She told police she was so upset that she might just drown herself in the Thames.

During the inquest on August 23 she was reminded several times that she was under oath. She claimed that on August 6 at 10:00 p.m., she and Martha Tabram began drinking with two soldiers in Whitechapel. The couples went their separate ways at 11:45. Throughout the Ripper investigation I've continued to wonder about the accuracy of when events occurred or were witnessed. What or who told Pearly Poll the time? The Whitechapel Church clock chiming? And was she counting?

At the inquest she testified to the coroner and jurors that she went up Angel Alley with the "corporal" while Martha headed toward George Yard with the "private." Both soldiers wore white bands around their caps. The last time Pearly Poll saw Martha and the private, they were walking toward the dilapidated tenement housing of George Yard Buildings on Commercial Street in the dark heart of the East End slums.

Pearly Poll claimed nothing out of the ordinary happened. Their encounter with the soldiers was pleasant enough. Maybe there was an argument. Some accounts claim Pearly Poll's soldier struck her with a stick. But there was nothing that might have set off even the faintest alarm in the two women, who certainly had seen it all. They had survived the streets a long time for good reason.

Two hours and fifteen minutes after Pearly Poll claimed she last saw Martha, Police Constable Barrett, #226 of Metropolitan Police H Division, was on routine patrol on Wentworth Street. It intersected with Commercial Street and ran along the north side of George Yard Buildings, and at 2:00 a.m., Barrett noticed a lone soldier. He appeared to belong to one of the regiments of foot guards who wore white bands around their caps.

Barrett said the solider was a private between the ages of twenty-two and twenty-six. He was five foot nine or ten with a fair complexion and a small dark-brown mustache turned up at the ends. He wore no medals on his uniform except a good-conduct badge. He told Constable Barrett that he was "waiting for a chum who had gone with a girl."

At the same time this brief exchange was taking place, a Mr. and Mrs. Mahoney of George Yard Buildings passed the landing where Martha's body was later found. They heard and saw nothing of note. It would seem Martha couldn't have been murdered yet. Perhaps she was nearby in the shadows waiting for the constable to resume his patrol so she could finish business with the soldier.

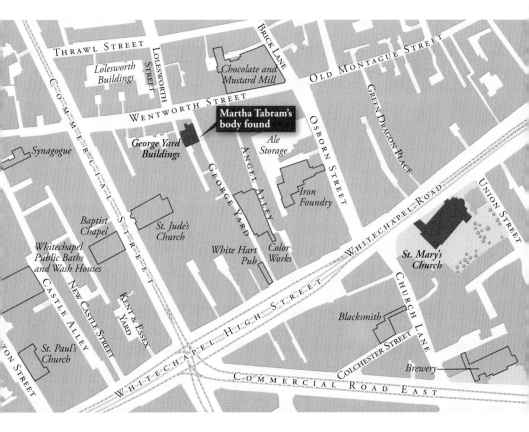

The body of Martha Tabram was found at 37 George Yard Buildings at 4:50 a.m. on Tuesday, August 7, 1888. Mary Ann Connolly, known on the streets as Pearly Poll, was the last to see Tabram alive, as Tabram was walking down Commercial Street with a soldier.

Or it could be that the soldier had nothing to do with Martha's murder and is simply a source of confusion. But it's evident that Police Constable Barrett's attention was piqued by a soldier alone in the street at 2:00 a.m. outside George Yard Buildings. Later Barrett, Pearly Poll and witnesses who had noticed Martha on the street were asked to take a look at soldiers in the guardroom at the Tower of London or in Wellington Barracks. Every man who seemed even remotely familiar had a believable alibi. A search through their belongings produced no evidence including blood, and Martha Tabram's killer would have been bloody.

Chief Inspector Donald Swanson of Scotland Yard's Criminal Investigation Department (CID) acknowledged in his special report that there was no reason to think Martha Tabram had been with anybody but the soldier she'd walked off with before midnight. Although it was possible, due to the "lapse of time," that she might have been with another client. She might have been with several.

The puzzle of the "private" seen with Martha at 11:45 and the "private" seen by PC Barrett at 2:00 a.m. nagged at Scotland Yard. This man was seen so close to when and where Martha was murdered. Maybe he did it. Maybe he really was a soldier. Or maybe her killer was disguised as one. What a brilliant bit of trickery that would have been. There were plenty of soldiers out on bank holiday nights, and cruising for prostitutes wasn't an uncommon activity among military men. It may seem a stretch to consider that Jack the Ripper might have donned a soldier's uniform and pasted on a fake mustache to commit his first murder, but this wouldn't be the last time a mysterious man in uniform would be connected with a Jack the Ripper–type crime.

Walter Sickert was familiar with uniforms. Years later during World War I when he was painting battle scenes he would admit to being especially "enchanted" by French ones. "I have got my Belgian uniforms today," he wrote in 1914. "The artillery man's forage cap with a little gold tassel is the sauciest thing in the world." As a boy Sickert frequently sketched men in uniforms and armor. As Mr. Nemo, his most critically acclaimed performance was in 1880 when he played a French soldier in Shakespeare's *Henry V.* In 1887 Sickert completed a painting he titled *It All Comes from Sticking to a Soldier.* It's an unsettling painting that depicts music hall performer Ada Lundberg singing to a crowd of leering men.

Sickert's interest in things military never waned throughout his life, and it was his habit to ask the Red Cross for the uniforms of soldiers who were disabled or dying. His motive, he said, was to outfit models for his

As a young man, Sickert enjoyed sketching men in uniforms or armor.

military sketches and paintings. An acquaintance recalled that at one time Sickert's studio was piled with uniforms and rifles.

"I am doing a portrait of a dear dead man, a Colonel," Sickert writes. He asked a friend to help him "borrow some uniforms from Belgians in hospital. One has a kind of distaste for using misfortunes to further one's own ends." He didn't really. He admitted more than once to his "purely selfish practice of life." As he himself said, "I live entirely for my work—or as some people put it, for myself."

It's surprising that the possibility of the Ripper wearing disguises hasn't been emphasized as a likely scenario. It would help explain why he seemed to vanish without a trace after his crimes. It might account for why witnesses gave such a variety of descriptions of the men supposedly last seen with his victims or in the area where the murders were committed. The use of disguises by violent offenders isn't uncommon.

Men dressed as police, firefighters, soldiers, maintenance workers, deliverymen, servicemen, paramedics and even clowns have been convicted of violent serial crimes. A disguise is a simple and effective way to gain access and lure the victim without resistance or suspicion. Disguises allow the perpetrator to return to the scene of the crime and watch the investigative drama or assist in it or attend the victim's funeral.

A psychopath intent on murder uses any means to con a victim out of life. Eliciting trust before the kill is part of the violent psychopath's script. To understand Jack the Ripper we must accept that violent psychopaths are human beings, often clever, attractive, charismatic ones. They are the next-door neighbor who's friendly with your kids, the colleague who's polite in the break room, the handsome former law student who walks you to your car at night to make sure you're safe, as serial killer Ted Bundy used to do with writer Ann Rule.

Her remarkable book about him—*The Stranger Beside Me*—launched her career when I was still a police reporter at the *Charlotte Observer*. I would meet her years later in 1988 when I was finishing my first Scarpetta novel, *Postmortem,* and was in Miami for the opening of the new Miami-Dade County Medical Examiner Department. Ann was on tour for her bestseller *Small Sacrifices*, and during brunch I asked her about Ted Bundy.

She said she met him in 1971 when both of them were night-shift volunteers at the Seattle Crisis Clinic. They were answering the suicide hotline.

At the time Ann also happened to be working on an investigative story about serial killings. It seemed incredible to me that she could have been sitting right next to the man committing them and not have a clue. Didn't she pick up on anything? Didn't she ever get a weird feeling that something was off? She told me that Bundy was a perfect gentleman. She liked him. She thought he had "cute knees," she exclaimed as if she were still in disbelief about it. He would walk her to her car in the dark parking lot and remind her to be careful.

Outwardly, violent psychopaths don't necessarily look different from anybody else. But ongoing scientific study indicates that inwardly they are hardwired in a way that isn't necessarily "normal." The psychiatric community defines psychopathy as an antisocial behavioral disorder. It's more dominant in males than females and statistically five times more likely to occur in the male offspring of a father suffering from it. Symptoms, according to the *Diagnostic and Statistical Manual of Mental Disorders*, include stealing, lying, substance abuse, financial irresponsibility, cruelty, running away from home, promiscuity, fighting, a lack of remorse and an inability to deal with boredom.

But as is true of "normal" people, each psychopath is unique. One might be promiscuous and lie but be financially responsible. One might fight and be promiscuous but not steal, might torture animals but not abuse alcohol or drugs, might torture people but not animals. A psychopath might commit multiple murders and be profligate with money but not be promiscuous. Sickert made it known that there were two vices he hated. One was stealing. The other was alcoholism, which ran in his family. Yet he showed no concern over behaviors of his that should have troubled him profoundly.

The combinations of antisocial behaviors are countless. But the most distinctive and profound characteristic is that psychopaths feel no remorse for their criminal acts and have no empathy. One of Britain's most infamous serial killers, Ian Brady, has said from the maximum-security psychiatric hospital where he is held that "sorry" is a word he'll never use. It's "meaningless." He considers his sadistic crimes entertaining. He's shown admiration for people who commit other bloody atrocities, including the two teenaged boys who massacred thirteen students at Colorado's Columbine High School in 1999. Violent psychopaths have no concept of guilt. They don't have a conscience. Typically they blame the victim.

I'd heard and read about a vicious killer named John Royster months before I actually saw him during a hearing in New York City in the winter of 1997. I was shocked by how polite and gentle he seemed. His pleasant looks, neat clothes, slight build and the braces on his teeth jolted me when he was seated at his defense counsel's table. Had I met Royster in Central Park and seen him flash his silver smile as I jogged by, I might not have felt the slightest breath of fear.

From June 4 through June 11, 1996, he attacked four women who were complete strangers to him. Grabbing them from behind, he threw them to the ground and repeatedly smashed their heads against pavement, concrete and cobblestone until he thought they were dead. He was calm and calculating. He would put down his knapsack and take off his coat before each assault. As his victims lay bleeding and battered on the ground, he raped them or attempted to, then calmly gathered up his belongings and left the scene. Bashing a woman's head to mush was sexually exciting to him, and he admitted to the police that he felt no remorse.

A more recent example of psychopathic behavior was the massive Ponzi scheming of Bernie Madoff, who is believed to have conned people out of $65 billion. In a *New York Times* story, former FBI profiler Gregg O. McCrary said, "Some of the characteristics you see in psychopaths are lying, manipulation, the ability to deceive, feelings of grandiosity and callousness toward their victims."

While McCrary says he never met Madoff and "can't make a diagnosis," he adds, "People like him become sort of like chameleons. They are very good at impression management. . . . They know what people want, and they give it to them." Madoff has been reported to say that he has no sympathy for his victims and blames them for being "greedy."

In the late 1880s this sort of antisocial behavioral disorder was diagnosed as "moral insanity." In his 1893 book on criminology, Arthur MacDonald defined this type of person as a "pure murderer." These people are "honest" because they aren't thieves "by nature" and many are "chaste in character." But all are "unconscious" of feeling "any repulsion" over their violent acts. As a rule, pure murderers begin to show "traces of a murderous tendency" when they're children.

Modern research on prison inmates diagnosed as psychopathic shows that more than 80 percent of those studied were abused as children. A substantial percentage of these show abnormalities of the frontal lobe, the master control for civilized human behavior. Many also have alterations in the amygdala, the area of the brain that's considered the seat of our emotions. In the mid-1900s the remedy for severe antisocial behavior was the prefrontal lobotomy. Typically an ice pick was hammered through the roof of an eye orbit to shear the wiring that connects the frontal part of the brain to the rest of it. Fortunately, modern medicine has less primitive ways of dealing with psychiatric disorders. The mission is to understand, not destroy.

Today scientists are using PET scans (positron emission tomography) and more recently fMRI (functional magnetic resonance imaging) to watch the living brain at work. While we don't completely understand exactly what creates a Jack the Ripper, we have a better idea than we did even a decade ago. Recent research studies by British neurocriminologist Adrian Raine estimate that as much as 25 percent of the male criminal population and as much as 1 percent of the entire male population is psychopathic. It's estimated these individuals commit as much as 65 percent of all crime.

Raine believes psychopaths are largely predetermined by genetics: "Some people are dealt a bad hand; some are born with a flush." It's also possible that some are born with both—like Bundy. He was handsome, charming and very bright but also suffered from an uncontrollable compulsion to commit sexual murder. Raine goes on to describe that functional imaging gives scientists a look in real time at "what goes on when a psychopath views disturbing photos or contemplates a moral dilemma, compared with the rest of us."

Research indicates that psychopaths have noticeably less neural activity in the frontal lobe. They have defects in the paralimbic system, a network of brain regions important to memory and the regulation of emotion.

This suggests that the inhibitions and constraints that keep most of us from engaging in violent acts or giving in to murderous impulses don't register normally if at all in the psychopathic brain. Such an individual may carefully plan and execute his crime but can't control what drives him to violence. The repeated sexualized murders Jack the Ripper committed were driven by an uncontrollable compulsion. They weren't a conspiracy with some logical motive.

Psychopaths are extraordinarily cunning and lead double lives, and "they don't grow out of it," Raine concludes. "They simply get better at it." The Ripper did. Assuming Martha Tabram was his first victim and it was his opening night, no amount of practice or attention to strategy could guarantee that the performance was going to be flawless. Mistakes happen and he may have made an amateurish one.

3

BY SOME PERSON UNKNOWN

WHEN MARTHA TABRAM accompanied her killer to the dark first-floor landing at 37 George Yard Buildings it's possible he relinquished control to her. He may have inadvertently introduced the risk that something could go wrong with his plan.

Her turf may not have been the killing ground he had in mind. Maybe something else happened that he didn't anticipate? An insult? A taunt? Prostitutes, especially intoxicated old veterans, weren't the sort to be sensitive. All Martha had to do was reach between his legs and say exactly the wrong thing. Sickert used the term "impotent fury" in a letter. His writings are peppered with similar violent and angry allusions. More than a century after the event it's impossible to re-create what actually happened in that pitch-black, fetid stairwell in the early morning hours of Tuesday, August 7, 1888. But the killer got enraged. He was frenzied.

To stab someone thirty-nine times is overkill. Such a loss of control can be prompted by an event or a word that sets off the killer in an unanticipated way. Sometimes simply resisting is enough to evoke a violent explosion. Attempting to escape or fight an attacker can result in carnage that far exceeds what was needed to end life.

The fact that overkill is evident in Martha Tabram's case doesn't mean her assailant didn't premeditate murder and set about to commit one.

When he decided to accompany her to the stairwell he had the means and possibly the intention of slashing or stabbing her to death. He'd brought a strong, sharp knife or dagger to the scene and he left with it. He may have been disguised as a soldier or maybe he wasn't. But he knew how to come and go undetected. He knew to be careful about leaving obvious evidence. A lost button, a cap, a pencil. The most personal forms of homicide are stabbings/cuttings, beatings and strangulation. All require the assailant to have physical contact with the victim, and stabbing someone dozens of times is emotional. But that doesn't mean the victim and assailant knew each other.

There's no reason to think that Martha was familiar with her killer. But she elicited a very personal reaction from him, perhaps when she did or said something that didn't follow his script. Martha was known for having fits. She could be quite difficult when she was drunk, and she'd been drinking rum and ale earlier with Pearly Poll. Residents of George Yard Buildings later stated that they heard "nothing" at the early hour of Martha's death. Their testimony doesn't count for much when considering the exhausted, inebriated condition of an impoverished people who were accustomed to drunken behavior, scuffles and violent domestic fights. It was best not to get involved. One could be hurt or get in trouble with the police.

At 3:30 a.m., an hour and a half after Police Constable Barrett spotted the loitering soldier outside George Yard Buildings, a resident named Alfred Crow was returning home from work. He was a cabdriver. Bank holidays were always busy and kept him out late. He must have been tired. He may even have unwound with a few pints after dropping off his last fare. As he passed the first-floor landing he noticed "something" on the ground that might have been a body. He didn't bother to examine it and went to bed. The creed of the East End, as Victorian economist and social reformer Beatrice Webb put it, was don't "meddle" with the neighbors. Crow later explained at the inquest that it wasn't uncommon to see drunks unconscious in the East End. No doubt he saw them all the time.

It seems it wasn't until 4:50 a.m. that anyone realized the "something" on the landing was a dead body. Waterside laborer John S. Reeves was heading out of the building and noticed a woman lying on her back in a pool of blood. Her clothes were disarrayed as if she'd been in a struggle,

Reeves recalled. He saw no footprints on the staircase. He didn't see a knife or any other type of weapon. He said he didn't touch the body but immediately located Police Constable Barrett, who sent for Dr. T. R. Killeen. The time of the doctor's arrival wasn't given but the lighting couldn't have been very good.

He deduced at the scene that the victim, whose identity would remain unknown for days, had been dead for approximately three hours. She was "36 years old," the doctor divined, and "very well nourished," meaning she was overweight. Most of the Ripper's victims, including those the police discounted as having been murdered by him, were either very thin or fat. All of them were "immoral." With rare exception, they were in their late thirties or early forties. It doesn't appear the Ripper preyed on the finer-bred women Sickert married, socialized with and stalked such as actresses Ellen Terry and in later years Gwen Ffrangcon-Davies.

Sickert mingled with the social elite and beautiful but they weren't what inspired his art. He preferred female studio models obese or emaciated. The lower their social class, the uglier, the better. In his letters he makes frequent references to women who were "skeletal" or "the thinnest of the thin like a little eel," and to the big women with wide hips and grotesquely pendulous breasts that he repeatedly depicts in his art. Other people could have the "chorus girls," Sickert writes, but leave him the "hags."

He often remarked that any woman who wasn't too fat or too thin was boring. In a letter he wrote to his American friends Ethel Sands and Nan Hudson he voiced delight over his latest models and how "thrilled" he was by the "sumptuous poverty of their class." He loved their "every day dirty, old, worn clothes." He added in another letter that were he twenty years old, he "wouldn't look at any woman under 40."

Martha Tabram was short, overweight, homely and middle-aged. When she was murdered, she was wearing a green skirt, a brown petticoat, a long black jacket, a black bonnet and sidespring boots, "all old," according to the police. Martha would have suited Sickert's taste. But victimology is an indicator and not a science. Victims of serial murder often share some trait that's significant to the killer but this doesn't imply that a violent psychopath is unbending in whom he picks. Why Jack the Ripper would have focused on Martha Tabram instead of some other prostitute of similar description can't be known. The explanation may be as pedestrian as opportunity.

Whatever his reason, he might have learned a valuable lesson from her murder. To lose control and stab a victim thirty-nine times was to cause a bloody mess. Even if he didn't track blood on the landing or elsewhere he would have had blood on his hands, his clothes, and the tops of his boots or shoes. That makes evasion riskier. It would also have been more difficult to control a victim who wasn't immediately disabled and rendered silent. Cutting her throat would be much more efficient.

There was no suitable mortuary in the East End. Dr. Killeen performed the postmortem examination at a nearby "dead house" or "shed" as these abysmal morgues were called. He attributed a single wound to the heart as "sufficient to cause death." Every detail helps the dead speak but Dr. Killeen's descriptions tell us so little that we don't know if the weapon was double- or single-edged. We don't know the angle of trajectory, and this would help position the killer in relation to Martha at the time of each injury. Was she standing or lying down? Were any of the wounds large or irregular, caused by the weapon twisting as she struggled? Were there contusions or abrasions that might indicate a knife with a guard between the blade and the handle?

Reconstructing how a victim died and determining the type of weapon used begin to paint a portrait of the killer. Details hint at his intent, emotions, activity, fantasies and even his occupation or hobbies. The height of the killer can also be conjectured. Martha was five foot three. If the killer was taller and the two of them were standing when he began stabbing her, then one would expect her initial wounds to be high up on her body and angled downward. If both of them were standing, it would have been difficult for him to stab her in the stomach and genitals unless he was short. Most likely those injuries would have been inflicted when she was on the ground.

Dr. Killeen assumed the killer was very strong. But if the Ripper was enraged and high on adrenaline and his weapon was pointed, strong and sharp, he didn't need to be muscle-bound to penetrate skin, organs, cartilage and bone. Dr. Killeen also mistakenly assumed that a wound penetrating the sternum or "chest bone" couldn't have been inflicted by a "knife." He jumped from that incorrect conclusion to his next one, that two weapons were involved, possibly a "dagger" and a "knife." This led to an early theory that the killer might be ambidextrous.

Even if he was, the image of a man simultaneously stabbing Martha with a dagger in one hand and a knife in the other in poor lighting if not total darkness seems bizarre if not absurd. Chances are good he would have stabbed or cut himself a few times. The medical evidence actually doesn't suggest an ambidextrous assault unless the person was dominantly right-handed. Martha's left lung was penetrated in five places. The heart, which is angled toward the left side of the body, was stabbed once. A right-handed person is more likely to inflict injuries to the left side of the body if the victim is facing him.

A penetration of the sternum doesn't merit the emphasis Dr. Killeen gave it because a sharp-pointed knife can penetrate bone, including the skull. In a case that occurred in Germany decades before the Ripper began his spree, a man murdered his wife by stabbing her through the sternum. He confided that the "table knife" penetrated the bone as easily as if it were "butter." The edges of the wound indicated that the table knife cleanly penetrated the bone once and went through the right lung, the pericardium and the aorta.

Dr. Killeen speculated that two weapons were used in Martha Tabram's murder because the stab wounds were different sizes. This can be explained if the blade was wider at the guard than it was at the tip. Stab wounds can be different widths depending on their depth, the twisting of the blade and the elasticity of the tissue or the part of the body penetrated. It's difficult to ascertain what he meant by a knife or a dagger but a knife usually refers to a single-edged blade while a dagger is narrow and double-edged and has a pointed tip.

In the early years of this investigation I explored the types of cutting instruments that might have been available to the Ripper. The variety is bewildering. British travelers to Asia returned home with all sorts of souvenirs, some better suited than others for stabbing or cutting. The Indian *pesh kabz* is a fine example of a weapon that could leave wounds of several different widths, depending on their depth. The strong steel blade of this "dagger," as it was called, could create an array of wounds that would perplex any medical examiner even now.

The curved blade is almost an inch and a half wide at the ivory handle. It becomes double-edged two-thirds of the way up where it begins to taper off to a point as thin as a needle. The one I bought from an antiques dealer was made in 1830 and including its sheath would easily fit in one's waistband, boot, coat pocket or up a sleeve. The curved blade of the Oriental dagger called a *djambia* (circa 1840) would also leave wounds of varying widths, although the entire blade is double-edged.

The Victorians enjoyed an abundance of beautiful weapons that were made for killing human beings. These were cavalierly collected during travels abroad or bought for a bargain at bazaars. In one day I discovered the following Victorian weapons at a London antiques fair and at the homes of two dealers in Sussex: daggers, kukris, a dagger stick disguised to look like a polished tree branch, daggers disguised to look like canes, tiny six-shot revolvers designed to fit neatly into a gentleman's vest pocket or a lady's purse, "cut throat razors", bowie-type knives, swords, rifles and beautifully decorated truncheons including a "Life Preserver" that is weighted with

Left: Victorian-era straight razors were also called "cut-throat" razors. However, a straight razor would likely have folded under the intensity of force used in Jack the Ripper's killings. *Right:* A German bowie knife from the late 1800s was a thick and sturdy type of hunting knife.

lead. If Jack the Ripper cruised for weapons he was blessed with an embarrassment of riches, although it is extremely unlikely he used a straight razor. When force is exerted, the blade folds back.

No weapon was ever recovered in Martha Tabram's murder, and since Dr. Killeen's autopsy report seems to be missing—as are many records related to the Jack the Ripper case—all I had to go on were the sketchy details of the inquest. Of course I can't determine with absolute certainty the weapon that took Martha's life. But I can speculate. Based on the frenzied attack and subsequent wounds it may very well have been a dagger with a strong blade, a sharp point, and a substantial handle designed to prevent one from losing one's grip and slicing oneself.

If it's true that there were no defense injuries such as cuts or bruises on Martha's hands or arms or elsewhere, this suggests she didn't put up much of a fight even if her clothing was "disarrayed." Without more detail one can't surmise whether she'd begun to undress when she was attacked. We can't know if the killer rearranged, undid, cut or ripped the layers of what she had on, and if so was it before or after her death?

In criminal cases of that era, clothing was important mainly for purposes of identifying the victim. Usually it was tossed out the dead-house door into an alleyway. As the Ripper's victim count went up, some socially minded people thought it might be a good idea to collect the clothing of the murdered women and donate it to paupers.

In 1888 there was no such thing as blood-spatter pattern analysis. Little was known about blood. It has a character all its own and a behavior that dutifully abides by the laws of physics. It's unlike any other liquid. When pumping at a high pressure it isn't going to simply drip or slowly drain when an artery is cut. An arterial pattern peaks and dips in rhythm with the heart, and at Martha's crime scene such a pattern high on a wall would indicate that the stab wound to her neck severed an artery and occurred while she was standing.

If the pattern was low on the wall this would suggest she was on the ground. If there was no arterial spatter she may have been dead by the time an artery was cut. The examination of these patterns helps establish the sequence of events during the attack. In none of the Ripper murders do we have the benefit of such information.

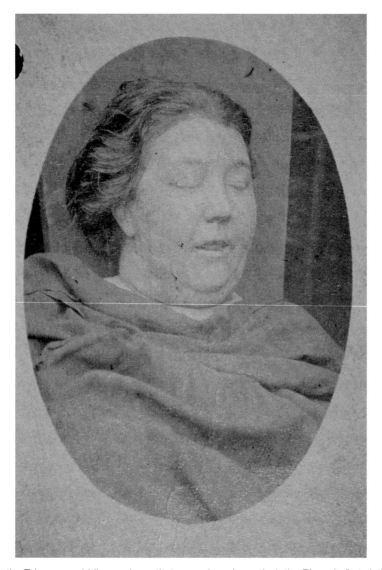

Martha Tabram, a middle-aged prostitute, may have been Jack the Ripper's first victim. Because of her low status in life, her death did not attract much attention.

The stabbing and cutting wounds to Martha Tabram's genitals indicate a sexual component to the crime. There was no indication of "connection," as the Victorians called intercourse. This seems to be consistent in all of the Ripper's murders. It was a pattern that should have been treated seriously but wasn't. Today it would tell us that we're dealing with a compulsive killer for whom the violent act takes the place of sex. Of course one has to wonder how a "connection" was determined. If the victim was a prostitute, she may have "connected" numerous times in one night. She didn't have the luxury of regular bathing or laundry and would have carried many layers of civilization on her clothing and body.

By today's standards Martha Tabram's murder was investigated so poorly it could hardly be called an investigation at all. Her violent death didn't overly excite the police or the press. There was no public uproar. There was very little in the news until the first inquest hearing on August 10. After that there was little follow-up. She wasn't important to anyone in particular. It was assumed, as we used to say when I worked in the morgue, that she simply died the way she lived.

Her murder was savage but it wasn't seen as the initial attack of an evil force that had invaded the Great Metropolis. Martha was considered

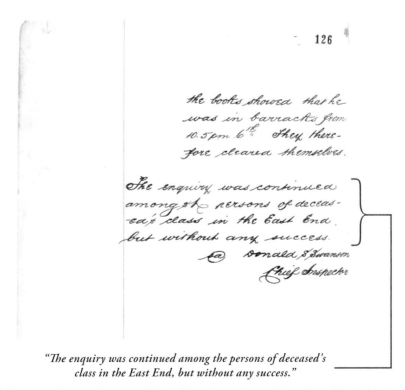

"The enquiry was continued among the persons of deceased's class in the East End, but without any success."

Chief Inspector Swanson's report of Martha Tabram's murder confirmed that officials did not expand the search for her killer outside of "persons of deceased's class in the East End."

a filthy worn-out whore who deliberately placed herself at great risk by the life she chose. The press pointed out that she willingly plied a trade that required her to elude the police as much as her murderer did. It was hard to feel much pity for the likes of her. Public sentiment then was really no different from what it is now. Somehow it's the victim's fault.

Chief Inspector Donald Swanson summarized in his report, "The inquiry was confined amongst persons of deceased's class in the East End, but without any success." The police already had decided what sort of man they were looking for. An East End thug. A lowlife. Someone uneducated and brutish. It was a stereotype that would persist throughout the Ripper's crimes. There are many people who hold the same belief today.

4

A GLORIOUS BOY

WALTER SICKERT WAS BORN in Munich, Germany, on May 31, 1860. One of England's most important artists wasn't English.

His father, Oswald Adalbert Sickert, was Danish, and his English-Irish mother was a beauty named Eleanor Louisa Moravia Henry. Walter was the firstborn of six children, five boys and a girl. Remarkably it appears likely that none of them would ever have children. One might wonder about genetics in the Sickert bloodline and whether nature dead-ended it.

Walter's younger brother Oswald Valentine would grow up to be a failed writer, penning one novel that was published in yellow paper covers by Walter's brother-in-law T. Fisher Unwin. Oswald complained about being afflicted with "the Spleen," which in the nineteenth century was a euphemism for melancholy or moodiness. "It's rather degrading when you think that a compound rhubarb pill can make you contented with life," Oswald says in a letter to arts patron Edward Marsh.

Walter's other siblings didn't fare much better. Robert would become a recluse and die after being hit by a lorry. Leonard was described as seeming strangely detached from reality and would die after a long battle with substance abuse. Bernhard was a failed painter and suffered from depression and alcoholism. A poetic observation their father, Oswald, wrote seems tragically prophetic about his offspring:

Where there is freedom, there, of course,
the bad thing has to be free, too, but it dies,
since it carries the germ of destruction within
itself and dies of its own consequence/logicality.

The Sickerts' only daughter, Helena, had a brilliant mind and a fiery spirit, but health problems plagued her all of her life. She was the only member of the family who seemed interested in humanitarian causes and other people, explaining in her memoirs that early suffering made her compassionate. It gave her a sensitivity toward others. At a young age she was sent off to a harsh boarding school where she was served terrible food and humiliated by the other girls because she was sickly and clumsy. The males in her home convinced her she was ugly. She was inferior because she wasn't a boy. She wasn't an artist in a family of them.

Walter Sickert's grandfather, Johann Jürgen Sickert, was so gifted as a painter that he earned the patronage of Denmark's King Christian VIII. Walter's father, Oswald, was an artist for the humorous German journal *Fliegende Blätter*. He didn't make a name for himself or much of a living. What little he earned he squandered, and his humor could be mocking and cruel. There were few photographs of him I could find but in one he has a long bushy beard and cold eyes that glint of anger.

A search of records turned up a small collection of his writings and art included in Walter's papers at Islington Libraries. It seems to be a Sickert trait that they are a people difficult to track and decipher. Oswald's handwritten High German had to be translated into Low German and then English. The process took about six months and produced only sixty fragments of pages. Most of what he wrote was impossible to read. What could be deciphered offers a glimpse of an extraordinarily strong-willed, complex and talented man who wrote music, plays and poetry.

His gift with words and theatrical flair made him a favorite for giving speeches at weddings, carnivals and other social events. Politically active during the Danish-German War of 1864, he traveled extensively to different cities, encouraging the workingmen to pull together for a united Germany. "I want your help," he said in an undated speech. "Every one of you needs to do his share . . . It is also up to those of you who deal with

Left: Walter Sickert's father, Oswald Sickert, came from Germany but raised his family in Denmark. He worked as an artist for the journal Fliegende Blätterand was politically active. *Right:* Walter Sickert's great-grandmother, pictured here, was German. Sickert's father, Oswald, was born in Germany but later moved to Denmark.

the workers, to the larger tradesmen, factory owners, among you, it is up to you to care for the honest worker."

Oswald could rouse the spirits of the oppressed. He could compose beautiful music and poetic verses full of tenderness and love. He could create cartoonlike artwork that reveals a cruel and fiendish sense of fun. Pages of his diaries show that when he wasn't sketching or giving talks he was wandering. It was a habit his eldest son, Walter, came by honestly.

Oswald was always on the move. In fact, one wonders when he got his work done. His walks might consume the better part of the day. Or he might be on a train somewhere until late at night. A sampling of his activities reveals a man who could scarcely sit still and constantly did what he pleased. His diary pages are incomplete and undated, but there's enough to get the image of a self-absorbed, moody, restless man, a compulsive peripatetic given to moving from place to place. It's unlikely his family always knew where he was or what he was doing.

An example of Oswald Sickert's movements over a seven-day period demonstrates this rather graphically:

On a Wednesday he traveled by train from Eckernförde to Schleswig to Echen to Flensburg in northern Germany. The next day, Thursday, he took a look "at the new road along the railroad" and walked "along the harbor to the Nordertor [North Gate]" and across a field "to the ditch and home." He ate lunch and spent the afternoon at "Notke's beer garden." From there he visited a farm and then returned home. Friday he "went by myself" and met up with a group of people, ate dinner with them, and at 10:00 p.m. returned home. On Saturday he "went for a walk by myself through the city."

Sunday he was out of the house all day. Then he had dinner. Afterward there was piano music and singing at home until 10:00 p.m. Monday he walked to Gottorf, then "back across over the property/estates and the peat bog." Tuesday he went by horse to Mugner's. He fished until 3:00 p.m. and caught "30 perch." Next he visited with acquaintances at a pub, "ate and drank," and returned home at 11:00 p.m.

Oswald's writings make it clear he hated authority, particularly police. His angry, mocking words eerily portend Jack the Ripper's own "catch me if you can" taunts.

"—Hooray! The watchman is asleep!" writes Walter Sickert's father. "When you see him like that, you wouldn't believe that he is a watchman. Shall I nudge him out of love for humanity and tell him what the bell has tolled [or what trouble he is in for]. . . . O no, let him slumber. Maybe he dreams that he has me, let him hold on to this illusion."

Oswald's sentiments about authority must have been voiced within the walls of his home. Walter couldn't have been oblivious to them. He couldn't have been unaware of his father's frequent visits to beer gardens and pubs, to his being "plied with punch."

"I have boozed away the money," Oswald writes. "I sleep during my leisure hours, of which I have plenty."

Whatever prompted his obsessive walks, frequent journeys and regular patronage of pubs and beer gardens, these preoccupations were costly. Oswald didn't earn enough to support his family. He didn't have disposable income to squander. As would be true of his famous artist son, it was the wife who had the money, and without it the family wouldn't have survived. Perhaps it's no coincidence that in a Punch and Judy script Oswald wrote (probably in the early 1860s), the sadistic puppet-husband Punch is spending the family money on booze and cares nothing for his wife and infant son.

PUNCH *appears in the box*:

Ah yes, I believe you don't know me . . . my name is Punch. This also used to be my father's name, and my grandfather's, too.

I like nice clothes. I am married by the way. I have a wife and a child. But that doesn't mean anything.

WIFE (JUDY):

No, I can't stand this anymore! Even this early in the morning, this awful man has drunk brandy!

Oh, what an unhappy woman I am. All earnings are spent on spirits. I have no bread for the children—

If Walter got his restlessness and financial irresponsibility from his father, he got his charm and good looks from his mother, Eleanor or "Nelly." He may have inherited a few of her less attractive attributes as well. His mother's bizarre childhood has an uncanny resemblance to Charles Dickens's *Bleak House*, a novel that Walter would cite as his favorite.

In Dickens's story an orphan girl named Esther is mysteriously sent to live in the mansion of the kind and wealthy Mr. Jarndyce, who later wants to marry her. As a child Nelly was neglected and abandoned. She ended up in the care of a kind and wealthy patron who may have had something more than a platonic regard for her.

Born in 1830, Nelly was the illegitimate daughter of a beautiful dancer who was a heavy drinker and finally ran off to Australia when Nelly was twelve. It was at this juncture in her life that she suddenly found herself in the guardianship of a wealthy, anonymous bachelor. He sent her to a school in Neuville-les-Dieppe on the English Channel in northern France, and over the next six years he wrote her affectionate letters he cryptically signed "R."

When Nelly turned eighteen and at last met her guardian, he revealed himself as Richard Sheepshanks, a former ordained priest turned

Walter Sickert's mother, Eleanor Sickert, was abandoned by her mother at the age of twelve after a turbulent childhood. She married Oswald Sickert, and together they had six children.

much-acclaimed astronomer. He was witty and dashing, everything a young woman might conjure up in her dreams, and she was intelligent and very pretty. Sheepshanks spoiled Nelly. He adored her even more than she adored him. He introduced her to the right people and placed her in the proper settings.

Soon she found herself going to parties, the theater, the opera, traveling abroad and learning new languages. She developed into a cultured young woman under the watchful eye of her doting benefactor. One day to her shock he confessed that he was her biological father. He made her promise to destroy all of his letters to her, and one wonders what was in them. It may very well have been a profession of more than fatherly love. That could explain his reaction when she told him she was getting married.

He was enraged. He accused her of being ungrateful, dishonest and unfaithful. He demanded that she break off the engagement immediately but Nelly refused. So he withdrew his generosity and returned to England. Sheepshanks wrote her several bitter letters before dying suddenly after a stroke. Nelly never got over his death and blamed herself for it. Honoring her promise, she destroyed all of his letters except one that she hid inside an old chronometer of his. "Love me, Nelly, love me dearly, as I love you," it says.

He left her nothing. Fortunately his sister, Anne Sheepshanks, came to Nelly's rescue, giving her a generous allowance that would make it possible for her to support a husband and six children. Her desolate childhood and ultimate betrayal and abandonment by her father would have left their scars. There's no record I could find of how she felt about her irresponsible dance-hall mother. We don't know how she felt about the seemingly incestuous love of a father who was little more than a romantic secret most of her young life. But it would make sense if Nelly suffered from deeply felt grief, anger and shame. She may have been emotionally distant.

Had her daughter, Helena Sickert, not grown up to be a famous suffragette and political figure who wrote her memoirs, it's safe to say that we would know very little about the Sickert family. We might know nothing about what her brother Walter was like as a boy. Almost every published reference to his early life can be traced back to Helena's memoirs. From her we also get a fairly detailed description of their mother, an intelligent, complex woman who could be fun, charming and independent. At other times she was strict, emotionally absent, manipulative and submissive.

The home Nelly Sickert made for her family was an inconsistent one, severe and harsh one minute, then suddenly blossoming into games and song. In the evenings she often sang while Oswald accompanied on the piano. She sang when she was at her needlework and when she took her children for romps in the woods or to swim. She taught them delightful ballads and nonsense songs such as "The Mistletoe Bough" and "She Wore a Wreath of Roses" and the children's favorite:

I am Jack Jumper the youngest but one
I can play nick-nacks upon my own thumb

From an early age, Walter was a fearless swimmer with a head full of pictures and music. He was blue-eyed with long blond curls. His mother used to dress him in "Little Lord Fauntleroy velvet suits," recalled a family friend. Helena's observations don't exactly mirror their mother's endless praises of his "beauty" and "perfect behavior."

Walter may have been lovely to look at but he was anything but obedient, gentle or sweet. Helena depicts him as a charming, energetic and quarrelsome little boy who made friends on command. He was indifferent to them once they no longer amused him or served a useful purpose. His mother often found herself having to console Walter's rejected playmates and fabricate excuses for her son's suddenly vanishing from their lives.

His coldness and self-absorption were obvious at a young age, and his mother's relationship with him might have been a contributing factor to the darkening shades of his character. Nelly may have adored her angelic-looking son but not necessarily for healthy reasons. It's possible he was nothing more than an extension of her ego. Her doting behavior might have been a projection of her own deeply rooted unrequited needs.

She may have treated him the only way she knew how. This very well could have included disconnecting from him emotionally the way her mother had from her. Nelly may have felt the inappropriate intensity that she'd experienced from her father. When Walter was a toddler, an artist named Fuseli insisted on painting the "glorious" little boy. Nelly kept the life-size portrait hanging in her sitting room until the day she died at the age of ninety-two.

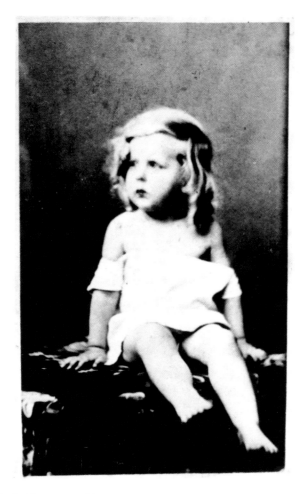

Walter Sickert at two years old.

There is little documentation that might reveal how she reacted to Oswald's pretense that he was head of the household. The dysfunctional playacting that went on with them may have validated Walter's habit of seeking women who would pander to his megalomania and every need. A ritual the children witnessed all too often was "Mummy" begging her husband for money while he dug in his purse and demanded, "How much must I give you, extravagant woman?"

"Will fifteen shillings be too much?" she would ask after going down the list of all their household needs.

Considered a clever child, Walter taught himself to read and write and was said to have a photographic memory.

With great fanfare Oswald would give her money that was hers to begin with, and his scripted generosity would be rewarded with his wife's kisses and expressions of delight. As would be true of his oldest son, Oswald was selfish. He was dominant, controlling and gave the appearance of power that he didn't really have. Women were to be subjugated. He had no patience with children and bonded with none of his own.

Helena recalls that he talked only to Walter, who in later years would claim that he remembered everything his father ever told him. There wasn't much that Walter didn't learn quickly and remember precisely. As a young child, he taught himself to read and write, and throughout his life his acquaintances would marvel at his photographic recall.

Legend has it that Walter was taking a walk with his father one day and passed by a church where Oswald directed his young son's attention to a memorial. "There's a name you will never remember," Oswald commented as he kept walking. Walter paused to read:

MAHARAJA MEERZARAM

GUAHAHAPAJE RAZ

PAREA MANERAMAPAM

MUCHER

K.C.S.I.

When he was eighty years old he could still recall the inscription and write it without error.

5

THORNS AND SHARP STONES

FROM AN EARLY AGE Walter couldn't resist drawing, painting and making models out of wax.

His father would take him to the Royal Academy at Burlington House, and Sickert claimed that what he knew of art history he'd learned from him. Searches through Sickert archives suggest that Oswald may have had a hand in Walter's development as a draftsman as well. Included in a remarkable collection at Islington are sketches originally attributed to Oswald but now believed by some historians and art experts to have been made by the father's talented eldest son. It's possible that Oswald critiqued Walter's early artistic efforts.

Many of the drawings clearly were made by the gifted but tentative hand of someone learning to draw street scenes, buildings and figures. But the creative mind guiding these efforts was disturbed, violent and morbid. There are grotesque scenes of men being boiled alive in a cauldron, and demonic characters with long pointed faces, tails and evil smiles. Absent is even a trace of whimsy. The fantasy behind the art is dark and scary.

A favorite theme is soldiers storming castles and battling one another. A knight abducts a buxom maiden and rides off with her. She looks terrified and seems to be pleading for her life. Sickert could have been talking about his own juvenilia when he described an etching made by Karel Du

Jardin in 1652: a ghastly scene of a "cavalier" on horseback pausing to look at a "stripped" and "hacked"-up "corpse," while troops "with spears and pennants" ride off in the distance.

The most violent amateurish drawing in the Sickert collection at Islington depicts a bosomy woman in a low-cut dress sitting in a chair, her hands bound behind her. Her head is thrown back as a right-handed man plunges a knife into the center of her chest at the level of her sternum. She has additional wounds on the left side of her chest, a wound on the left side of her neck and possibly a wound below her left eye.

Her killer's only facial feature is a slight smile. He's dressed in a suit. Around him is a crowd of rowdy people, one of them a man who appears to be wielding a scalpel. Opposite this sketch on the same scrap of rectangular

The young Sickert's sketches often featured morbid and disturbing scenes, such as this one of heads boiling in a cauldron.

A particularly violent pair of early Sickert sketches depict a man stabbing a woman and another man leaping out at a woman on the street.

paper, a crouching, frightening-looking man is about to spring on a woman dressed in a long skirt, shawl and bonnet.

I've found no evidence that Oswald Sickert was sexually violent. But he could be mean-spirited and stony. His favorite target was his daughter, Helena. Her fear of him was so great that she would tremble in his presence. When she was bedridden with rheumatic fever for two years, he showed no sympathy. After she recovered at age seven, she was very weak and had poor control of her legs. She dreaded it when her father began forcing her to take walks with him.

During these outings he never spoke, and she was forced to keep up with his relentless pace. If she clumsily bumped into him, "he would then silently take me by the shoulder," she writes, "and silently turn me into the opposite direction, where I was apt to run into the wall or gutter." Her mother didn't intervene, and doesn't come across as particularly interested in her homely redheaded daughter. Nelly preferred her "pretty little fellows" with their fair hair and sailor suits.

Walter was by far the prettiest of the fair little fellows and the "cleverest," according to his sister. He usually got his way through manipulation, deception or charm, and other children did his bidding even if his "games" were unfair or unpleasant. When playing chess he thought nothing of changing the rules as it suited him. When he was a bit older, after the family had moved to England in 1868, he began recruiting friends and siblings to perform scenes from Shakespeare. Some of his stage direction was nasty and degrading.

In an unpublished draft of Helena's memoirs, she recalls:

> *I must have been a child when [Walter] roped us in to rehearse the three witches to his Macbeth in a disused quarry near Newquay, which innocently I thought was really called 'The Pit of Achaeron.' Here he drilled us very severely I was made (being appropriately thin and red-haired) to discard my dress & shoes & stockings, in order to brood over the witches cauldron, or stride around it, regardless of thorns and sharp stones, in my eyes the acrid smoke of scorching seaweed.*

This account and others were sanitized or deleted by the time Helena's autobiography was published in 1935. Were it not for a six-page handwritten remnant donated to the National Art Library of the Victoria and Albert Museum, little would be known about Walter's youthful tendencies. I have no doubt that much has been censored and favorably slanted by virtually everyone who's ever written about him, including contemporary art experts and biographers.

In the Victorian era and early 1900s it was unheard of to "tell all." Queen Victoria's family could have burned down one of the palaces with the conflagration made of her private papers after she died. By the time Helena published her autobiography, *I Have Been Young*, her brother Walter was seventy-five years old and a British icon hailed by young artists as the *roi*, the "king." His sister might have had second thoughts about disparaging him in her book. It's a shame we don't have more than six pages to tell us what she witnessed and felt before she refined and enhanced her account of him. It's hard to imagine that their regard for each other was admiring or warm.

He had no use for feminists, and Helena was one of the few women he couldn't dominate. The two of them were never close. It seems she didn't really know what to make of him. He was "at once the most fickle and the most constant of creatures . . . unreasonable, but always rationalizing," she writes. "Utterly neglectful of his friends and relations in normal times and capable of the utmost kindness, generosity and resourcefulness in crises—never bored, except by people."

Sickert scholars agree that he was a "handful." He was "brilliant" with a "volatile temperament." By the time Walter was three his mother told a family friend that he was "perverse and wayward"—a physically strong boy whose "tenderness" easily turned to "temper." Like his father, Walter was disdainful of religion. Authority didn't exist any more than God did.

"I hate Christianity!" Sickert once yelled at a Salvation Army band.

In school he was energetic and intellectually keen but he didn't abide by rules. Those who have written about him are vague and elusive about his "irregularities," as one of his biographers, Denys Sutton, describes them. When Sickert was ten he was "removed" from a boarding school in Reading where he found the "horrible old schoolmistress" intolerable, he would later say.

He was expelled from University College School for reasons unknown, and around 1870 he attended Bayswater Collegiate School. After that he was a student at King's College School for two years. In 1878 he made first class honors on the matriculation exam all schoolchildren took in their last year. But he didn't attend a university. By his late teens, he was pursuing acting, and in 1879 he would meet Whistler and become his pupil, his apprentice. Sickert grew up to be a physically striking man with the emotional maturity of a little boy. He often hurt, ridiculed and betrayed those who cared for him, and this same "difficult" and often cruel spirit is also found in the writings of Jack the Ripper.

After fifteen years of studying the some 250 Ripper-related notes, letters and telegrams that survive in archives, I've formed a horrifying image of a furious, spiteful and cunning child who was the master controller of a brilliant, talented and strong adult. This mocking, hateful personality is recognizable in a startling number of the Jack the Ripper communications. I don't accept the assumption that most of them are hoaxes or the rantings of mentally unbalanced people.

A careful examination of Walter Sickert's and Jack the Ripper's communications is chilling. The way they expressed themselves in their writings and the types of paper and artistic media they used can't be dismissed if one is tenacious and engages the analysis of experts. After years of research I've become increasingly persuaded that a great number of the letters attributed to Jack the Ripper at The National Archives in fact were written by the killer. The majority of those in the London Metropolitan Archives most likely weren't.

Forensic paper analysis wasn't implemented or even known about at the time of the Ripper crimes.

There would have been no reason for police to place much importance on these peculiar and violent communications beyond noting the content and postmark. In some instances they may have resorted to the psychological interpretation of handwriting known as graphology. Analyzing the language in these letters would be done very differently today. Forensic psychologists and FBI profilers would be quite interested in the Ripper's childish, hateful teases and mocking comments. Examples of his taunts include the following:

"Ha Ha Ha"

"Catch me if you can"

"It's a jolly nice lark"

"Love, Jack the Ripper"

"Just to give you a little clue"

"Hold on tight you cunning lot of coppers"

"You might remember me if you try and think a little Ha Ha."

"you donkeys, you double-faced asses"

"The police pass me close every day, and I shall pass one going to post this."

"you made a mistake, if you thought I dident [sic] see you . . ."

"Au revoir, Boss."

"a good Joke I played on them"

"ta ta"

"P.S. You can't trace me by this writing so its [sic] no use"

"I think you all are asleep in Scotland Yard"

"I am now going to make my way to Paris and try my little games"

"Oh, it was such a jolly job the last one."

"Kisses"

"What fools the police are."

"The police now reckon my work a practical joke, well well Jacky's a very practical joker ha ha ha"

"You never caught me and you never will"

Such bravado doesn't mean the Ripper didn't spend his years paranoid and on the run. Walter Sickert writes to his friend Edward Marsh (circa 1914), "you will never know how hunted I have been during the years I have known you." In another letter to artist Sir William Eden (circa 1900), Walter Sickert complains of being "irritable to a pitch of madness, nervous, apprehensive, agonies of fear of nothing!"

He goes on to say that he hides these moods from other people, which is the "worse for me, perhaps." He claims his fearfulness is why at that time he had chosen to live in Normandy or "in the country" as he puts it.

Several years after the Ripper crimes began, Sickert had left London. He wouldn't return until 1905.

My lawyer father used to say that you can tell a lot by what makes a person angry. A careful review of the letters, particularly those in The National Archives, reveals that Jack the Ripper was intellectually arrogant. It angered him when people considered him primitive or stupid. Even when he disguised his handwriting to give the appearance that a letter was penned by someone ignorant or crazy, he didn't like to hear that he was any such thing.

The Ripper couldn't resist reminding people he was literate and superior. Some letters from him show off his perfect spelling and his neat and at times beautiful script, and his excellent vocabulary reveals how well informed he was. As the Ripper protests more than once in communications that would be increasingly ignored by the police and the press, "I ain't

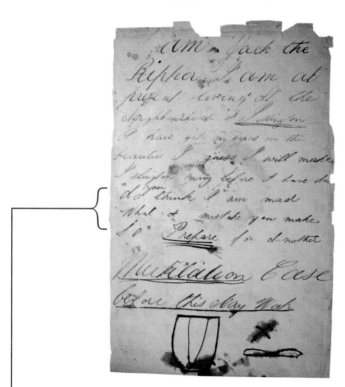

Jack the Ripper loved to taunt readers of his letters. In this one, he says, "Do you think I am mad? What a mistake you make."

a maniac as you say I am to dam [*sic*] clever for you" and "Do you think I am mad? What a mistake you make."

In all likelihood an illiterate person wouldn't use the word *conundrum*. Someone uneducated wouldn't sign a letter "Mathematicus." But the Ripper did. In 1888, Mathematicus was also a pseudonym used in at least one letter to the editor of *The Times*. In another letter to the editor, a writer using the pseudonym Pomingolarna references "the correspondent Mathematicus." The Pomingolarna letter was published September 17,

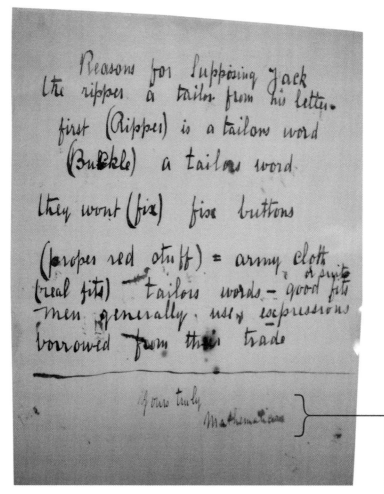

Despite the misspellings in his letters, the Ripper showed his intellect through his vocabulary. In this one, he signs it "Mathematicus."

1888. That happens to be the date of possibly the first Ripper letter where the name Jack the Ripper appears.

It was the killer himself who created his own public persona. Had he not written letters and signed them with variations of Jack the Ripper, we wouldn't know the name. All we might be aware of is that in the summer and fall of 1888 someone began killing and mutilating prostitutes in London's East End. Sadly such crimes were common—unless the histrionic and narcissist Jack the Ripper was involved.

He scripted violent high drama and riddles that are so intricate they are maddening. Whoever pursues him is left frustrated, baffled and overwhelmed. Are we making connections that don't exist? Are we missing allusions he deliberately makes in this "catch me if you can" game of his? Pomingalarna is an area of Australia on the outskirts of Wagga Wagga. It's a place that was a key element in the Tichborne case, one of the most celebrated trials of the nineteenth century and another obsession of Sickert's.

In 1854 Roger Charles Tichborne, the heir to a family fortune, was lost at sea and a year later declared dead. His bereft mother sent out inquiries around the world, hoping someone might have information. In 1865 a butcher in Wagga Wagga named Arthur Orton claimed to be her son, and the result was a long-drawn-out, highly publicized trial that Orton lost. One has to wonder why in September of 1888 someone writing a letter to the editor of *The Times* would allude to an area of Australia made famous by the Tichborne case. When Pomingolarna answered Mathematicus, was it the same individual writing a letter under one odd name and answering it under another? More fun? Another "Ha Ha"? Or simply a coincidence?

"You can't trace me by this writing," the Ripper brags on November 10, 1888.

He uses vulgarities such as "cunt" and often goes out of his way to misspell, mangle or write in snarls. Then he mailed at least some of his violent, mocking letters—"I have not got a stamp"—from Whitechapel as if to imply that Jack the Ripper was a low-life resident of the slums. Few Whitechapel paupers could read or write. A large percentage of that population was foreign and didn't speak English—and an ignorant brute isn't likely to refer to the people he has murdered as "victims."

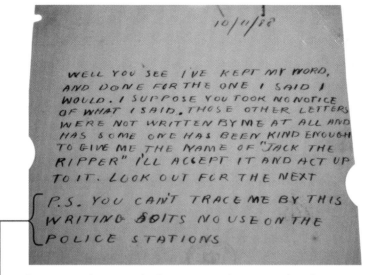

10/11/88

WELL YOU SEE I'VE KEPT MY WORD,
AND DONE FOR THE ONE I SAID I
WOULD. I SUPPOSE YOU TOOK NO NOTICE
OF WHAT I SAID. THOSE OTHER LETTERS
WERE NOT WRITTEN BY ME AT ALL AND
HAS SOME ONE HAS BEEN KIND ENOUGH
TO GIVE ME THE NAME OF "JACK THE
RIPPER" I'LL ACCEPT IT AND ACT UP
TO IT. LOOK OUT FOR THE NEXT

P.S. YOU CAN'T TRACE ME BY THIS
WRITING SO IT'S NO USE ON THE
POLICE STATIONS

"P.S. You can't trace me by this writing so it's no use on the police stations."

In his November 10, 1888 letter, the Ripper taunts the police, claiming his letter is untraceable.

He probably wouldn't describe mutilating a woman as giving her a "CeaSerzain Operation."

Words such as *games* and *ha ha* also weren't commonly used by the British. They were, however, favorite expressions of the American-born James McNeill Whistler. His "ha ha" or "cackle," as Sickert called it, was often described as a much-dreaded laugh that grated against the English ear. Whistler's "ha ha" could stop a dinner party conversation. When it preceded him into a room, his enemies would freeze or get up and leave. One can read hundreds of letters written by Victorians and not see a single "ha ha," but the Ripper letters are filled with them. Some of Sickert's extant writings have "ha ha" in them too.

Generations have been misled to think the Ripper letters are pranks or the work of a journalist bent on creating a sensational story. They're dismissed as the drivel of lunatics because that was what the press and the police thought at the time. Investigators and those intrigued by the Ripper crimes have focused on the handwriting more than the language. But handwriting is easy to disguise. It's often obvious when it has been. Squiggly strokes and hesitation marks are clues that the pen or pencil

Ripper letters were sometimes riddled with mocking language and a distinctive American-style "Ha. Ha."

paused as the person thought about how to write a word. Natural writing is a reflex. It's clear that much of the Ripper's writing is faked.

A typical style of disguise in ransom notes is block printing, which no longer is the person's handwriting at all. I once wrote my name five different ways and asked a forensic document examiner to take a look. Could he recognize the writing was mine? He said no. The handwriting comparison of the Ripper and Sickert letters will never be the strongest evidence in this case. But the unique and repeated use of linguistic combinations in multiple texts is the fingerprint of a person's mental wiring, emotions, background and education.

Like his father, Walter Sickert had an ugly habit of calling people "fools." The Ripper was fond of this disparagement and believed he was more clever and intelligent than everyone else. Psychopaths are confident they can outsmart those trying to catch them. These cunning manipulators love to play games, to harass and taunt. What a thrill to set so much chaos in motion and sit back and watch. Jack the Ripper wasn't the first psychopath to play games and get away with murder. But he may be the most original, creative and highly functioning killer in the history of criminalistics.

Sickert probably had the IQ of a genius. As a draftsman he was better than most of his peers, his work revered but not always enjoyed. Much of his art is gloomy, violent and morbid, showing no hint of whimsy, no tender touches. But he never pretended to paint pretty pictures. He was a *Mathematicus*, a technician. "All lines in nature . . . are located somewhere in radiants within the 360 degrees of four right angles," he writes. "All straight lines . . . and all curves can be considered as tangents to such lines."

He would teach his students that "the basis of drawing is a highly cultivated sensibility to the exact direction of lines . . . within the 180 degrees of two right angles." By his definition, "Art may be said to be . . . the individual co-efficient of error . . . in [the craftsman's] effort to attain the expression of form."

Sickert's precise way of thinking and calculating was evident not only in his own description of his work but also in the way he executed it. His method in painting was to "square up" his sketches, enlarging them geometrically to preserve the exact perspectives and proportions. In some of his pictures the grid of his mathematical method is faintly visible behind the paint. In Jack the Ripper's games and violent crimes the grid of who he was is faintly visible behind his machinations.

6

WALTER AND THE BOYS

B Y AGE FIVE, Sickert had undergone three major surgeries for a fistula. Over the past decade, his physical defect has become the source of considerable uproar.

At the time of my original research I wasn't aware that anyone had explained the exact nature of this fistula or why three life-threatening operations were required to repair it. Since this book was first published, however, various people have rallied to the Sickert cause and claimed that his fistula was a defect of his anus. That's certainly not what his nephew John Lessore told me on July 6, 2001.

In a conversation that took place at his painting studio in Peckham, I asked him about the fistula mentioned in several books I'd read. He replied without hesitation that Sickert had "a hole in his penis." As I was driving away, moments after this conversation, I wrote down what had transpired: "W.S. had a fistula of the penis according to his nephew John, who was a *lovely* man." I underlined *lovely* twice. "I bought 5 of his [John Lessore's] paintings—they are gentle and kind as he is. Of course he says W.S. in addition to being such a marvelous and important artist absolutely was not J the R. I also got a book with W.S. notes and a WS [*sic*] painting table."

This conversation was witnessed by my then chief of staff, Irene Shulgin, and on November 25, 2007, she and I exchanged e-mails about it. "We were in John's studio, he was in his wheelchair, and I asked him about Sickert's fistula," I wrote to her, "and he literally jumped in—almost interrupted me—and said, 'he had a hole in his penis.'"

Irene replied, "I remember the meeting with John Lessore the same way you did. We were both shocked by the way he just came out with the information. Like it was old news."

I don't think John Lessore placed any significance in what he said to me that July day when we were having such a pleasant chat. He suggested I write a biography of his famous uncle. What I eventually wrote wasn't exactly what Lessore had in mind. Since the first edition of this book was published, his comment about Sickert's fistula seems to have been relegated to family lore. I suppose we're to assume that a nephew of Sickert's third wife was simply repeating a rumor or was mistaken.

Worse are public criticisms that I twisted the facts. Supposedly, I make the ridiculous argument that "penile mutilation is the mark of a serial killer," as was stated in *The Art Newspaper* in December of 2002. Matthew Sturgis claims in his biography of Sickert that my theory about him having "a malfunctioning penis" is "demonstrably false." I'm not sure how such a thing can be demonstrated. Especially at this late date in time.

There may well be confusion about the anatomical location of Sickert's fistula. The malformation could have been an external opening between the urinary tract and the rectum. It could have involved both the penis and the anus. What's a certainty is that the repeated painful and mutilating surgeries on the anus, the penis or both would have been devastating, especially if the patient was a young child. It's indisputable that by the time he was five, Walter had undergone three serious surgeries. He would have suffered some physical and psychological effect from them.

In 1975 the *International Journal of Psychiatry in Medicine* published an article that offered the following interesting speculation about nightmarish medical experiences and the Ripper:

It is possible that Jack the Ripper can be understood in terms of doctor-identification borne of one or more terrifying experiences he may have had with doctors during his childhood. The fantasies acted out by this primitive murderer are similar

*to the fantasies experienced by people who have been surgically
traumatized as children. The evidence suggests that the activities
of Jack the Ripper resemble the acting-out of a horror story in
which he, as the main character, played to the population of
London as an actor plays to his audience.*

Other than what John Lessore said about Sickert's fistula, I've discovered nothing else that might tell us it was a penile one. It's also unlikely that the deformity of one's genitals would be openly discussed with friends, colleagues and biographers. It's entirely possible that people outside Sickert's most intimate circle wouldn't have known such a detail about him.

References to his problem say little more than that he underwent two failed surgeries "for fistula in Munich," according to Denys Sutton. In 1865 while the Sickert family was in Dieppe, his great-aunt, Anne Sheepshanks, suggested a third attempt by a prominent London surgeon. Helena Sickert doesn't mention her elder brother's medical history in her memoirs, although Walter Sickert himself obliquely alluded to his fistula when he used to joke that he came to London to be "circumcised."

In the nineteenth century, fistulas of the anus, rectum and vagina were so common that St. Mark's Hospital in London was dedicated to treating them. There are no references to fistulas of the penis in the medical literature I found. But the term could have been loosely if not euphemistically used to describe penile anomalies such as the one Sickert may have suffered from. The word *fistula* is Latin for "reed" or "pipe." Such an abnormal opening or sinus can cause such atrocities as a rectum connected to the bladder, to the urethra or to the vagina.

A fistula can be congenital. Often it's caused by an abscess that takes the path of least resistance, burrowing through tissue or the skin surface to form a new opening for urine, feces and pus to escape. Fistulas could be extremely uncomfortable, embarrassing and even fatal. Early medical journals cite harrowing cases of miserably painful ulcers, bowels emptying into bladders, bowels or bladders emptying into vaginas or uteri, and menstruation through the rectum.

During the mid-1800s, doctors attributed the cause of fistulas to all sorts of things: sitting on damp seats or outside on omnibuses after

ST. MARK'S HOSPITAL.

When Walter was a child, St. Mark's Hospital in London treated him for an ailment rumored to be a fistula.

physical exertion, swallowing small bones or pins, the "wrong" food, alcohol, improper clothing, the "luxurious" use of cushions or sedentary habits associated with certain professions. Dr. Frederick Salmon, the founder of St. Mark's Hospital, treated Charles Dickens for a fistula. Supposedly it was caused by the great writer's sitting at his desk too much.

St. Mark's was established in 1835 to relieve the poor of rectal diseases and their "baneful varieties," and in 1854 moved to City Road in Islington. In 1865, the hospital suffered financial devastation when its secretary fled from London after embezzling £400, or one-quarter of the annual income. A fund-raising dinner hosted by the fistula-free Dickens was proposed. He declined the honor.

In the fall of that same year, Walter Sickert arrived at St. Mark's to be "cured" by its recently appointed surgeon, Dr. Alfred Cooper, who later married the daughter of the Earl of Fife and was knighted by King Edward VII. Dr. Cooper was a twenty-seven-year-old medical star rapidly on the rise in his profession, his specialties the treatment of rectal and venereal diseases. Searches of his published writings and other literature failed to unearth any mention of his treating fistulas of the penis.

Possible explanations for Sickert's defect range from fair to awful. Nature may have slighted him with a genetically inherited malformation of the genitals called hypospadias. In such a case the urethra terminates just below the tip of the penis or somewhere along the shaft or behind the scrotum. German medical literature published at the time of Sickert's birth indicates that a case of simple hypospadias was "trifling" and more common than generally known. A "trifling" case meant the fistula wouldn't interfere with procreation and wasn't worth the risk of a surgical procedure that could cause infection and death.

Since Sickert's malformation required three surgeries, his problem certainly wasn't "trifling." Obviously whatever was wrong with him was extremely serious. In 1864 Dr. Johann Ludwig Casper, professor of forensic medicine at the University of Berlin, wrote about more serious forms of hypospadias. He describes an opening in the urethra at the "root" or base of the penis. Even worse is epispadias, when the urethra is divided and runs like a "shallow gutter" along the back of a rudimentary or incompletely developed penis. In mid-nineteenth-century Germany such cases were considered a type of hermaphroditism or "doubtful sex."

When Sickert was born in Germany his gender may have been ambiguous, suggesting his penis was small, possibly misshapen and imperforate (lacking a urethra). If the bladder was connected to a canal that opened near the anus at the base of the penis there may have been a cleft in the scrotum that resembled the female clitoris, vagina and labia. It's possible that Sickert's gender wasn't clearly established until his testicles were discovered in the folds of the so-called labia and it was determined that he had no uterus. In cases of ambiguous genitalia, if the gender turns out to be male, he's usually masculine and healthy in all respects as he matures. The exception is the penis. It may be acceptably functional but certainly not normal. In the early days of surgery, attempts to repair seriously deformed genitalia usually resulted in mutilation.

Without medical records I can't know exactly what Sickert's anomaly was. But if his problem was only "trifling" hypospadias, why did his parents resort to risky surgery? Why did his mother and father wait so long before attempting to correct what must have been a very unpleasant affliction? He was five when he underwent surgery the third time. One wonders how soon this occurred following the first two operations.

We know that his great-aunt interceded to bring him to London. This suggests his disability was acute and that the two previous operations may have been recent and resulted in complications. If he was three or four when this nightmarish medical ordeal began, it could be that his parents delayed corrective procedures until they were certain of his gender. I don't know when Sickert was named Walter Richard. I'm unaware of a birth certificate or record of a christening that might tell us.

In Helena's memoirs she writes that when she was a child "we" always referred to Walter and his brothers as "Walter and the boys." Whom was she referring to when she wrote *we*? I doubt her brothers referred to themselves as *Walter and the boys*. I would be surprised if Helena came up with the phrase on her own. Four years younger than Walter, she wasn't born when he had his first surgery. I'm inclined to suspect that the reference to *Walter and the boys* originated with one or both parents.

Given Helena's portrayal of a young Walter as bright, controlling and a law unto himself, it may be that he wasn't placed in the same category as the other sons. Possibly the phrase *Walter and the boys* was a way of acknowledging his precocity. It also could be that he was physically different from his brothers or maybe from all healthy boys. The repeated use of the phrase could have been humiliating and emasculating for young Walter. He was further traumatized by nightmarish medical procedures. When corrective surgery for hypospadias occurs after the age of eighteen months, it can create fears of castration.

If Sickert's surgeries involved his penis, the sequelae would have been strictures and scarring that could have made erections painful or impossible. He may have suffered partial amputation. I find it interesting that his art doesn't seem to include nude males, with the exception of two sketches

I found that appear to have been done when he was in his teens or in art school. In each the nude male figure has a vague stub of a penis.

More than a dozen Ripper letters include phallic drawings of knives. All are long daggerlike instruments except for two strange, short truncated blades. One of the stubby-knife letters was mailed on July 22, 1889, some eight months after the police seemed convinced the murderous spree had ended. Penned in black ink on two pages of cheap paper, the Ripper says, "Not a very big blade but sharp." Following his signature is a postscript that trails off in the very clear letters "R. St. w." Possibly he literally meant *R Street west*. Possibly the cryptic initials are a double entendre, another "catch me if you can."

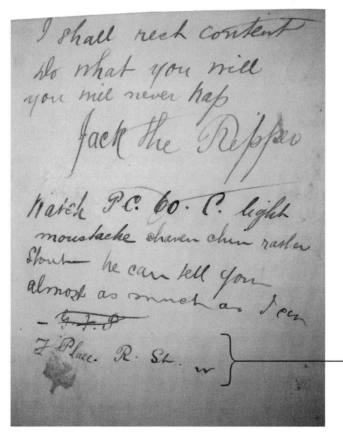

A Ripper letter closes with the ambiguous initials "R. St. w." Sickert sometimes abbreviated his last name as "St."

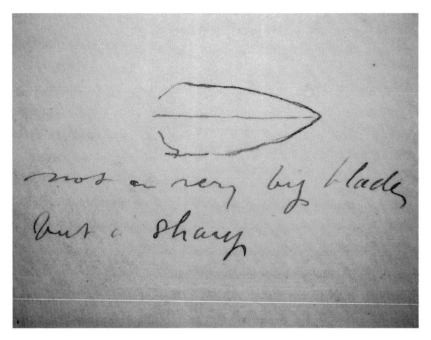

A July 1889 Ripper letter features a sketch of a short phallic blade and reads, "not a very big blade but sharp."

On a number of Sickert's paintings, etchings and sketches he abbreviates Sickert as St. In later years he puzzled the art world by deciding that he was no longer Walter Sickert. He was Richard Sickert and he signed his work "R.S." or "R. St." In a Ripper letter dated September 30, 1889, two months after the one I just described, there's another similarly drawn truncated knife blade. In addition there is what appears to be a scalpel or straight razor with the initials R (possibly W) S on the blade as if faintly etched there.

There's no indication I could find that Sickert ever suffered from infections or other complications of his bowels, rectum or anus. But we know from his letters that in later life he periodically suffered from abscesses and boils that would send him to bed. He would attempt to recover on his own. Throughout his life he assiduously avoided doctors. His trouble with urinary tract infections was consistent with strictures caused by repeated surgeries to the penis, and in a letter he wrote to artist Sir William Eden (circa 1901), Sickert mentions how much he wants "a sound cock again."

I don't know if his unsound "cock" was a temporary disability due to another urinary tract infection or if he was referring to a permanent deformity. But whatever caused these infections, they were damaging to his health. When he died on January 22, 1942, his cause of death was recorded as uremia (kidney failure) due to chronic nephritis (kidney disease), with a contributing factor of myocardial degeneration (heart disease that can accompany kidney disease).

An exact diagnosis of Sickert's congenital deformity and any other health problems associated with it may always remain elusive. But something was wrong. In 1899 he refers to his "organs of generation," to having "suffered all his life" with "physical misery." St. Mark's patient records don't exist prior to 1900, and it doesn't appear that Sir Alfred Cooper kept any papers that might reveal information about Sickert's surgery in 1865. In that era, whatever ordeal he went through couldn't have been pleasant, especially if the surgery involved his penis.

Anesthetics such as ether, nitrous oxide (laughing gas) and chloroform had been discovered some thirty years earlier but it wasn't until 1847 that Great Britain began using chloroform. This may not have helped young

A second Ripper letter depicting a stubby blade shows the initials "R" (possibly "W") and "S" inscribed on the scalpel-like tool.

Walter much. Unlike Queen Victoria, who decades earlier had insisted on chloroform during childbirth, Dr. Salmon, the head of St. Mark's, didn't believe in anesthesia. He didn't allow the use of chloroform in his hospital because it was prone to cause death if the dose wasn't just right.

It's uncertain whether Walter was chloroformed during his two surgeries in Germany. He does mention in a letter to Jacques-Émile Blanche that he remembered being chloroformed while his father looked on. It's hard to know exactly what Sickert was referring to or when or how many times or even if he was telling the truth. He may or may not have been given anesthesia in London when Dr. Cooper operated on him in 1865. What's most amazing is that the little boy didn't die.

Only a year earlier in 1864 Louis Pasteur had proven that germs cause disease. Three years later in 1867 Joseph Lister would argue that germs could be combatted by using carbolic acid as an antiseptic. There was no such thing as antibiotics. Infection was such a common cause of hospital deaths that many people refused to be operated on. They preferred to take their chances with cancer, gangrene, injuries and other potentially fatal maladies.

One can only imagine Walter's terror when at the age of five he was whisked away by his father to the foreign city of London. Leaving behind mother and siblings, Walter found himself in the care of a parent not known for compassion or warmth. Oswald Sickert doesn't seem the sort to hold a little boy's hand. He may not have offered words of love and comfort when he helped his son into the horse-drawn taxi that would take them to St. Mark's.

His father may have said nothing at all when he left Walter at the hospital with his small bag of belongings, turning him over to the care of the matron, possibly Mrs. Elizabeth Wilson. A seventy-two-year-old widow, she was a stickler for protocol and discipline. She would have assigned Walter a bed, placed his belongings in a locker, deloused and bathed him. Then she would have read him the hospital rules. At that time Mrs. Wilson had one assistant nurse. There was no nurse on duty at night.

I could find no record of how long Walter was in the hospital before Dr. Cooper performed the surgical procedure. I don't know whether chloroform or an injection of a 5 percent solution of cocaine or any other type of anesthesia or pain reliever was used. Since anesthetizing patients didn't become standard practice at St. Mark's until 1882, one might suspect the worst. One can only imagine his terror when he was brought inside the operating theater where an open coal fire blazed to warm the room and heat the irons used to cauterize bleeding.

Only steel instruments were sterilized. Dressing gowns and towels weren't. Most surgeons donned black frock coats not unlike the ones butchers wore in slaughterhouses. The stiffer and filthier with blood, the more it boasted of a surgeon's experience and rank. Cleanliness was considered to be finicky and affected, and a London hospital surgeon of that era compared washing a frock coat to an executioner manicuring his nails before chopping off a person's head.

St. Mark's operating table was a bedstead. One would assume it was an iron one with head- and footboards removed. What a ghastly impression Walter must have had of an iron bedstead. On his ward he was confined to one. He was operated on one. It would be understandable if he associated an iron bedstead with bloody, painful terror and rage. He was alone. His father may not have been very reassuring and might have viewed his son's birth defect with shame or disgust. Walter was German. This was his first time in London. He was abandoned and powerless in an English-speaking prison where he was surrounded by suffering and subjected to the orders, probing, scrubbings and bitter medicines of a no-nonsense nurse.

Assuming Mrs. Wilson was on duty at the time of Walter's surgery, she would have assisted in the procedure by placing him on his back and separating his thighs. Typically in operations on the rectum or the genitals, the patient was virtually hog-tied, with arms straightened, legs arched, wrists bound to ankles. Walter may have been restrained with cloth ligatures. As an extra precaution the nurse may have firmly held his legs in place while Dr. Cooper took a scalpel and cut along the fistula's entire track according to the hospital's standard procedure.

If Walter was lucky, the ordeal began by his feeling suffocated as his nose and mouth were covered with a chloroform-soaked rag that was guaranteed to make him violently nauseated later. If he was an unlucky little boy, he was wide awake and experienced every horror happening to

This surgical kit is similar to those that would have been used during Sickert's childhood.

him. It's no wonder Sickert would go through life with no love for "those terrible hospital nurses, their cuffs, their enemas & their razors," as he would write more than fifty years later.

Dr. Cooper may have used a blunt knife for separating tissue and a curved director (steel probe) to pass through the opening in the penis. He may have selected a trocar to puncture tender flesh and passed a section of stout thread through the track of the new opening. He would have tied a firm knot at the end to strangulate the tissue over time in much the same way a thread or post keeps the hole in a newly pierced ear from closing.

It all depends on what was really wrong with Walter. But Dr. Cooper's corrective procedures would have been more extensive and painful after two earlier surgeries in Germany. There would have been scar tissue. There could have been other disastrous sequelae such as strictures and possibly partial or almost complete amputation. His published medical procedures don't mention malformations of the penis. But his method when performing typical fistula operations on a child was to operate as quickly as possible to prevent shock and ensure that the "little patient" wasn't "exposed" or left with open wounds "more than absolutely necessary." At the end of this ordeal he would close any incisions with silk sutures called "ligatures" and pack absorbent cotton wool into the wounds.

While Walter was going through all this and who knows what else, the elderly Mrs. Wilson or some other nurse in her starchy uniform would have assisted as needed. She would have done her best to quiet straining limbs and screams if he hadn't been anesthetized. If he had been, her face may have been the last one he saw as the sickly sweet chloroform knocked him out. She may have been the first person he saw when he woke up throbbing with pain and retching.

In 1841 Charles Dickens was operated on without anesthesia. In a letter he describes: "I suffered agonies, as they related all to me, and did violence to myself in keeping to my seat. I could scarcely bear it." Surgery on the penis, the rectum or the anus would have been a terrifying torture, especially if the patient was a five-year-old foreigner who couldn't have possessed the coping skills, the insight or perhaps sufficient fluency in English to understand what was happening to him. It's awful to consider what he might have imagined when a nurse changed his dressings, administered his medicines or appeared at his bedside with a supply of leeches if he had an inflammation believed to be due to an excess of blood.

The nurse may have had a sweet bedside manner. She may have been strict and humorless. A typical requirement in those days was that she was single or widowed, ensuring that all her time could be devoted to the hospital. Nurses were underpaid. They worked long, grueling hours and were exposed to extraordinarily unpleasant conditions and risks. It wasn't uncommon for them to "get into drink," to run home for a nip, to show up at work a bit mellow.

Walter's hospital stay must have seemed to him an endless stretch of bleak, scary days. Breakfast at 8:00 a.m. was followed by milk and soup at 11:30, then a late-afternoon meal, with lights out at 9:30 p.m. There he lay in pain day in and out with no one on duty at night to hear him cry or comfort him in his native tongue. Had he hated Nurse Wilson or whoever tended to him, no one could blame him. Had he believed this authoritative medical woman was the one who mutilated him and caused him so much anguish, it would be understandable. Had he hated his mother for being far away from him during his ordeal, it would come as no surprise.

In the nineteenth century if one was illegitimate or the child of an illegitimate parent it was a terrible stigma. In the narrow minds of many Victorians when Sickert's maternal grandmother had sex out of wedlock she enjoyed it, meaning she suffered from the same genetic disorder that prostitutes did. The common belief was that this congenital defect was passed down the bloodline. It was a "contagious blood poison" routinely described in the newspapers as a "disease that has been the curse of mankind from an early period in the history of the race, leaving its baneful effects on posterity to the third and fourth generations."

Sickert might have blamed his boyhood agonies, his humiliations and his possibly maimed masculinity on a genetic defect or "blood poison" that he inherited from his immoral dance-hall grandmother and his illegitimate mother. The psychological overlays to young Walter's physical curse are tragic to contemplate. He was damaged. His language as an adult reveals a significant preoccupation with "things medical" when he was writing about things that weren't.

Throughout his letters and art reviews he uses medical terms as metaphors, such as *operating table, operation, diagnosis, dissection, laying bare, surgeon, doctors, fateful theater, castrated, eviscerated, all your organs taken out, anesthetized, anatomy, ossify, deformation, inoculated, vaccinating.* Some of these images are quite shocking and revolting when suddenly they appear in the middle of a paragraph about life or art.

His violent metaphors and descriptions are startling: *morbid horror, horrors, deadly, dead, death, dead ladies' hearts, hacking himself to pieces, terrify, fear, violent, violence, prey, cannibalism, nightmare, stillborn, dead work, dead drawings, blood, putting a razor to his throat, nailing up coffins, putrefied, razor, knife, cutting.* In a 1912 article for *The English Review* he wrote, "Enlarged photographs of the naked corpse should be in every art school as a standard of drawing from the nude."

7

THE DAUGHTERS OF COBDEN

E LLEN MILLICENT ASHBURNER COBDEN was born on August 18, 1848, in Dunford, England. By all accounts she was fragile and far too sensitive.

Letters she wrote as a young girl visiting Paris depict a kind, tender soul who delighted in saving a sparrow that had fallen out of its nest in the garden. "A dear little tame thing it will eat out of my hand and perch upon my finger," she describes to a pen pal in 1860, the year Walter Sickert was born.

Ellen's early years seem happy and full of adventure. She describes her mother, Kate, planning a lovely children's party with fifty or sixty guests. Best of all, Ellen was going to the circus. Afterward they would have a picnic in an "enormous tree" with a staircase leading to a table on top. Ellen had just learned a special trick of "putting an egg in a wine bottle," she writes cheerily.

Life back in England was not so enchanting for her famous politician father, Richard Cobden. In a letter he wrote to her at the time he describes a violent storm that slammed the family estate in West Sussex, tearing up thirty-six trees by the roots. A severe cold front destroyed most of the shrubbery including the evergreens. The vegetable garden would be barren come summer.

Richard Cobden, Ellen Sickert's father, rose from a difficult childhood to become a famous politician.

The report seems a foreshadowing of the evil that had entered the world through a distant city in Germany. Ellen's future husband soon enough would cross the Channel and settle in London, where he would uproot and destroy countless lives, including hers. Walter Sickert couldn't have been more unlike the father she idolized.

Numerous biographies have been written about Richard Cobden. All of them portray him as a courageous, kind man intimately acquainted with suffering. One of eleven children, he endured a desolate, harsh childhood, much of it spent away from home while his father's disastrous business sense spiraled the family to ruin. During Cobden's growing-up years he worked for his uncle, a merchant in London, and attended a school in

Yorkshire. This period of his life was so physically and emotionally difficult that in years to come he could scarcely bring himself to speak of it.

Suffering bears the fruits of unselfishness and love in some people, and it did with him. There was nothing bitter or unkind about him, not even when he was battered by his most derisive detractors during his polarizing political career. His great passion was people. He was never far from his pained memories of watching farmers, including his own father, lose everything they owned. Cobden's compassion inspired his determination to repeal the Corn Laws, a terrible piece of legislation enacted in 1815 when the Napoleonic Wars left England almost in a state of famine.

Bread was precious. The Corn Laws (*corn* meant *grain*) kept people poor and hungry by making it illegal for a baker to sell his loaves until after they had been out of the oven for at least twenty-four hours. If bread was stale, people weren't as likely to overeat. They would "waste not, want not," and the penalty for defying this law was severe. Bakers were fined as much as five pounds and court costs. As a small boy, Cobden watched the desperate come to Dunford and beg for alms or food that his own family couldn't afford.

Only well-off farmers and landlords profited, and they made sure that the price of grain remained as high in good times as it had been in bad. Landlords who wanted to keep prices inflated were the majority in Parliament, and the Corn Laws weren't difficult to pass. The logic was simple. Place impossibly high duties on imported foreign grains, and the supply in England stays low, the prices artificially high. The enactment of the Corn Laws was disastrous for the common worker. Riots broke out in London and other parts of the country.

The laws would remain in effect until 1846, when Cobden won his fight to repeal them. To honor him for this, the vestry of St. Pancras erected a statue of him in Camden Town. His future son-in-law, Sickert, would later have a habit of riding past in a hansom and making mocking remarks. He could never measure up to Cobden, and likely had heard far too much about him from Ellen. She worshipped her humanitarian father.

Respected at home and abroad, Cobden was invited to stay in the White House during his first trip to America, where he gained the admiration and friendship of author Harriet Beecher Stowe (best known for *Uncle*

Tom's Cabin, and according to genealogies and family lore believed to be an ancestor of mine). She visited Cobden at Dunford in 1853, and the two of them discussed the importance of "cultivating cotton by free labour." In an essay she wrote a year later she described him as a slender man of small stature who had "great ease of manner" and "the most frank, fascinating smile." He was a peer to every powerful politician in England including Sir Robert Peel, the father of the police force that would one day take on Jack the Ripper and lose.

A devoted family man, Cobden became the only stability in his five daughters' young lives after his only son, Richard Brooks, died of scarlet fever at age fifteen in 1856 while away at a boarding school near Heidelberg. The story is made all the more tragic by an almost unforgivable blunder. The headmaster contacted a Cobden family friend and each man assumed the other had wired the father about his beloved son's sudden death.

The boy had been buried by the time Richard Cobden got the news in a most heart-wrenching way. Having just sat down to breakfast in his London hotel room on Grosvenor Street, he was going through his mail and found an April 3 letter from his son. Cobden eagerly read it first, then opened another letter that consoled him over his terrible loss. Stunned and beside himself with grief, Cobden immediately began the five-hour journey to Dunford, anguishing over how to tell his family, especially Kate. She'd already lost two children. She was unhealthily attached to her only son.

Cobden appeared at Dunford ashen and drawn, and broke down as he told the family what had happened. The shock was more than Kate could bear. After several days of denial, she fell into an almost catatonic state, sitting "like a statue, neither speaking nor seeming to hear," Cobden writes. Hour by hour he watched his wife's hair turn white.

Seven-year-old Ellen had lost her brother and now she'd lost her mother. Kate Cobden was emotionally stricken, stumbling "over [Richard's] corpse as she is passing from room to room," as her husband described it. She became addicted to opiates, and Ellen found herself in a role too overwhelming for any young girl to assume. Just as Richard Brooks had become his mother's best friend, Ellen became a replacement helpmeet for her father. It was the same role she would play with Sickert.

On September 21, 1864, when she was sixteen, her father asked her in a letter to please look after her four younger sisters. "Much will depend on your influence & still more on your example," he writes. "I wished to have told you how much your Mamma & I looked to your good example." He goes on to say that he expects Ellen to help "bring [your sisters] into a perfect state of discipline." This was an unrealistic expectation for a sixteen-year-old struggling with her own losses. The burden and pain must have become almost unendurable when her father died a year later.

Cobden was susceptible to respiratory infections that sent him to the seaside or the countryside where the air was better than the sooty soup of London. His last trip to London before his death was in March 1865, and Ellen accompanied him. They stayed in a lodging house on Suffolk Street, reasonably close to the House of Commons. Immediately he was laid up with asthma as black smoke gushed from chimneys of nearby houses and the east wind blew the noxious air into his room.

A week later he lay in bed praying that the winds would mercifully shift, but his asthma worsened and he developed bronchitis. Cobden sensed that the end was near and made out his will. His wife and Ellen were by his bed when he died on Sunday morning, April 2, 1865, at the age of sixty. Ellen's "attachment to her father seems to have been a passion scarcely equaled among the daughters," said Cobden's lifelong friend and political ally John Bright. She was the last one to let go of her father's coffin as it was lowered into the earth. She never let go of his memory. She never forgot what he expected of her.

Bright would later tell biographer John Morley that Cobden's "was a life of perpetual self-sacrifice. . . . I little knew how much I loved him until I had lost him." The day after Cobden's death, Benjamin Disraeli said to Members of Parliament in the House of Commons, "There is this consolation . . . that these great men are not altogether lost to us." Cobden would not be forgotten, his friends and admirers promised, and he wasn't.

Today in the Heyshott village church, a plaque on his family pew reads, "In this place Richard Cobden, who loved his fellow men, was accustomed to worship God." But what would become of his family was another matter. He left an unstable wife to take care of five spirited girls, and despite the many promises made by influential friends at the funeral, the "daughters of Cobden," as the press called them, were on their own.

In 1898 Ellen was reminded by her sister Janie that "all those who professed such deep admiration and affection for [our] father during his lifetime forgot the existence of his young daughters, the youngest but 3½ years old. Do you remember Gladstone at father's funeral telling mother that she might always rely on his friendship & her children also— The next time I met him, or spoke to him . . . was more than 20 years later. Such is the way of the world!"

Ellen held the family together as she'd promised her father she would. She handled the finances while her mother moved numbly through her unhappy life. Had it not been for Ellen's dogged cajoling and firm supervision of the family affairs it's questionable whether bills would have been paid. Young Annie might not have gone to school. The sisters might not have left their mother's house to move into a London flat at 14 York Place on Baker Street. Ellen's yearly stipend was £250. It's likely that each daughter received the same amount, securing a comfortable existence while creating a vulnerability to men whose intentions may have been questionable.

When Cobden died, Richard Fisher was engaged to daughter Katie and rushed her into marriage before the family had stopped writing letters on black-bordered mourning stationery. Over the years his greedy demands would prove a constant source of irritation to his sisters-in-law. In 1880, when Walter Sickert entered their lives, Katie was married, Maggie was too spirited and frivolous to serve any useful purpose to an ambitious, manipulative man, and suffragettes Annie and Janie were far too savvy for Sickert to get near. He chose Ellen.

Both of her parents were dead. She had no one to advise her or raise objections. It's doubtful that Sickert would have gained the approval of Richard Cobden, a wise and insightful man who may not have been fooled by the artist's acts or charm. Cobden would have detested the handsome twenty-year-old's lack of compassion, a trait noted by others including Whistler, who would later use words such as "reckless" and "treacherous" to describe his former apprentice.

ELLIOTT & FRY.   55 BAKER ST
PORTMAN SQ^R

Ellen's sister, Janie Cobden, with whom she was always close. But Ellen kept secrets about Walter from even Janie.

"Mrs. Sickert and all her sons were such pagans," Janie would write Ellen in later years when the marriage to Sickert was about to end in divorce. "How sad that fate has ever brought you into their midst."

The differences between Ellen's father and Sickert should have been obvious. But in her eyes the two men might have appeared to have much in common. Richard Cobden didn't have an Oxford or Cambridge education. In many ways he was self-taught. He loved Shakespeare, Byron, Irving and Cooper. He was fluent in French. As a young man he had fantasized about being a playwright. His love of the visual arts would be a lifelong affair even if his attempts at writing for the stage were a failure. He also wasn't adept at handling finances. He wasn't interested in money unless he had none, and at one point his friends had to raise sufficient funds to save the family home.

Cobden was driven by idealism and his sense of mission. He wasn't a spendthrift. He simply had loftier matters on his mind, and this may have impressed Ellen as a noble flaw. How fortuitous that John Morley's long-awaited two-volume biography of Cobden was published in 1881, the year Sickert and Ellen met. Sickert certainly could have known enough to script a very persuasive role for himself. The glib, charming actor could easily convince her that he and the famous politician shared some of the same traits. They loved the theater and literature. They had an attachment to all things French. They shared a higher calling that wasn't about money. Sickert might have persuaded Ellen that he was an advocate of women's suffrage. He wasn't.

"I shall reluctantly have to support a bitches suffrage bill," Sickert would complain some thirty-five years later. "But you are to understand I shall not by this become a 'feminist.'"

Richard Cobden believed in the equality of the sexes. He treated his daughters with respect and affection. He would have applauded their political activism as they matured. The 1880s were a time of social activism and fights for equality. Women were forming Purity and political leagues that lobbied for contraception, for reforms to help the poor. Women demanded the right to vote and to have representation in Parliament. Feminists like the Cobden daughters wanted to enjoy the same human dignity as men. They warred against entertainment and vices that degraded women, the very things that intrigued Walter Sickert. Prostitution. The lasciviousness of London's music halls.

He must have sensed that Ellen's life belonged to her father. There was nothing she would do to smear his name. Years later when she and Sickert finally divorced, Janie's prominent publisher husband, T. Fisher Unwin, contacted the chief editors of London's major newspapers and requested that they print "nothing of a personal nature" in their papers. "Certainly," he insisted, "the family name should not appear." Any secret that might have hurt Richard Cobden was safe with Ellen. We'll never know how many secrets she took to her grave. For Richard Cobden, the great protector of the poor, to have a son-in-law who slaughtered them was inconceivable. The question will always be how much Ellen knew.

It's possible that at some point and on some level she suspected the truth about her husband. She may have discovered clues or even evidence he inadvertently left or he may have flaunted his secret life to torment and control her. We may never know what went on between the two of them but she was no match for him. Despite her liberal feminism she was weak in body and spirit. Her fragility may have been genetic. She would have been further damaged by her well-meaning father's desperate needs. She couldn't live up to his expectations. In her own eyes she was a failure long before she and Walter Sickert met. It was her nature to blame herself for whatever went wrong in the Cobden family and in her marriage.

No matter how often Sickert betrayed her, lied to her, abandoned her or made her feel unloved or invisible, she remained loyal. She would do anything she could for him. His happiness and health mattered to her many years after they were divorced and he was married to someone else. Emotionally and financially, Sickert used and abused her. Not long before she died she confided in Janie, "If only you knew how much I long to go to sleep for good & all. I have been a troublesome sister in many ways. There is a strain of waywardness in my character which has neutralized other qualities which should have helped me thru life."

Janie didn't blame Ellen. She blamed Sickert. The strong, shrewdly observant Janie had formed her opinion of him early on when she encouraged Ellen to go away on trips, to stay at the family estate in Sussex or at the Unwins' apartment at 10 Hereford Square in London. Janie's biting observations about Sickert wouldn't become blatant until Ellen finally decided to separate from him in September 1896. Then Janie forcefully spoke her mind. She was infuriated by his ability to fool other people, particularly his artist friends, who "have quite an exalted idea of his character," she writes to Ellen on July 24, 1899. "They cannot know what he really is as you do."

The ever-sensible Janie tried to convince her sister of the truth. "I fear to say that W.S. will never change his conduct of life—and with no guiding principles to keep his emotional nature straight he follows every whim that takes his fancy—you have tried so often to trust him, and he has deceived you times without number." But it seemed that nothing would dissuade Ellen from loving Walter Sickert and hoping he would change.

A gentle, needy woman, Ellen was a daddy's girl. Her identity was defined as his daughter. She politicked for the right causes. She said and did the right things. She was always appropriate, perpetuating her father's missions as much as her limited strength and courage would allow. Ellen deeply cared about the poor. She campaigned for free trade and home rule for Ireland until she became too worn down to accompany her words with her feet. While Janie would move on to become one of the most prominent women suffragettes in Great Britain, Ellen would drift deeper into depression, illness and fatigue.

She and Sickert would have no children. There's no real evidence that he ever had children with anyone unless the much-publicized claim of an artist and picture restorer named Joseph Gorman is true. In the spring of 1970 he legally changed his surname to Sickert, claiming that the artist had befriended him as a child and revealed that he was his biological father. Sickert also allegedly said that the boy's grandfather was the Duke of Clarence, second in line to the throne.

Another story has persisted that Sickert had an illegitimate son by Madame Villain, a French fishwife he stayed with in Dieppe after his separation from Ellen. In a letter he refers to Madame Villain as a mother figure who took care of him at a low point in his life. Supposedly the illegitimate son's name was Maurice, and Sickert would have nothing to do with him. Maybe the story is true. Madame Villain was said to have had many children by many different men.

In a July 20, 1902, letter from French artist Jacques-Émile Blanche to novelist André Gide, Blanche says that Sickert's "life more and more defies everyone. . . . This immoralist has ended up living alone in a large house in a working class suburb so that he doesn't have to do anything regarded as normal and can do what ever he likes whenever he likes. He does this without having a legitimate family in England and a fishwife in Dieppe, with a swarm of children of provenances which are not possible to count."

Artist and devoted friend Cicely Hey had a very different opinion about Sickert being the "immoralist." In a letter she wrote to John Woodeson on February 5, 1973, she refers to having spent ten years and "many long hours" alone with Sickert in his studios. The accusations that he was a womanizer and had fathered "innumerable illegitimate children" caused her great indignation. She was emphatic that he had no children and "had told me that himself."

The medical implications of Sickert's early surgeries would suggest that he may have been unable to father children. But without hospital records all one can do is speculate. He wouldn't have wanted the responsibility of children even if he could have fathered them. Ellen probably wouldn't have wanted them either. She was almost thirty-seven and he was twenty-five when after a four-year engagement they married at the Marylebone Registry Office on June 10, 1885. He was starting his career and didn't want children, his nephew John Lessore told me in 2001.

Ellen may also have been an advocate of the Purity League, which encouraged women not to engage in intercourse. Sex held women back and victimized them. Ellen and Janie were ardent feminists, and Janie had no children either. Both women agreed with the Malthusians, who relied on Thomas Malthus's essay on population as the basis for promoting contraception—even if the Reverend Malthus himself was actually opposed to contraception.

Ellen's diaries and correspondence reveal an intelligent, decent and socially sophisticated woman who was idealistic about love. She was also very careful. Or someone was. Over the thirty-four years she knew and loved Walter Sickert, she mentions him very few times. Janie mentions him more often but not with the frequency one might expect from a thoughtful woman who should have cared about her

Sickert was twenty-five years old when he married Ellen Cobden.

sister's spouse. Gaps in the some four hundred extant letters and notes the sisters wrote to each other suggest that much of their correspondence has vanished. I found only thirty-some letters from 1880 to 1889. In none of them is there so much as an allusion to Ellen's wedding.

Based on the list of witnesses on the marriage certificate, no one in the Cobden or Sickert family was present at the Registry Office. In those days it was a very odd place for a first marriage, especially when the bride was the daughter of Richard Cobden. There doesn't appear to be a single letter from Ellen when she was on her honeymoon in Europe. In no archival source did I discover correspondence between Ellen and Sickert or between Ellen and Sickert's family or between Sickert and his family or between Sickert and the Cobden family.

If such letters existed they may have been kept out of public circulation or destroyed. I find it strange that a husband and wife apparently didn't write or telegraph each other when they were apart, which was more often than not. If Sickert did write to Ellen, it's significant that as legacy minded as she was, she didn't preserve his letters or other communications. She believed in his genius. She was convinced he was destined to become an important artist.

"I know how good it is," Ellen wrote to Blanche about Sickert's art. "*I have always known.*"

By 1881, the young, beautiful, blue-eyed Walter had attached himself to a woman whose yearly stipend was as much as £250. It was more than what some young physicians earned then. There was no reason why he shouldn't enroll in the prestigious Slade School of Fine Art in London. At that time it was offering courses strong in the sciences, etching, sculpture, archaeology, perspective, chemistry of materials used in painting, and anatomy. On Tuesdays and Thursdays there were lectures on "the bones, joints and muscles." Dr. Thomas Openshaw, mentioned in one of the most infamous Ripper letters, may have been involved with the Slade.

By the time the Ripper crimes began, Dr. Openshaw had worked for eleven years at what was then the London Hospital Medical College, his most recent position an "assistant demonstrator of anatomy." In the spring of 1888 he was appointed curator of the hospital's pathological museum.

He prided himself on his "intimate knowledge of normal anatomy," he cites in his March 16 application for the position. Included was his detailed anatomical rendering of a liver. Dr. Openshaw also taught anatomy to aspiring artists, I was told by Royal London Hospital archivist Jonathan Evans. It's possible Sickert might have heard Dr. Openshaw lecture.

During Sickert's time at the Slade he was friendly with Whistler, but how and precisely when they actually met is hazy. One story is that the two of them were in the audience at the Lyceum Theatre while Ellen Terry was

This photo of Dr. Thomas Openshaw, never before published, was taken in his consulting room. Openshaw was an esteemed surgeon who often gave lectures on human anatomy. He also received a famous letter from Jack the Ripper.

performing. During the curtain call, Sickert hurled roses weighted with lead onto the stage and the fragrant missile almost hit Henry Irving, who wasn't amused. Whistler's infamous "ha ha!" could be heard in the crowd. As the audience was filing out, the great artist made a point of meeting the audacious young man. It's also possible Sickert met Whistler through Henry Irving. His theater company had employed Sickert when he was an actor. Irving and Whistler correspondence indicates they had been friends since at least 1876.

Other accounts suggest that Sickert "ran into" Whistler somewhere or followed him into a shop or met him at a party or through the Cobden daughters. Sickert was never accused of being shy or reticent about whatever it was he wanted at the moment. Persuaded by Whistler to stop wasting his time with art school, Sickert left the Slade to become his apprentice. Possibly this was in 1882, the year he stopped living with his mother, according to a letter written by his sister, Helena. Sickert worked side by side with the master but what his days with Ellen were like remains blank.

References to the early years of Ellen and Walter's marriage don't indicate an attraction to each other or the slightest hint of romance. In Jacques-Émile Blanche's memoirs he refers to Ellen as so much older than Sickert that she "might have been taken for his elder sister." He thought the couple were well matched "intellectually" and observed that they allowed each other "perfect freedom." During visits with Blanche in Dieppe, Sickert would disappear in the narrow streets and courtyards. He would sequester himself in his rented "mysterious rooms in harbour quarters, sheds from which all were excluded." Ellen wasn't welcome in her husband's secret places. He paid little attention to her.

Their divorce decree states that Sickert was guilty of "adultery coupled with desertion for the space of 2 years & upwards without reasonable excuse." Yet in fact it was Ellen who eventually refused to live with him, and there's no real evidence he had even one sexual transgression. Ellen's divorce petition states that Sickert deserted her on September 29, 1896, and some two years later he committed adultery with a woman whose name was "unknown." This alleged tryst supposedly occurred on or about April 21, 1898, at the Midland Grand Hotel in London. On May 4, 1899, he supposedly committed adultery again with a woman whose name also was "unknown."

Nothing I've read would indicate that Sickert was amorous toward women or given to inappropriate touching or invitations even if he did use vulgar language. His artist friend Nina Hamnett, later called the Queen of Bohemia, rarely turned down liquor or sex. She writes in her autobiography that Sickert would walk her home when she was drunk, and she stayed with him in France. Yet the kiss-and-tell Nina says not a word about Sickert so much as flirting with her.

Ellen may really have believed Sickert was a womanizer, and maybe he was. Maybe he'd had affairs and fathered illegitimate children, one of whom might have been Joseph Gorman or a French boy named Maurice. Despite the enormous attention Sickert has gotten, especially in recent years, I'm not aware of anyone other than Joseph coming forward to make such a claim. It's also possible that Ellen's claims of infidelity may have been something of a red herring if the humiliating truth was that the couple never consummated their marriage. In the late nineteenth century a woman had no legal grounds to leave her husband unless he was unfaithful and cruel or deserted her. She and Sickert agreed to these claims. He didn't fight her.

One would assume that if he had a damaged penis she knew about it unless the brotherly and sisterly couple never undressed in front of each other or attempted sex. During their divorce proceedings Ellen wrote to Janie that Sickert promised if she would "give him one more chance he [would] be a different man, that I am the only person he has ever really cared for—that he has no longer those relations with [unknown]."

Her lawyer would convince her to go through with the divorce. He felt Sickert was "sincere—but that taking into consideration his previous life—& judging as far as he could of his character from his face & manner," Ellen confides to her sister, "he does not believe he is capable of keeping any resolve that he made, and his deliberate advice to me is to go on with the divorce. I am dreadfully upset & have hardly done anything but cry ever since. I see how far from dead is my affection for him."

These "relations" Sickert supposedly had and allusions to his "previous life" appear to remain "unknown," and one might wonder if they are a veiled reference to something other than adultery. One wonders why in all of Ellen's correspondence—at least what I could find—there's not so much as an allusion to the Ripper crimes or her husband's preoccupation with the very type of women being murdered. If Ellen knew her husband was Jack the Ripper or even suspected it, would she have continued to preserve her family name by covering for him? It makes sense that the caretaker Ellen, who blamed herself for everything, would have kept a secret like that. What an insult to the Cobden name, and she wouldn't have wanted her husband hanged.

8

THE GENTLEMAN SLUMMER

THE HEAVIEST RAIN of 1888 fell during the last week of August. On average the sun burned through the mist no more than an hour each day.

Temperatures remained unseasonably cool. Coal fires burned inside dwellings, gushing black smoke that added to the worst pollution in London's history. There was no such thing as monitoring air quality during the Victorian era but the problems created by coal were nothing new.

It had been known since the English stopped using wood for fuel in the seventeenth century that smoke from burning coal damaged life and all of its edifices. This didn't dissuade people from using it. In the 1700s there were 40,000 houses with 360,000 chimneys in the metropolis. By the late 1800s coal consumption had gone up, especially among the poor. The approaching visitor smelled London many miles before he saw it. Skies were sodden and blotchy. Streets were paved with soot, and limestone buildings and ironworks were being eaten away.

The polluted, thick mist lingered longer and became denser as it took on a different hue than it had in the past. Watercourses dating from Roman times were so foul they had to be filled in. A public health report written in

1889 declared that at the rate London was polluting itself, engineers would also be forced to fill in the Thames, which was fouled with the excrement of millions every time the tide seeped in. There was good reason to wear dark clothing. On some days the sulfurous, smoky air was so hellish and the stench of raw sewage so disgusting that Londoners walked about with burning eyes and lungs, handkerchiefs held over their faces.

The Salvation Army reported in 1890 that in the Great Metropolis population of approximately 5.6 million, 30,000 were prostitutes, and 32,000 men, women and juveniles were in prison. A year earlier, 160,000 people were convicted of drunkenness, 2,297 committed suicide, and 2,157 were found dead on streets and in parks and hovels. Almost one-fifth of Londoners were homeless, in workhouses, asylums and hospitals, ravaged by poverty and near starvation. Most of the "raging sea" of misery, as the founder of the Salvation Army, General William Booth, described it, was located in the East End, where a cunning predator like Jack the Ripper could easily ply his murderous trade.

London had a shockingly large population of homeless children in the 1890s, especially in the city's East End, where the Ripper murders took place.

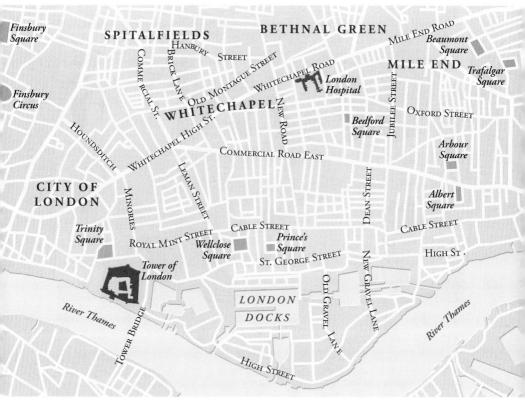

The neighborhood of Whitechapel, where most of Jack the Ripper's alleged victims were found, lies at the heart of London's East End.

When he was terrorizing the East End, the population there was estimated at a million. If one includes the overcrowded nearby hamlets, that number doubles. The London docks and run-down areas of Whitechapel, Spitalfields and Bethnal Green were bordered on the south by the River Thames, to the west by the City of London, to the north by Hackney and Shoreditch, with the River Lea to the east. The growth of the East End was heavy. The road leading from Aldgate to Whitechapel to Mile End was a major artery for leaving the city, and the earth was level and easy to build on.

The anchor of the East End was the London Hospital for the poor, still located on Whitechapel Road but now called the Royal London Hospital. When New Scotland Yard's John Grieve took me on retrospective visits to what is left of the Ripper crime scenes, our meeting place was the

In 1900, Whitechapel High Street was a major road that led from Aldgate all the way out of the city.

Royal London Hospital, a grim Victorian brick building. It doesn't seem to have been modernized much. The depressiveness of the place is but a faint imprint of what a pitiful pit it must have been in the late 1800s when Joseph Carey Merrick, mistakenly called John Merrick by the showman who "owned" him last, was granted shelter in two of the hospital's first-floor back rooms.

Merrick, the "Elephant Man," was rescued from torment and certain death by Sir Frederick Treves. A courageous and kind physician, he was on the London Hospital's staff in November 1884 when Merrick was a slave to the carnival trade across the street inside a deserted greengrocer's shop. In front, a huge canvas advertised a life-size "frightful creature that could only have been possible in a nightmare," as Dr. Treves described years later when he was Sergeant-Surgeon to King Edward VII.

For twopence one could gain admittance to this barbaric spectacle. Children and adults would file inside the cold, vacant building and crowd around a red tablecloth hanging from the ceiling. The showman would yank back the curtain to "oohs!" and "aahs!" and cries of shock as the hunched figure of Merrick cowered on his stool, dressed in nothing but an oversized pair of filthy, threadbare trousers. Dr. Treves lectured on anatomy. He had seen just about every conceivable form of disfigurement and filth. But he'd never encountered or smelled any creature quite so disgusting.

Joseph Merrick suffered from von Recklinghausen disease, caused by mutations in genes that promote and inhibit cell growth. His physical aberrations were bony deformations so grotesque that his head was almost three feet in circumference. A mass projected from his brow like a "loaf" and occluded one eye. The upper jaw was similar to a tusk; the upper lip curled inside out, making it very difficult for Merrick to speak. "Sack-like masses of flesh covered by . . . loathsome cauliflower skin" draped from his back, his right arm and other parts of his body, his face frozen in an inhuman mask incapable of expression. Until Dr. Treves intervened it was believed that Merrick was obtuse and mentally impaired. In fact he was an extremely intelligent, imaginative and loving human being who hadn't turned bitter or hateful despite the abominable way he'd been treated all his life.

How could Merrick be kind and sensitive when he'd known nothing but mockery and cruel abuse? How could anyone be born with more against him? As Dr. Treves pointed out, Merrick would have been better off insensible and unaware of his hideous appearance. In a world that worships beauty, what greater anguish can there be than to suffer from such revolting ugliness? Few would dispute the notion that Merrick's deformity was more tragic than Walter Sickert's. It's possible that at some point the handsome young artist paid his twopence and took a peek at "the frightful creature."

By 1884, Sickert was making sketches and etchings of the East End. He and Whistler knew the slums of Shoreditch and Petticoat Lane. They loved to explore, and Sickert also roamed the sordid squalor on his own. The "Elephant Man" was just the sort of cruel, degrading exhibition that Sickert would have found amusing, and perhaps for an instant Merrick and Sickert were eye to eye. It would have been the perfect metaphor. Each was the other inside out.

In 1888 Joseph Merrick and Walter Sickert were simultaneously living secret lives in the East End. Merrick was a voracious reader and keenly curious. He would have been all too aware of the horrible murders beyond his hospital walls. A rumor began to circulate that it was the "Elephant Man" who went out in his black cloak and hood at night and slaughtered unfortunates. It was the monster Merrick who butchered women because they wouldn't have him. To be deprived of sex would drive any man mad, especially such a beast as that carnival freak who ventured out into the hospital garden only after dark. Fortunately no rational person took such nonsense seriously.

Merrick's head was so heavy he could scarcely move it. The stalk of his neck would snap if he moved the wrong way. He didn't know what it was like to settle into a pillow at night. In his fantasies he lay himself down to sleep and prayed the Lord would one day bless him with the sweet caresses and kisses of a woman, best of all a blind one. Dr. Treves thought it a tragic irony that Merrick's "organs of generation" were nothing like the rest of him. Merrick was perfectly capable of the sexual love he'd never have. He slept sitting up, his huge head hung low. He couldn't walk without a cane.

It isn't known whether the baseless rumors that he was the Whitechapel killer ever reached his safe little rooms crammed with signed photographs of celebrities and royalty, some of whom had come to see him. He was a favorite of Queen Victoria's, and members of the royal family met him on several occasions. What a great act of benevolence and tolerance to visit the likes of him and not outwardly register horror. What a story to relate to one's friends, to dukes and duchesses, to lords and ladies or to Her Majesty herself.

Queen Victoria was obsessed with life's morbidities and curiosities. She was quite fond of Tom Thumb, an American midget named Charles Sherwood Stratton who was only forty inches tall. It was easy, even gratifying to enter the cloistered world of harmless and amusing mutants or freaks. Certainly it was more pleasant to be entertained by them than to wade through the "bottomless pit of decaying life," as Beatrice Webb described the East End, where rents were steep because overcrowding gave slumlords the upper hand.

What was the equivalent of a dollar to a dollar-fifty a week in rent might be a fifth of a worker's salary. When one of these Ebenezer Scrooge slumlords decided to raise the rent, a large family found itself homeless with nothing but a handbarrow to tote away all its worldly goods. In 1902 American writer Jack London went undercover in the East End to see for himself what it was like. He related terrible stories of poverty and filth, describing an elderly woman found dead inside a room so infested with vermin that her clothing was "gray with insects." She was skin and bones, covered with sores, her hair matted with "filth" and a "nest of vermin," London wrote. In the East End an attempt at cleanliness was a "howling farce." When rain fell it was "more like grease than water."

This greasy rain fell in drips and drizzles in the East End most of Thursday, August 30. Horse-drawn wagons and barrows splashed through the garbage-strewn muddy water of narrow, crowded streets where flies droned in clouds, and the poor struggled for the next penny. An unfortunate couldn't get out of the weather and find a bit of food unless she could convince a man to take her in or give her small change so she could rent a bed for the night in a doss-house.

Doss was slang for bed. A typical doss-house was a decaying dwelling where men and women paid four- or fivepence to sleep in communal rooms filled with small iron bedsteads covered with gray blankets. Supposedly linens were washed once a week. The casual poor, as the guests were called, sat around in crowded dormitories, smoking, mending, sometimes talking, maybe joking or telling a morose tale. In the kitchen men and women gathered to cook whatever they'd been able to find or steal during the day. Children begged and were beaten for getting too close to the fire.

Inside these inhumane establishments one abided by strict, degrading rules posted on walls and enforced by the doorkeeper or warden. Misbehavior was rewarded by banishment to the mean streets. Early in the morning lodgers were herded out the door unless they paid in advance for another night. Doss-houses were usually owned by a better class of people who lived elsewhere, what today we would call slumlords. They didn't supervise properties they may have never seen. For a little capital one could own a piece of a poorhouse and perhaps have no idea that a "Model Lodgings" investment was an abomination supervised by "keepers" who used dishonest and abusive means to maintain control over the desperate residents.

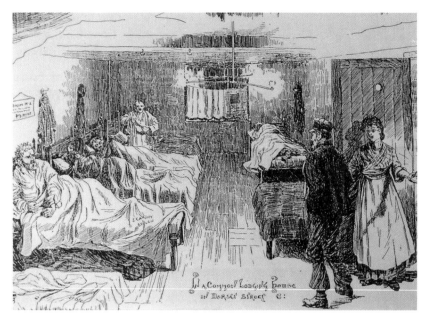

Doss-houses were common in the East End. Crime was typical in these last-resort shelters.

Many of these doss-houses catered to the criminal element, including the unfortunates who on a good night might have pennies for lodging. Perhaps the unfortunate might persuade a client to take her to bed. That was certainly preferable to sex on the street. Another breed of lodger was the "gentleman slummer." Like thrill-seeking men of every era he would leave his respectable home and family to enter a forbidden world of low-life pub-hopping, music halls and cheap, anonymous sex. Some men from the better parts of the city became addicted to this secret entertainment. Walter Sickert was one of them.

Sickert was in a class that was above suspicion if he wanted to commit murder. He was a genius at becoming any number of different characters in every sense of the word.

It would have been easy and exciting for him to disguise himself as an East End man or a gentleman slummer and voyeuristically prowl the pubs and doss-houses of Whitechapel and its nearby hellholes. He was an artist capable of changing his handwriting and designing taunting letters. But the police weren't looking for the likes of him. It wouldn't be until 117 years later that art historian Anna Robins, paper conservator Anne Kennett, forensic paper expert Peter Bower and others would begin examining the original Ripper documents and realize their remarkable character.

Using scientific techniques and instruments such as Fourier Transform Infrared Spectroscopy (FTIR), high magnification, forensic imaging software, laser beams, presumptive blood tests and the keen eyes of experts, many discoveries have been made that were completely unknown before this investigation. What had always been assumed to be human or animal blood on at least some Ripper letters turns out to be sticky brown etching ground or perhaps a mixture of inks that remarkably resembles old blood. It's possible blood may have been added to the artist's palette. Under a microscope it's obvious that some of these bloody-looking smears, drips and splotches were applied with an artist's brush or are imprints left by fabrics or fingers.

Apparently no one, including the police, paid any attention to the different watermarks found on letters dismissed as hoaxes contrived by journalists or illiterate or deranged pranksters. Apparently no one asked whether such a prankster was likely to possess drawing pens, colorful inks, lithographic or chinagraph crayons, etching ground, an artist's paints and paper or fine stationery. The police weren't looking for a talented, clear-headed and calculating killer who had an intense curiosity about anything that might catch his artist's eye.

There was much to appeal to Walter Sickert on the Thursday night of August 30, 1888. A brandy warehouse on the London docks caught fire around 9:00 p.m. and illuminated the entire East End. People came from miles away to peer through locked iron gates at an inferno that defied the gallons of water dumped on it by the fire brigades. Unfortunates drifted toward the blaze, curious and eager to take advantage of an unplanned opportunity for sexual commerce.

In the finer parts of London other entertainment lit up the night as Richard Mansfield continued to thrill theatergoers with his brilliant

Author Patricia Cornwell examines one of Sickert's artists' palettes at the Islington Local History Centre in September 2001. A blood-like substance used on a Ripper letter may have been mixed on a palette.

performance as Dr. Jekyll and Mr. Hyde at the Lyceum. The farce *Uncles and Aunts* had just opened, and *The Paper Chase* and *The Union Jack* were going full tilt. The plays began at 8:15, 8:30 or 9:00. By the time they ended, the fire on the docks still roared. Warehouses and ships along the Thames were backlit by an orange glow visible for many miles. Whether Sickert was home or at one of the theaters or music halls he was unlikely to miss the drama at South and Spirit Quays that was attracting such an excited crowd.

Of course it's purely speculative to say that Sickert wandered toward the water to watch a brandy warehouse burn. He might not have been in London on this night. But there's no proof he wasn't. I've found no letters, documents, news accounts or works of art that might indisputably show where Sickert might have been. He wasn't interested in people knowing his business or whereabouts. He was notorious for his lifelong habit of renting multiple secret "studios" at a time. These hovels were scattered about in locations so private, unexpected and unpredictable that his wife, colleagues and friends had no idea where they were.

His known flats and studios are believed to have numbered at least thirty during his life. They were described by acquaintances as slovenly "small rooms" filled with chaos that "inspired" him. Sickert worked alone behind locked doors. It was rare he would see anyone. A visit to these rat holes required a telegram or a special knock. In his older years he erected tall black gates in front of his door and chained a guard dog to one of the iron bars.

As is true of any good actor, Sickert knew how to make an entrance and an exit. He had a habit of vanishing for days or weeks without telling Ellen or his second or third wives or his acquaintances where he was or why. He might invite friends to dinner and not show up. He would reappear as he pleased, no explanation offered. Outings often turned into a vanishing act.

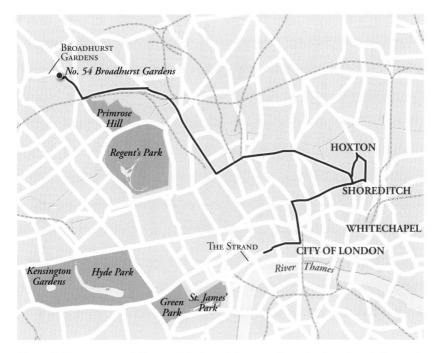

Walter Sickert frequented the music halls and theaters along the Strand and often took the long way home through the slums.

He liked to go to the theater and music halls alone, and afterward wander during the late night and early morning hours. His routes were peculiar and illogical, especially if he was returning home from central London along the Strand.

Denys Sutton wrote that Sickert often walked north to Hoxton, then retraced his steps to end up in Shoreditch on the western border of Whitechapel. From there he would have to walk west and north to return to 54 Broadhurst Gardens, where he lived with his wife Ellen during the early Ripper crimes. He had a studio on the top floor. According to Sutton the reason for these strange peregrinations and detours into a dangerous part of East London was that Sickert needed "a long silent tramp to meditate on what he had just seen" in a music hall or theater.

The artist pondering. The artist observing a dark, foreboding world and the people who lived in it. The artist who liked his women ugly.

9

A BIT OF BROKEN LOOKING GLASS

MARY ANN NICHOLS was approximately forty-two years old and missing five teeth.

She was five foot two or three, plump with a fleshy, plain face, and brown eyes and graying dark-brown hair. During her marriage to a printer's machinist named William Nichols she'd given birth to five children. The oldest was twenty-one, the youngest eight or nine at the time of her murder.

For the past seven years or so she and William had been separated because of her drinking and quarrelsome ways. He would later tell police he discontinued his weekly support of five shillings when he learned she was living the life of a prostitute. Mary Ann had nothing left, not even her children. Years before she'd lost custody of them when her ex-husband informed the courts that she was living in sin with a blacksmith named Drew. Soon enough he left her too. The last time William saw Mary Ann alive was in June of 1886 at the funeral of a son who had burned to death when a paraffin lamp exploded.

During her desolate times, Mary Ann had been an inmate at numerous workhouses. These were huge barracks packed with as many as a thousand men and women who had nowhere else to go. There were always long lines on cold mornings as the destitute waited in hopes of admission into what were called "casual wards." Often the workhouse was full. If the porter took in a new boarder, the person was carefully interrogated and searched for money.

The discovery of even a penny sent one back out on the street. Tobacco was confiscated. Knives and matches weren't allowed. Every inmate was stripped and washed in the same tub of water and dried off with communal towels. They were given workhouse-issue clothing and directed to stinking, rat-infested wards where canvas beds stretched out between poles like hammocks.

Breakfast at 6:00 a.m. might be bread and a gruel called "skilly" made with oatmeal or moldy meat. Then the inmate was put to work performing the same cruel tasks used to punish criminals for hundreds of years. Pounding stones, scrubbing, picking oakum (untwisting old rope so the hemp could be reused). They were sent to the infirmary or mortuary to clean up after patients or tend to the dead. It was rumored that the incurably ill were "polished off" with poison. Dinner was at 8:00 p.m. Sometimes the inmates got leftovers from the infirmary. Now and then there was suet soup.

Guests of the casual wards were required to stay at least two nights and one day. To refuse to work was to end up homeless again. Rosier accounts of these degrading places can be found in gilded publications that tend to mention only "shelters" for the poor that provided clean beds and "good meat soup" and bread. Such civilized charity wasn't to be found in London's East End unless it was at Salvation Army shelters. They were avoided by the street-smart who'd gotten cynical. Ladies of the Salvation Army regularly visited doss-houses to preach God's generosity to paupers who knew better. There was no hope for a fallen woman like Mary Ann Nichols. The Bible couldn't save her.

She'd been in and out of the Lambeth Workhouse several times between the previous Christmas and April of 1888. In May she vowed to change her ways and took a coveted job as a domestic servant in a respectable family home. Her optimistic resolutions didn't last. In July she left after stealing clothing valued at three pounds, ten shillings. She sank deeper into her drunken ways and returned to the life of an unfortunate.

For a while she and another prostitute named Nelly Holland shared a doss-house bed in the maze of decaying buildings on Thrawl Street, which ran east to west from Commercial Street to Brick Lane.

After a while Mary Ann moved to White House on nearby Flower and Dean Street. She stayed there until August 29. The following night she walked the streets wearing everything she owned. Her black straw bonnet was trimmed in black velvet, and a brown ulster (overcoat) was fastened with big brass buttons engraved with the figures of a man and a horse. A list of her personal effects in police records indicates that her many layers also included a brown linsey frock, two gray woolen petticoats with the stenciled marks of the Lambeth Workhouse, two brown stays (stiff bodices made of whalebone), flannel underclothing and ribbed black woolen stockings. Her men's sidespring boots had been cut on the uppers, tips and heels for a better fit. In a pocket she tucked a white handkerchief, a comb and a bit of broken looking glass.

Mary Ann was spotted several times between 11:00 p.m. and 2:30 the following morning. In each sighting she was alone. She was noticed on Whitechapel Road, then at the Frying Pan public house. At around 1:40 a.m. she was in the kitchen of her former lodging house at 18 Thrawl Street, where she claimed to be penniless. She asked that her bed be kept for her, promising to return soon with money for payment. Witnesses said she was intoxicated. On her way out the door she bragged about the "jolly" bonnet she recently had acquired.

Mary Ann was last seen alive at 2:30 a.m. when her friend Nelly Holland happened upon her at the corner of Osborn Street and Whitechapel Road, across from the parish church. Mary Ann was drunk and staggering along a wall. She told Nelly that so far this night she'd earned three times what she needed for her bed at the lodging house. She'd spent all of it. Despite her friend's pleas that she come with her and go to bed, Mary Ann insisted on trying one last time to earn a few pennies. The parish church clock chimed as Mary Ann wove her way along Whitechapel Road, dissolving into darkness.

Approximately an hour and fifteen minutes later and half a mile away on a street called Buck's Row in Whitechapel, a carman (delivery man) named Charles Cross was walking to work. He passed a dark shape against some gates on a footpath near a stable yard. At first he thought it was a tarpaulin. On closer inspection he realized it was a woman lying motionless, her bonnet on the ground by her right side, her left hand up against the closed gateway. As Cross tried to get a better look, he heard footsteps. Another carman named Robert Paul appeared. He crouched down and put a hand on the woman's chest. He thought he felt a slight movement. "I believe she is still breathing," he said.

The clothing was disarrayed, her skirt raised above her hips, and the men chastely rearranged it. They didn't notice any blood because it was too dark. Paul and Cross walked off and happened upon Jonas Mizen, 55 H Division, who was making his rounds at the nearby corner of Hanbury and Old Montague Streets. The men informed the constable that there was a woman on the pavement either dead or "dead drunk."

By the time Mizen reached the stable yard on Buck's Row, Constable John Neil had arrived at the scene and was alerting other police in the area by shouting and flashing his bull's-eye lantern. It appeared the woman's throat had been slashed, and Dr. Rees Ralph Llewellyn, who lived nearby at 152 Whitechapel Road, was roused from bed and summoned. Mary Ann Nichols's identity was unknown at this time. According to Dr. Llewellyn, she was "quite dead." Her wrists were cold, her body and lower extremities still very warm. He was certain she'd been dead less than half an hour and that her injuries were "not self-inflicted." He also observed that there was little blood around her neck or on the ground.

He ordered the body moved to the nearby Whitechapel Workhouse mortuary, a private dead house for workhouse inmates and not intended for any sort of proper postmortem examination. Dr. Llewellyn said he'd be there shortly, and Constable Mizen sent a man to fetch the handcart from the Bethnal Green Police Station. Victorian London hospitals didn't have ambulances. There was no such thing as a rescue squad.

The usual means of rushing an extremely sick or injured person to the nearest hospital was for friends or Good Samaritans to carry the patient by the arms and legs. Sometimes the cry "Send for a shutter!" rang out and the afflicted one would be carried on a window shutter. Ambulances were used by police. Most stations had an unwieldy wooden-sided handcart with a lashed-in, sturdy black leather bottom that was equipped with thick leather

A drawing of the era titled *Saturday Night in Whitechapel Road*.

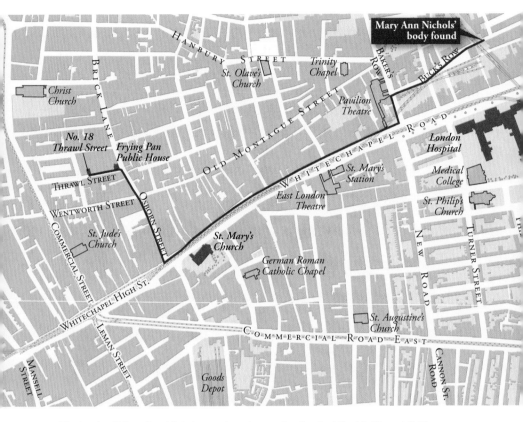

The body of Mary Ann Nichols was found on a street called Buck's Row at 3:45 a.m. on August 31, 1888. Witnesses saw her at the Frying Pan Public House, at her lodgings, and in front of the parish church in the hours before her death.

straps. A tan leather convertible top could be unfolded but probably did little more than offer partial protection from prying eyes or bad weather.

In most cases an ambulance was used to remove a drunk from a public place. But occasionally the cargo was the dead. It must have been quite a chore for a constable to navigate a handcart at night along unlighted, narrow, rutted streets. It was extremely heavy even without a patient and very difficult to steer. Based on the one I found in Metropolitan Police storage, the type of handcart that transported Mary Ann Nichols likely weighed several hundred pounds. It would have been a challenge to haul up the gentlest hill unless the constable at the handles was strong and had a good grip.

This morbid means of transportation was one that Jack the Ripper would have seen had he lingered in the dark and watched his victims taken away. It must have been thrilling to spy on a constable huffing and straining as Mary Ann's nearly severed head lolled from side to side while the big wheels bounced and her blood speckled the street.

Sickert is known to have drawn, etched and painted only what he saw. Without exception this seems to be true. One of his unsigned, undated paintings is titled *The Hand Cart, Rue St. Jean, Dieppe*. In some catalogues it's referred to as *The Basket Shop*, and it depicts a handcart that is almost identical to the one I saw in police storage. The perspective is from the rear. It has what looks very much like a folded-down tan convertible top. Stacked in front of a shop across the narrow deserted street are what appear to be large long baskets, similar to what the French used as stretchers for the dead.

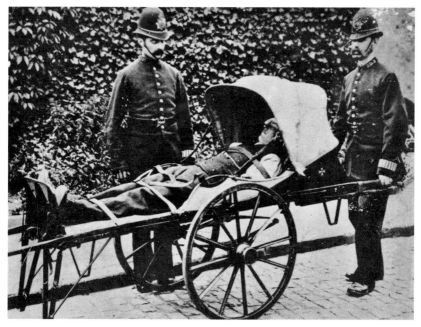

Handcarts used to carry sick or dead people were sometimes equipped with a leather convertible top to offer meager protection from weather or curious eyes.

A barely visible figure, possibly a man wearing some sort of hat, is walking along a sidewalk and looking over to see what's inside the cart. At his feet is an inexplicable black square shape that might be a piece of luggage. But it could be part of the sidewalk, rather much like an open sewer trap. Newspaper reports of Nichols's murder mention that the police didn't believe the "trap" in the street had been opened, implying that the killer hadn't escaped through the labyrinth of vaulted brick sewers that ran beneath the Great Metropolis.

A trap is also an opening in stage floors that gives actors quick and easy access to a scene in progress to the surprise and delight of the unsuspecting audience. In many productions of Shakespeare's *Hamlet*, the ghost enters and exits through the trap. The former actor Sickert would have known quite a lot about stage traps. In 1881 he had played the ghost in Henry Irving's *Hamlet* at the Lyceum Theatre. The dark shape at the figure's feet in Sickert's painting could be a theater trap. It could be a sewer trap. It could be a detail he created to tease or perhaps hint of something sinister.

Mary Ann Nichols's body was lifted off the street and placed inside a wooden shell that was strapped into the ambulance. Two constables accompanied the body to the mortuary, where it was left outside in the yard. By now it was after 4:30 a.m. While the constables waited at the mortuary for Inspector John Spratling to arrive, a boy named John Green, who lived near the gateway where Mary Ann Nichols's body was found, helped the police clean up the crime scene. Pails of water were splashed on the ground. Blood flowed into the gutter, leaving only a trace between the stones.

Police Constable John Thain later testified that as he watched the washing of the pavement he noticed a "mass of congealed" blood about six inches in diameter. He said it had been under the body. Contrary to what Dr. Llewellyn said, there was quite a lot of blood, Thain recalled. It had flowed from the murdered woman's neck, seeping under her back and as far down as her waist. Dr. Llewellyn might have noticed the same details had he turned over the body.

Inspector Spratling arrived at the mortuary and impatiently waited in the dark for the keeper to arrive with the keys. By the time Mary Ann

Nichols's body was carried inside, it must have been after 5:00 a.m. She'd been dead for approximately two hours. The shell bearing her body was lifted onto a wooden bench or table typical of those used in mortuaries then. Usually they were acquired secondhand from butchers at the local slaughterhouses. Inspector Spratling pulled up Mary Ann's dress for a closer inspection in the gas lamp's gloom and discovered that her abdomen had been slashed open, exposing the intestines.

The next morning, Saturday, September 1, Dr. Llewellyn performed the autopsy. That same day Wynne Edwin Baxter, the coroner for the South Eastern District of Middlesex, began the inquest, which was open to the public in Great Britain then and would be today. It's an unfamiliar and rather jolting concept when considering the United States, where grand jury proceedings are closed to everyone except the prosecution, jurors and those subpoenaed.

In an 1854 treatise on the office and duties of coroners it was noted that while it may be illegal to publish evidence that could prove important in the trial, these facts were routinely published anyway. It was believed they benefited the public. Details might serve as a deterrent. By knowing the facts, especially when there are no suspects, the public becomes part of the investigative team. People might read about the case and realize they have helpful information.

In 1888 coroners' inquisitions and ex parte proceedings were fair game to journalists. As incomprehensible as this may seem to anyone unaccustomed to the publication of evidence and testimony before the actual trial, were it not for Britain's open policy there would be virtually no death investigation details about Jack the Ripper's crimes. With the exception of a few pages here and there, the original autopsy notes and reports have disappeared.

It's frustrating that so many documents are missing. Much more could be learned if we had access to all of the original police reports, photographs, memorandums and whatever else has vanished. Over the decades much was lost, misplaced or spirited away, and I suspect some of it ended up in the hands of collectors. At the beginning of this investigation, I bought an alleged original Ripper letter for $1,500 that apparently someone found in an old dresser.

It's written in red pencil or crayon and dated August 22, possibly 1889. The poor condition makes it difficult to read, but it opens with the Ripper asking the press to "just put in yours paper a word for me just to put the police on my track." I later donated it to New Scotland Yard's Crime Museum, where it is displayed as an exhibit.

At some point this letter may have disappeared from the case files. It's also possible that communications sent to individuals or newspapers weren't turned over to the police at all. How many Ripper documents were thrown out or tucked in drawers or are in private collections? I was told by officials at New Scotland Yard that the overriding reason all Ripper files were finally moved to The National Archives in Kew was that so much had vanished. It was feared that eventually there would be nothing left except reference numbers linked to empty folders.

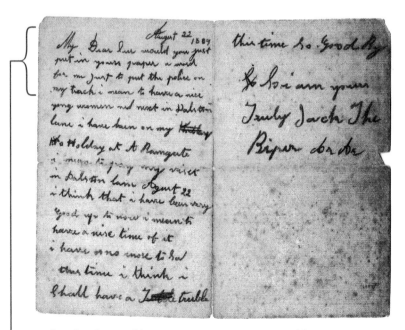

"My dear boss would you just put in yours paper a word for me just to put the police on my track."

Ripper letters like this one were often tucked away in private collections. Author Patricia Cornwell donated this rarely published letter to Scotland Yard's Crime Museum in 2007.

Unfortunately, when records aren't accounted for or accessible it's fodder for scandalous theories about cover-ups and conspiracies. There are plenty of them that have made their way into blogs, books and movies, accusations that Scotland Yard has always known who the Ripper was but protected him. He was tucked into an asylum and the public wasn't informed. The government didn't care about murdered women of the dustbin, and the police didn't try very hard. The Royal Family was involved. Queen Victoria herself might have been. These accusations have been further fueled by intriguing stories about the Home Office ordering the Ripper case records sealed for a hundred years. That's not accurate either but it's not entirely false, according to historian Paul Begg.

He explains that the Ripper files were really never closed, but nothing new had been added since the end of the Victorian era, and certainly there wasn't the interest in these documents then that there is today. In the 1950s New Scotland Yard transferred these and other records to what's now The National Archives in Kew. At this point it was decided to keep the files closed for a period of time that was based on when the case last had generated active investigative reports. This was a standard practice, Paul Begg says, as the intention was to protect the names and reputations of the people involved, and to demonstrate sensitivity toward the victims. It wouldn't be until 1976 that the information was made readily available to researchers.

This wasn't due to a conspiracy but rather to the typical landscape one navigates when dealing with any government bureaucracy. Maggie Bird was the archivist in New Scotland Yard's Records Management Branch when I visited in 2001, and she offered her perspective on the missing records. In the late nineteenth century it was routine to destroy all police personnel files once the officer turned sixty-one, she said, and this might help account for the absence of significant information about the police involved in the Ripper investigation.

As a matter of routine, she added, even now-high-profile murder cases are sealed for twenty-five, fifty or seventy-five years. It depends on the nature of the crime and whether a privacy issue remains for the family of the victim or victims. If the Ripper case records hadn't been kept out of circulation for decades there might not be anything left of them at all. It took only two short years after the records were opened to the public for "half of them" to "go missing" or be stolen, Ms. Bird told me. Today all New Scotland Yard files are stored in a huge warehouse, the boxes labeled, numbered and logged into a computer system. Ms. Bird claimed "with hand on heart" that no Ripper files are lurking about or lost in those boxes. All were turned over to The National Archives. She attributes any gaps in the records to "bad handling, human nature or pinching, and the bombings of World War II" that partially destroyed the headquarters where the records were stored.

Suspicions about a conspiracy to conceal who Jack the Ripper was and why he got away aren't likely to dissipate. But if anyone covered up anything it was people in Walter Sickert's inner circle and not the government or law enforcement. If those closest to him had the vaguest sense of what he was doing in his secret life, they didn't tell anyone who might have done something about it. People like Ellen might have been in denial. They didn't want to ask. They didn't want to know. It's possible the Ripper's victim selection was almost acceptable, almost palatable. At least he wasn't killing people of high standing, and unfortunates were unpleasant. They were sinners, most if not all of them criminals. Some members of the public may have viewed these women as disposable like trash, and had very little sympathy for what happened to them.

One thing is certain. Most of what went wrong in the Ripper case was due to ignorance. He was a modern killer born a hundred years too soon to be caught. He must have grown frustrated by the inadequacy of his opposition, and there can be no question he was personally interested in those out to get him. They were a challenge, something for him to taunt and laugh about.

The Ripper's favorite authority figure to mock was the senior military man Charles Warren. An intellectual soldier-scholar, he'd been appointed commissioner of the Metropolitan Police specifically to bring much-needed discipline to the force.

He was well educated and progressive, and didn't deserve the negative reputation he'd earned by the time the Ripper crimes began in 1888. The year before, the radical press turned venomous when Warren forbade a socialist demonstration in Trafalgar Square on November 13, which became known as Bloody Sunday. His order was considered illegal. It was ignored by socialist reformers Annie Besant and Charles Bradlaugh, and fearing a mob that might turn violent, Warren sent in his troops.

Mounted police charged in, "rolling men and women over like ninepins," Annie Besant wrote. According to her account, soldiers arrived preparing to fire upon the crowd. They were swinging truncheons, and "peace-loving, law-abiding working men and women" were left with shattered limbs. Two were dead, many were wounded, people were imprisoned without representation, and the Law and Liberty League was formed to defend all victims of police brutality. *The Times* told a different story of demonstrators who were ruffians motivated by a "simple love of disorder [and] hope of plunder."

Walter Sickert's brother-in-law, T. Fisher Unwin, published Annie Besant's autobiography, and Sickert painted Charles Bradlaugh's portrait twice. Neither was a coincidence. Sickert knew them. His wife Ellen and her family were active Liberals and moved in those political circles. In the early days of Sickert's career, Ellen helped him professionally by introducing him to well-known figures whose portraits he might paint. Sickert was a news junkie who despised authority. He was well aware of what was going on socially and politically in London. He would have loathed the likes of a Besant, a Bradlaugh, a Charles Warren. But Jack the Ripper's crimes had nothing to do with them or what they stood for, despite what the press began to suggest.

Some newspapers started publishing stories about a rather lofty motivation for the Ripper's ghastly murders. They were a socialist statement directed at graphically exposing the underside of the class system and the dirty secrets of the greatest city in the world. In fact, the Ripper was driven by no such thing. His inner demons ran his show. His victims were easy. They were in poorly lit conditions. They were intoxicated and unarmed. Ambushing and killing them had nothing to do with his making some grand noble statement.

The Ripper was propelled by what aroused him—sexual violence and his insatiable need for attention. He wasn't making some socialist political point, regardless of what he might boast in his letters to the police and the press. He killed to satisfy his uncontrollable, violent psychopathic compulsions. When the papers and public hinted at motive, especially a social or ethical one, the Ripper must have enjoyed a secret delight and rush of power. He taunted and teased that maybe they were right.

"[H]a! ha! ha!" he wrote. "To tell you the truth you ought to be obliged to me for killing such a deuced lot of vermin, why they are ten times worse than men."

10

THE DARK LANTERN

DURING THE EARLY YEARS of the eighteenth century, robbers ruled the high roads and byways. Most villains could buy their way out of trouble with a bribe.

London was protected by night watchmen armed with staves, lanterns and wooden noisemakers called rattles that made a startling clack-clack-clack sound when the head was spun. It wasn't until 1750 that times began to change when Henry Fielding, better known as an author than a magistrate, gathered a faithful group of constables under his command. With £400 allotted by the government, Fielding formed the first squadron of "thief-takers" to break up gangs and apprehend other scoundrels who terrorized Londoners.

After Henry Fielding moved on in his career, he was followed by his brother, Sir John Fielding, for whom justice was truly blind. He'd lost his eyesight and was famous for wearing a bandage over his eyes when he confronted prisoners. He was said to recognize criminals by voice. Under his supervision the thief-takers were headquartered on Bow Street. They became known as the Bow Street Patrol and then the Bow Street Runners.

At this stage policing was somewhat privatized. A Bow Street Runner might investigate the burglary of a resident's town house for a fee or simply find the perpetrator and coax him to agree on a settlement with the victim. In a curious way, criminal and civil law were combined. While it was unlawful to commit bad deeds, order could be restored and a lot of fuss and bother could be avoided through deal making. Better to have half of one's belongings returned than none at all. Better to give back half of what one had stolen than to end up in prison, and some Bow Street Runners retired as wealthy men.

Unfortunately, nothing much could be done about riots and murders, and they were rampant as were other evil deeds. Dogs were stolen and killed for their hides. Cattle were tortured by "bullock-baiting," the sporting mobs chasing the pain-crazed animals until they collapsed and died. Until 1868 executions had been public and drew tremendous crowds. Hanging days were holidays, and the gruesome spectacle was considered a deterrent to crime and proof that justice had been served.

During the era of thief-takers and Bow Street Runners, violations of the law punishable by death included horse stealing, forging and shoplifting. In 1788, thousands gathered at Newgate to watch thirty-year-old Phoebe Harris burned at the stake for counterfeiting coins. Highwaymen were heroes. Spectators cheered them on as they dangled from ropes, and a convicted member of the upper class was ridiculed no matter the crime.

When Governor Joseph Wall was convicted of flogging a soldier to death and was hanged in 1802, onlookers fought over the executioner's rope, paying a shilling per inch. Five years later a crowd of forty thousand gathered to watch the execution of two convicted murderers, and people were trampled to death. Not every prisoner died quickly or according to plan. Some of the agonal scenes were a horror. The knot slipped or didn't catch just right and the strangling prisoner flailed violently as men grabbed his kicking legs and pulled down hard to hasten death. Often the condemned lost his pants and twisted and writhed naked in front of the screaming mob. In the old days of the axe, a refusal to place a few coins into an executioner's hand could result in bad aim that required a few extra chops.

In 1829, Sir Robert Peel convinced government and the public that they had a right to sleep safely within their own homes and walk the streets without worry. The Metropolitan Police Force was established and headquartered at 4 Whitehall Place. Its back door opened onto Scotland Yard, possibly the former site of a Saxon palace that had served as a residence for visiting Scottish kings. By the late seventeenth century most of the palace had fallen to ruin and was demolished, and what remained was used as offices for the British government.

Many well-known figures once served the crown from Scotland Yard, including the architects Inigo Jones and Christopher Wren, and the great poet John Milton when he was the Latin secretary for Oliver Cromwell. Architect and playwright Sir John Vanbrugh built a house on the old palace grounds that Jonathan Swift, author of *Gulliver's Travels*, compared to a "goose pie." Few people realize that *Scotland Yard* is a metonym like *Hollywood*. The Yard has always been a place and not the actual police organization. Since 1829 it has been the location of the Metropolitan Police headquarters. That remains true today although the official name now is New Scotland Yard, which at this writing is in the process of relocating to the neoclassical Curtis Green Building on the Victoria Embankment, close to Parliament Square.

From its earliest days the Yard and its uniformed divisions were resented by the public. Policing was viewed as an affront to the Englishman's civil rights and associated with martial law and the government's practice of spying and bullying. When the Metropolitan Police Service was first organized it attempted to avoid a military appearance by dressing its force in blue coats and trousers. These were topped off with rabbit-skin stovepipe hats reinforced with steel frames in case an apprehended criminal decided to knock an officer on the head. The hats also came in handy as footstools for climbing into windows or over fences and walls.

At first the Metropolitan Police had no detectives. It was bad enough having bobbies in blue but the idea of men in ordinary garb sneaking about to collar people was angrily opposed by citizens. Uniformed police resented detectives for getting better pay and were suspicious that the real purpose of these plainclothesmen was to tattle on the rank and file. By 1842 there was a solid detective division that within a few years included plainclothes officers. But this wasn't without setbacks and fumbles such as the unenlightened decision to hire educated gentlemen who had no police training. One can only imagine such a person interviewing a drunk East End husband who's just smashed his wife in the head with a hammer or taken a straight razor to her throat.

The Criminal Investigation Department (CID) wasn't formally organized until 1878, ten years before Jack the Ripper began terrorizing London. By 1888 public sentiment about detectives hadn't changed much. Law enforcers weren't supposed to entrap or arrest citizens by artifice. Scotland Yard strictly enforced the rule that plainclothes policing could take place only when there was ample evidence that crimes in a certain area were being committed repeatedly. This approach was enforcement, not prevention, and it delayed the decision to order undercover measures when the Ripper began his slaughters.

But the Yard was completely unprepared for a sadistic serial killer like him, and after Mary Ann Nichols's murder, the public began to cast its eye on the police more than ever. They were criticized, belittled and blamed. Mary Ann's murder and inquest hearings were obsessively reported on by every major English newspaper. Her case made the covers of tabloids such as *The Illustrated Police News* and the budget editions of *Famous Crimes* that one could pick up for a penny. Artists rendered sensational, salacious depictions of the homicides, and no one in charge, not Commissioner Warren or even Queen Victoria herself, had the slightest comprehension of the problem or its solution.

When the Ripper began making his bloody rounds there were only uniformed officers walking their beats, all of these men overworked and underpaid. They were issued the standard equipment of a whistle, a truncheon, a rattle. Perhaps they were given a bull's-eye lantern, nicknamed a "dark lantern" because all it really did was vaguely illuminate the person holding it. A dangerous, cumbersome device, it was comprised of a steel cylinder ten inches high that included a chimney shaped like a ruffled dust cap. The magnifying lens was three inches in diameter and made of thick, rounded ground glass. Inside was a small oil pan with a wick.

The brightness of the flame could be controlled by turning the chimney, which rotated the inner metal tube. This blocked out as much or as little of the flame as needed, allowing a policeman to flash his lantern and signal another officer out on the street. I suppose the word *flash* is a bit of an exaggeration if one has ever seen a bull's-eye lantern lit up. I found several rusty but authentic Hiatt & Co. Birmingham ones that

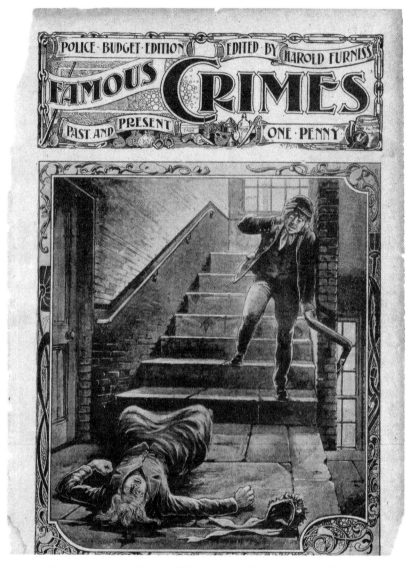

Popular publications such as *Famous Crimes* covered Mary Ann Nichols's murder.

were manufactured in the mid-1800s, very similar to what was used by the police during the Ripper investigation.

I waited until dark to carry one of these antique contraptions out to the patio and light a small fire in the oil pan. The lens turns into a

Officers often carried bull's-eye lanterns, also known as "dark lanterns" because they gave off very little light.

reddish-orange wavering eye. The convexity of the glass causes the light to vanish when viewed from various angles. I held my hand in front of the lantern, and at a distance of six inches could barely see a trace of my palm. Smoke wisped out the chimney. The cylinder got hot enough, according to police lore, to brew tea. I imagined a poor constable walking his beat and holding such a device by its two metal handles or clipping it to his leather snake-clasp belt. It's a wonder he could see where he was going and didn't burn himself.

The typical Victorian may not have had a clue about the inadequacy of bull's-eye lanterns or even what they looked like. Magazines and penny tabloids show constables shining intense beams into the darkest corners and alleyways while frightened suspects reel back from the blinding glare. Unless these cartoonlike depictions were deliberately exaggerated, they lead me to suspect that most people had never seen a bull's-eye lantern. That shouldn't come as a surprise. Police patrolling the safer, less crime-ridden areas of London would have little or no need to light their way. It was in the forbidden places that the lanterns shone their bloodshot eyes as they blearily probed the constables' beats. Most civilized people traveling by foot or in horse-drawn cabs didn't frequent those parts of the Great Metropolis.

Walter Sickert was a man of the night and the slums. He would have had good reason to know exactly what a bull's-eye lantern looked like because it was his habit to wander the forbidden places after his visits to the music halls. During what is called his Camden Town period in the early 1900s, when he was producing some of his most blatantly violent works of art, he used to paint murder scenes in the spooky glow of a bull's-eye lantern. This was witnessed by fellow artist and friend Marjorie Lilly, who shared his house and one of his studios. She described his behavior as "Dr. Jekyll" assuming the "mantle of Mr. Hyde."

A shrewd observer like Sickert would have been aware of the difficulties and discomforts faced by police whose dark-blue woolen uniforms and capes couldn't keep them warm and dry in bad weather. When days were hot it must have been unbearable. A constable wasn't permitted to loosen his belt or tunic or take off his military-shaped helmet with its shiny Brunswick star. If the ill-fitting leather boots he'd been issued maimed his feet, he could either buy a new pair with his own pay or suffer in silence. When smog enveloped the streets at night, a "dark lantern" wouldn't light his way. A clack-clack-clack of his rattle didn't assure a hasty response from comrades on foot blocks away.

In an anonymous 1893 article published in *Police Review and Parade Gossip*, a Metropolitan policeman gave the public a glimpse of what the average constable's life was like in 1887. He tells the story of his wife and their dying four-year-old son living in two rooms in a lodging house on Bow Street. Almost half of his weekly salary of twenty-four shillings went to rent. It was a time of great civil unrest, he writes, and animosity toward the police was intense.

With little more than a small truncheon tucked into a special pocket of a trouser leg, officers went out day after day and night after night, "well nigh exhausted with [our] constant contact with passionate wretches who had been made mad with want and cupidity." Angry citizens screamed vile insults

An officer of the Metropolitan Police on night duty carries a bull's-eye lantern.

and accused the police of being "against the people and the poor," the anonymous writer says. Better-off Londoners sometimes waited four to six hours before summoning the police after a robbery or burglary, and then publicly complained that responding men in blue were unable to bring offenders to justice.

Not only was policing a thankless job, it was also an impossible one. One-sixth of the approximately 14,000-member force was out sick, on leave or suspended on any given day. The supposed ratio of 1 policeman per 450 citizens was misleading. The number of men actually on the street depended on which shift was on duty. The number always doubled during night shift (10:00 p.m. to 6:00 a.m.). This meant that during day shift (6:00 a.m. to 2:00 p.m.) and late shift (2:00 p.m. to 10:00 p.m.) there were approximately 2,000 beat officers working each shift.

That's a ratio of 1 policeman to every 4,000 citizens or 1 policeman to cover every 6 miles of street on foot. In August 1888 when the Ripper's crime spree began, the ratio got even worse. As many as 2,000 men took

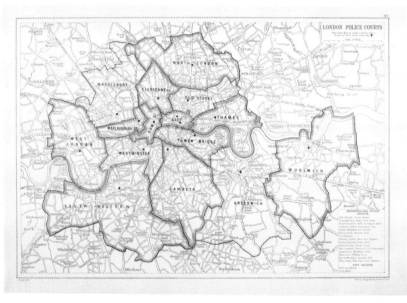

There were not enough police officers to cover the Greater London area. At night, the city was vastly underpatrolled.

vacation leave. During the night shift, a constable was expected to walk his beat in ten to fifteen minutes at an average pace of two and a half miles per hour. By the time the Ripper began his crimes this requirement was no longer enforced but the habit was deeply ingrained, and criminals and others up to no good could recognize a constable by his measured shoe-leathery gait.

The Greater London area was seven hundred square miles, and even if the police ranks doubled during the early morning hours, the Ripper could have prowled East End passageways, alleys, courtyards and back streets without seeing a single Brunswick star. If a constable was drawing near, the Ripper was forewarned by the unmistakable walk. He could slip into the shadows and wait for the body to be discovered, then eavesdrop on the excited conversations of witnesses, the doctor and the police. Jack the Ripper could have seen the moving orange eyes of the lanterns without any threat of the police seeing him.

Psychopaths love to watch the drama they script. It's common for serial killers to return to the crime scene or insert themselves into the investigation. A murderer showing up at his victim's funeral is so common that today's police often have plainclothes officers clandestinely surveil the mourners. Serial arsonists get off on watching their fires burn. Rapists love to work for social services. Ted Bundy was a volunteer for a crisis clinic while he was committing murder. When Robert Chambers strangled Jennifer Levin to death in New York's Central Park in 1986, he sat on a wall across the street from his staged crime scene. He waited two hours to watch the body be discovered, the police arrive and the morgue attendants zip up the pouch and load it into an ambulance. "He found it amusing," recalled Linda Fairstein, the prosecutor who sent him to prison.

Jack the Ripper would have been obsessed with watching the police and doctors examining the bodies at the scenes. He might have lingered in the dark long enough to see his victims carted away. He might have followed at a distance to catch a glimpse of the bodies being locked inside the mortuaries, and he could have attended the funerals. In the early 1900s, Sickert did an etching of two women gazing out a window, and inexplicably titled the work *The Passing Funeral*.

Several Ripper letters make taunting references to his watching the police at the scene. He hints that he was present for the victim's burial. "I see them and they cant see me," he writes.

One Sickert etching titled *The Passing Funeral* features two women staring out a window. The funeral procession itself is not visible.

11

THE ROYAL CONSPIRACY

D R. LLEWELLYN TESTIFIED at Mary Ann Nichols's inquest that she had a slight laceration of her tongue. He deduced that a bruise on her lower right jaw was from the blow of a fist or the "pressure of a thumb."

What the well-intentioned doctor didn't seem to consider was that she could have gotten these bruises earlier, perhaps from a scrap with a client or even a row with another prostitute. I could find no detailed description of Mary Ann's bruises that might give us insight into their age. The photograph taken of her in the mortuary is too washed out to tell us much.

Contusions or bruises are caused by trauma that results in blood leaking into the skin and other tissue. There are significant variables to consider if one is to determine when the blows or crushing injuries might have occurred. For example, someone who abuses alcohol or suffers from a blood disorder such as hemophilia or von Willebrand disease will bruise easily, and it's safe to say that Mary Ann Nichols was a heavy drinker. It might not have required much finger or thumb pressure to leave marks on her jaw and face.

Assuming the bruises were caused by the Ripper, this might suggest he attacked her from behind. He may have grabbed her chin, yanking her head back to expose her throat before slashing it in two places. One

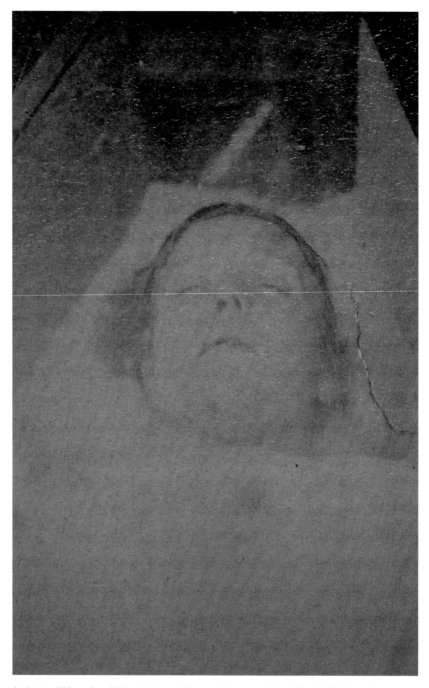

A photo of Mary Ann Nichols taken at the mortuary provides little insight into the manner of her death.

incision began below the left ear and was four inches long, and the second incision Dr. Llewellyn described as "circular." It also began on the left side of her neck, approximately one inch lower than the other incision and "a little forward of the ear." I don't know what he meant by "circular" but I suspect he was suggesting the incision encircled her neck, almost decapitating her. That vicious wound was eight inches long, severing all blood vessels, muscle tissue and cartilage, and nicking the cervical vertebra before terminating three inches below her right jaw.

Dr. Llewellyn's recital of other injuries also is unspecific. A jagged incision on her left side was "just about at the lower part of the abdomen." In addition there were "three or four" similar cuts that ran in a downward direction on the right side of the abdomen and "several" cuts running across it. She also had small stabs to her "private parts." He concluded that the abdominal wounds were sufficient to cause death, believing they were inflicted before her throat was cut. He based this on the lack of blood around her neck at the scene, failing to mention to the coroner or the jurors that he'd neglected to turn over the body. It's possible that by the time of the inquest he still didn't know he'd overlooked a large quantity of blood and a six-inch clot.

The injuries were from left to right, Dr. Llewellyn testified, and this led him to the conclusion that the killer was "left handed." The weapon, and there was only one this time, he speculated, was a long-bladed "moderately" sharp knife used with "great violence." The bruises on the jaw and face also were consistent with a left-handed assailant. From that assumption he went on to suggest that the killer placed his right hand over Mary Ann's mouth to stop her from screaming as he used his left hand to repeatedly slash her abdomen.

In the scenario Dr. Llewellyn describes the killer would have been facing Mary Ann when he launched his attack. Either they were standing or the killer already had her on the ground. Somehow he managed to keep her from shrieking and thrashing as he shoved up her clothes and started cutting through skin and fat, all the way down to her bowels. It's difficult to envision because such a scenario is awkward and defies logic.

A calculating, stealthy killer like Jack the Ripper wouldn't slash open a victim's abdomen first. Imagine her ferocious struggle as she suffered

In his official report, Dr. Llewellyn describes Mary Ann Nichols as having stabbing wounds to her abdomen and "private parts."

2

130

cut in several places and,
two small stabs on private
parts, which in his opinion
may have been done with
a strong bladed knife. At
first the Doctor was of
opinion that the wounds
were caused by a left
handed person but he is
now doubtful.

31st Aug. 88 The body was identified by
Ellen Holland of 18 Thrawl
Street, E. as that of Mary
Ann Nichols of the same
address, – a common lodging
house, – & subsequently by the
husband, Wm Nichols of 37
Coburg Road, Old Kent Rd –
printers' machinist.

There was no money in pocket of
deceased & there was nothing left behind
by the murderer.

The results of Police enquiries are
as follows: –

2.30 a.m. 31st Aug 88 Mrs Nichols was last
seen alive at 2.30 am 31st Aug
1888

Thrawl St.

*". . . along right side, under pelvis to left of stomach, there the wound
was jagged: the coating of the stomach was cut in several places and
two small stabs on private parts, which in his opinion may have been
done with a strong bladed knife."*

unimaginable terror, panic and pain. Imagine her screams. Had the coroner carefully questioned Dr. Llewellyn about the relevant medical details, a very different reconstruction of Mary Ann Nichols's murder might have emerged. Maybe the killer didn't approach her from the front. Maybe he never said a word to her. Maybe she never saw him.

A hint of how the Ripper attacked his victims might be found in Sickert's celebrated series of paintings and etchings called *Ennui*. In all five versions of what is considered his most famous work, a bored older man sits at a table, his cigar lit, a tall glass of what may be gin in front of him. He stares off deep in thought, completely uninterested in the woman behind him. She leans against a dresser, resting her head on her hand, gazing unhappily into a corner of the room.

In one version of *Ennui* there is a painting on the wall that depicts a woman surrounded by darkness. She wears a reddish-brown evening dress that covers her left shoulder, upper arm and breast. Behind her is a curious vertical crescent, rather fleshy-white with a slight bump on the left side that looks very much like an ear. What we see in an image is subjective. But it appears to me that this crescent could be a man's face half in the shadows, and the woman is barely turning as if she senses his approach. Under low magnification the half-shadowed face of the man is more apparent and the woman's face begins to look like a skull.

In 2001, I photographed this version of *Ennui* at the Tate and sent a transparency to documents expert Chuck Pruitt at the Virginia Institute of Forensic Science and Medicine. Perhaps we could get a sharper look with forensic imaging software that detects hundreds of gray shades that the human eye can't see. While this forensic technology is effective when used on blurry bank video recordings or poor-quality photographs, it doesn't work on paintings.

All our efforts accomplished was to separate Sickert's brushstrokes until we ended up with the reverse of what he was doing when he put them together. Another "ha ha," the joke on me. Sickert's *Ennui* was mentioned in the Ripper theories long before I'd ever heard of the artist or his famous series of paintings. It's been suggested that Sickert left us a clue in another version of *Ennui* that includes yet another curious shape in the painting on the wall, possibly a bird shape above the woman's bare left shoulder.

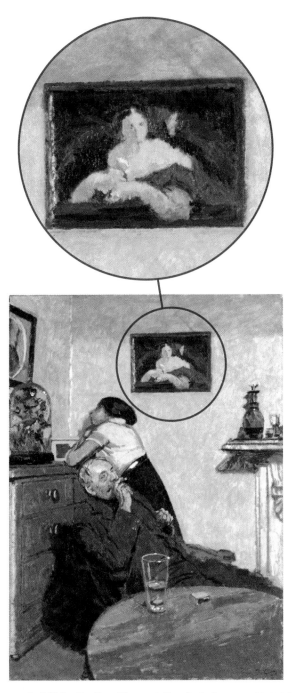

In the background of Sickert's *Ennui* is a painting featuring a woman and possibly a shadowy figure.

When Joseph Gorman went public with his claims that Sickert was his biological father, he said that Sickert had cleverly introduced a "gull" into a painting to point the finger at Jack the Ripper's true identity: Queen Victoria's Physician-in-Ordinary, Sir William Gull, who since has become a popular Ripper suspect, absurdly I might add. Dr. Gull was almost seventy-one years old and had already suffered a stroke by the time the murders began. He was in failing health and would die in January 1890. He doesn't exactly seem a likely candidate for someone committing vicious serial crimes.

Even so, when I began this investigation I was remiss in completely ignoring him and other Ripper suspects and theories. I dismissed them as illogical and silly. But I should have taken a close look at what Stephen

Sir William Gull, Queen Victoria's physician, also has been suspected of being Jack the Ripper, though he was in poor health at the time.

Knight argued in *Jack the Ripper: The Final Solution* (1976). It purports that Dr. Gull, Walter Sickert and a man named John Netley committed five Ripper murders. This "solution" was based in part on stories told by Joseph Gorman, and at the time I began my research I chose not to interview Knight or read his book.

I also paid no attention to what Jean Overton Fuller presented in her investigation, *Sickert and the Ripper Crimes*. Published in 1990, it asserts that Sickert accused Dr. Gull of being the Ripper but in fact it was Sickert who committed the murders. I chose not to interview Ms. Fuller when I first started my work on this case. I didn't read her book. I had no interest whatsoever in anything associated with the prevailing and all-time favorite Ripper theory known as the Royal Conspiracy. It wouldn't have occurred to me then that there could be an actual connection between Ripper killings and incredible dramas involving the Royal Family that I will touch on now.

Suffice it to say that since the early days I've completely changed my mind. I now believe it is important to consider seemingly outlandish tales that may actually fit with what Sickert spun to at least two individuals who had no connection to each other. Joseph Gorman and Sickert's artist friend Florence Pash never met. They recounted anecdotes about the Royal Conspiracy that they couldn't have gotten from each other.

As the convoluted conspiratorial theories go, and admittedly my summary of them is a simplistic one, Princess Alexandra asked Walter Sickert to teach art to her son the Duke of Clarence, Albert Victor Christian Edward, affectionately known as Prince Eddy. He began clandestinely showing up for lessons at Sickert's studio on Cleveland Street. This is where the prince, who was second in line to the throne, is said to have met Annie Elizabeth Crook, a confectionary assistant near Sickert's studio and also one of his models.

Her alleged affair and secret marriage to Prince Eddy produced a child named Alice Margaret Crook, who was born in the Marylebone Workhouse on April 18, 1885, according to her birth certificate. In some versions of this account, she ended up in Sickert's care because the Royals wished to keep her scandalous existence a secret. As the story goes, Sickert's fostering of Alice Margaret became sexual in later years, resulting in yet another illegitimate child, this one Joseph, who was raised by the Gormans. He saw the famous artist infrequently, Joseph would later claim. He said it was during occasional visits that he learned about his supposed royal lineage, and while Sickert was at it, he confided in the boy about the Jack the Ripper murders. Supposedly Sickert told Joseph that Annie Elizabeth Crook was friends with eventual Ripper victim Mary Kelly, who in turn was acquainted with other eventual Ripper victims Mary Ann Nichols, Annie Chapman and Elizabeth Stride. All of them made the mistake of deciding to blackmail the Royal Family because of Prince Eddy's secret marriage and illegitimate child. Sir William Gull took care of the messy problem through murder.

Joseph explained all this to Stephen Knight and others, only to retract his story after the publication of Knight's *Final Solution* in 1976 when ugly intimations began circulating about Walter Sickert. According to Joseph's widow, Edna, her late husband wasn't prepared for the avalanche of sensationalism his stories caused. By the time I considered talking to Joseph it was too late. He died on January 9, 2003, barely two months after the first edition of this book was published.

Joseph Gorman was born in Camden Town on October 22, 1925. His birth certificate lists his father as William Gorman, a fish curer, and his mother as Alice Crook. If she's the same Alice Crook who was born in the Marylebone Workhouse, she would have been forty when she gave birth to Joseph. If Sickert really was the biological father, he would have been sixty-five at the time.

The Gormans' address was 195 Drummond Street in West St. Pancras, not even half a mile from where Sickert had kept a studio. Since he died in 1942, if he really did tell these Ripper stories then it had to have been when Joseph was no older than his midteens. Completely ridiculous? Maybe not. In earlier years Sickert had produced some of his most important works including *Ennui* in his studio at 19 Fitzroy Street. It was a gathering place for other artists. It's where he and artists Spencer Gore and Charles Ginner formed the Fitzroy Street Group that would evolve into the Camden Town Group.

Joseph grew up but a few minutes' walk from an area of London that Sickert was intimate with and frequented. Their paths may have crossed. It's possible he filled Joseph's head with fantastic, murderous tales, a claim that wasn't refuted by Andrina Schweder, the sister of Sickert's second wife,

Christine Drummond Angus. When the theory of the Royal Conspiracy became public Ms. Schweder claimed to Stephen Knight that she saw her brother-in-law, Walter Sickert, constantly and with "great intimacy." In her October 20, 1976, letter to Knight she didn't say that Joseph was Sickert's son. But she didn't deny it either.

She also didn't dismiss Joseph's stories as fabrications or confabulations. Indeed her major criticism was that by the time Joseph was old enough to have listened to such things, Sickert was in his dotage. She thought it was rather "mean" of Joseph to have "cashed in" on such tales. Possibly without intending to she managed to affirm that Sickert did indeed tell outrageous stories to a young Joseph, including ones about Jack the Ripper that ultimately may have been the genesis of the Royal Conspiracy.

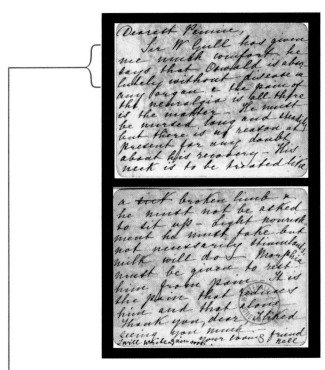

"Sir W. Gull has given me much comfort—he says that Oswald is absolutely without disease . . ."

In a letter to a friend, Walter Sickert's mother implies that Dr. William Gull was one of their family doctors.

Joseph's claims about what Sickert told him become more interesting when one considers another detail that has been ignored in Ripper lore. Sickert's mother knew Dr. William Gull. Apparently he was a Sickert family doctor. She says in an undated letter she wrote to her close friend Pennie Muller: "Sir W. Gull has given me much comfort—he says that Oswald is absolutely without disease in any organ & the pain of the neuralgia is all there is in the matter. . . . Your loving friend, Nell."

If the Oswald she refers to is her husband then it's likely the letter was written between 1872 when Dr. Gull was created a baronet and December 1885 when Oswald Sickert died. However, it's also possible and more likely that Mrs. Sickert is writing about her son, Oswald Valentine, who suffered chronic health problems. The Sickert family connection to Dr. Gull is significant. It might hint that the introduction of him as a Ripper suspect came from Walter Sickert himself.

In a story published by Stephen Knight on December 7, 1973, in the *East London Advertiser* Joseph claimed it was his alleged father, Sickert, who had told him about Gull. Of course it's also possible Joseph got the idea from the November 1970 edition of the *Criminologist*, where Dr. Thomas Stowell theorized that Prince Eddy and Sir William Gull were responsible for the Ripper crimes. The story was picked up by the *Sunday Times* and became an international sensation.

We can't know the truth. It's likely we never will. But I have no doubt that Joseph believed the claims he made. That was clear to me four years after his death, on October 15, 2007, when I visited the Gorman flat in Kentish Town. An easel, palettes and artwork still filled a corner of the living room, and I was shown a portrait he had painted of Sickert. The two men seemed to bear a resemblance to each other. Unquestionably Joseph worshipped and emulated him. The Gorman family was passionate and sincere about what Joseph believed, and his widow, Edna, repeated his stories of being a boy and visiting the artist he thought was his father.

"He went to Walter Sickert's home many times," she said. When I last talked to her, in the fall of 2013, she recalled that Joseph's childhood nickname for Sickert was "Teethy because he had large teeth." She went on to explain that Sickert's teeth were a dominant feature to the boy, perhaps because Sickert laughed and smiled while enchanting and entertaining him. Certainly Sickert was famous for being witty, dramatic and charismatic. Edna said that Sickert also would visit young Joseph at the Gorman home on Drummond Street. She added that she wasn't surprised by the opposition and criticism her late husband eventually got. There was good reason for certain people to dismiss him entirely as a liar or a crackpot.

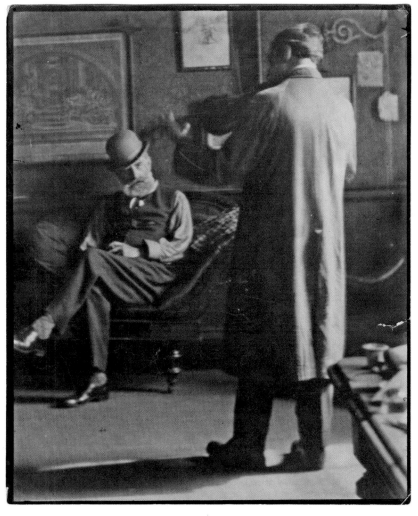

Sickert, around the age he was when the young Joseph Gorman spent time at his home, listens critically to a violinist in his Highbury Place studio.

If he really was Sickert's biological child, this possibly could have thrown quite a monkey wrench into who owns the Sickert copyright or any of his art that might have been retained by his third wife's relatives. Not to mention, there could be the untidy problem of Joseph having royal blood in his veins, assuming there's any truth to his grandfather having been Prince Eddy. During my visit to the Gorman Kentish Town home, Edna presented a possible source of her late husband's DNA, a small spot of his blood on a favorite jacket he'd worn. A DNA scientist who accompanied us removed the stain, which supposedly was too contaminated for analysis. Barring an exhumation, tracing Joseph Gorman's genetic ancestry would be a difficult task. There may never be answers to the questions he raised about his identity. But it was clear when I was with his family that they had no hesitation about using any means possible to "prove" Joseph was Walter Sickert's son.

There are other strange teases that might make us wonder if he was. From a very young age Joseph had latched on to artist Harry Maude Jonas. They spent considerable time together and would be lifelong close friends. Born in London in 1893, Jonas may have encountered or even been acquainted with Sickert in the late 1920s and beyond. This could have been how young Joseph connected with Sickert, although the possibility has been categorically denied by Sickert biographer Matthew Sturgis. "Jonas had never known Sickert," Sturgis writes. Overall he dismisses Joseph as a delusional aspiring artist for whom the "idea of a kinship with the great [Sickert] was part of Joseph's self-mythologizing."

I don't know where Sturgis got his information about Sickert and Jonas but it appears he's incorrect. In the January 1950 edition of the *St. Pancras Journal* it states: "[Sickert] seems to have had a peculiar habit of using several addresses at the same time. The distinguished painter, Mr. Harry Jonas, who knew Sickert in his Fitzroy days, recalls that the artist was frequently to be seen walking across the street from one studio to another—with his palette in one hand and his canvas or easel in the other."

The likelihood that Jonas and Sickert were acquainted is further supported by a letter dated May 5, 1929, to Walter Sickert from a Jack (or Jock) Brady. It certainly seems that Sickert knew, did business with or was interested in Harry Jonas. "As Mr. Jonas is away on holiday," Brady writes to Sickert, "I have been left in charge of the above address. And I cannot get in touch with Mr. Wilson Steer." The artist Steer was a friend of Sickert's, and the "above address" Mr. Brady refers to was Thackeray House, 35 Maple Street, and according to an April 21, 1969, article in *The Times*, Jonas there lived for thirty-five years.

When Sickert had returned from France in 1905, he'd taken the studio at 19 Fitzroy Street, a five-minute walk from 35 Maple Street. In 1922 he'd done a moody, desolate oil painting titled *Maple Street*, depicting a man and a woman on an empty street of closed-up shops. Some sort of parcel is by their feet. The scene is typically evocative of something bad about to happen, and one imagines the artist himself out in the early morning hours, watching a man and a woman who seem vulnerable.

It's remotely possible the Mr. Jonas referred to in the letter from Mr. Brady isn't Harry Jonas, but likely it was. A letter Jonas wrote to an art historian in 1943 lists the same Thackeray House address. Even so, that certainly doesn't prove that any relationship Jonas and Sickert might have had also included Joseph Gorman. I don't know the answer. But the addition of Jonas into the mix is yet one more detail that is curious and unsettling. Then there's the odd financial connection between Joseph Gorman and Sickert that only adds to the intrigue.

Among Joseph's papers is a statement dated September 19, 1989, that had accompanied a check for £154.88 from a literary agency. This payment was a permission fee and a 50 percent share of an advance due to Joseph for the use and paperback release of *A Free House!*, a compilation of Walter Sickert's writings edited by Osbert Sitwell. The book originally was published by Macmillan, London, in 1947, and one has to ask how it's possible Joseph Gorman was entitled to any revenues from it.

On March 10, 2005, the literary agency involved offered a written explanation:

> *It is our understanding that Joseph Sickert was Walter Sickert's son and inherited the copyright in his father's work. . . . Our original contact for the Estate was Walter Sickert's widow. Our files indicate that we received instruction in 1989 that future income was to go to Joseph Sickert so presumably it was at that point that he inherited copyrights.*

A spokesperson for that agency (which requested anonymity) would later state in October of 2012 that the source of this original directive can't be clarified. Maybe the instruction came from the Sickert estate. Maybe it came from Joseph Gorman or someone else. A riddle wrapped up in a mystery, and it concludes with the enigma of a 1926 drawing by Sickert. It's of an infant in a pram and captioned "Boy Jos," presumably short for Joseph. In 1926 Joseph Gorman would have been about one.

Joseph Gorman, who claimed to be Sickert's illegitimate son, said Sickert confided many details about the Ripper case to him. This sketch from 1926 by Walter Sickert may depict Joseph Gorman, hinting at a close relationship between them. The abbreviated name "Jos" in the caption is likely short for "Joseph," and the child in the drawing is the right age.

12

DREADFUL BLEEDING CORPSES

O N OCTOBER 14, 2007, I went to see Jean Overton Fuller in the small village of Wymington, England, where she lived in a stone and brick cottage covered with red ivy and roses.

She was ninety-two, dressed that day in a colorful cardigan and green slacks. I found her elegant and articulate, and I was keenly interested in the story I'd come to hear about her theory of Jack the Ripper. In 1990 it was the basis of her book *Sickert and the Ripper Crimes*. She was an author, a theosophist, and I couldn't understand why she chose to write something so far afield if not weird considering her background and other publications.

She was raised by her Army doctor grandfather and her mother, Violet, and after a brief career as an actress Jean Overton Fuller graduated with honors from the University of London. According to her obituary published in *The Guardian* on May 18, 2009, she worked in London as an examiner in the postal service during the Second World War. She wrote books on a range of subjects including spiritualism, literary criticism and studies of Victor Neuburg, Shelley, Swinburne, Francis Bacon and others.

Jean Overton Fuller wrote a book about her Jack the Ripper theory, titled *Sickert and the Ripper Crimes*.

When we met at her home she'd just finished her autobiography, *Driven to It*, and was quite proud to show me her big black antique Olympia typewriter. We sat in a living room comfortably cluttered with books and art, and she told me about her mother's strange encounter in France with artist Florence Pash, a close friend and confidant of Walter Sickert's. Ms. Fuller was a young girl at the time, and she recalled her mother as having just returned to London, "bubbling over with information."

As I took notes in my journal, Ms. Fuller went on to explain that Florence Pash had told "the most amazing story" about having been with Walter Sickert, who shocked and frightened her with what he confided. "He said he knew who Jack the Ripper was," Ms. Fuller recalled, "and that he could never get out of his mind the dreadful bleeding corpses. I was very puzzled by this. How did he come to see the dreadful bleeding corpses? If he saw *all* of the bleeding corpses that makes him Jack the Ripper."

As she continued to tell what she recalled, it sounded all the more farfetched. Certainly it doesn't fit with what I believe happened in the Ripper case. But the details she shared are remarkable nonetheless and may not be completely wrong. I also was intrigued that her era overlapped Sickert's.

She was the only person I met during this investigation who remembered hearing about him from people who were witnesses with direct knowledge of what he did and said. She had information she'd gotten long ago. She struggled with what it meant.

Sickert claimed a member of the Royal Family "in direct line to the throne" had an illegitimate child he deserted, she said. The implication was that the Royal who did the deserting was Prince Eddy, the Duke of Clarence. The mother, whose name Ms. Fuller didn't know, deposited her infant daughter on Sickert's doorstep, so to speak, asking him to keep an eye on the little girl in his studio while he painted. Some Royal Conspiracy theories place this studio at 15 Cleveland Street, but Ms. Fuller said she didn't recall the location if she ever knew it. Apparently Sickert told Florence Pash that eventual Ripper victim Mary Kelly was at that time working as a tobacconist assistant in a shop across from his studio. Sickert said that Mary had much to say about "bringing up a child that wasn't his."

Sickert's portrait of Florence Pash, circa 1896–97.

He told Ms. Pash he was unhappy about not getting paid for his caretaking efforts and that Mary Kelly convinced him to "raise the matter" with the Royal Family. She suggested he threaten to go to the police, to take a "tougher line. . . . If he was good enough to bring the child up he should get some money for it" were Ms. Fuller's words that I wrote down in my journal. Sickert said Mary Kelly "was as good as telling him to blackmail the Royal Family, which he had no intention of doing." Instead, as Ms. Fuller's story goes, he went to the Palace and discussed the matter with Sir William Gull.

After that Sickert took it upon himself to take care of the Royal indiscretion by murdering Mary Kelly, who was busy "writing letters to the

Palace." She was attempting blackmail. The four other East End prostitutes of the so-called canonical five were either in league with her or were accidentally murdered while the Ripper was after Mary. In other words Sickert confessed he began killing people "because Sir William Gull wanted him to."

This was how Gull, Queen Victoria's physician, became a Ripper "suspect" when the Royal Conspiracy theory became big news in the late 1970s. As I've pointed out, Sickert certainly would have been familiar with his family doctor, Sir William Gull, and I find the link significant since it was Joseph Gorman who connected the name Gull with the Ripper crimes in a story published by Stephen Knight (December 7, 1973, *East London Advertiser*). Joseph claimed it was his alleged father, Walter Sickert, who had told him about Gull, and these words gain new meaning when one realizes Sickert knew Gull or at least knew of him.

It seems that Sickert also mentioned Gull to Florence Pash, supposedly telling her that his most famous series of paintings and etchings, titled *Ennui*, feature a gull on Queen Victoria's shoulder as a clue. (Most art experts see neither a gull nor Queen Victoria in *Ennui*, and I didn't either when I looked at a version of it at the Tate Britain.) The reason Sickert gave Florence Pash for his divulging such a bizarre and unsettling story was that he wanted what he'd done to be known, "but not during his lifetime." He went on to show Ms. Pash a number of "murder paintings that he later burned."

Ms. Fuller's story sounds very similar to Joseph Gorman's, but there are differences. Significantly, the account he gave Stephen Knight makes no mention of Florence Pash or a number of the details that supposedly came from her. Gorman and Jean Overton Fuller were acquainted but there's no indication they got their information from each other. Their stories about Sickert were published fourteen years apart, Knight's book in 1976 and Fuller's in 1990. In a letter she wrote to Ripper expert Keith Skinner on August 9, 2007, she said that after *Sickert and the Ripper Crimes* was published she and Joseph had a conversation about it. He said that what she'd written "told him something he had never known—who Florence was."

He'd heard about her from his mother, who'd always told him that "Florence Pash was a person whom he had to respect," but never explained who she was, Ms. Fuller said. When I met with her several months after she'd written this letter she concluded her story about Sickert and Florence Pash by simply summarizing, "It makes no sense she [her mother] would make it up."

Maybe Violet Overton Fuller didn't make it up. Maybe Florence Pash and Joseph Gorman didn't either, although I don't believe that a conspiracy is why women were being slaughtered in the late summer and fall of 1888 and beyond. Sexual homicides don't fit what sounds like a violent fairy tale that involves a royal palace, a prince and a love child left in the care of strangers. Nonetheless I don't doubt that Sickert might have told such things to Florence Pash, Joseph Gorman and possibly to others.

I don't doubt that he might have confabulated myths to give meaning, motive and even nobility to cowardly, cruel crimes. His wild, ugly yarns also would have been a way to obsess openly about fantasies and memories that would have been alive and well in his psyche. Violent sexual psychopaths endlessly replay their horrific acts. Sickert may have been proud of what he'd done. He might have been excited by allusions he felt safe to make to a nonthreatening audience such as an easily frightened female artist friend or a gullible little boy. Sickert also may have been frustrated. By the time he made his confession to Florence Pash, Jack the Ripper was the most infamous killer in history. Sickert himself would never be as well known as that, and he was getting older. Maybe he was becoming disinhibited. Maybe he wanted the credit.

I've yet to locate any documentation about what Florence Pash claims Sickert told her in France. But the two of them certainly were together in Dieppe in 1921 when she was painting his portrait, and the conversation could have taken place then. Perhaps there are no letters or diaries that would verify Jean Overton Fuller's story, but she isn't the only one who has relayed odd and disturbing memories that go beyond Sickert's simply being eccentric, as his apologists continue to portray him.

I can't verify what Joseph Gorman and Jean Overton Fuller claimed. But I can address the motive for the Ripper crimes that Sickert supposedly offered. It has no ring of truth. I've immersed myself in criminal investigations for more than half my life and witnessed the ugly spoils of violence

Florence Pash painted this portrait of Sickert in the French city of Dieppe in 1921.

firsthand, and rarely are there elaborate, fantastic motives in murder. The Royal Conspiracy continues to sound ludicrous to me.

If the point in murdering a prostitute named Mary Kelly was to shut her up, then why mutilate her body beyond recognition? Why rip up any of the victims and steal body parts? Why send violent confessional communications? Why repeatedly goad the police to "catch me if you can," and threaten to kill and mutilate others? It's absurd to think that prostitutes had to be slashed to death because they were trying to blackmail the Royal Family. If that were really the motive, discretion would have been mandated. Simply make the women disappear.

It's been estimated that in 1887 some eighteen thousand people were reported missing in London, half of them never accounted for. Transient, homeless and desperate prostitutes could have vanished or turned up dead and never made the news or created a stir. "Strange Disappearance of Ladies" was a headline in the *York Herald* on December 26, 1888. The journalist claimed that the London police "have been informed of a large number of disappearances," including "members of the aristocratic class . . . and some startling rumors are afloat."

As British historian Paul Begg points out, "The government could and no doubt would have been able to get rid of half a dozen blackmailing prostitutes quietly and almost unnoticed." He reasons that if the goal was to get rid of problematic people it wouldn't make sense "to leave their mutilated corpses on the streets to kick start an international sensation." Why would the Duke of Clarence and Sir William Gull involve themselves in something as risky and loathsome as that?

To this day both of them continue to be popular Ripper suspects. It doesn't seem to matter that there's absolutely no evidence either of them were involved in violence or would have condoned it or even been capable of cunning calculations. It's doubtful they could have expended the effort required by the Ripper's crimes. Prince Eddy in particular would have found them distasteful. It would seem his major preoccupation was his dazzling uniforms and fine clothes, and he's described as sweet, sensitive and lazy. It's unfair his name has been forever linked to grisly homicides that continued after his sudden death in 1892 at the age of twenty-eight.

The Duke of Clarence, second in line to the throne, was born two months prematurely after his mother watched her husband play ice hockey. Apparently she spent too much time being "whirled" about in a sledge. Not feeling well, she was taken back to Frogmore, where there was only a local practitioner to oversee her son's unexpected birth. His developmental difficulties probably had less to do with his premature birth than with the small royal gene pool that spawned him. He was gentle but obtuse. He was

The Duke of Clarence, "Prince Eddy," has been a popular suspect in modern Ripper theories. The case against him isn't based on evidence and most likely is the product of confabulation.

congenitally prone to deafness, and as another curious aside so are Joseph Gorman's children.

Prince Eddy was sensitive, courteous and kind but a dismal student. He could barely ride a horse and was consumed by vanity. He didn't have the traits needed to be a strong king or leader. He was slow, lacking in motivation and couldn't resist temptations that wouldn't hold him in good stead were he to rule the most powerful empire on the planet. Out of frustration his father, the Prince of Wales, and Queen Victoria tried to toughen up Prince Eddy by sending him on long voyages to distant lands. Maybe it was also a good idea to make him scarce from time to time because of sexual indiscretions that may have included homosexual dalliances.

I found no real evidence that he was homosexual or bisexual but there's no question he was involved with women. His emotional attachments were to them, especially to his beautiful, doting mother, Princess Alexandra, who didn't seem unduly concerned that he cared more about clothes than the crown. On July 12, 1884, Prince Eddy's unhappy father wrote to his son's German tutor, "It is with sincere regret that we learn from you that our son dawdles so dreadfully in the morning. . . . He will have to make up the lost time by additional study." In this seven-page missive that the future king wrote from Marlborough House he's emphatic that his son "must put his shoulder to the wheel."

It's extremely unlikely that Prince Eddy had either the stamina or the interest to go about preying on prostitutes because they supposedly were attempting to extort money from him. On the nights of at least three of the murders, it's reported he wasn't in London or even close by. But strangely enough he was indeed being blackmailed not long after the Ripper crimes began, referring to what sounds like a sordid mess in letters he wrote to his formidable and famous barrister, George Lewis.

In late 1890 and early 1891 Prince Eddy claims to have gotten himself into a compromising situation with two ladies of low standing, one of them a "Miss Richardson." He was trying to disengage himself by paying for the return of letters he'd written to her and another lady friend. "I am very pleased to hear you are able to settle with Miss Richardson," Prince Eddy writes Lewis on November 17, 1890, "although £200 is rather expensive for letters." He goes on to promise to "do all I can to get back" the letters he wrote to "the other lady and if unsuccessful will ask your assistance on the matter."

Two months later he writes from his cavalry barracks and includes a gift "in acknowledgement for the kindness you showed me the other day in getting me out of that trouble I was foolish enough to get into." But apparently "the other lady" wasn't so easily appeased and the Prince had to send a friend to "ask her to give up the two or three letters I had written to her . . . you may be certain that I shall be careful in the future not to get into any more trouble of the sort."

The content of the letters the Duke of Clarence wrote to Miss Richardson and "the other lady" has never been revealed as far as I can determine. But one might infer that he acted in a manner bound to cause the Royal Family embarrassment. He was well aware that news of his involvement with the sorts of women who might blackmail him wouldn't have been well received by the public and certainly not by his grandmother the Queen.

What this attempted extortion seems to suggest is that Prince Eddy's inclination in such an indelicate situation wasn't to have the offending parties butchered but to pay them off. However, it's only fair to point out that his rumored relationship with a twenty-three-year-old woman named Lydia Manton didn't end up quite so innocuously as payments for the return of potentially embarrassing communications. She met with a tragic and mysterious end after she was forced to break off a relationship with someone anonymous and extremely important. It's believed her lover was Prince Eddy.

A popular chorus girl at the Gaiety Theatre, Lydia Manton was known for her beauty, refinement and expensive clothing and jewelry. She lived in a West End apartment in Burlington Mansions, described as a luxurious building with elevators and full service staff. It was suspected she was being kept by a rich man, and on October 1, 1891, she ordered lunch for two sent up to her sitting room. According to a waiter, at 2:40 that afternoon Lord Charles Montagu, a son of the Duke of Manchester, arrived and stayed but a few minutes. When the waiter returned to clear away the untouched luncheon, he found Lydia very upset. Some five hours later a maid discovered her dead body sprawled across the bed, a bottle of carbolic acid nearby. A story circulated that Lydia and Montagu were lovers, but there were serious doubts about that.

Montagu was a spendthrift and a sponge, and it was improbable he could have supplied Lydia with an expensive lifestyle. In fact none of the Gaiety chorus girls were aware of a relationship between the two of them, although it was suspected she was seeing someone of extreme importance whose name she never mentioned. She'd spent much of the summer in the seaside village of Broadstairs and the night before her death had returned from a visit there. She was described by friends as in extremely high spirits, and soon after her alleged suicide, rumors began circulating that Lord Montagu was a front for someone of extraordinarily high class who'd been having an affair with her. It was suggested in a number of newspapers that on the October afternoon of her death, Montagu was sent to tell her that her lover would not be coming to lunch because the relationship was over.

The inquest into her death was attended by George Lewis, although he had no active role in the case. *The Star* newspaper reported: "It was quite

"London Gaiety Co."

949 BROADWAY. N.Y.

On October 1, 1891, chorus girl Lydia Manton was reportedly visited in her luxurious apartment by Lord Charles Montagu, a son of the Duke of Manchester. Later that day, she was found dead.

certain that everything that money could do would be done to prevent publicity at the inquest. Was it because there was a crime to conceal? Or was it because some exalted personage was involved—some person whose foolings could not endure the penalty of exposure?" The implication made by a number of newspapers was that the "exalted personage" was the Duke of Clarence.

Certainly it's a fact that George Lewis was his attorney, and why else might he attend Lydia Manton's inquest? It's also noteworthy that her alleged suicide occurred at 23 Cork Street in Mayfair, known for its commercial art galleries and the Royal Academy of Arts at Burlington House. It was an area of London that was quite familiar to Walter Sickert, and he also happened to be acquainted with George Lewis. A review of Whistler correspondence shows that in May or June of 1888 Sickert was trying to arrange a meeting with Lewis.

Sickert would have further entanglements with the flamboyant attorney in 1897. Lewis would represent American artist and author Joseph Pennell, who sued Sickert for damaging his reputation through a series of attacks on his technique of transfer lithography to produce prints. Whistler was Lewis's star witness. Coincidentally, Sickert's former master was fond of the Gaiety Theatre where Lydia Manton performed, and he created at least one drawing of it, titled *Souvenir of the Gaiety*. Sickert also was quite familiar with the Gaiety. He refers to it in a letter he wrote to the *Pall Mall Gazette* on February 2, 1889.

It's possible Sickert, who loved gossip and freely mingled with well-known people, might have been aware of Lewis's intervention in Prince Eddy's blackmail case. Sickert also might have known about Lydia Manton's unfortunate and controversial death. Certainly it was publicized, and these dark stories seem eerily similar to elements of the Royal Conspiracy theory. This again suggests that the origin was confabulations Sickert may have told others over the years, including a young Joseph Gorman and the artist Florence Pash.

Although my intention in this work has never been to focus on who the Ripper wasn't, I will emphasize there's no basis in fact for suspecting Sir William Gull. There's no justification for blaming Prince Eddy, whose style doesn't seem to include neutralizing an indiscretion through blatant murder and mutilation and then sending taunting letters to the police, press and others. Another suspect who should be dismissed while we're at it is a cotton merchant named James Maybrick. He supposedly wrote the notorious Ripper Diary that came to light in 1992 and has since been pronounced a fraud.

An arsenic addict, Maybrick lived in Liverpool, and long before the Ripper murders began was visiting a chemist as often as five times a day to obtain potentially lethal doses. By June of 1888 Maybrick was complaining of headaches and numbness of his limbs from his abuse of arsenic and other poisonous drugs such as strychnine. It's difficult to accept that someone compromised by a severe and chronic drug addiction could have committed the Ripper crimes and successfully evaded detection. Then there is the problem of motive. Supposedly Maybrick discovered his wife, Florie, was having an affair, and enraged, he began killing prostitutes in London. But the chronology doesn't work.

Newspaper articles in addition to Florie's correspondence indicate it wasn't until March of 1889 that the couple quarreled over the suspected affair and Maybrick supposedly beat her. Original documents also indicate that Florie's alleged affair with the young cotton broker Alfred Brierley occurred many months after the Ripper began his notorious rampage in London's East End.

On August 7, 1889, Florie was convicted of murdering her husband with arsenic, the very poison he was addicted to, and she was sentenced to death. There was no evidence except high levels of arsenic in the arsenic-addicted Maybrick's blood. Perhaps the outrageous miscarriage of justice in her case was best summed up in a letter that a seventy-year-old physician named James Adams wrote to Lord Charles Russell on March 24, 1891: "I never heard such an unfair trial and unjust verdict in the whole course of my experience."

On May 29, 1895, after six years of imprisonment, solitary confinement and failing health, Florie writes, "I have met with so many disappointments at the hands of Her Majesty's representatives, that I feel almost too disheartened to make any further efforts for my relief. Were it not for the sake of my dear children & my mother, whose health is failing so greatly under the strain of deferred hope, I should not presume to recall myself to your memory . . . As a prisoner, I am powerless to help myself or my cause."

Queen Victoria rarely showed compassion toward prisoners but in this case she eventually yielded to public pressure, and Florie's life was spared. Sentenced to fifteen years, she was released in 1904 and changed her name. She moved to America, became a housekeeper and died a recluse. One might wonder if James Maybrick would have been associated with the subtle, sinister allusions in the controversial Ripper Diary had it not been for the international outrage created by his wife's conviction for a crime she didn't commit.

Otherwise why would anyone have heard of him? Why would his name jump to mind when reading an alleged Ripper diary about "pills" and "numb" extremities or personal references to Maybrick's home and family that might not be recognizable if we didn't already know who he was? Why would anyone think to fabricate a diary that suggests the dead arsenic-addicted cotton merchant was the most notorious killer of all time? The likely answer is that Maybrick would have been too obscure for such a "hoax" if his name hadn't been all over the news when his wife was accused of his murder.

To date it's not known who wrote the infamous Ripper Diary. It didn't surface until 1992 and the album it was written in is inconsistent with the period, possibly from the early 1900s. The tiny, snarled handwriting in perfect straight lines doesn't remotely resemble Maybrick's, and according to forensic paper expert Peter Bower, the handwriting isn't of the Victorian era at all and could be as recent as twenty or thirty years old. The diary "is absolute rubbish," Bower said to me in London on September 26, 2012.

Florie Maybrick's tragic story could have been known by anyone who followed the news and had a voyeuristic interest in people, especially those accused of murder. What happened to her also serves as a reminder of the prejudice against any woman considered immoral or a "whore" in Victorian London. Had the Ripper's crimes not been so brutal, so recurrent and most of all so sensationalized by his written taunts, it's likely the murders of East End unfortunates wouldn't have created much of a stir.

13

INSTANT
DEATH

A CALCULATING PREDATOR like Jack the Ripper would have watched Mary Ann Nichols, determining how drunk and aware she was before he struck.

He may have drifted up to her in the dark and showed her a coin, maybe giving her a line before stepping behind her for sex. Or he may have materialized out of the darkness, ambushing her by shoving up her jaw to force her head back, causing her to bite her tongue. That could account for the abrasion Dr. Llewellyn found, and if she tried to twist away it would explain why one incision was a failed attempt requiring the Ripper to try again, this time almost cutting off her head.

Based on Dr. Llewellyn's descriptions of the two incisions to her neck, they were made from left to right, suggesting the Ripper held the knife in his right hand and was behind Mary Ann. This plan of attack would have prevented him from being splashed by arterial blood spurting out of her severed left carotid artery. It's difficult to imagine he wanted blood spattering his face, especially the blood of a victim who probably had diseases, including sexually transmitted ones.

When Mary Ann was on her back, the Ripper moved to the lower part of her body and shoved up her clothes. But her injuries made it impossible to scream. She may have made no sound except the wet choking rushes and gurgles of air and blood sucking in and out of her severed windpipe. She may have aspirated her own blood and drowned in it, and all of this can take minutes. Coroners' reports including Dr. Llewellyn's tend to assure us that the person "died instantly" but there's virtually no such thing unless one is decapitated, blown to bits or vaporized in an explosion. One might be disabled instantly by a sniper gunshot to the head that transects the medulla and pons (brain stem), for example. But it takes minutes for someone to bleed to death, suffocate, drown or cease all bodily functions due to a stroke or cardiac arrest. It's possible that Mary Ann Nichols was aware of what was happening when the Ripper began slashing through her abdomen. She may have been barely alive when he left her body in the courtyard.

Robert Mann was the Whitechapel Workhouse inmate in charge of the mortuary the morning her body was brought in. During the inquest on September 17 he testified that at some point after 4:00 a.m. the police arrived at the workhouse and ordered him out of bed. They said there was a body parked outside the mortuary, to hurry along, and he accompanied them to the ambulance parked in the yard. They carried the body inside, and Inspector Spratling and Dr. Llewellyn appeared briefly to take a look. The police left, and Mann recalled it must have been around 5:00 a.m. when he locked the mortuary door and went to breakfast.

An hour or so later he and another inmate named James Hatfield returned and began to undress the body without police or anyone else present. No one had instructed them not to touch the body, Mann swore to Coroner Baxter during the inquest. Mann also was sure the police weren't present. He was absolutely certain of it, he would say. Then again, well, maybe he wasn't. He could be mistaken, he admitted. He couldn't remember, he added. If the police said they were there, maybe they were. Mann grew increasingly confused during his testimony and "was subject to fits . . . his statements hardly reliable," *The Times* reported.

Wynne Baxter was a solicitor and an experienced coroner, who two years later would preside over the inquest of Joseph Merrick, the "Elephant Man." Baxter wouldn't tolerate lying in his courtroom, and he had no use for the abuse of proper protocol in a case. He was more than a little irked that inmates had removed Mary Ann Nichols's clothing. He relentlessly questioned the confused, fitful Mann, who steadfastly maintained that the clothing wasn't torn or cut when the body arrived. All he and Hatfield did was strip the dead woman naked and wash her before the doctor showed up so they could save him time.

Mary Ann was wearing many layers, some of them stiff with drying blood, and it's very difficult to pull clothing over the arms and legs of a body that's becoming rigorous. The inmates cut and tore the clothing to speed things along and make their chore a bit easier, and what this means is it isn't possible to know which cuts or tears were made by the Ripper. When Hatfield took the stand, he agreed with everything Mann had said, recalling that the two of them unlocked the mortuary after breakfast. They were by themselves when they cut and tore off the dead woman's clothing. They were alone with her body when they washed it. They had no reason to think there was anything inappropriate about it.

Transcripts of their testimonies at the inquest give the impression that the men were frightened and bewildered. They didn't think they'd done anything wrong. They didn't understand what the fuss was about. So what if they were alone with a murdered woman's naked body before it had been examined by the police surgeon? What was the big deal if they cut and ripped up her clothing? The Whitechapel Workhouse mortuary wasn't supposed to handle police cases anyway. It was just a whistle-stop for dead inmates on their way to a pauper's grave.

Not knowing with certainty the condition of Mary Ann's clothing when her body arrived at the mortuary is a significant loss. Whatever the Ripper did would reveal more about him and his emotions at the time of his murders. Based on the descriptions of the body at the scene, it seems likely he shoved up her ulster, woolen petticoats, flannel underclothing and skirts but he escalated his violence this time by mutilating the victim. Dr. Llewellyn described these injuries as a jagged incision, and "three or four" quick slashes downward and "several" across almost in the pattern of a grid. A few small stabs to the genitals and the Ripper was gone, vanished in the dark.

Without reviewing autopsy diagrams or photographs it's very difficult if not impossible to reconstruct injuries, to re-create what a killer did and what he might have been feeling. Wounds can be fierce or they can be tentative. They can show hesitation or rage. Three or four shallow incisions on a wrist in addition to the deep one that severed veins tell one story in a suicide, and a single decisive cut tells another. A slash to the neck that almost decapitates is bold and confident while frenzied stab wounds hint at inexperience or experimentation or a loss of control.

Psychiatrists interpret mental states and emotional needs based on a patient's demeanor, confessed moods and behavior. The physicians of the dead rely on the language of injuries old and new. They analyze debris found on the body and the way the victim was positioned or undressed, and where and when death occurred. Listening to the dead speak is a unique gift and demands highly specialized training. The silent communication is difficult to interpret but the dead don't lie. They may be hard to understand and we might misinterpret them or fail to find them before what they have to say has begun to fade. But their veracity is unimpeachable, and sometimes they continue to talk long after they've been reduced to bone.

It's startling what the dead communicate. I never cease to be amazed and pained. One young man was so determined to end his life he shot himself in the chest with his crossbow and then pulled out the bolt and shot himself again. Anger. Desperation. Hopelessness. No turning back. I want to die but I'll go ahead and make family vacation plans. I'll write down the details of my funeral so I don't inconvenience anyone. I'll put on makeup and fix my hair and shoot myself in the heart because I don't want to ruin my face. I'll shoot you in the mouth, bitch, because I'm tired of hearing you nag. I'll throw your body in the tub and dump acid all over it. That's what you get for screwing around on me. I'll stab you in the eyes because I'm tired of your staring. I'll drain your blood and drink it because aliens are taking all of mine. I'll dismember you and boil you piece by piece so I can flush you down the toilet. No one will ever know. Hop on the back of my Harley, you slut, and I'll take you to a motel. I'll cut you with a razor and scissors and watch you slowly die because that's the initiation I gotta do before I can be a member of the gang.

Mary Ann Nichols's wounds tell us that Jack the Ripper didn't want her to struggle or scream. He was ready for the next step of taking his knife below her throat and destroying her body. But he wasn't a master of this move yet and could go only so far. Maybe he got interrupted. He didn't remove her bowels or organs, and his cuts to her abdomen were only so deep. He took no body part with him as a trophy or a talisman that might inspire violent sexual fantasies when he was alone in one of his secret rooms. Perhaps for the first time, the Ripper had ripped but we can't say that for sure. It's possible he may have killed in the past or engaged in dry runs or had failed attempts. But what's beyond debate is that he would continue feeding his violent cravings and compulsions.

On October 5, 1888, the Ripper writes, "I like the work." He indicates he wants "some more blood."

"I must have some more," he says the following month on November 2.

As best we know it was in the controversial letter dated earlier, on September 17, when Jack the Ripper would publicly call himself by that infernal name. Why did he pick it? It could be that the moniker was an echo of a childhood tune popular in the Sickert house: *I am Jack Jumper the youngest but one / I can play nick-nacks upon my own thumb. Jack* was street slang for sailor or man and *Ripper* is someone who rips. But Walter Sickert was never obvious. A scan through a dozen dictionaries and encyclopedias dating from 1755 to 1906 offers possibilities that include a few from Shakespeare. In his plays a *jackanapes* is an insult, an allusion to a dolt

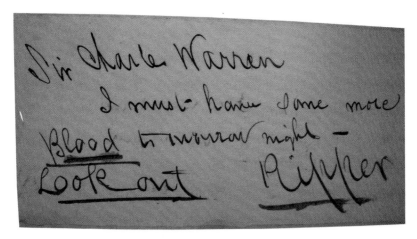

On November 2, 1888, Ripper writes, "I must have some more blood tomorrow night—look out." He now routinely signs his letters "Ripper."

or an ape. A common theme in Ripper letters is that the police assume he is an uneducated idiot, someone primitive, a savage. The Sickert brothers were all "Shakespeare mad," their sister, Helena, recalled in her autobiography, and Walter was known for standing up at dinner parties and delivering long soliloquies from Shakespeare plays.

Definitions of *Jack* include boots, a diminutive of John used contemptuously to mean a saucy fellow (the Ripper also called himself Saucy Jack), a footboy who pulls off his master's boots, a scream, a male. It's American slang for a stranger or a jackass. It's a cunning fellow who can do anything, such as a jack-of-all-trades. Definitions of *Ripper* include one who rips, tears, cuts, or he could be a fine fellow who dresses well. It might be a good fast horse, a good play or part. "Every Jack-slave hath his belly-full of fighting," Shakespeare writes.

The Ripper boasts in a letter that he ripped "up the womb of your dear mother England," and one wonders if Sickert might have felt he'd been ripped from his own mother's womb. It would be understandable if not a certainty that he must have felt savaged or "ripped" during his early surgeries. He came into this world a victim and he would repay.

14

WIDE STARING EYES

MARY ANN NICHOLS'S EYES were wide open when her body was discovered on the pavement. She stared blindly in the weak glow of a bull's-eye lantern.

In Charles Darwin's *The Expression of the Emotions in Man and Animals*, wide staring eyes are indicative of the "horror" he associates with "extreme terror" or the "horrible pain of torture." It's a centuries-old fallacy that whatever emotion was felt at that moment of death is frozen on the victim's face. Symbolically at least, Mary Ann's expression captured the last thing she saw in life—the dark silhouette of her murderer cutting her up.

The police made note in their reports of her wide-eyed dead stare, and their attention to that detail may hint of what they were beginning to feel about the Whitechapel murderer. He was a monster. He was a phantom who in Metropolitan Police Inspector Frederick Abberline's words didn't leave "the slightest clue." A woman with her throat slashed and staring wide eyes is a ghastly image one doesn't forget, and Sickert wouldn't have. More than anyone else he would have remembered her stare as life fled from her. In 1903 he drew a sketch of a woman whose eyes are wide open and staring. She looks dead. There's an inexplicable dark line around her throat. The sketch is blandly titled *Two Studies of a Venetian Woman's Head*.

Three years later Sickert followed that sketch with a painting of a nude woman grotesquely sprawled on an iron bedstead. He titled that picture *Nuit d'été*, or *Summer Night*. Mary Ann Nichols was murdered on a summer night, and the women in the sketch and the painting look eerily similar. Their faces are reminiscent of Mary Ann's in a photograph taken after she had been "cleaned up" by workhouse inmates Hatfield and Mann.

Mortuary photographs were made with a big wooden box camera that could shoot only directly ahead, and bodies had to be stood up or propped upright against the dead-house wall. Sometimes they were hung with hooks, nails or pegs, and a photograph of a later Ripper victim, Catherine Eddowes, shows her nude body suspended by the nape of her neck or her hair, one foot barely touching the floor. These grim, degrading photographs were for purposes of identification. They weren't made public, and at the time of Mary Ann Nichols's murder there were but a few ways to know what her dead body looked like. Someone would have had to view it at the crime scene or in the mortuary or convince a police investigator to share a picture or two.

Sickert's 1903 sketch *Two Studies of a Venetian Woman's Head* evokes the cleaned-up postmortem photo of Ripper victim Mary Ann Nichols.

In 1906, Sickert painted *Nuit d'été*, or *Summer Night*, which again evokes Mary Ann Nichols and eerily recalls the women in his pencil sketch from three years prior.

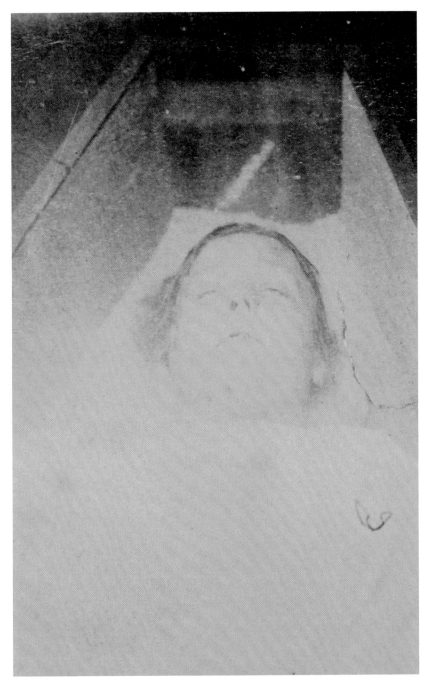

Mary Ann Nichols was found dead on Buck's Row in the early morning hours of August 31, 1888. This mortuary photo was taken after the blood had been cleaned from her body.

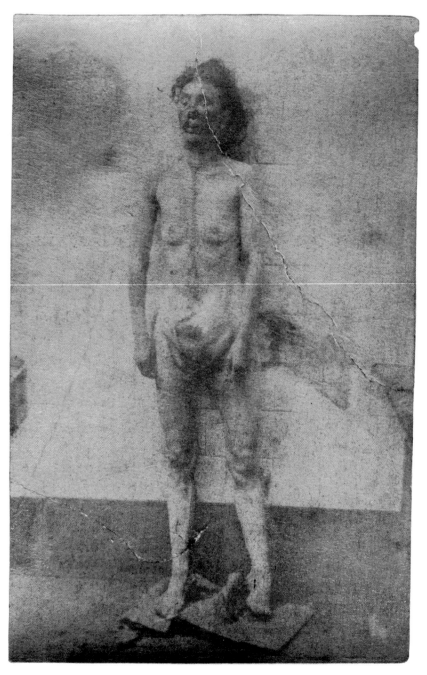

Catherine Eddowes's body is suspended from the mortuary wall by her hair in order to position her properly in front of the box camera.

Sickert was quite capable of charming his way into seeing whatever he wanted. He had a morbid curiosity, and one could argue that he knew what the victims looked like because he asked to view them. It wouldn't surprise me if he did but I have no evidence of it, and certainly I don't claim that disturbing similarities between the murdered women and figures in Sickert's art prove he was the Ripper. He also could have been influenced in later years by Alexandre Lacassagne's *Vacher l'éventreur et les crimes sadiques* (1899), which includes photographs of Ripper victims Mary Kelly and Catherine Eddowes.

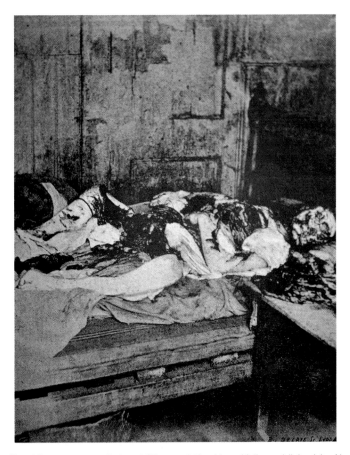

Images like this gruesome photo of Ripper victim Mary Kelly, published in Alexandre Lacassagne's 1889 book *Vacher l'éventreur et les crimes sadiques*, may have influenced Sickert's artwork.

Jack the Ripper was the sort of cunning psychopath who would have returned to his carnage if given the chance. It would have thrilled and empowered him, and given him a sexual rush. He could have disguised himself as a man of the slums and offered the ruse that he might know who the dead woman was. In other words, he easily could have shown up at the mortuary like any other concerned citizen who claimed he or she might recognize the victim. The type of deranged and ignorant killer the police were looking for wouldn't do something like that. It's likely they never considered that the Ripper might return to his crime scenes or wander into a dead house or ask to see photographs of his victims' naked dead bodies.

Unfortunately, few photographs exist, and the ones preserved at The National Archives and Scotland Yard's Crime Museum are small. They have poor resolution that has gotten only worse since I first looked at them in 2001. From the beginning of this investigation I've used experts in forensic image processing to sharpen what we see, and it's been helpful. But we're still left straining to make out what might have been missed even as we wonder if our imagination is running away with us. When the software revealed odd shapes that I'll describe later, we questioned if something is really there. Or are we seeing it because we want it to be true?

Sickert's sketch *Killed His Father in Fight* mirrors the body position of Ripper victim Mary Kelly, as documented in one of the few crime scene photos from Jack the Ripper's killings.

In today's forensic cases, bodies are photographed multiple times and from many angles with a variety of photographic equipment. But during the Ripper's violent spree it was rare to call for the unwieldy box camera. It would have been even more unusual for a mortuary or a dead house to be equipped with one. Technology hadn't advanced enough for photographs to be taken at night. There is but a scant visual record of Jack the Ripper's crimes unless one browses through a Walter Sickert art book or takes a look at his "murder" pictures and nudes that hang in fine museums and private collections. Artistic and scholarly analysis aside, many of his sprawling nudes look mutilated and dead.

A number of his female subjects have bare necks with black lines around them as if to suggest a cut throat or decapitation. Some dark areas around a throat are intended to be shadows and shading, but the solid black lines I'm referring to are cryptic. They aren't jewelry. If it's true Sickert drew and painted what he saw, then what is the explanation? The mystery intensifies when one looks at *Patrol* (circa 1921). In this painting a policewoman has bulging eyes and an open-neck tunic that reveals a solid black line around her throat.

What's known about *Patrol* is murky. Sickert may have painted it from a photograph, possibly of Birmingham policewoman Dorothy Peto. Or it could be Margaret Damer Dawson of the Women's Police Service. Whoever she was, it appears she or someone eventually donated the life-size Sickert portrait to the Metropolitan Police Service. When I first saw *Patrol* it was hanging behind a locked door and chained to a wall. No one seemed quite sure what to do with it. I suppose it's another Ripper "ha ha" that New Scotland Yard owns a painting by the most notorious murderer it never caught.

Patrol isn't exactly a tribute to women or law enforcement, and in fact seems more the product of angry, mocking, scary fantasies. The frightened expression on the policewoman's face undermines the power of her profession, and in typical Sickert fashion the painting has the patina of violence, of something very bad about to happen. The wooden-framed canvas is a dark mirror in the bright galleries of the art world, and references to it and reproductions weren't easily found at the time of my earliest research.

Author Patricia Cornwell views Sickert's oil painting *Patrol*, which depicts a police-woman. The bulging eyes and black line around the policewoman's neck may be a reference to Ripper's victims. The painting, ironically, was hanging in a back room at New Scotland Yard.

During those early days of this investigation, I did my best to rely on only primary research materials. In addition to looking at original art, letters, police reports and other documents whenever possible, I wanted access to the newspapers that would have been read by Londoners during the Ripper's crimes. I didn't want copies or facsimiles of anything if it could be avoided, and in the summer of 2001 I asked London rare book dealer Pom Harrington if he could find *The Times* newspapers in their entirety for 1888 through 1891. Newsprint from that era had such a high cotton fiber content that the papers could be ironed, sewn together and bound good as new. Each volume weighs about fifty pounds.

It was a cumbersome process going through these weighty tomes, and I would do this on the floor or at a big table, copying information by hand into a journal. The details in those very old pages are amazingly rich. I was able to find out what the weather was at various hours. Was it foggy? Was it cold? What was going on in the theaters or politically or on holidays? What about letters to the editor or other unusual events that might have been more of the Ripper's game playing? My big newspaper books enabled me to re-create his world accurately and palpably. Then Pom Harrington made another fascinating find, a ledger book.

It's filled with *Weekly Dispatch* and *News of the World* articles written about the Ripper murders and other cases that might be related. The clippings were rather sloppily cut out and crookedly pasted into the ledger from August 12, 1888, through September 29, 1889, and what prompted someone to do this continues to puzzle. The ledger was purchased at an auction. As far as I know its provenance remains unknown or for some reason has been kept confidential. Added to the mystery are the dozens of pages that appear to have been cut out. One wonders what was removed and why.

On remaining pages are fascinating annotations written in blue and black ink and also in gray, blue and purple pencil. Who went to all this trouble and why? Where had the ledger been for more than a century? The annotations themselves suggest they were written by someone quite familiar with the crimes and how the police were working them. When I first acquired the ledger I fantasized that it might have been kept by Jack the Ripper himself. It seems whoever cut out the clippings was personally if not obsessively focused on reports of what the police knew.

These handwritten notes both agree and argue with details of the investigation. For example, information is crossed out as if it's inaccurate, and scribbled next to certain details are comments such as "Yes! Believe me" or "unsatisfactory" or "unsatisfactory—very" or "important. Find the woman"—and most peculiar of all, "7 women 4 men." Sentences are underlined, especially if they relate to descriptions witnesses gave of men the victims were seen with last. I doubt we'll ever know if a journalist kept this ledger. Maybe a policeman did. But the handwriting is inconsistent with what I saw in police reports, most of the ones I reviewed written in a very good or beautiful hand. The penmanship in the ledger is small and very sloppy. It's uncharacteristically bad for an era when script was consistently well formed, if not elegant.

In fact the handwriting in the clippings book reminds me of the rather wild and sometimes completely illegible way Walter Sickert wrote. His handwriting is markedly different from the average Englishman's of the time, and maybe the explanation is that the precocious Sickert taught himself to read and write (according to family legend). He wasn't schooled in traditional calligraphy, but his sister, Helena, says he was capable of a "beautiful hand" when it suited him.

No one seems to have any idea who kept the ledger or why, but the articles add another dimension to the reportage of the day. The journalist who covered crime for the *Dispatch* is anonymous, which isn't surprising because bylines then were as rare as female reporters. Whoever was the owner of the ledger, this person had an excellent eye and a very inquisitive mind. Assuming it was a man, his deductions, questions and perceptions add new facets to the cases.

In Mary Ann Nichols's murder, for example, the police suspected it was committed by a gang. At that time in London, roving packs of violent young men preyed upon the weak and poor, and these hooligans were vindictive when they attempted to rob an unfortunate who turned out to have no money. In the *Dispatch* accounts the police wrongly maintained that Mary Ann wasn't killed where her body was found. Martha Tabram wasn't either, they claimed, and that's yet another incorrect assumption. Each victim had been left in the "gutter of the street in the early hours of the morning," and no screams were heard. The conclusion was they were murdered elsewhere and their bodies dumped, and that's simply not the case based on police and coroner reports.

In some of the *Dispatch* articles it's obvious the anonymous reporter suggested to Dr. Llewellyn that the killer attacked Mary Ann Nichols from behind—and not from the front. This would have made the killer right-handed—contrary to what Dr. Llewellyn claimed. Imagine the killer standing behind the victim when he cut her throat, the reporter brazenly countered. The deepest wounds would be on the left side and trail off to the right, he summarized like a pathologist or the Ripper himself.

15

RED FINGERPRINTS

THE MOST COMMON CAUSES OF DEATH for people of the East End were the miseries of poverty.

Infections and diseases such as tuberculosis, pleurisy, emphysema and pneumoconiosis persistently ended life prematurely. Men, women and children were fatally burned and scalded by accidents at home and at work. Starvation killed, as did cholera, whooping cough and cancer. Parents and their children weakened by malnutrition and surrounded by filth and vermin didn't have immune systems that could fight off what should have been nonlethal illnesses.

Colds and flu became bronchitis, pneumonia and death. Many infants weren't long for the world of the East End, and the people who lived and suffered there hated the London Hospital. They avoided it if they could. To go there was to get worse. To let a doctor touch them was to die. Often this was true. An abscessed toe requiring amputation could lead to a bone infection such as osteomyelitis and death. A cut requiring sutures could lead to a staph infection and death.

A sampling of hospital admissions for suicides shows that in 1884 five men tried to kill themselves by cutting their throats. Four women did the same and two slit their wrists. In 1885 five women are listed as suicides or attempted suicides by poisoning and one by drowning. Eight men slashed

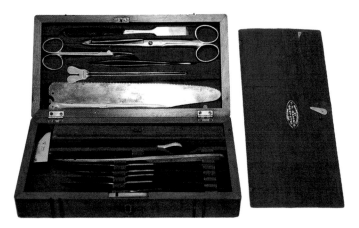

An amputation kit like the kind that was used at the London Hospital in the late 1800s.

their throats, one used a gun and another a noose. In 1886 five women attempted suicide by cutting their own throats. Twelve women and seven men tried to poison themselves. Another twelve men cut their own throats or stabbed or shot themselves.

It simply isn't possible to sort out who really committed suicide and who might have been murdered. If the individual was a person of the dustbin and the death or attempted death was witnessed, the police tended to accept whatever they were told. In a case where a woman's drunk, abusive husband hurled two lit oil lamps and set her on fire, she told police in her dying breath that it was entirely her fault. Her husband wasn't charged. Her death was listed as an accident.

Unless the circumstances were obvious, there was no certainty that the manner or cause of death would be accurate. If a woman's throat was cut indoors and the weapon was nearby, the police decided she'd killed herself. Such assumptions including those made by the well-meaning Dr. Llewellyn only sent police down a false trail. If they bothered following up at all, bad diagnoses and wrong determinations of injury and death could destroy a case in court. Forensic medicine wasn't sophisticated in Dr. Llewellyn's day. It was virtually nonexistent, in fact, and that's the most likely explanation for his hasty, baseless conclusions.

Had he examined the pavement after Mary Ann's body was picked up and loaded into the ambulance, he would have noticed the blood and the blood clot that Constable Thain observed. Dr. Llewellyn might have noticed blood or a bloody fluid trickling into the gutter. Visibility was very poor, and maybe he should have thought to wipe up some of this fluid to determine whether it was blood. Its stage of coagulation would have offered another clue about time of death.

Taking the ambient temperature of the crime scene to compare with the temperature of the body wasn't standard then for determining time of death. But Dr. Llewellyn should have noted the progression of rigor mortis or stiffness that occurs when lactic acid builds up in muscles that can no longer contract. He should have checked for the reddish discoloration of livor mortis due to blood no longer circulating and settling in certain parts of the body. Depending on the temperature and other variables, livor mortis typically becomes fixed after about eight hours. Rigor and livor mortis could have suggested the time of Mary Ann Nichols's death. They could have told Dr. Llewellyn whether her body had been moved at some point after her murder.

Time of death is a symphony of many details that play in concert with each other. Rigor mortis is hastened along by the victim's muscle mass, the temperature of the air, the loss of blood, and even the activity preceding death. The nude body of a thin woman who hemorrhaged to death outdoors in chilly weather will cool faster and stiffen more slowly than if she was clothed in a warm room and had been strangled.

Ambient temperature, body size, clothing, location, cause of death and many more postmortem minutiae can be subtle little talebearers. They can confuse or fool experienced experts as to what really happened. Livor mortis can be mistaken for fresh bruises. An object pressing against the body will leave a pale area or blanching in the shape of that object. If this is misinterpreted as "pressure marks," then a case of nonviolent death can suddenly turn criminal.

There's no telling how much was hopelessly garbled in the Ripper murders. It's depressing to consider what evidence might have been lost. But one can be sure that the killer left traces of his identity and daily life. They would have adhered to the blood on the body and the ground, and he carried away evidence when he left the scene. In 1888 it wasn't standard practice for police or doctors to look for hairs, fibers or other minuscule amounts of evidence that might have required microscopic examination. Fingerprints were called "finger marks" and simply meant that a human being had touched a mirror or a glass windowpane, for example. Even if a patent (visible) fingerprint with well-defined ridge detail was discovered, it didn't matter. It wouldn't be until 1901 that Scotland Yard would establish its Central Fingerprint Bureau.

Five years earlier in 1896, two fingerprints in red ink were left on a Ripper letter the police received on October 14. The prints appear to have been made by the first and second fingers of the left hand, and more than a century later after much excitement and repeated examination the joke was on forensic scientists and me. There was no discernible ridge detail. In retrospect I doubt there ever was. Perhaps the featureless, useless prints were left deliberately, another "ha ha."

By 1890 Sir Arthur Conan Doyle had published his first two Sherlock Holmes novels. They introduced a rigorous scientific approach to police

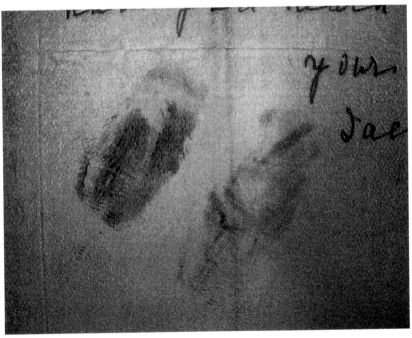

Two fingerprints in red ink were left on an 1896 Ripper letter, but there were no visible identifying characteristics (minutiae). Either such features vanished over time, or they were never there to begin with.

detection that included utilizing fingerprints and footprint evidence. Sickert very well may have read *A Study in Scarlet* and *The Sign of the Four*. He certainly would have been familiar with their author and may have met him. Doyle moved in Whistler's circle as did Oscar Wilde, and Henry Irving and his Lyceum Theatre business manager, Bram Stoker, the Irish novelist best known for *Dracula*.

Strange to imagine Sickert perhaps rubbing shoulders with the creator of Sherlock Holmes. He may have been the only sleuth in the Victorian era capable of catching Jack the Ripper. Sickert was the sort to know the latest criminal investigative technology. Deliberately leaving worthless fingerprints on Ripper letters would have amused him enormously. At this writing we still don't have Sickert's fingerprints, and it continues to be hard to accept that he didn't leave them in paint or ink on any of his works. But if he didn't, maybe it's no accident. Maybe he was deliberately careful. If anyone in the late Victorian era might have predicted that fingerprints or biological materials such as blood, skin cells, saliva or semen could be incriminating evidence in the future it would have been Sickert. He was forward-thinking and scientifically brilliant, and he was shrewd.

He may have been meticulously mindful of not leaving evidence but that hasn't stopped my team of scientists and historians from trying for what's now fifteen years. One of our biggest obstacles is the expected and necessary limitations placed on what we've been allowed to do, as the top priority is to preserve original documents that truly are a British national treasure. To date our efforts have included using nondestructive microscopes, forensic lights and infrared cameras on hundreds of Sickert paintings, drawings and etchings, and original documents. We found nothing of significance. The only fingerprint discovered is a barely visible one left in ink on the back of a Sickert copper etching plate. There wasn't sufficient ridge detail for a match, assuming there were Ripper prints for comparison, and of course it's possible that the print on the etching plate wasn't left by Sickert.

Fingerprints were known about long before the Ripper began his murders. Ridge detail on human finger pads gives us a better grip and is unique to every individual including identical twins. It's believed that the Chinese used fingerprints some three thousand years ago to sign legal documents.

In India fingerprints were used as a means of signing contracts as early as 1870, and seven years later an American microscopist published a journal article suggesting that fingerprints should be used for identification. This was echoed in 1880 by a Scottish physician working in a hospital in Japan. As is true with every major scientific breakthrough including DNA, fingerprints weren't instantly understood. They weren't immediately utilized or readily accepted in court.

During the Victorian era, the primary means of identifying a person and linking him or her to a crime was anthropometry, developed in 1879 by French criminologist Alphonse Bertillon. He believed that people could be identified and classified by facial characteristics and body measurements including height, reach, head width, and length of the left foot. Bertillon maintained that skeletons were highly individualized, and his method continued to be used to classify criminals and suspects until the turn of the century. Anthropometry was not only flawed but dangerous.

It was based on physical attributes that aren't as individualized as originally assumed. Today we would call this profiling at its worst, a pseudoscience that places far too much emphasis on what a person looks like. During the Ripper's time, police also consciously or subconsciously were seduced by yet another pseudoscience called physiognomy, which similarly asserts that criminality, morality and intellect are reflected in a person's body and face. Thieves tend to be "frail" while violent men usually are "strong" and "in good health." All criminals have superior "finger reach." Most female offenders are "homely, if not repulsive." Rapists tend to be "blond." Pedophiles often are "delicate" and look "childish."

If people today have difficulty accepting that a psychopathic killer can be attractive, likeable and intelligent, imagine the difficulty in the Victorian era when standard criminology books included long descriptions of anthropometry and physiognomy. Victorian police were programmed to identify suspects by their skeletal structure and facial features. Investigators assumed that a certain "look" could be linked to a certain type of behavior.

Walter Sickert wouldn't have been tagged as a suspect or even a person of interest during the time of the Ripper murders. The "young and beautiful Sickert" with "his well known charm," as artist Edgar Degas once described him, couldn't possibly be capable of cutting a woman's throat and slashing open her abdomen or flaying her to the bone. I've heard it naively suggested in recent years that if an artist like Sickert had violent proclivities he would have sublimated them through his creative work and not acted them out. I really can't blame people for having a hard time believing that Jack the Ripper could have been a handsome, successful, brilliant man who was respected and admired in the highest levels of society. How bizarre to think that the Ripper was an apprentice to Whistler and later gave painting lessons to Winston Churchill.

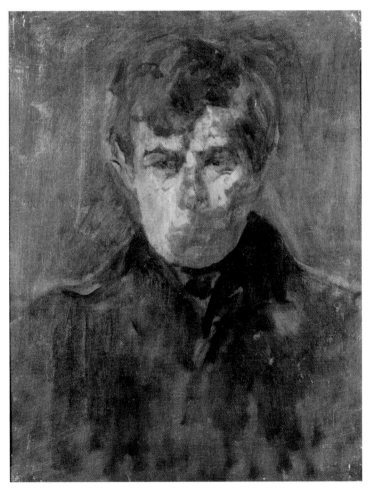

James McNeill Whistler painted this portrait of his apprentice, Walter Sickert, with his face in shadow.

When the police were looking for the Ripper a great deal of importance was placed on witness descriptions of men last seen with the victims. Investigative reports reveal that much attention was paid to hair color, complexion and height. The police didn't take into account that all of these characteristics can be disguised. Height not only varies in an individual depending on posture, hats and footwear but it can be altered by trickery. Actors can wear tall hats and special lifts in their shoes. They can pull caps low. They can stoop and slightly bend their knees under voluminous coats or capes, giving the appearance that they are inches shorter. I've experimented with such disguises in front of the mirror, and it's remarkable the false impressions even a novice can manage. I admit rather shamefully that as a child I engaged in such a ruse by changing my costume and height so I could go out trick-or-treating twice in one night.

Early publications on medical jurisprudence and forensic medicine reveal that much more was known about criminal investigations than was actually applied. In 1888, cases continued to be made or lost based on witness descriptions instead of physical evidence. If the police knew anything at all about forensic science there was no practical way to get evidence tested. The Home Office that oversees New Scotland Yard didn't have forensic laboratories then, and a physician such as Dr. Llewellyn might never have touched a microscope. He might not have known that hair, bone and blood could be identified as human.

During the Ripper investigation no attempt was made to identify the source of biological evidence. Unless blood was on the body or near it or on a weapon at the scene, the police couldn't say that it was related to the crime. Maybe it was human. Maybe it came from a horse or a sheep or a cow. In the 1880s the streets of Whitechapel near slaughterhouses were putrid with blood and entrails. A man walking about with blood on his clothing and hands wasn't necessarily a cause for suspicion.

Dr. Llewellyn attended the London Hospital Medical College and had been a licensed physician for thirteen years. His private practice surgery or medical office was no more than three hundred yards from where Mary Ann Nichols was murdered. The police knew him well enough to request him by name when her body was discovered but there's no reason to suppose that he was a divisional surgeon for Scotland Yard. In other words

In the crowded environs of Whitechapel, blood on the street or on a man's clothing may not have drawn curious looks, thanks to the slaughterhouses in the area.

Dr. Llewellyn wasn't a physician who offered his services part-time to a particular division, in this instance the H Division covering Whitechapel.

The job of a divisional surgeon was to tend to the troops. Free medical care was a benefit of working for the Metropolitan Police, and a police surgeon was to be available when needed. He was to examine prisoners or go to the local jail to determine if a citizen was drunk or ill. He would determine whether someone was suffering from an excess of "animal spirits," presumably excitement or hysteria. In the late 1880s the divisional surgeon also responded to death scenes for a fee of one pound, one shilling per case. If he performed the autopsy he was paid two pounds, two shillings. He wasn't expected to be well acquainted with the microscope, the nuances of injuries and poisonings, and what the body can reveal after death.

Dr. Llewellyn was a local doctor the police felt comfortable calling on. He was a Fellow of the British Gynecological Society and would have been accustomed to being summoned at all hours of the night. When the police rapped on his door on the cool, overcast early morning of August 31 he probably got to the scene as quickly as he could. He wasn't trained to do much more than determine that the woman was dead. He offered educated guesses about almost everything else.

16

HUE AND CRY

MEDICOLEGAL DEATH INVESTIGATION had its beginnings eight centuries ago with King Richard I, later known as King Richard the Lionheart. During his reign it was decreed that officers in every county of His Majesty's realm would ensure the "pleas of the crown," and these men were called crowners. Eventually the name evolved into coroner.

Elected by the freeholders of the county, a coroner was required to be a knight of good standing. He was to be financially secure so as to prevent any conflict of interest when he decided matters pertaining to money and property. An unexpected death was a source of revenue for the king. If one of these elected officers decided the person had caused his or her own demise, then someone was going to pay. Even a failure to act appropriately at the discovery of a dead body could result in punishment and financial penalty. One had better respond with the expected hue and cry.

When there was a sudden and unexpected death in medieval England, the coroner was to be notified immediately. He would appear and assemble a jury for what would later be called an inquest. It's frightening to consider how many deaths were labeled evil deeds when the person simply choked on his mutton, had a stroke or dropped dead at a young age from a congenitally bad heart or an aneurysm. Suicides and homicides were sins against God and the King. When a person took his or her own life or someone else did, if the coroner and jury determined wrongdoing, the entire estate could end up in the crown's coffers. This placed the coroner in a tempting position. He might bargain a bit and ride off with coins jingling in his pockets.

Eventually the coroner's power placed him in a seat of judgment, and he became an enforcer of the law. People he pursued had no place to hide. Even seeking refuge in the church didn't spare one the face-to-face confrontation with a coroner, who would demand a confession and arrange the seizure of assets. He might resort to the gruesome practice of trial by ordeal. Proving innocence meant showing no pain or injury while being burned or enduring other dreadful tortures as the coroner sat nearby and watched.

If a forensic pathologist today were the equivalent of a coroner of old, the person would be male and have no medical or legal training. He would drive a van or truck to a death scene where he would glance at the body and listen to witnesses and find out how much the decedent is worth. He might decide that a sudden death from a bee sting was a homicidal poisoning. He might test the wife's role in it by holding her head underwater. If she didn't drown after five or ten minutes, the coroner would conclude she was innocent. If she died, wrongdoing would be the verdict and the family estate would go to the Queen or in the United States to the IRS. In death investigations of long ago, jurors were easily bribed. Coroners got rich. Innocent people could lose everything they owned. They might be hanged.

Times began to change for the better in the sixteenth century when the coroner's role was reduced to investigating sudden deaths only. He was to stay clear of any sort of enforcement or imaginative tortures that might prove who did what. In 1860, the year Walter Sickert was born, a committee recommended that the election process for coroner should be treated as seriously as voting for Members of Parliament. The importance of competent postmortem examinations and the proper handling of evidence added further value and prestige to the office of coroner. In 1888 a governmental act mandated that death investigation findings would no longer render any sort of financial benefit to the crown.

These groundbreaking pieces of legislation are rarely mentioned in connection with the Jack the Ripper case. The change in law meant a change of mindset that allowed and encouraged the coroner to concentrate on justice and not insidious political pressure. The crown had nothing to gain by interfering with the inquests of Martha Tabram, Mary Ann Nichols or the Ripper's other victims, and the coroner had plenty to lose if the freewheeling press depicted him as an incompetent fool, a liar or a greedy tyrant. Men such as Wynne Baxter supported themselves through respectable legal practices. They didn't add much to their incomes by presiding over inquests, and placed their livelihoods at risk if their integrity and skills were impugned.

By 1888, the evolution in the coroner's system and police investigation had reached a new level of objectivity and seriousness. For sure, mistakes were made. Poor judgment was used and naivete abounded. But I don't believe there was deliberate impropriety or "a cover-up" during the Ripper murders, even if the elusiveness of the investigator who tried hardest to solve them unwittingly added fuel to conspiratorial fires. So much is made of Frederick Abberline. So little is known about this legendary sleuth whose briefings about the Ripper investigation would have reached the ear of Queen Victoria. The murders had become a frustration for her. She complained that the lighting was inadequate in the East End and was incensed if she deemed certain officials were unsympathetic toward the people this fiendish killer was terrorizing.

Wynne Baxter was a coroner who ran a respectable practice.

Quite the detective herself, she told Home Secretary Henry Matthews that the police should step up their surveillance and keep a sharp eye out for single men living alone. Cattle and passenger boats could be checked, Her Majesty directed, and of course all those slaughterhouses were part of the problem. It had to be a bad influence on people to witness animals being butchered and to see blood flowing in the streets, Queen Victoria pointed out.

By all accounts, Frederick George Abberline was a modest, courteous man of high morals. He was as reliable and methodical as the clocks he repaired before he joined the Metropolitan Police in 1863.

During his thirty years of service he earned eighty-four commendations and awards from judges, magistrates and the commissioner of police. As Abberline himself matter-of-factly put it, "I think [I] was considered very exceptional." Admired by his colleagues and the public he served, he wasn't the sort to deliberately outshine anyone but took great pride in a job well done. There don't seem to be many photographs of him, but I found one and also a few sketches published in magazines that didn't always spell his name right. Artistic renderings of him show an indistinct-looking man with muttonchops, small ears, a straight nose and a high forehead.

Inspector Abberline kept a clipping book on cases he investigated, but he did not comment on the Ripper case, likely because it was so sensitive.

Pension details about him in the Metropolitan Police Service records describe him as rather tall, close to five foot ten. He had dark eyes. In 1885 it appears he was losing his brown hair. He may have slumped a bit. His love of clocks and gardening says a great deal about him. These are solitary, gentle pursuits that require patience, concentration, tenacity, meticulousness, a light touch and a love of life and the way things work. I can't think of many better qualities for a police investigator except honesty, and there's no reason to doubt that Frederick Abberline was as true as a tuning fork.

He never wrote his autobiography or allowed anyone else to

tell his story. But he did keep a diary of sorts, a hundred-page clipping book about crimes he worked interspersed with comments written in his graceful, generous hand. Based on the way he assembled these clippings, it would seem that he didn't get around to it until after his retirement. When he died in 1929 his collection of newsprint remnants was passed on to a friend. In 1988 it was donated to the Metropolitan Police Historical Collection. I knew nothing about it until early 2002 when an official with New Scotland Yard showed it to me.

Abberline's clipping book isn't confessional or full of details about his life. But facets of his personality are revealed by the way he worked cases and in the comments he wrote. A brave, intelligent man, he kept his word and abided by rules. This included not divulging the very sort of information I hoped to find within his clipping book's covers. Abberline's entries abruptly stop with an October 1887 case of "spontaneous combustion" and don't resume until March 1891 when he investigated "trafficking in infants."

There's not so much as a hint about the investigations we really want to hear about. He makes no allusion to Jack the Ripper. One won't find a single word about the 1889 Cleveland Street male brothel scandal that must have been a briar patch for Abberline. Some of the accused or suspected of engaging in homosexual activity were aristocrats and men close to the throne such as the Duke of Clarence. To read the clipping book is to think the Ripper murders and the Cleveland Street scandal never happened. It would seem Abberline deliberately excluded what he knew would be the most sought-after and controversial details of his investigative career.

On pages 44–45 he offers an explanation for his silence:

> *I think it is just as well to record here the reason why as from the various cuttings from the newspapers as well as the many other matters that I was called upon to investigate— that never became public property—it must be apparent that I could write many things that would be very interesting to read.*
>
> *At the time I retired from the service the Authorities were very much opposed to retired Officers writing anything*

for the press as previously some retired Officers had from time to time been very indiscreet in what they had caused to be published and to my knowledge had been called upon to explain their conduct—and in fact—they had been threatened with actions for libel.

Apart from that there is no doubt the fact that in describing what you did in detecting certain crimes you are putting the Criminal Classes on their guard and in some cases you may be absolutely telling them how to Commit Crime.

As an example in the Finger-Print detection you find now the expert thief wears gloves.

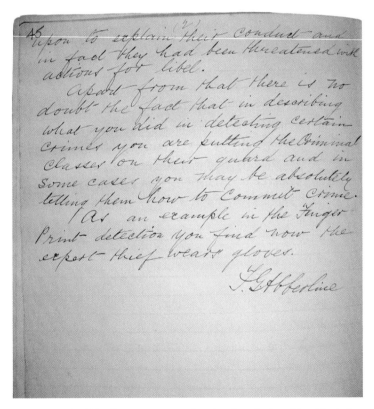

In his clipping book, Abberline wrote an explanation for why he did not include certain high-profile cases: the police asked retired officers to be discreet and not to disclose their methods.

Opposition to former officers' writing their memoirs didn't deter everyone. While I was writing the first edition of this book I kept three autobiographical works on my desk: Sir Melville Macnaghten's *Days of My Years*, Sir Henry Smith's *From Constable to Commissioner* and Benjamin Leeson's *Lost London: The Memoirs of an East End Detective*. All include Jack the Ripper anecdotes and analyses that are as baseless as those offered by people who weren't alive at the time of the crimes.

Major Henry Smith was appointed Acting Commissioner of the City of London Police in September of 1888. He modestly writes of the Ripper investigation, "There is no man living who knows as much of those murders as I do." He declares that after the "second crime" (possibly referring to Mary Ann Nichols, who wasn't murdered in his jurisdiction), he

Major Henry Smith became Acting Commissioner of the City of London Police in the fall of 1888.

"discovered" a suspect he was fairly sure was the Ripper. Smith describes him as a former medical student. He had been in a lunatic asylum and had spent "all of his time" with prostitutes he cheated by passing off polished farthings as sovereigns.

Smith conveyed this intelligence to Sir Charles Warren, who failed to find the suspect according to Smith. It was just as well. The former lunatic–medical student turned out to be the wrong man. I feel compelled to add that a sovereign would have been an unusually generous payment for prostitutes accustomed to exchanging sexual favors for pennies. Smith managed to perpetuate the notion that the Ripper was a doctor, a medical student or someone with surgical skills. I don't know why Smith made such an assumption as early as the "second case" when no victim had yet been disemboweled. No organs had been taken. Following Mary Ann Nichols's murder there was no suggestion that the weapon was a surgical knife or that the killer possessed even the slightest surgical skills. Unless Smith simply has the timing wrong in his recollections there was no reason for the police to suspect a medically trained individual this early on.

Smith's overtures to Charles Warren apparently evoked no satisfactory response. So Smith took it upon himself to put "nearly a third" of his City of London police force in plainclothes. He instructed them to "do everything which, under ordinary circumstances, a constable should not do," he says in his memoirs. These clandestine activities included sitting on doorsteps smoking pipes and lingering in public houses, gossiping with the locals. Smith jumped in to help. He visited "every butcher's shop in the city," quizzing slaughterhouse workers about suspicious-looking men of their profession who might be going about cutting up women.

Sir Melville Macnaghten altered the Ripper theories permanently with his certainties that weren't based on firsthand information or police experience. In 1889, Macnaghten joined the Metropolitan Police as assistant commissioner of CID. His background included twelve years of work on his family's tea plantations in Bengal, where he went out each morning to shoot wildcats, foxes and alligators or maybe have a go at a good pig sticking (spearing wild boar). When his memoirs were published in 1914, four years after

Sir Melville Macnaghten became an assistant commissioner of CID in 1889.

Smith published his, Macnaghten engaged in a bit of literary pig sticking. He alluded to Henry Smith being "on the tiptoe of expectation" and having a "prophetic soul" since he was in hot pursuit of the Ripper weeks before the first murder had even happened. Smith like many others considered the slaying of Martha Tabram as the Ripper's debut while Macnaghten was certain that the first victim was Mary Ann Nichols on August 31.

Macnaghten goes on to recall those terrible, foggy evenings and the "raucous cries" of newsboys shouting out that there had been "Another horrible murder . . . !" I suppose it's possible he heard those raucous cries and experienced those fatal foggy nights but it's more likely he simply knew about them. I doubt he was anywhere near the East End. He'd just returned from India and was still working for his family. He wouldn't begin at Scotland Yard until some eight months after the Ripper murders supposedly stopped and were no longer a priority.

This didn't deter Macnaghten from narrowing down the suspects to three and the number of victims to five. He stated with confidence that the Ripper had murdered "5 victims - + 5 victims only": Mary Ann Nichols, Annie Chapman, Elizabeth Stride, Catherine Eddowes and Mary Kelly. His theory took root and continues to flourish. The incorrect "canonical five" continues to be perpetuated in books, movies, even in Wikipedia, and it continues to be extremely frustrating as it subliminally galvanizes the ridiculous theory that the Ripper's sexually driven psychopathic crimes were motivated by blackmail linked directly to the Royal Family.

It's important to remember that the Royal Conspiracy is a modern theory (1970s) and similarly Macnaghten's tallying of victims was long after the fact, about a quarter of a century later (1914). During the actual time of the Ripper crimes the number of victims varies. Some said six. Others said seven, and police continued to be bothered by later cases that fit the Ripper's pattern of slashing throats and mutilating. And what about the dismembered torsos and body parts that started showing up even as the Ripper's bloody fall of 1888 was going full tilt? What about the additional Ripper letters that continued for the better part of a decade? There was much uncertainty until Melville Macnaghten published his memoirs in 1914, a year after he retired, and by then he was absolutely certain the Ripper was dead.

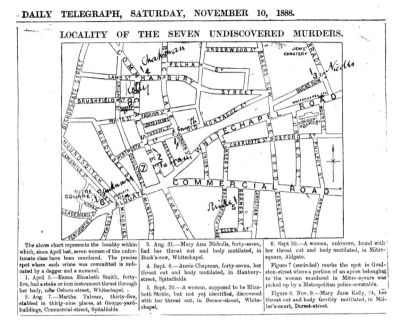

The Murder of Mary Jane Kelly.
9th Nov. 1888.

DAILY TELEGRAPH, SATURDAY, NOVEMBER 10, 1888.

LOCALITY OF THE SEVEN UNDISCOVERED MURDERS.

The above chart represents the locality within which, since April last, seven women of the unfortunate class have been murdered. The precise spot where each crime was committed is indicated by a dagger and a numeral.
1. April 3.—Emma Elizabeth Smith, forty-five, had a stake or iron instrument thrust through her body, near Osborn-street, Whitechapel. ·
2. Aug. 7.—Martha Tabram, thirty-five, stabbed in thirty-nine places, at George-yard-buildings, Commercial-street, Spitalfields.

3. Aug. 31.—Mary Ann Nicholls, forty-seven, had her throat cut and body mutilated, in Buck's-row, Whitechapel.
4. Sept. 8.—Annie Chapman, forty-seven, throat cut and body mutilated, in Hanbury-street, Spitalfields.
5. Sept. 30.—A woman, supposed to be Elizabeth Stride, but not yet identified, discovered with her throat cut, in Berner-street, Whitechapel.

6. Sept. 30.—A woman, unknown, found with her throat cut and body mutilated, in Mitre-square, Aldgate.
Figure 7 (encircled) marks the spot in Goulston-street where a portion of an apron belonging to the woman murdered in Mitre-square was picked up by a Metropolitan police-constable.
Figure 8. Nov. 9.—Mary Jane Kelly, 24, her throat cut and body terribly mutilated, in Miller's-court, Dorset-street.

In the 1880s and 1890s, police suspected there might have been seven victims of the Ripper in total.

It was his "rational theory" that after the "fifth" murder of November 9, 1888, the Ripper's "brain gave way altogether" and he most likely committed suicide (violent psychopaths almost never do). This added yet another popular suspect to the list, the depressed young barrister Montague John Druitt. When he drowned himself in the Thames toward the end of 1888, he unwittingly cast himself as a main character in the Ripper's bloody drama.

Two other favorite suspects for Macnaghten were a Polish Jew named Aaron Kosminski, who was "insane" and "had a great hatred of women," and Michael Ostrog, a Russian doctor committed to a "lunatic asylum." Pointing a finger at Kosminski wasn't new. Four years earlier, in 1910, Chief Inspector Donald Swanson jotted his name as a suspect in his copy of Sir Robert Anderson's memoir, *The Lighter Side of My Official Life.*

For some reason Macnaghten thought that Montague Druitt was a doctor, thus explaining the notion that the Ripper had surgical skills. It's unclear where Macnaghten got his information. Perhaps he was confused because Montague Druitt had medical men in his family. His uncle Robert Druitt was a prominent physician and medical writer. His father, William, was a surgeon. Montague or "Monty" likely will always be stigmatized as a Ripper suspect, and it's baseless. It's tragic for descendants of the Druitt family.

In 1876 Montague Druitt was a handsome, athletic nineteen-

A Russian physician named Michael Ostrog was one of Macnaghten's top suspects.

year-old enrolled at New College, Oxford University, and five years later he was admitted to the Inner Temple in London to pursue a career in law. A good student and exceptionally talented cricket player, he worked a part-time job as an assistant at Valentine's School, a boys' boarding school in Blackheath. In the fall of 1888 the thirty-one-year-old bachelor was fired from the school and soon after committed suicide. Macnaghten claimed in his memoir that Druitt was "sexually insane," and in the Victorian era that could have referred to homosexuality. Macnaghten backs up his accusation with nothing more than so-called reliable information that he supposedly destroyed.

Mental illness was in Druitt's genetic code. His mother was committed to an asylum in the summer of 1888 and had attempted suicide at least once. One of Druitt's sisters later committed suicide. When he drowned himself in the Thames in the late fall or early winter of 1888, he left a suicide note. He indicated he feared he would end up like his

Montague John Druitt, a well-educated man who committed suicide in late 1888, was another of Macnaghten's Ripper suspects.

mother and thought it best to kill himself. I couldn't find this note. Maybe it was one of the documents Macnaghten saw fit to get rid of or misplaced.

Druitt became a suspect in the Ripper murders allegedly based on unknown information given to the police. More to the point, it was convenient if he happened to kill himself not long after what Macnaghten considers the last Ripper strike, Mary Kelly's murder on November 9, 1888. The young barrister was probably guilty of nothing more than a hereditary mood disorder, most likely depression. Maybe he was gay or, worse, attracted to underaged boys. At the time, homosexuality was considered as morally depraved and destructive to society as pedophilia, and police had little or no understanding about sexual violence. It wasn't considered that a lust murderer tends to target the object of his lust—which possibly wasn't women in Druitt's case. We'll probably never know, but what seems to have tipped the scales fatally for him was his acute distress over whatever happened to get him fired from Valentine's School.

We can't know his mind or feelings at that point in his life but his despair was sufficient for him to stuff rocks in his coat pockets and jump into the frigid, polluted Thames. Druitt's body was recovered from the water the last day of 1888, and it was supposed that he'd been dead for about a month. It could have been much longer than that. The cold temperatures would have significantly delayed decomposition. He may have killed himself before Mary Kelly's murder. At his inquest in Chiswick, the jury returned a verdict of "suicide whilst of unsound mind."

It seemed to be open season on doctors, suspected homosexuals and lunatics, especially Jewish ones. Perhaps Frederick Abberline refrained from writing about the Ripper investigation because he was smart enough not to trot out what he didn't know. Every case he included in his clipping book was one he personally investigated and solved. He wasn't given to guesswork, wild goose chases and witch hunts. His comments about the news articles he pasted on pages and underlined precisely with a straight-edge aren't copious or enthusiastic. He made it plain that he worked very hard and wasn't always happy about it. On January 24, 1885, when the Tower of London was bombed, for example, he found himself "especially overworked, as the then home secretary Sir Wm. Harcourt wished to be supplied every morning with the progress of the case and after working very hard all day I had to remain up many nights until 4 and 5 a.m. the following morning making reports for his information."

If Abberline was up all night in the bombing case, one can imagine his exhaustion during the Ripper crimes of 1888. I suspect the fabled investigator spent much of his time walking the streets, especially at night, speculating, deducing, trying to coax leads out of the dark, dirty air. His colleagues, friends, family and the merchants of the East End gave him a retirement dinner in 1892. They presented him with a silver tea and coffee service to honor his extraordinary career. He was praised for his tireless efforts in the Jack the Ripper case.

According to the *East London Observer*, H Division's Superintendent Arnold told those who had gathered that during the Ripper murders, "Abberline came down to the East End and gave the whole of his time with the object of bringing those crimes to light. Unfortunately, however, the circumstances were such that success was impossible." It must have been painful and infuriating in the fall of 1888 when Abberline was forced to confess to the press "not the slightest clue can at present be obtained."

He was used to outwitting criminals. Reportedly he worked so hard to solve the Ripper murders that he "almost broke down under the pressure." Often he went days without sleep. It wasn't uncommon for him to wear plainclothes and mingle with the "shady folk" in doss-house kitchens until the early hours of the morning. But no matter where he went, the "miscreant" wasn't there. At least this was Abberline's belief, and he may have been wrong. The killer wasn't the uneducated brute the police were looking for, and Abberline may have chatted with Jack the Ripper more than once and been none the wiser. He may have had pleasant conversations with a former actor disguised as a local.

"Theories!" Abberline would later thunder when someone brought up the Ripper murders. "We were lost almost in theories; there were so many of them." By all indications it wasn't a pleasant subject to bring up with him in later years after he'd moved on to other cases. Better to let him talk about the improved sanitation in the East End. Better to discuss how he solved a long string of bond robberies by tracing clues that led to an unclaimed hatbox in a railway station.

For all his experience and gifts he didn't solve the biggest case of his life. It's sad if that failure gave him pain and regret for even a moment in his retirement years. He went to his grave having no idea what he'd been up against. For reasons not imagined at the time, Jack the Ripper was a murderer unlike any other.

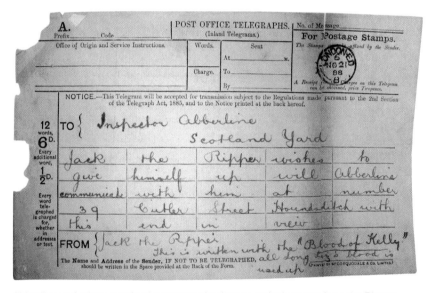

Abberline and others received many taunting letters and telegrams from the Ripper.

17

CROCHET WORK AND FLOWERS

MARY ANN NICHOLS'S BODY remained at the mortuary in Whitechapel until Thursday, September 6. She was enclosed in a "solid-looking" wooden coffin and loaded into a horse-drawn hearse that carried her to the City of London's Little Ilford Cemetery. One can find her grave today. On it is a granite marker that reads: "Victim Of 'Jack The Ripper.'"

The sun shone only five minutes on the day of her burial. It was misty and rainy. The next day the weather was worse, with no sunshine reported, and squalls roared in from the north. Heavy rain and sleet smacked down, and Londoners moved about in a cold mist going to and from work and later to the theaters, where *Dr. Jekyll and Mr. Hyde* was still drawing large audiences at the Lyceum, and a parody of it called *The Real Case of Hide and Seekyll* had opened at the Royalty. The play *She* at the Gaiety was reviewed in that day's paper as "a formidable experiment of dramatizing," offering a murder and cannibals. At the Alhambra, one of Walter Sickert's favorite music halls, the doors opened at 10:30 p.m. with a cast of dancing women and Captain Clives and his "marvelous dog."

The Friday night of September 7, Annie Chapman was sleeping off her last glass of spirits while London's early nightlife was going on. The week had been a bad one. Times were harder than usual for Annie, forty-seven and missing her two front teeth. She was five feet tall, overweight with blue eyes and short brown wavy hair—as the police later put it, "she had seen her better day." On the street she was known as "Dark Annie." In some accounts her estranged husband, John, was said to be a veterinary surgeon but he actually was a coachman and domestic servant employed by a wealthy gentleman who lived in the Royal Borough of Windsor. Annie's drunken behavior would have made her unwelcome on the estate where her husband worked, and finally the couple separated.

They had no contact with each other and she made no inquiries into his life until her weekly allowance of ten shillings suddenly stopped in late 1886. One day a woman having the appearance of a tramp showed up at the Merry Wives of Windsor public house and inquired about John Chapman. She said she'd walked twenty miles from London, staying in a lodging house along the way. Annie wanted to know if her husband was ill or using that as an excuse not to send money, and it was then she was informed that John had died. He left her nothing but two estranged children, her son an inmate of the Cripples' Home and her well-educated daughter living in France.

Annie moved in with a sieve maker for a while. When he left her, she borrowed small sums from her brother, who finally cut her off. She had no further contact with any members of her family. When her health allowed, she made pennies by selling crochet work and flowers, and acquaintances described her as "clever" and industrious by nature. As her addiction to alcohol tightened its grip on her life she became more desperate to earn her keep.

During the four months before her death Annie had been in and out of the infirmary. She was spending her nights in Spitalfields doss-houses, the most recent one located at 35 Dorset Street, which joined Commercial and Crispin Streets like a short rung on a ladder. There were an estimated five thousand lodging-house beds in the hellish dens of Spitalfields. *The Times* later observed at Annie's inquest that the "glimpse of life . . . was sufficient to make [jurors] feel there was much in the 19th century civilization of which they had small reason to be proud." In Annie Chapman's world the poor were "herded like cattle" and were "near starvation." Violence smoldered day and night, fueled by misery, alcohol and rage.

Four nights before her death, Annie got into an altercation with another lodger named Eliza Cooper, who confronted her in the lodging-house kitchen, demanding the return of a scrap of soap. Annie angrily threw a halfpenny on the table and told her to go buy soap herself. The two women carried their disagreement to the nearby public house, where Annie slapped Eliza across the face and Eliza punched Annie in the left eye and chest.

Annie's bruises were still noticeable the early Saturday morning of September 8 when John Donovan, the deputy of the lodging house on Dorset Street, demanded payment of eight pennies for a bed if she planned to stay. She replied, "I have not got it. I am weak and ill and have been in the infirmary." Donovan reminded her that she knew the rules. She replied that she would go out and get the money, asking him not to let her bed to someone else. Donovan would later tell police that she "was under the influence of drink" when the night watchman escorted her off the property.

Annie took the first right on Little Paternoster Row, where the night watchman saw her making her way through the narrow alley. Had she headed but a short distance away to Commercial Street, she would have reached Shoreditch, where there were several music halls including the Shoreditch Olympia, Harwood's and Griffin's. A little farther north was Hoxton, the very route Walter Sickert sometimes took when he walked home to 54 Broadhurst Gardens after evenings at music halls, theaters or wherever it was he went on his obsessive wanderings late at night and in the early morning hours.

At 2:00 a.m. when Annie emerged onto London's East End streets it was fifty degrees and sodden out. She was dressed in a black skirt, a long black jacket, an apron, wool stockings and boots. Around her neck was a piece of a black woolen scarf tied in front with a knot, and under it she wore a handkerchief that she recently had bought from another lodger. On the wedding ring finger of her left hand she wore three base metal or "flash" rings. In a pocket on the inside of her skirt were a small comb case, a piece of coarse muslin, and a torn bit of envelope that she had been seen to pick off the lodging-house floor and use to tuck away two pills she had gotten from the infirmary. The torn envelope had a red postmark on it. If anyone saw Annie alive over the next three and a half hours, no witness came forward.

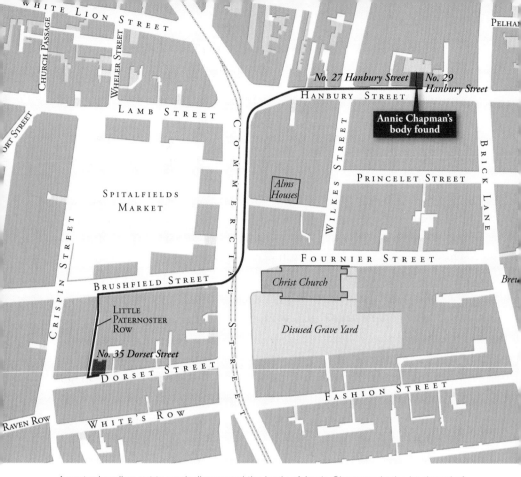

A porter heading out to work discovered the body of Annie Chapman in the backyard of 29 Hanbury Street at 5:55 a.m. on Sept. 8, 1888.

At a quarter of five, thirty-seven-year-old John Richardson, a porter at the Spitalfields Market, headed toward 29 Hanbury Street, a rooming house for the poor. Like so many other dilapidated dwellings in Spitalfields it once had been a workplace for weavers to toil on hand looms, until steam power put them out of business. Richardson's mother rented the house and sublet half of its rooms to seventeen people. She ran a packing-case business, and two months earlier someone had broken into the cellar and stolen two saws and two hammers.

Richardson had dropped by just as he always did when he was up early, and he went through a passage that led into the backyard to check that the cellar was safely locked. Then he sat on the steps to cut a bother-some piece of leather off his boot, his knife "an old table knife," he would testify at Annie Chapman's inquest. It was "about five inches long" and he'd used it earlier to cut "a bit of carrot." He estimated he sat on the steps no longer than several minutes, his feet resting on flagstone very close to where Annie's mutilated body would be found. He didn't hear or see anyone, he later claimed. Tucking his knife into a pocket, he laced up his mended boot and headed to the market as the sun began to rise.

Albert Cadosch lived next door at 27 Hanbury, his backyard separated from 29 Hanbury by a wooden fence that was approximately five-and-a-half feet high. He would later tell police that at 5:25 a.m. he walked into his backyard and heard a voice say "No" from the other side of the fence. Several minutes later something heavy fell against the palings. He didn't check to see who or what had caused the noise. Five minutes later at 5:30 a.m. Elizabeth Long was walking along Hanbury Street, heading west to Spitalfields Market, when she noticed a man talking to a woman on the street. They were in front of 29 Hanbury Street where Annie Chapman's body would be found in the backyard barely half an hour later. Mrs. Long testified at the inquest that she was "positive" the woman was Annie Chapman. She and the man were talking loudly but seemed to be getting along, Mrs. Long recalled. The only fragment of the conversation she overheard as she made her way down the street was the man asking, "Will you?" and the woman identified as Annie replying, "Yes."

Obviously the accounts given by witnesses conflict. It was never made clear at the inquest how all of them happened to be certain what time it was when they walked past acquaintances or strangers or stumbled onto a dead body. Most people told time by their routines, the position of the sun in the sky, and various clocks that chimed the hour or half or quarter hour. A cat meat (cat food) saleswoman named Harriet Hardiman of 29 Hanbury Street testified at the inquest that she was certain it was 6:00 a.m. when she was awakened by excited voices outside her ground floor window.

Afraid the building was on fire, she awakened her son and told him to go outside and look. When he returned he exclaimed that a woman had been murdered in the yard. Both mother and son had slept soundly all night, and Harriet Hardiman later testified she often heard people on the stairs and in the passage that led into the yard. But all had been quiet. John

Richardson's mother, Amelia, had been awake half the night. Certainly she would have been aware had someone been arguing or screaming, and she also claimed she hadn't heard a sound.

Residents were continually in and out of the rooming house at 29 Hanbury Street, and the front and back doors were always kept unlocked. It would have been easy for anyone to pass through the house and enter the backyard, and this is what Annie Chapman must have done just before she was murdered. At 5:55 a.m., John Davis, a porter who lived in the rooming house, headed out to market and had the shock of discovering a gory sight between the fence and the stone steps where Richardson had been sitting about an hour earlier mending his boot.

Annie Chapman was on her back. Her left hand was on her left breast, her right arm by her side, her legs bent, her disarrayed clothing pulled up to her knees. Her throat was cut so deeply that her head was barely attached, and her abdomen was slashed open. Her bowels and a flap of her belly were in a puddle of blood on the ground above her left shoulder, an arrangement that some view as intentionally symbolic. I doubt it was.

Most likely the Ripper's placement of organs and tissue was for the practical purpose of getting them out of his way as he targeted the kidneys, uterus and vagina. He also intended terror and horror, and he succeeded. John Davis fled to the street for help. The mutilated body was covered with a tarpaulin, and soon after Inspector Joseph Chandler of the Commercial Street Police Station arrived. When he saw what he was dealing with he sent for Dr. George Bagster Phillips, a divisional surgeon.

A crowd was gathering and voices cried out, "Another woman has been murdered!" With little more than a glance Dr. Phillips determined that the victim's throat had been cut before her "stomach" was slashed open. Rigor mortis was just beginning to set in. She'd been dead about two hours. He noted that her face seemed swollen and her tongue was protruding between her front teeth. Next he deduced she'd been strangled before her throat was cut, and he noted "six patches" of blood on the back wall about eighteen inches above Annie's head.

The droplets ranged from very small to the size of a sixpence and each "patch" was in a tight cluster. In addition there were "marks" of blood on the fence in back of the house. At Annie's feet were a bit of coarse muslin and a comb. There was a piece of bloody torn envelope that had the Sussex Regiment coat of arms on it and a London postmark with the date August 20, 1888, and nearby were two pills. Her cheap metal rings were missing, and an abrasion on her finger indicated that they had been forcibly removed.

On an undated, unsigned postcard mailed to James Fraser, Commissioner of the City of London Police, the Ripper drew a childish cartoon figure with a cut throat. He writes "poor annie" and claims to have her rings "in my possession." The cartoon's face and round head resemble a Sickert

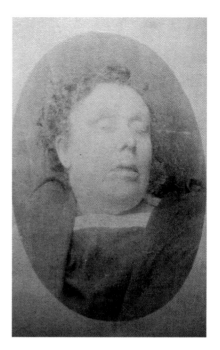

Annie Chapman's neck and abdomen were cut open.

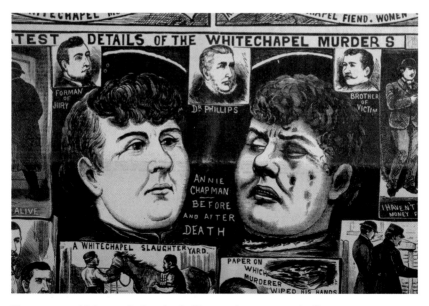

Newspapers widely reported on Annie Chapman's gruesome death.

doodle on a letter he wrote in 1893 to his artist friend William Rothenstein. That particular letter is on paper with a *Joynson Superfine* watermark. Several Ripper letters are also on *Joynson Superfine* watermarked paper. It was one of the stationeries Sickert was using in the summer and fall of 1888.

None of Annie Chapman's clothing was torn, and her boots were on, her black coat still buttoned and hooked. The neck of the coat was soaked with blood, and Dr. Phillips also pointed out drops on her stockings and

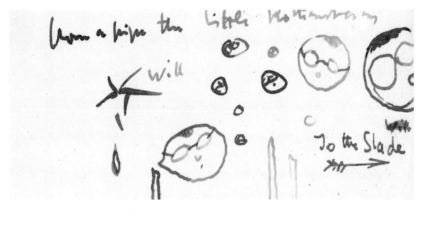

The round-headed cartoons in a Ripper letter *(bottom)* bear resemblance to drawings in a Sickert letter from 1893 *(top)*.

left sleeve. It wasn't mentioned in the newspaper or police reports but he or someone else must have scooped up her intestines and other body tissues and tucked them back inside her abdominal cavity before covering her with sacking. Then police helped place her into the same shell that had transported Mary Ann Nichols's body, and Annie was transported by hand ambulance to the Whitechapel workhouse mortuary.

It was daylight now. Hundreds of excited people were hurrying to the enclosed yard at 29 Hanbury Street. Neighbors on either side of the rooming house began charging admission to step inside for a better view of the bloodstained area where Annie had been slain. In a letter dated October 10, 1888, Jack the Ripper writes:

> *HAVE YOU SEEN THE "DEVIL"*
> *If not*
> *Pay one Penny & Walk inside*

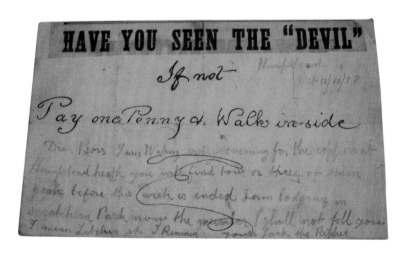
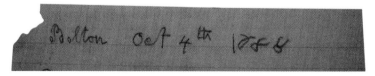

A Ripper letter mocks those who charged admission to view the bloodstained site of Annie Chapman's murder.

On the same mocking note he adds, "I am waiting every evening for the coppers at Hampstead heath," a sprawling parkland famous for healing springs and bathing ponds. The area was popular with writers, poets and painters including Dickens, Shelley, Pope, Keats and Constable. On bank holidays as many as one hundred thousand people might visit the rolling farmlands and dense copses, and Walter Sickert's home in South Hampstead was a twenty- or thirty-minute walk from there.

Ripper letters were being sent fast and furiously and began to reveal an emerging geographical profile. Many of the locations mentioned, some of them repeatedly, are places and locations that were well known to Sickert. Here are examples:

- Postmarks and references in close proximity to the Bedford Music Hall include Hampstead Road, King's Cross, Tottenham Court, Somers Town, Albany Street and St. Pancras Church.

- Locations in close proximity to Sickert's home at 54 Broadhurst Gardens include Kilburn, Palmerston Road (mere blocks from his house), Princess Road, Kentish Town, Alma Street and Finchley Road, a main artery in North London that one could take to Broadhurst Gardens.

- Locations of businesses that might have been of interest to Sickert include Piccadilly Circus, Haymarket, Charing Cross, Battersea (near Whistler's studio), Regent Street, Mayfair, Paddington (where Paddington Station is located), York Street (near Paddington), Islington (where St. Mark's Hospital is located), Worcester (a favorite place for painters), Greenwich, Gipsy Hill (near the Crystal Palace), Portman Square and Conduit Street (both of them not far from the Fine Art Society, one of Whistler's art dealers).

While it's true that many of the Ripper letters were mailed in the East End, many of them weren't. Sickert was in a position to mail letters from a variety of areas that he knew quite well. Certainly he was familiar with the

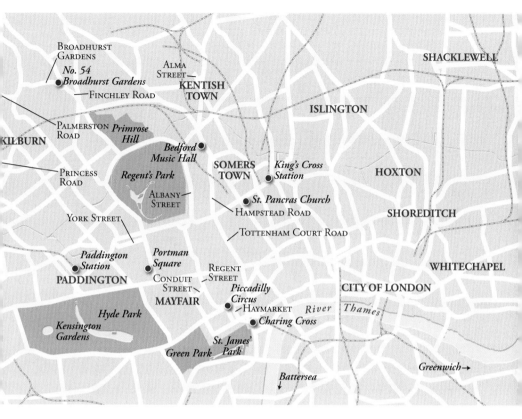

Locations all over Greater London were referenced in Ripper letters. Many of these locations would have been familiar to Walter Sickert.

East End and probably knew that run-down part of London better than most policemen did. The Ripper had all of the advantages and none of the restrictions or rules that those out to get him did. The orders of the day didn't allow Metropolitan Police to enter pubs or mingle with the neighbors at will. Constables were supposed to stay on their beats. To enter lodging houses or pubs without cause or to stray from one's measured walks around assigned blocks was to invite reprimand or suspension. But Sickert could mingle and meander as he pleased. No place was off-limits to him. He may have started getting frustrated that taunts and clues of his identity and whereabouts were being completely ignored.

Ripper letters were postmarked or addressed from distant cities and countries outside of England.

The police seemed to suffer from East End myopia. No matter how much the Ripper tried to lure them into investigating other locales or likely haunts, no one was listening. It doesn't appear that the police paid attention to the postmarks or locations of Ripper letters not mailed from the East End, especially those written or mailed from other cities in Great Britain and abroad. Unfortunately, not all envelopes have survived, many of them thrown out at the time because they weren't viewed as important. Without a postmark one has only the location that the Ripper wrote on his letter, and this may or may not have been where he really was at the time.

Distant cities where he gives the appearance of having been include Birmingham, Liverpool, Manchester, Leeds, Bradford, Dublin, Belfast, Limerick, Edinburgh, Plymouth, Leicester, Bristol, Clapham, Woolwich, Nottingham, Portsmouth, Croydon, Folkestone, Gloucester, Leith, Lille

(France), Lisbon (Portugal) and Philadelphia (USA). A number of these places seem unlikely. Portugal and the United States, for example. It also would have flown in the face of commonsense that someone could have mailed letters from London, Lille, Birmingham and Dublin on the same day, October 8. But when so many envelopes and their postmarks are missing, when evidence is cold and witnesses are dead, it's not possible to know for a fact that letters were written on a given date and where they were mailed. Only postmarks and eyewitnesses could swear to that.

The month of October 1888 was a busy letter-writing period for the Ripper. Some eighty letters still exist. There probably were many more than that, ones that were lost, pinched or never turned over to the police. These letters weren't taken particularly seriously in the beginning of the Ripper's crimes. As weeks passed the police began to assume that almost all of the communications were hoaxes, and this mind-set remains today if you talk to Ripperologists or even those who maintain the Ripper archives. From the beginning of this investigation I have maintained my belief that in fact few alleged Ripper letters are the handiwork of pranksters, disturbed people or ambitious journalists attempting to create a spectacle.

It's a shame distant locations weren't taken seriously. It would make sense for the Ripper to be on the run after multiple closely spaced murders. Whitechapel was getting too hot for him, the Ripper writes, and he was seeking peace and quiet in distant ports. We know from modern cases that some serial killers move around, virtually living in their cars or on the rails. October would have been a convenient time for Sickert to travel in and out of London and other cities, and going to and from France was easy. There's no telling where he went at a time when his wife Ellen was part of a Liberal delegation that was holding meetings in Ireland to support home rule and free trade. She was away from England much of the month. Apparently she planned to return to London on October 20, based on a letter she wrote from Carrick on the eleventh.

If she and Sickert had any contact at all during this separation, no communications to each other seem to have survived. But there's a hint found in a letter from Sickert's mother to her friend Penelope (Pennie) Muller dated simply as "Sunday Morning, 1888": "Nelly [Ellen] Sickert is back from Ireland, and she and Walter came to supper on Sunday, and now they have gone to Midhurst, where they have a cottage they shared with Janie Cobden [Ellen's sister]—and which I am to go and see." If Ellen was returning to London on Saturday, October 20, then the Sunday her mother-in-law mentions might have been the next night, the twenty-first. Midhurst is in West Sussex, some fifty-five miles southwest of London, and I've found no reference to how long Sickert and Ellen stayed there or if one or both of them actually did at all. But the information in his mother's and wife's letters indicates he may have been in the London area close to the time of the Mary Kelly murder on November 9.

In Ellen's absence, her husband had plenty of opportunity to move about unnoticed and without suspicion. A compulsive writer, he could create and send as many threatening and degrading communications as he liked. Indeed, Sickert had such a knack for stirring up news that letters and articles by and about him amounted to as many as six hundred in one year. It was daunting to go through his archives and look at his reams of clippings that he began gathering himself around the turn of the century. After that he used clipping services to keep up with his seemingly endless publicity, yet throughout his life he was known as a man who refused to give interviews.

Sickert managed to create the myth that he shied away from attention, and that couldn't be further from the truth. In fact his obsession with writing letters to the editor, reviews and articles became an embarrassment at some newspapers. Editors squirmed when they got yet another Sickert communication about art or the aesthetic quality of telephone poles or why all Englishmen should wear kilts or the disadvantages of chlorinated water. Most editors didn't wish to insult the well-known artist by ignoring him or relegating his prose to a small, inconspicuous space.

For example, from January 25 through May 25, 1924, Sickert delivered a series of lectures and articles that were published in the *Southport Visiter* in Southport, north of Liverpool on the coast. Although these articles came to more than 130,000 words, apparently that wasn't enough. On May 6, 12, 15, 19 and 22 Sickert wrote or telegraphed W. H. Stephenson of the *Visiter*: "I wonder if the Visiter could bear one more article at once. . . . If so you should have it at once" and "delighted writing" and "please ask printer to express early six copies" and "do let me send you just one more article" and "if you hear of any provincial paper that would care to carry series over the summer let me know."

Throughout Sickert's life his literary prolificacy was astonishing. His newspaper clippings book contains more than twelve thousand news items about him and letters he wrote to editors in Great Britain alone, most of them between 1911 and the late 1930s. He published some four hundred lectures and articles, and I'm convinced these known writings don't begin to represent the entirety of his literary output. He was an obsessive writer who enjoyed persuading, manipulating and impressing people with his words. He was a narcissist who craved an audience. He was addicted to seeing his name in print, and it would have been in character for him to write a startling number of the Ripper letters, including some of those mailed from all over the map.

He may have written far more of them than some document examiners would be inclined to believe based on their examinations of the Ripper correspondence. But it's a mistake to judge the likes of Walter Sickert by the usual handwriting-comparison standards. He was a multitalented artist with an amazing memory. He was multilingual, a voracious reader and skilled mimic. A number of books on graphology were available at the time, and the handwriting in many Ripper letters is similar to examples of writing styles associated with various occupations and personalities. Sickert could have opened any number of graphology books and imitated the styles he found there. That likely would have amused him.

Using chemicals and highly sensitive instruments to analyze inks, paints and paper is scientific. Handwriting comparison isn't. It's an investigative tool that can be powerful and convincing, but it can be frustrating or impossible if a suspect is adept at disguising his writing. The police investigating the Ripper cases were eager to pinpoint similarities or differences in handwriting, but they didn't seem to explore the possibility that the killer might use many different styles. Other leads such as watermarks or cities the Ripper mentions and postmarks on envelopes weren't pursued. Had they been it would have been discovered that types of paper and cities shared points in common, including theaters and racecourses. Many of these locations and paper manufacturers would have been quite familiar to Sickert, and letters purportedly mailed from Manchester are a good example.

There were reasons for him to know that city and visit it. His wife's family owned property in Manchester. His sister, Helena, lived there as did some of his friends and professional connections. When he was an actor, it also was a stop on his theater tour. One Ripper letter with a Manchester connection is dated November 22, 1888, and has a partial *A Pirie & Sons* watermark. Another November 22 letter that the Ripper claims to have written from East London has a partial *A Pirie & Sons* watermark, the same watermark on stationery Walter and Ellen Sickert began using after they were married on June 10, 1885.

18

A CAUTIOUS INDICATOR

IN 1999, I HAD AN IDEA I presented to Dr. Paul Ferrara, the director of the Virginia crime labs at the time, and to James Gilmore, who was the governor.

What an amazing thing it would be if we could assemble the best and the brightest forensic scientists and pathologists to further police and death investigative training. Active practitioners in the labs and the medical examiner's office were recruited for the faculty, and the Virginia Institute of Forensic Science and Medicine was born. It would never have occurred to me in my wildest fantasies that I might one day need these skilled experts to help with Jack the Ripper. In retrospect, I've had as much good fortune in this case as I've had bad.

When it all began in the spring of 2001, I asked the institute's codirector, Dr. Ferrara, if he could help with the forensic science. One of my thoughts was just maybe we could recover DNA from the backs of envelopes and stamps of Ripper-related documents. Apparently this had never been requested or done, and I was stunned that so few people had bothered to analyze the original evidence with lightboxes and microscopes at the very least.

That summer we received permission to conduct nondestructive forensic testing on the letters, envelopes and Ripper victim photographs preserved at The National Archives and the London Metropolitan Archives. Dr. Ferrara assembled a team that included himself, DNA analyst Lisa Schiermeier and forensic document examiner and image-processing expert Chuck Pruitt, and we set off for London. I had no idea what we were getting into or that chasing after the Ripper's DNA would go on for another seven years with a result that wasn't particularly helpful. I also had no forewarning that the letters and envelopes at The National Archives had been laminated in cellulose acetate films. It was a devastating discovery that to this day remains a sad disappointment. We'll never know just how much these priceless documents were compromised by a process that involves handling and heat.

As we stood around a table with our cotton gloves on and surgical masks in hand, we looked at each other in dismay. Dr. Ferrara picked up a Ripper envelope that was stiff and completely sealed with what felt like plastic. He politely informed archivists that these films would have to be removed before envelope flaps and stamps could be peeled back and swabbed. Why should they agree to such a thing? I didn't think they would. I was certain we'd be returning to Virginia empty-handed the following day. But just in case, we went ahead and swabbed ourselves and the archivists for exclusionary purposes. And we waited.

For the better part of a dejected hour we felt sure we would have nothing to show for our plans and efforts, and what this meant for me was that I would quit the project immediately. Without science I couldn't in good conscience proceed. I would need to call my literary agent, Esther Newberg. I imagined telling her I was sorry but there was no book after all. Fortunately I hadn't signed the contract yet, and even as I was contemplating such matters, Mario Aleppo, head of Collection Care at the time, made an unexpected decision.

He basically said we should give it a try. Under his watchful eye his staff began to remove the acetate films, revealing the fragile documents underneath. Next Dr. Ferrara and Lisa Schiermeier began gently collecting samples with cotton-tipped swabs and sterile water. Photographs were taken. Forensic light sources and microscopes were used. Each document was placed on a lightbox, and handwriting, paper, watermarks, inks and media that include pencils, artist crayons and paints were patiently examined. The process was painstaking and slow, and the story these precious documents began to tell was incredible.

There was less to swab at the London Metropolitan Archives. But we examined each document and collected samples from any envelope that seemed to make sense. From there we went on to other archival collections, swabbing Whistler documents and looking for watermarks at the University of Glasgow, where his massive archival collection includes letters Sickert wrote to him. At the West Sussex Record Office we swabbed and examined the letters in the Cobden family archives. Obviously Ellen Cobden Sickert and Whistler have never been suspects in the Ripper murders, but Walter Sickert worked in Whistler's studio. The apprentice Sickert mailed letters for his master and was in close physical contact with him and his belongings. It's possible that Whistler's and Ellen's DNA could have contaminated Sickert evidence.

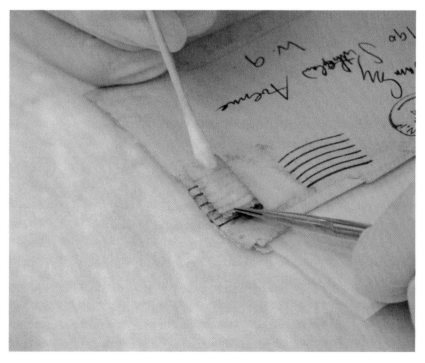

Author Patricia Cornwell and a team of forensic scientists examine Ripper and Sickert documents, September 2001.

In the process of examining documents in West Sussex, we coincidentally discovered some of Montague Druitt's family correspondence including a single letter written by him, dated 1876, while he was a student at Oxford University. The mitochondrial DNA results we would get from the envelope yielded one of only three single-donor profiles in this case. Of course it certainly can't be established whose profile it is. It might be Montague Druitt's. It might not be.

We also tried our luck with the Duke of Clarence since I happened to own several original letters of his that interestingly enough discuss the sensitive subject of blackmail. My thought was that for privacy reasons he might have addressed and sealed the envelopes himself as opposed to a secretary doing it. In the end we would get nothing useful from Prince Eddy, and while it would have been extremely gratifying to clear his and Montague Druitt's names for good, DNA wasn't going to help—not that there is anyone left to indict and convict since Jack the Ripper has been dead for many decades. But there's no statute of limitations on homicide, and his victims and those falsely accused of his crimes deserve the justice denied them.

That was the main motivation in attempting DNA analysis to begin with, and those of us involved knew up front it was a long shot. Ultimately it would be decided by some that the results aren't statistically important enough to merit the trouble and expense. I've been told we shouldn't have attempted it, that it was a waste of time. I've since been warned that the analysis was blighted from the onset and everything about it should be ignored. But I maintain that attempting multiple rounds of genetic testing was something we had to try. Having done so I maintain that it would be less than honest for me not to include the results and any possible interpretations of them.

I was never optimistic we would get a nuclear DNA match. All the same, I was surprised and quite crestfallen when the first results of testing in 2001 turned up not a single sign of human life in fifty-five samples tested. We tried again, this time swabbing different areas of the same envelopes and stamps. Still we came up with nothing. There are a number of possible explanations for the disappointing outcome.

Perhaps the one-billionth of a gram of cells in human saliva that might have been deposited on a stamp or envelope flap didn't survive the years. Maybe the heat used to laminate Ripper letters for conservation destroyed the nuclear DNA. Or possibly suboptimal storage had degraded and destroyed it. We also were suspicious of the adhesive. Called a "glutinous wash" in the mid-nineteenth century, it was derived from plant extracts such as the bark of the acacia tree.

During the Victorian era the postal system underwent an industrial revolution, with the first Penny Black stamp mailed from Bath on May 2, 1840. Five years later the envelope-folding machine was patented. Many people didn't want to lick envelopes or stamps for sanitary reasons, and used a moistened sponge. It wasn't possible for us to know who had licked or handled anything we examined. Yet we didn't give up. When two attempts failed, the only genetic option left was to go after mitochondrial DNA.

When one reads about DNA tests used in modern criminal or paternity cases what's usually being referred to is the nuclear DNA, which is located in virtually every cell in the body and passed down from both parents. Mitochondrial DNA is found outside the nucleus of the cell. Think of an egg. The nuclear DNA is the yolk and the mitochondrial DNA is the egg white. While the mitochondrial region of a cell contains thousands more "copies" of DNA than the nucleus does, the testing is very complex and expensive.

The results can be limited and statistically unimpressive because the mitochondrial DNA is passed down only from the mother, and the more-than-a-century-old Ripper-related documents are a very difficult medium. They can't be cleaned like tooth and bone. One can't scrub away surface contaminants from the paper and adhesives. So chances were good if not a certainty that the original donor was going to be masked by the DNA of other people including police and archivists. But that didn't stop us from trying every logical means we possibly could.

Extracts of all samples were sent to the Bode Technology Group, an internationally respected private DNA service with clients that include law enforcement, crime labs and disaster management organizations. As I traveled back and forth to England, I anxiously waited for the lab results. When I finally got the call I was in The National Archives with art and paper experts and other members of my team, and I excitedly found a quiet place to hear the news. Dr. Paul Ferrara informed me that Bode had finished the testing of the first fifty-seven samples. We'd gotten mitochondrial DNA on almost every one of them, but there wasn't reason to break out the champagne.

At best I would describe the results as inclusionary. A hint at identity. A taunt like so much in the Jack the Ripper case. Overall the analysis showed that the results we got are "a cautious indicator," Dr. Ferrara told me. He added that Sickert and Ripper mitochondrial DNA sequences may have come from the same person, but they might not have either. "The matching sequences might be a coincidence," he said. "They might not be a coincidence." The possible Ripper single-donor profile from the Openshaw envelope, Dr. Ferrara explained, excludes 99 percent of the population as having left that DNA on the back of a partial stamp.

While this sounds impressive and conclusive, it's not. One percent of the population is one out of a hundred people. The results are better than nothing but not nearly enough to convict anyone of a crime for a number of reasons. For starters we can't know the source of that single-donor profile. Second, there are no DNA references such as Sickert's profile for comparison, and most significantly, the evidence is contaminated. The majority of the genetic profiles we got were a mishmash of individuals, and none of it would hold up in court. But that doesn't mean the results should be thrown out entirely.

When I began work on the revision of this book, I decided to include the original lab information. Let others decide whether it matters that seven samples from Ripper/Sickert documents had the same mitochondrial DNA sequence components that were found on the envelope of a Ripper letter written to Dr. Thomas Openshaw. When the Ripper crimes began, Openshaw was the curator of the London Hospital Museum, and as I mentioned earlier he also may have taught anatomy at the Slade School of Fine Art. I find it interesting that the Openshaw letter and

Stamps on an envelope containing a Ripper letter written to Dr. Openshaw yielded the best DNA profile, although the results remain inconclusive in this case due largely to the age, contamination and degradation of the samples. The samples were taken at The National Archives in London, September 2001.

its envelope had been in private hands until a few months prior to our appearing at The National Archives to swab them. The documents hadn't been laminated yet.

It can be withering to look at DNA results, and all of the significant ones are in the appendix. But I list the single-donor profiles here:

- From a Whistler document: 16311 T-C 93 A-G

- From the Druitt document: 16223 C-T 16278 C-T 73 A-G 263 A-G

- From the Openshaw document: 16294 C-T 73 A-G 263 A-G

The three components (markers) of the Openshaw clean sequence were found in other Ripper/Sickert samples that showed a mixture of base positions or "locations" in the mitochondrial region. This likely means the samples were contaminated by the DNA of other people, and to better understand what I mean by contamination think of a map drawn in pastels that smear. On this map are only three "markers" or features: the National Mall, the White House and the Smithsonian Museum of Natural History. Together these constitute a sequence or "profile" that's single-donor or from the same city, in this example, Washington, DC. To continue with the analogy, imagine other pastel-drawn maps with other features from other cities coming in contact with our "Ripper" map. Chalky imprints of features from these other cities will be transferred, and what had been single-donor becomes contaminated, in other words a mixture.

It's in keeping with the frustrations when dealing with the ever-elusive Walter Sickert that he never offered us his DNA profile. It would have answered so many questions if we'd had it to compare to DNA recovered from Ripper documents. But no matter what we tried, we came up empty-handed. A swabbing of Sickert's white coveralls donated to the Tate was fruit-less, possibly because they'd been laundered, and neither fabric nor paper are good sources for DNA because they can't be cleaned of contaminants. A hair found in a satchel of Sickert's, also at the Tate, had too much insect damage for testing.

A last-ditch effort would have been to exhume his remains. In addition to the mere thought of it causing an uproar, doing so most likely would have been pointless even if one could get permission. When Sickert was cremated in 1942, our best evidence went up in flames. Unless we eventually find a viable sample of his blood, skin, hair, teeth or bones we'll never resurrect Walter Richard Sickert in a laboratory. But that doesn't mean we didn't find pieces of him. The single-donor sequence recovered from the partial stamp on the back of the Openshaw envelope was our best discovery.

These seven other Sickert/Ripper samples shared components in common with it:

- The front stamp from the Openshaw (i.e., Ripper) envelope

- Three other Ripper envelopes

- A Walter Sickert envelope flap

- A stamp from a Walter Sickert envelope

- An envelope from a letter written by Sickert's first wife, Ellen

These six samples had mixtures of the Openshaw (i.e., Ripper) components:

- Two envelopes from Sickert letters

- Two envelopes from Ripper letters

- Two envelopes from Ellen Sickert

The Ellen Sickert results may mean nothing. But supposing the components are from her husband, this could be explained if she moistened the envelope and stamp with the same sponge he used. Or Walter Sickert might have touched or licked the adhesive on the flap or stamp perhaps because he mailed letters for her. If it's true that the profile on the Openshaw letter is Sickert's, then there's also the extremely remote possibility that Ellen had the same mitochondrial DNA sequence he did. We didn't get a single-donor profile on any samples derived from swabbing envelopes and stamps in her collection of family correspondence.

Without a genealogical study of Sickert's family, which would require an exhumation of his mother or siblings or any provable offspring, we'll never be able to say without a doubt what Walter Sickert's DNA profile was. The same holds true for Montague Druitt, the Duke of Clarence, Whistler and Ellen. But it's of note that the source of the most promising single-donor DNA sequence was written on stationery, the watermark of the stationery Sickert was using at the time. This document, the Openshaw letter, was postmarked October 29, 1888, mailed in London, and it reads:

Envelope:

DR. OPENSHAW
PATHOLOGICAL CURATOR
LONDON HOSPITAL
WHITE CHAPEL

Letter:

Old boss you was rite it was
the left kidny i was goin to
hopperate again close to your
ospitle just as i was goin
to dror mi nife along of
er bloomin throte them
cusses of coppers spoilt
the game but i guess i wil
be on the job soon and will
send you another bit of
innerds
Jack the ripper

O have you seen the devle
with his mikerscope and scalpul
a lookin at a Kidney
with a slide cocked up

As is true of many Ripper letters this one is blatantly contrived. The bad handwriting looks disguised and is jarringly inconsistent with the handwriting of someone who had access to pen and ink and fine-quality watermarked stationery. The address on the envelope would appear to be the work of someone educated and is vastly different from the overblown illiteracy of the letter with its inconsistent misspellings such as *kidny* and *Kidney*, *wil* and *will*.

The Ripper letter to Dr. Openshaw was written on paper with the same watermark found on Sickert's stationery.

Ripper experts Stewart P. Evans and Keith Skinner point out in their book *Jack the Ripper: Letters from Hell* that the postscript in the Openshaw letter is reminiscent of a verse in an 1871 Cornish folktale:

> *Here's to the devil,*
> *With his wooden pick and shovel,*
> *Digging tin by the bushel,*
> *With his tail cock'd up!*

Such an allusion wouldn't seem to make much sense if we're supposed to believe the Openshaw letter was written by an uneducated homicidal maniac who ripped a kidney from a victim. But it would be understandable if Walter Sickert recalled and wrote it. He visited Cornwall as a boy. He spent months there with Whistler in 1883 and 1884. Sickert knew Cornwall and the Cornish people, and at the time the Ripper crimes began, Sickert was at war with the Newlyn school, the art colony headed by Stanhope Forbes located near Penzance, Cornwall. Sickert was well read and familiar with folk tunes and music hall songs. It's unlikely that a poor, uneducated person from London spent time in Cornwall or sat around in the slums reading Cornish folktales.

19

A PAINTED LETTER

JACK THE RIPPER was a forensic scientist's worst adversary. He was like a twister tearing through a lab.

He created investigative chaos with his baffling varieties of papers, pens, paints, postmarks and disguised handwritings. He constantly moved about without leaving a trail that could be trusted, and he fooled everyone. But some of what he did would get him into serious trouble today. I believe his communications to the police, press and others would be his downfall and get him caught.

A Ripper letter received by the police on October 18, 1889, isn't exactly a normal document. The paper is an 11-by-14-inch sheet of azure laid foolscap, the lettering first drawn in pencil, then beautifully painted over with a fine brush in brilliant red ink. Apparently no one thought it unusual that a lunatic or an illiterate or even a prankster would elaborately paint a letter that reads:

Dear Sir

I shall be in Whitechapel on the 20th of this month—And will begin some very delicate work about midnight, in the street where I executed my third examination of the human body.

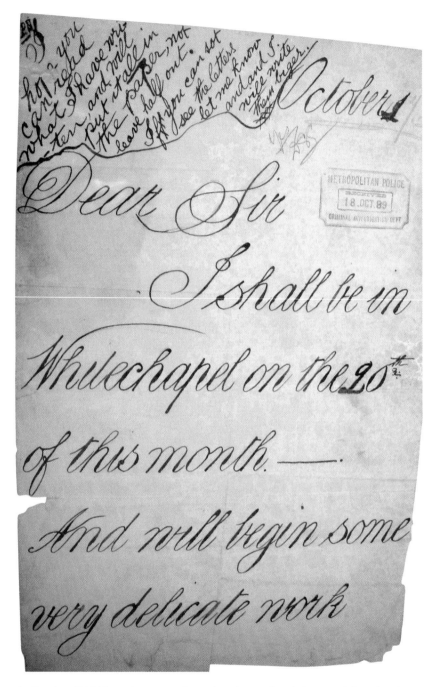

An October 1889 Ripper letter was first written in pencil and then carefully painted over in red ink with a fine brush.

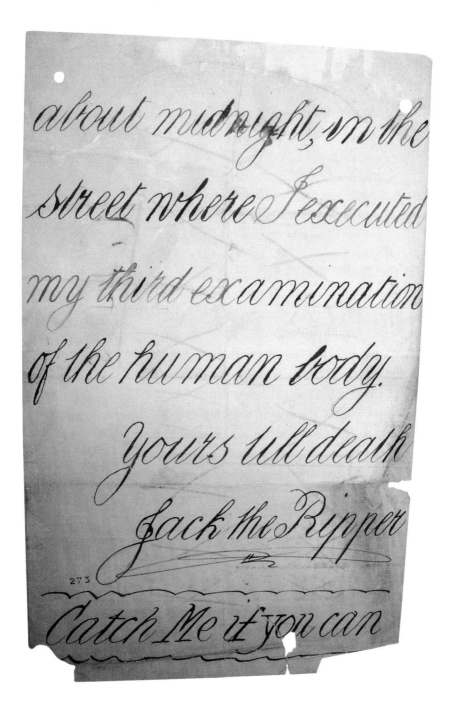

Yours till death
Jack the Ripper
Catch Me if you can

[postscript at the top of the page]

PS

*I hope you can read what I have written, and will put it all
in the paper, not leave half out. If you can not see the letters
let me know and I will write them biger.*

He misspells *bigger* as an illiterate would, and I don't believe the glaring inconsistency was an accident. The Ripper was playing one of his little games. He was showing what "fools" the police were. An alert investigator certainly should have questioned why someone would correctly spell *delicate* and *executed* and *examination* and yet misspell the simple word *bigger*.

Police should have asked what sort of individual would contrive puzzles and riddles that more than a century later would require a forensic light source to coax out what if anything lurked under heavy black ink he'd supposedly used to obliterate a clue. In a letter dated September 24, 1888, the Ripper offers the police a fill-in-the-blanks challenge for his "name" and "address." But in yet another one of his teases he blots out the "information" with dark black rectangles and coffin shapes.

Using a forensic light, we were able to make out *ha* and the barely legible and partial signature *Ripper*. Another bit of fun was to glue a strip of paper on the front of an envelope as if to entice someone to do what Dr. Ferrara did in 2001. He performed long, delicate surgery to lift that strip. There was nothing under it. Another joke. Another "ha ha," and we couldn't help but feel duped. At least we bothered to look but there was no sign the police ever did. The artistic and taunting touches to these infamous communications seemed to have been ignored at the time the Ripper was at work. Of course details that seem obvious to us now have the benefit of hindsight and the analysis of modern scientists and art experts.

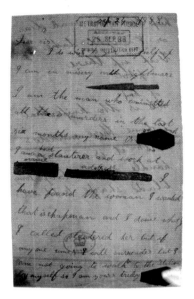

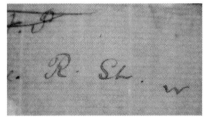
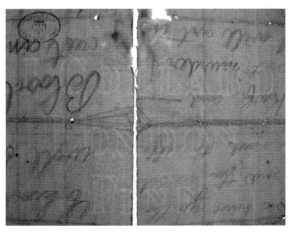

In his letters, the Ripper laid out tricks and puzzles that he said contained hints for the police. He often suggested that important information was concealed under black boxes of ink or obscured by sketches. Author Patricia Cornwell and her forensic team examined many different letters for obscured or hidden clues.

According to art historian and Sickert expert Anna Robins, many of the illustrations in Ripper letters are works of art. For example, a drawing of a Neanderthal-looking thug is actually a print made by an elaborately carved woodcut. This was never noticed until she examined the original letter on a lightbox and under a hand lens in 2001.

Some four years later in October 2005 a team of us that included forensic scientists and art conservators from Harvard's Fogg Museum traveled to London to reexamine the Ripper letters. This time in addition to microscopes, we used a VSC-5000 video spectral comparator combined with an electrostatic imaging system. The hope was to detect artistic media such as inks, obliterated information and other features by using magnification and lights of varying wavelengths. We also wanted to have a go at checking for indented writing caused by a pen or pencil bearing down on paper and leaving an imprint on underlying sheets.

No indented writing was detected but we weren't surprised. If it had been there in the past, the fragile imprints might have faded or been eradicated when documents were laminated. But we did make some important discoveries, including a startling number of hints that an artist or someone

The brutish face in this Ripper letter is actually a woodcut created by carving the image into wood and using ink to transfer it to paper. Sickert would have been very familiar with this printmaking technique, and the image is extremely skillful.

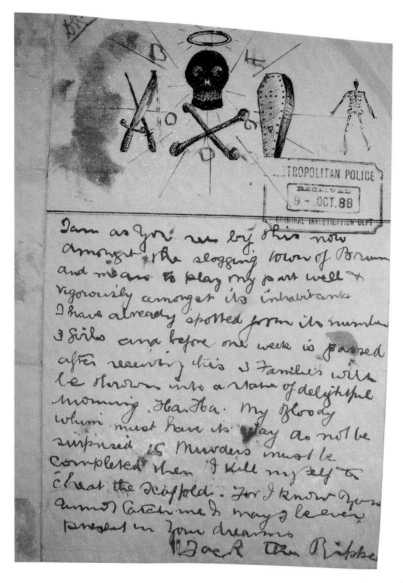

The images at the top of this Ripper letter may also have been created with hand-carved woodcuts.

who had access to art supplies created a number of these fiendish communications. Harvard art and paper conservator Anne Driesse determined that media used on 392 letters and envelopes examined over the course of five days include the following:

Art historian Anna Robins claims many of the "drawings" from Ripper letters are actually examples of professional art.

- Paintbrushes

- Blue copy pencil (typically used to copy documents or drawings onto damp paper in a copying press)

- Fountain pens

- Graphite pencils

- Colored pencils

In 2005, the author and her team used a VSC-5000 video spectral comparator combined with an electrostatic imaging system to thoroughly examine Ripper artifacts. Letters were tested at both The National Archives and the London Metropolitan Archives.

- Colored inks

- Black ink containing powdered carbon pigment
  (usually lampblack)

- Etching ground (a waxy material used to coat the surface of
  a copper printing plate)

- Brownish accretions that might be etching ground or blood
  or both

Driesse's analysis reveals that forty-two documents were written in red ink, eight in red pencil, seven in blue pencil, three in purple pencil, and fifty-nine documents have watermarks. In at least three documents the lettering may have been painted with a brush in red, purple and black ink. Sixteen documents have "a golden-brownish accretion and smears on the paper surface," and at least five of those may also have involved the use of a paintbrush. As many as thirty-five documents contain drawings or inkblots and splotches or other design elements such as "bloody smears."

It doesn't appear that unusual characteristics such as the delicate, feathery strokes of a paintbrush were ever noticed in the past, not at the time of the Ripper crimes or prior to our examination of the original documents during my ongoing research that began in 2001. One explanation is that police dismissed these communications as hoaxes. Another is that facsimiles such as photocopies or photographs (what most Ripper enthusiasts really relied on) aren't the appropriate means of discovering subtle details. One needs a lightbox and magnification for that. Most of all one needs experts who can interpret what they are seeing.

As was true in 1888, science can't solve crimes without the human element of deductive skills, teamwork, thorough investigation and smart prosecution. But in this case there will always be the problem of what the evidence really means. Even if we'd gotten an irrefutable DNA match linking Sickert to a Ripper letter, any sharp defense attorney would say that someone writing a letter or two or even a dozen doesn't prove he murdered anyone. Perhaps Sickert simply composed a number of Ripper letters

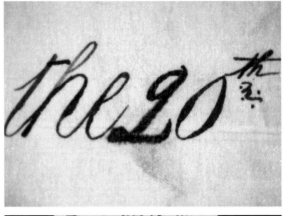

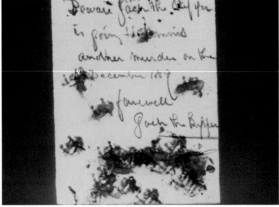

Materials used in creating the Ripper letters include various colors of ink and pencil, etching ground, and brownish accretions.

because he had a wacky, warped sense of humor. But a good prosecutor would counter that if Sickert wrote even one of those Ripper letters, he was in trouble. The letters are confessional. They're violent and full of hateful taunts and mockery.

In them the Ripper claims to have murdered and mutilated people he calls by name. He threatens to kill government officials and police. Unlike deranged individuals who make false confessions, the Ripper's statements don't evolve over time to reflect the most recent details in the news. In fact he ridicules accounts when they are wrong or stupid according to him. In some instances he goes on to correct details such as the various physical descriptions and supposed social status of the killer.

Dozens of Ripper letters have splotches and smears.

Today the flaunting of artistic skills in a serial murderer's letters would snag the attention of an experienced, well-trained investigator or criminal intelligence analyst (profiler). The paper evidence would be considered of great importance. Were Sickert a suspect in modern times, his paper trail would lead right to him. He'd have some explaining to do as to why three Ripper letters and eight Sickert letters have the *A Pirie & Sons* watermark, for example.

It seems that from 1885 to 1887 the Sickerts' 54 Broadhurst Gardens stationery was *A Pirie & Sons*. Folded at the middle like a greeting card, the front was bordered in pale blue. The embossed address also was pale blue, the *A Pirie & Sons* watermark centered on the crease. In three Ripper letters with the *A Pirie & Sons* watermark, the stationery was torn along the crease and only half of the watermark remains. Unless Jack the Ripper was incredibly obtuse he would have removed the side of the folded stationery that was embossed with the address. This isn't to say that criminals haven't been known to make numbskull oversights such as leaving a driver's license at a crime scene or writing a stickup note on a deposit slip that includes an address and phone number. But the Ripper didn't make errors that would have done him in. He didn't believe he would ever be caught and was justified in thinking that those in pursuit were no match for him.

Sickert must not have been worried about the artwork or watermarks on any Ripper letters he wrote. If it's a fact he left strange shapes or cartoonish art on a wall inside Mary Kelly's bedroom, he wasn't concerned about that either. Perhaps these were more of his "catch me if you can" taunts and teases or he may simply have been too arrogant to think paper or crude cartoons would matter. And he was right. They didn't. But today they would.

The *A Pirie & Sons* watermarks we found on Sickert stationery include a watermarked date of manufacturing that was divided by the fold. When the paper was torn along the fold in three different Ripper letters with that watermark, the remaining partial dates are 18 and 18 and 87. It's safe to conclude the manufacturing date for at least one of these torn sheets of stationery was 1887 and consistent with the time frame when Sickert was using this type of stationery.

Repeated trips to multiple archives turned up other watermarks that became familiar the more we looked. Letters Sickert wrote to Jacques-Émile Blanche in 1887 are on stationery with the address embossed in black and a *Joynson Superfine* watermark. A search through the Blanche–Sickert correspondence in the Bibliothèque de L'Institut de France in Paris shows that during the late summer and fall of 1888 and in the spring of 1889 Sickert was using *Joynson Superfine* paper with the return address of 54 Broadhurst Gardens embossed with no color or in bright red with a red border.

Letters Ellen Sickert wrote to Blanche as late as 1893 with a return address of 10 Glebe Place, Chelsea, are on stationery that also has the *Joynson Superfine* watermark. In the Whistler collection at Glasgow there are seven Sickert letters with the *Joynson Superfine* watermark, and it would appear that Sickert was using this stationery about the same time he was using *A Pirie & Sons*.

In the Sir William Rothenstein collection at Harvard University's Modern Books and Manuscripts Collection I found two other Sickert letters with the *Joynson Superfine* watermark. The artist and critic Rothenstein was someone Sickert trusted enough to ask him to lie under oath. As I've pointed out, during the late 1890s Sickert lived with the Frenchwoman

Madame Villain, a fishwife in Dieppe he referred to as "Titine" (and with whom it was rumored he might have had an illegitimate child named Maurice). For five pounds a quarter he rented a small space in her house for his bedroom and studio. Whatever the nature of his relationship with Titine, his cohabitating with her would have been used against him in court had he contested Ellen's divorce suit in 1899.

"If subpoenaed," Sickert writes to Rothenstein, "you might truly remain as you are in ignorance of Titine's very name. You might say I always call her 'Madame.'" Rothenstein wasn't ignorant of Titine. He knew very well who she was. Both *Joynson Superfine* watermarked letters that Sickert wrote to him are undated. One of them written in German and Italian is on stationery that must have belonged to Sickert's mother because the return address is hers. A second *Joynson Superfine* watermarked letter to Rothenstein includes mathematical scribbles, a cartoonish face and the word *ugh*. It has a return address of 10 Glebe Place, Chelsea, the same return address on Ellen Sickert's 1893 letter to Blanche. The cartoonish face bears some resemblance to cartoonish faces in a Ripper note on *Gurney Ivory Laid* paper that I will go into more detail about later.

Another Ripper letter has a partial *Joynson Superfine* watermark, and it appears that Sickert used *Joynson Superfine* watermarked paper from the late 1880s through the late 1890s. I've found no letters with this watermark after his divorce in 1899, the same year he moved to Continental Europe. As these watermarks continued to turn up in the earliest days of this investigation, Tate Britain suggested I consult with Peter Bower, one of the most respected paper experts and paper historians in the world. Art experts wanted to hear what he had to say. You might say he was sicced on me because I certainly had the distinct impression at the time that it was expected he would derail what Sickert apologists considered my imaginative and silly project. I'll never forget when I first saw him striding along a corridor headed in my direction at The National Archives. I was truly apprehensive as I watched this mythical blue jean–clad paper savant with his white ponytail, microscope and jeweler's lens. It seemed this would be the end of my investigation, and yet quite the opposite occurred. Bower's findings would prove to be the most incriminating evidence in the case.

Cartoonish faces on a Sickert letter *(below)* and a Ripper letter *(above)* bear a resemblance to each other.

A frequent expert witness in court, he is best known for his work on the types of paper used by Michelangelo, J. M. W. Turner, Constable and others. He's a master sleuth at rooting out counterfeit and fraud, and as he began the analysis in the Ripper investigation, he was quick to point out that matching watermarks don't always mean the paper was from the same batch or roll. Simply comparing watermarks on a lightbox as Dr. Ferrara and I did is far from conclusive.

To ascertain a match, Bower uses a 30X lens to study features such as measurements, fiber content, and the distances between chain lines that determine whether different sheets of paper were made in the same wire mold. Paper from different batches or rolls can have the same watermark and a very similar fiber content. But the individual sheets usually have slight differences in measurements due to the speed of drying or the way the machine cut them. These characteristics are the paper's Y profile, and if these Y profiles match it indicates the paper came from the same batch. This can be hugely important statistically in document comparisons.

Bower says it's common for an individual to have stationery with the same watermark but from many batches. Often when the paper is ordered from the stationer, there are different batches mixed in even if the watermarks, embossing or engraving are the same. The subtle differences in the Sickert and Ripper watermarked letters are due to their measurements. For example, the Openshaw letter with the *A Pirie & Sons* watermark is from the same batch as a November 22 *A Pirie & Sons* Ripper letter mailed from London. But it's not from the same batch as another November 22 *A Pirie & Sons* letter the Ripper claims he mailed from Manchester. Clearly he had paper on hand from different batches of *A Pirie & Sons* stationery when he wrote the two November 22 letters— unless one wishes to make the case that there were different individuals who just happened to write Ripper letters on *A Pirie & Sons* stationery on the same day.

In some instances, differences in measurements might be due to conservation. When heat was used to apply a protective plasticized membrane as was done at The National Archives, the paper might have shrunk slightly. Differences also can be explained by reorders from the stationer. During the late 1880s, personalized stationery was usually purchased in a quire of twenty-four sheets that included unprinted second sheets. A reorder of the same personalized stationery on the same type of paper with the same watermark could come from a different batch. Or perhaps the stationer used a different standard size such as Post Quarto, which was approximately 7 by 9 inches. Or Commercial Note, which was 8 by 5 inches. Or Octavo Note, which was nominally 7 by 4 ½ inches.

An example of a discrepancy in paper size is a Ripper letter with a *Joynson Superfine* watermark that was sent to the City of London Police. The torn half of the folded stationery measures 6 ¹⁵⁄₁₆ inches by 9 ⁹⁄₁₀ inches. Another Ripper letter on the same type of paper with the same watermark was sent to the Metropolitan Police, and that stationery is Commercial Note or 8 by 5 inches.

A Sickert letter written on paper with a *Monckton's Superfine* watermark measures 7 ⅛ inches by 9 inches, and a Ripper letter with that same watermark sent to the City of London Police measures 7 ⅛ inches by 8 ⁹⁄₁₀ inches. Most likely this suggests that the *Monckton's Superfine* stationery is from different paper batches. But this by no means indicates that it was from different Ripper letter writers. Bower says that after a lifetime of studying artists' paper, he "would expect to find variations like this." But he also made stunning paper matches that have no variations at all, and statistically it's almost impossible to dismiss this as coincidence.

Two Ripper letters written to the Metropolitan Police and one Ripper letter written to the City of London Police are on matching cheap pale-blue paper. For three letters to come from the same batch of paper strongly indicates that the same person wrote them. After the initial publication of this book in 2002, there were other absolute matches when Anna Robins discovered a small number of Sickert letters at the Getty Research Institute in Santa Monica, California. I went to see them and was frustrated that I wasn't allowed to take photographs. So I did the next best thing.

Putting on white cotton gloves, armed with pencils and a notebook, I made measurements of the stationery. I described watermarks and the paper, drawing what I saw and sending the information to Bower. He called to let me know rather excitedly that the stationery with the watermark *Gurney Ivory Laid* may be crucially important. He was sufficiently convinced to travel from London to the Getty so he could examine the original letters himself. What he ultimately confirmed is that two Sickert letters at the Getty were written on his mother, Nelly Sickert's, *Gurney Ivory Laid* stationery. They match a third Sickert letter Bower discovered at the British Library (circa 1890), written to a woman named Miss E. Case, who had invited Sickert and his first wife, Ellen, to a social gathering. The three sheets of stationery exactly match two pieces of paper Ripper letters were written on.

Gurney Ivory Laid was manufactured in relatively small runs, and Bower explained that the paper was roughly guillotined to size and then folded and divided into quires of twenty-four sheets. Each individual quire of paper was then given a final trim in a hand-fed guillotine. Every guillotining would produce slightly different trims. The match between the short-edge cuts of these five Sickert/Ripper letters shows they came from the same quire of paper or group of twenty-four sheets. This is extremely compelling. It's not exactly what some people had in mind when they decided that Bower should be brought in as a devil's advocate.

His conclusions are based on a multitude of other details including: the fibers used to make the paper; the way these fibers were processed; the wire profile of the forming surface; the weight, bulk and opacity of the sheet; the surface finish. "One can only assert that two sheets come from the same batch if everything matches," Bower concluded, and they do in these five critically important Sickert/Ripper documents that I list here:

- Ripper letter received by the City of London Police on October 4, 1888, which has doodles and three cartoonish faces on it (London Metropolitan Archives: CLA/048/ CS/02/380)

- Ripper letter postmarked October 31, 1888 ("Dear Boss, I am living 129 C Rd . . .") (The National Archives: MEPO 3/142 ff. 508-509)

- Sickert letter to D. C. Thomson (undated) written from 12 Pembroke Gardens (Getty)

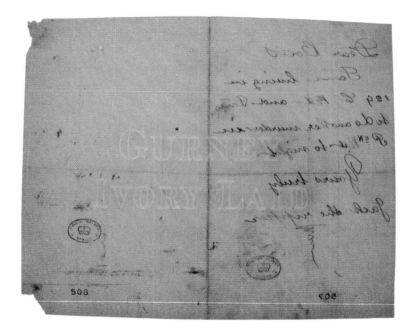

Above: A Ripper letter postmarked October 31, 1888, with the *Gurney Ivory Laid* water-mark. *Below:* Ripper letter received by the City of London Police on October 4, 1888, with the Gurney Ivory Laid watermark. (London Metropolitan Archives)

- Sickert letter to D. C. Thomson (undated) written from 12 Pembroke Gardens (Getty)

- Sickert letter to Miss Case (undated but possibly circa 1890) written from 12 Pembroke Gardens (British Library Department of Manuscripts: Add.50956 f.109)

As Peter Bower's paper investigation continued, he came up with even more evidence that strongly suggests Sickert wrote a number of Ripper letters. Five of them catalogued in the "Whitechapel Murders" file at the London Metropolitan Archives were signed "Nemo." As I've pointed out, Sickert's stage name when he was an actor was "Mr. Nemo." The dates of these Nemo letters are October 2, 1888; December 9, 1888; January 22, 1889; January 29, 1889; and February 16, 1889. Two of them were written on *Joynson Superfine* paper.

After more than fifteen years of research to date, I'm convinced that Jack the Ripper didn't always sign his communications with his various versions of the Ripper name. In some instances the signature seems to depend on the content and intended recipient. Many of these documents that aren't signed "Jack the Ripper" are supposed to seem helpful to the investigation. But they strongly hint of mockery and attempts to manipulate police into following through with rather ludicrous suggestions. Since these letters aren't obviously from Jack the Ripper, one might wonder how many others were tossed out. One might wonder just how many letters the Ripper wrote using a variety of names, and the answer I suspect would be staggering. The paper matches likely would be overwhelming if we had the benefit of examining all documents created by Sickert and the Ripper. We have but a shard, a fragment. Here is a sampling of other definite and probable paper matches that would be significant evidence in court today:

- Two Nemo letters that probably match a letter Sickert wrote on *Joynson Superfine* stationery to art dealer D. C. Thomson (circa 1890; Getty Research Institute)

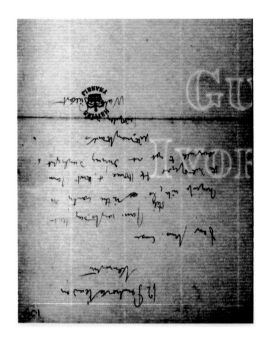

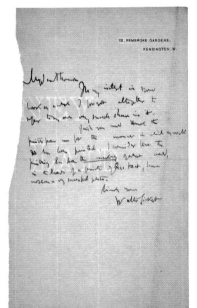
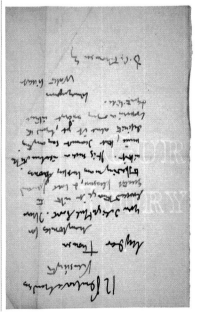

Above: Sickert sent this undated letter to Miss Case from 12 Pembroke Gardens, on another piece of *Gurney Ivory Laid* paper. *Below:* Sickert wrote these two undated letters to D. C. Thomson while living at 12 Pembroke Gardens. Note the *Gurney Ivory Laid* watermarks.

- One Nemo letter that definitely matches a letter on *Joynson Superfine* Sickert wrote to his friend William Rothenstein (Harvard)

- One music hall drawing on paper with a partial *Brookleigh Fine* watermark (1888; Walker Art Gallery) that probably matches two Ripper letters (The National Archives)

- One Sickert letter with the *Monckton's Superfine* watermark (Sickert Archives) that probably matches a Ripper letter (London Metropolitan Archives)

Trade directories list some nearly 1,200 different watermarks in use in the late 1880s, with some papermakers producing over a hundred different varieties. When one considers this vast number of differently watermarked papers available in London, it's hard to believe it's mere chance that the same small groups of paper occurred again and again in Sickert and Ripper letters. One manufacturer alone, Peter Bower explained, might have had as many as one hundred different watermark designs available to stationers. To find so many matches and probable matches in the Ripper case makes the statistical probability extremely strong that the letters came from a single source.

No documents or fine art were destroyed or even damaged during my investigation. It's important I clear this up, as there have been so many stubborn claims to the contrary. In fact, in 2001, I was publicly called "monstrously stupid" for supposedly ripping up the Walter Sickert painting *Broadstairs*.

"I can't believe she has done this," said art historian Richard Shone (*The Guardian*, December 8, 2001). "It all sounds monstrously stupid to me."

In a letter to the editor for *The Sunday Telegraph* on December 8, 2002, Bernard Dunstan wrote: "Patricia Cornwell says that she 'knows' that Walter Sickert was Jack the Ripper, and has cut up one of his pictures to help prove her point—oblivious, apparently, of the fact that he was perhaps the finest English artist of the last century. . . . I suppose Miss Cornwell has to be allowed her theories but I do hope she does not find it necessary to cut up any more paintings."

Sickert biographer Matthew Sturgis claims I spent "millions buying up (if not cutting up) Sickert pictures, letters, and related artifacts." The suggestion that I ripped up any art, letters or anything at all is reckless and patently false. No acts of vandalism in the name of science or otherwise ever happened. Scientists meticulously swabbed the backs of envelopes and stamps, and any forensic light sources used were nondestructive. During our examination of Sickert art, nothing was damaged or cut including the painting *Broadstairs*, which was dry rotted and had been improperly packaged, as it turned out. The painting was transported from London to the Virginia crime labs in 2001, and the canvas arrived with a large hole punched in it.

The genesis of this misunderstanding about my handling of historic documents and fine art was an ABC *Primetime Live* television documentary about my Ripper investigation. Unfortunately, the scripted narration incorrectly implied that forensic scientists and I cut up Sickert art while looking for evidence. I don't think the misinformation was intentional. The film crew was rolling their cameras as we were examining Ripper-related materials in the Richmond-based labs, and apparently it was assumed the damage to the painting *Broadstairs* was due to some sort of scientific extraction. Had that been true, it would have been senseless.

What we were looking for when we examined Sickert art in Virginia and years later at Harvard's Fogg Museum was any indication there might be images beneath the painting not visible to the unaided eye. To accomplish this we used infrared (IR) light, and we did find some images that were curious at least. We were looking for fingerprints on the edges and backs of canvases. We were interested in the types of paint Sickert used. We wondered if blood might have been mixed in but we never actually checked for it. To do so would have indeed required damaging art, and there wasn't sufficient cause to start punching out even tiny holes in valuable paintings for DNA analysis.

On January 7, 2002, I addressed my alleged monstrous stupidity in a five-page handwritten letter to John Lessore, the nephew of Sickert's

Sickert's *Broadstairs* was damaged en route to the Virginia crime labs in 2001, as can be seen in frames from video footage that captured Patricia and her team unwrapping the painting from its shipping materials.

third wife, Thérèse Lessore. John Lessore had written to me first. He was unhappy for a number of reasons, not the least of which was what he'd heard about my supposedly destroying a painting.

I replied to him:

> Let me say that it is patently false that I destroyed a Sickert painting. In fact, the painting in question was sold to me . . .

for some 27,000 [pounds] and flown by private jet back to the U.S. When it was unwrapped we were horrified to find a large hole punched through the middle of it. This painting did go to the labs but was only examined by non-destructive light sources. . . . What you should know however is that I would not hesitate to "cut up" a Sickert or anything else if it was the only way to expose a terrible crime and ensure justice. No work of art is worth as much as a human life.

20

A MAN IN ORDINARY LIFE

ON OCTOBER 4, 1888, *The Times* published a letter to the editor that was signed "Nemo." Unlike the Nemo letters sent to the police, this one supposedly was from a concerned citizen, and in it the writer described "mutilations, cutting off the nose and ears, ripping up the body, and cutting out certain organs—the heart, & c.—"

It's curious that Nemo mentioned the removal of a heart. As far as we know the Ripper had yet to take the heart from any of his victims.

The writer who called himself Nemo goes on to say:

> *Unless caught red-handed, such a man in ordinary life would be harmless enough, polite, not to say obsequious, in his manners, and about the last a British policeman would suspect.*
>
> *But when the villain is primed with his opium, or bang, or gin, and inspired with his lust for slaughter and blood, he would destroy his defenceless victim with the ferocity and cunning of the tiger; and past impunity and success would only have rendered him the more daring and restless.*
>
> *Your obedient servant*
> *October 2 NEMO*

Other unusual signatories in the Ripper letters at the London Metropolitan Archives are suspiciously reminiscent of some at The National Archives: "Justitia," "Revelation," "Ripper," "Nemesis," "A Thinker," "Maybee," "A friend," "an accessary" and "one that has had his eyes opened." Quite a number of these were written in October 1888, and also include art and comments similar to those found in Ripper letters at The National Archives. For example, in a letter to the editor of the *Daily News Office*, October 1, 1888, the Ripper says, "I've got someone to write this for me." In an undated letter at the London Metropolitan Archives, the anonymous sender says, "I've got someone to write this for me."

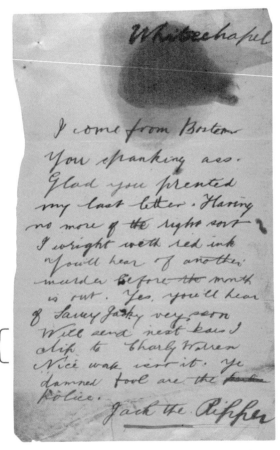

The author of this letter announces that he will "send next ears I clip to Charly Warren."

Other "Whitechapel Murder" letters in the City of London archives include a postcard dated October 3, with the anonymous sender using many of the same threats, words and phrases found in Ripper letters in Kew: "send you my victims ears," "It amuses me that you think I am mad," "Just a card to let you know," "I will write to you again soon" and "My bloody ink is running out."

On October 6, 1888, "Anonymous" offers a suggestion that the killer might be keeping "the victims *silent* by pressure on certain nerves in the neck." This writer adds that an additional benefit if the killer subdues his victim is that he can "preserve his own person and clothing comparatively unstained." In October 1888, an anonymous letter written in red ink uses the terms "spanking ass" and "Saucy Jacky" and promises to "send next ears I clip to Charly Warren."

Another riddle found in the London Metropolitan Archives is an undated letter that includes a bit of newspaper attached by a rusty paper clip. When removed what's revealed on the clipping's verso is the phrase "author of works of art." In a letter dated October 7, 1888, the writer signs his name "Homo Sum," Latin for "I am a man." In a July 1889 letter, the writer signs his letter "Qui Vir," Latin for "Which Man." In a letter Sickert wrote in 1897, he sarcastically and irreverently refers to his former "impish master" Whistler as "Ecce homo" or "Behold the man." In the "Qui Vir" letter, the writer suggests that the killer is "able to choose a time to do the murder & get back to his hiding place."

Approximately 20 percent of these London Metropolitan Archives letters have watermarks, including *Joynson Superfine* and *Monckton's Superfine*. A letter Sickert wrote to Whistler in the mid to late 1880s also has a *Monckton's Superfine* watermark. While I wouldn't begin to claim that all of the anonymous letters were written by the Ripper, some of them fit the profile of a violent psychopath who taunts police and inserts himself into the investigation.

Watermarks and language aside, the problem of handwriting remains a hot debate. I've heard countless times that it's impossible for one person to write in so many different hands. This isn't necessarily true. Peter Bower says he has seen "good calligraphers" who can write in an incredible number of different hands but "it takes extraordinary skill." His wife, Sally, is a much-respected letterer, an expert in how a person forms the letters strung together in words. When she looked through Ripper letters, she connected a number of them by how the hand made the writing or how the words were formed. There's no reason to doubt that Sickert had an amazing ability to alter his handwriting. For him it would be just another form of drawing.

In a letter he wrote to artist Sir William Eden, Sickert mentions a woman named Janon who couldn't read his handwriting. "I have written again in a copperplate hand," Sickert says. As a skilled draftsman, an artist, he was capable of a variety of styles of writing including writing backward, as is evident on a number of his etchings. For his signature not to be reversed on the print, he had to etch a mirror image of it on the copper plate. Typical of Sickert's many personas and disguises, his handwriting and signature in his correspondence is inconsistent and at times unrecognizable. In some instances Sickert's *T*'s, *S*'s and *W*'s are formed in so many different ways it's hard to believe the same person wrote them.

"I can write 5 hand writings," the Ripper boasts in a letter on October 19, 1888. "You can't trace me by this writing," he brags in another letter on November 10. He clearly didn't fear that the police would notice

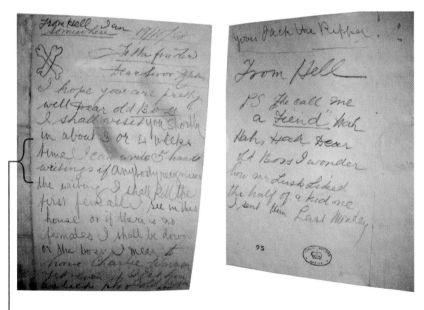

The Ripper brags, "I can write 5 hand writings."

or question the artwork in his mocking, violent, obscene letters or detect subtle similarities in disguised handwriting. Or perhaps he assumed that even if a shrewd investigator like Abberline zeroed in on the uniqueness of some of the Ripper letters, the path would never lead to 54 Broadhurst Gardens. After all, the police were "idiots." Most people were stupid and boring. Sickert often said as much. "I think the future, my Billy, is ours. *No one* else has *any* intelligence at all!" he writes Rothenstein (circa late 1890s).

Few people were as brilliant, clever, cunning or fascinating as Walter Sickert. Few people were as enigmatic, self-centered and vain. He just might not show up at dinners and other gatherings if he wasn't going to be the center of attention. He didn't hesitate to admit that he was a "snob" and divided the world into two classes of people: those who interested him and those who didn't. As is typical of psychopaths, Sickert believed that no investigator could touch him. His delusional thinking lured him into leaving far more incriminating clues than he ever imagined.

The distant locations associated with a number of Ripper letters would have reinforced the assumption that most of them were hoaxes. Police had no reason to believe that this East End murderer might be in one city one day and in another the next. No one seemed interested in considering that perhaps the Ripper moved around. It likely didn't dawn on anyone that there might be a link between cities that were on Henry Irving's theater company's schedule, which was published daily in the newspapers.

Every spring and fall Irving's company toured the major theater cities of Glasgow, Edinburgh, Manchester, Liverpool, Bradford, Leeds, Nottingham, Newcastle and Plymouth, to list a few. Often actress Ellen Terry made the grueling journeys. "I shall be in a railway train from Newcastle to Leeds," she dismally reports in a letter written during one of these tours, and one can feel her exhaustion. As I've mentioned, before his apprenticeship with Whistler, Sickert had toured with Henry Irving's company.

Most of these theater cities also had major racecourses, and several Ripper letters mention horse racing and offer the police a few lucky betting tips. Sickert painted pictures of horse racing and was quite knowledge- able about the sport. In the March 19, 1914, *The New Age* literary journal, he published an article he titled "A Stone Ginger," which is racing slang for an absolute certainty. He tossed in a few other bits of racing slang for good measure: "welsher" and "racecourse thief" and "sporting touts." Racecourses would have been a venue where Sickert could disappear into the crowd, especially if he was wearing one of his disguises and the race was in a city where he wasn't likely to encounter anybody he knew. At the races, prostitutes were plentiful, and those who lived in the area would have been accustomed to vast crowds of strangers showing up on race days.

In a December letter (circa 1892) to arts patron and civil servant Edward Marsh, Sickert mentioned he'd just been to the Ascot Racecourse in Windsor, where he found "the Guards officers standing around in the pride of their scarlet uniform." He described the women as magnificent and athletic looking as they talked of "bay mares and steppers." Horseracing, gambling in casinos, and boxing were interests of Sickert's although very little has been written about them in the books and articles I've seen.

I have no evidence that he bet on horseraces, but I'm not aware of anything that proves he didn't. Gambling may have been a secret addiction. It could help explain how he managed to go through money so quickly. By the time he and the parsimonious Ellen divorced, she was financially crippled and would never recover. Sickert's organized brain seemed to fail him when it came to money. He thought nothing of hiring a cab and leaving it sitting all day. He gave away armfuls of paintings or let them rot in his studios. He rented numerous rooms at a time, bought painting supplies and stationery, read multiple newspapers daily and must have had quite a wardrobe of costumes or disguises. It wasn't without expense to frequent the theaters and music halls. He also moved around quite a bit, although it isn't likely he went for the best seats in the house or traveled first class. After their divorce, Ellen wrote, "To give him money is like giving it to a child to light a fire with."

She began conspiring to buy his paintings through Jacques-Émile Blanche. He would purchase them, and she secretly reimbursed him. Sickert "must *never never* suspect that it comes from me," she writes Blanche. "I shall tell no one," she adds. Apparently Ellen kept their secret even from her sister Janie in whom she'd always confided. Ellen knew what Janie thought of Sickert and his exploitative ways, and Ellen also knew that helping her former husband financially wasn't really helping him. No matter how much he got, it would never be enough. But she couldn't seem to help herself when it came to helping him. Ellen Cobden Sickert was the classic enabler.

"He is never out of my mind day or night," she writes Blanche in 1899. "You know what he is like—a child where money is concerned. Will you again be as kind as you were before & buy one of Walter's pictures at the right moment to be of most use to him? And will you not forget that this will be of no good unless you insist on arranging how the money is to be spent. He borrowed £600 from his brother in law (who is a poor man) & he ought to pay him interest on the sum. *But I cannot.*"

Addiction to drugs and alcohol ran in Sickert's family. He likely had an addictive predisposition, and it could explain why he avoided alcohol in his younger years and then abused it later on. Maybe he also had a gambling problem. Whatever the truth, money seemed to vanish when he touched it. Yet he managed to live his life as he pleased, funded by his women. His career didn't require him to keep regular hours, and

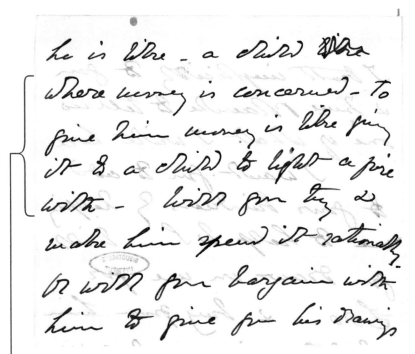

In a never-before-published letter written after the divorce, Sickert's ex-wife, Ellen, writes, "To give him money is like giving it to a child to light a fire with."

he didn't have to account to anyone, especially once his apprenticeship with Whistler had ended. In the late summer of 1888, the celebrated but cantankerous American artist was in France on his honeymoon, and Sickert was no longer bound to do as the master demanded. Ellen and Janie were away in Ireland much of October, not that Ellen needed to be away for Sickert to vanish for a night or a week. Disappearing in Great Britain was relatively easy as long as the trains were running. It was no great matter to cross the English Channel in the morning and have dinner in France that evening.

Whatever caused his chronic "financial muddle," to borrow Ellen's words, it was serious enough to push her to the extraordinary lengths of secretly funneling money his way after she divorced him for adultery and desertion. Sickert's financial irresponsibility was serious and chronic. When he died in 1942 he had only £135 to his name.

21

STYGIAN BLACKNESS

IVE HOURS AFTER Annie Chapman's body was carried inside the Whitechapel mortuary, Dr. George Bagster Phillips arrived and discovered she'd been stripped and washed. Furious, he demanded an explanation.

Robert Mann, the mortuary supervisor who had caused so much trouble in Mary Ann Nichols's case, replied that workhouse authorities had instructed two nurses to undress and clean the body. No police or doctors had witnessed this, and as the angry Dr. Phillips looked around the mortuary, he noticed Annie's clothing piled on the floor in a corner. Obviously Mann had ignored the doctor's earlier directive that the body wasn't to be touched by inmates, nurses or anyone else unless the police instructed otherwise. Mann didn't care. He'd heard it all before.

DR PHILLIPS

Dr. Phillips examined bodies in the Whitechapel mortuary, including that of Annie Chapman.

The mortuary was nothing more than a cramped, filthy, stinking shed with a scarred wooden table darkened by old blood. In the summer it was stuffy and warm. In the winter it was so cold Mann could barely bend his fingers. What a job his was, Mann must have thought, and maybe Dr. Phillips should have been grateful that two nurses had saved him some trouble. Besides, it didn't take a doctor to see what had killed the poor woman. Her head was barely attached to her neck and she'd been gutted like a hog hanging in a butcher's shop. Mann didn't pay much attention as Dr. Phillips continued to vent his disgust, complaining that his working conditions were unsuitable and dangerous to his health. It was a point the doctor would elaborate on during the inquest, and Coroner Wynne Baxter agreed.

He announced to jurors and the press it was a travesty that there was no proper mortuary in the East End. He said if any place needed an adequate facility for handling the dead it was this impoverished area of the Great Metropolis. In nearby Wapping, bodies recovered from the Thames had "to be put in boxes" for lack of anywhere else to take them, he pointed out. There used to be a mortuary in Whitechapel but it was destroyed when a new road was put in, and for one reason or another London officials hadn't gotten around to building a new facility to take care of the dead.

Details of the inquest reveal that by the time Dr. Phillips began his examination of Annie Chapman's body it was in full rigor mortis, which would have been slower to form because of the cool temperature. His estimate that she had been dead two or three hours by the time she was found may have been reasonably accurate. But he was misinformed to conclude that the small amount of food in her stomach and the absence of liquid meant she was sober when she died. Without testing body fluids such as blood, urine and the vitreous humor of the eye it wasn't possible to know such a thing. Her lungs and brain showed signs of advanced "disease," but he didn't specify. Despite her obesity she was malnourished, he testified.

The cuts to her neck were on the "left side of the spine" and were parallel and separated by approximately half an inch. The killer had attempted to disarticulate the vertebrae, indicating great force and a possible attempt at decapitation, Dr. Phillips decided. Since the cuts were deepest on the left side and trailed off to the right, he went on to say that her assailant was holding the knife in his right hand, assuming he attacked her from behind. He concluded that death was caused by compromised respiration and a dramatic drop in blood pressure.

A qualified forensic pathologist would clarify that blood pressure drops when anyone is dying. This is a symptom of death and not the cause of it. Breathing stops, the heart stops, digestion stops, brain waves go flat. Saying a person died of cardiac or respiratory arrest or syncope is like saying a person's blindness is due to his not being able to see. A more accurate description would have been that Annie's death was caused by either exsanguination or an air embolism due to cutting injuries of the neck.

During her inquest, a juror interrupted Dr. Phillips to ask him if he'd taken a photograph of her eyes. Maybe her retinas captured the image of her killer. He answered that he hadn't looked. Maybe he didn't assume the notion was silly. He abruptly concluded his testimony by telling Coroner Baxter that the details given were sufficient to account for the victim's death. To describe anything further would "only be painful to the feelings of the jury and the public." Of course, he added, "I bow to your decision."

Baxter wasn't of the same opinion. "However painful it may be," he replied, "it is necessary in the interests of justice" that the details of Annie Chapman's murder be given. Dr. Phillips countered, "When I come to speak of the wounds on the lower part of the body I must again repeat my opinion that it is highly injudicious to make the results of my examination public. These details are fit only for yourself, sir, and the jury, but to make them public would simply be disgusting." Coroner Baxter asked all ladies and boys to leave the crowded room. He added that he'd "never before heard of any evidence requested being kept back."

Dr. Phillips didn't waver. He repeatedly requested that the coroner spare the public any further details. The doctor's requests were denied and he was given no choice but to reveal all he knew about the mutilation of Annie Chapman's body, and the organs and tissue the killer had taken. He testified that had he been the murderer, he couldn't possibly have inflicted such injuries in less than fifteen minutes. To cause such damage with deliberation and skill would have taken "the better part of an hour."

The more information Dr. Phillips was forced to divulge, the farther off course he drifted. He reemphasized the illogical assertion that Mary

Ann Nichols's abdomen was slashed first and then her throat. He then went on to say that the motive for Annie Chapman's murder was the taking of the "body parts." He added that the killer must possess anatomical knowledge and possibly was associated with a profession that exposed him to dissection or surgery. Next the suggestion of using bloodhounds came up and Dr. Phillips suggested this might not be helpful since the blood belonged to the victim and not the killer. It didn't seem to occur to him or perhaps to anyone else at the inquest that bloodhounds aren't called bloodhounds because they're capable of picking up the scent of blood.

The conflicting witness statements weren't resolved during the inquest and never have been since. If Annie was murdered as late as 5:30 a.m. then according to that day's weather report she was attacked shortly before the sun began to rise. It would be incredibly risky to grab a victim in a populated area, cut her throat and disembowel her just before sunrise, especially on a market day when people would be out early.

Perhaps the most plausible scenario was suggested by the foreman of the coroner's jury. He offered that when John Richardson sat on the steps to trim his boot, the back door was open and blocked his view of Annie's body. Richardson admitted he didn't go into the yard but he couldn't say with certainty that the body wasn't there while he was trimming his boot. He didn't think so. But it was still dark when he stopped by his mother's house. His interest was in the cellar door and his boot, not in the space between the back of the house and the fence.

It's difficult to accept Elizabeth Long's claim that she saw a woman talking with a man at 5:30 a.m. and was certain the woman was Annie Chapman. If this is true, then Annie was murdered and mutilated at dawn and had been dead less than half an hour when her body was discovered. Elizabeth told the police she didn't get a good look at the man and wouldn't recognize him if she saw him again. But she described him as wearing a brown deerstalker and perhaps a dark coat. He was a "little" taller than Annie, which would have made him quite short since she was only five feet tall. He appeared to be a "foreigner," had a "shabby, genteel" appearance and was more than forty years old. This is quite a lot of detail for Elizabeth to have observed as she walked past two strangers in the predawn dark. Prostitutes and their clients frequented the area, and more than likely Elizabeth Long knew to keep to her own business. She might not have paused to stare. If she thought the conversation between the man and woman was friendly she might not have been inclined to take much notice anyway.

The truth is we don't know how reliable any of these witnesses were. It was a cool, misty morning. London was polluted. The sun wasn't up yet. How good was Elizabeth's eyesight? How well did Richardson see? Corrective lenses were luxuries to the poor. What can be stated with reasonable certainty about Annie Chapman's murder, however, is she wasn't "suffocated" or strangled into unconsciousness. Otherwise she should have had fresh bruises on her neck. It may be that her face appeared "swollen" because it was fleshy and puffy. Her tongue might have seemed to protrude because she was missing her front teeth.

Coroner Baxter concluded the inquest with his belief that "we are confronted with a murderer of no ordinary character, [whose crimes are] committed not from jealousy, revenge, or robbery, but from motives less adequate than the many which still disgrace our civilization, mar our progress, and blot the pages of our Christianity." The jury returned the verdict of "Murder against a person or persons unknown."

Three days later, on Tuesday afternoon, a young girl named Laura Sickings noticed strange "marks" in the yard behind 25 Hanbury Street, very close to where Annie Chapman was killed. The girl immediately found a policeman, and it was decided the marks were dried blood that formed a trail five or six feet long leading toward the back door of another decaying house overcrowded with lodgers.

Police concluded that the Ripper left the blood as he passed through or over the fence separating the yards. Perhaps in an attempt to remove some of the blood from his coat, he'd taken it off and knocked it against the back wall of number 25. This might explain a bloody smear and a "sprinkle." Police then found a blood-saturated piece of crumpled paper that they believed the Ripper used to wipe his hands before fleeing the crime scene the same way he'd entered it.

In an interview given to *The Star*, Inspector Joseph Chandler decided that the "sprinkle" was urine. If nothing else his conclusion continues to make the point that at the time there really was no such thing as forensic science in police investigations. It also didn't seem to be seriously considered that someone as calculating and meticulous as the Ripper would have familiarized himself with the best route for a safe escape. It's doubtful he left the scene by climbing over rickety, haphazardly spaced palings separating the yards. Had he done so, he most likely would have smeared blood on the boards or broken a few. It would make more sense for him to exit the scene the same way he'd entered it, passing through the house and emerging back onto the street.

From there he could have woven in and out of doors and passages of "Stygian blackness, into which no lamp shone where a murderer might, if possessed of coolness, easily pass unobserved," as one reporter described the area. Along Hanbury Street, doors were unlocked. Weathered palings enclosed yards and "waste grounds" where houses had been demolished. Even if the Ripper was spotted, as long as he wasn't acting in a way that aroused suspicion he would have been just one more shadowy figure, especially if he'd dressed to fit the surroundings. He may even have bid a stranger good morning.

It's possible the "patches" of closely clustered blood droplets noticed on the wall not far above her head were cast-off spatter from the weapon. Each time the Ripper slashed her body and drew back the knife to slash again, blood flew off the blade. Since we don't know the number, shape and size of the blood droplets we can't determine if she was upright or on the ground when her throat was cut. But it would make sense that she was standing when that happened, and once she was down and on her back, the Ripper inflicted the deep cuts to her abdomen. It's likely the attack was swift. It's possible that whoever she was seen with wasn't the person who murdered her.

The Ripper may have been in the habit of watching prostitutes with their clients before moving in for the kill. He may have watched Annie in the past and been aware that she and other prostitutes used the backyards of 29 Hanbury and neighboring houses for "immoral" purposes. He may have been watching her the morning he murdered her. "Peeping" at people dressing or undressing or engaging in sex is consistent in a lust murderer's history. Violent psychopaths are voyeurs. They stalk, spy and fantasize, and watching a prostitute sexually service a client could have been the Ripper's foreplay. He might have approached Annie Chapman immediately after her last customer left. He might have solicited sex from her, gotten her to turn her back to him and then attacked.

Or he might have appeared out of the dark, grabbed her from behind and jerked back her head by her chin, explaining the bruises discovered on her jaw. The cuts to her throat severed her windpipe. She wouldn't have been able to speak as she aspirated her own blood. Within seconds her killer could have had her on the ground, shoving up her clothing to slice open her abdomen. It takes no time or skill to disembowel someone. It doesn't take a forensic pathologist or surgeon to find the uterus, ovaries and other internal organs.

Much has been made of Jack the Ripper's alleged surgical skills. It doesn't seem to occur to people even today that it requires no medical training to hack out a uterus and part of the belly wall including the navel, the upper part of the vagina and the greater part of the bladder. But Dr. Phillips was sure that the Ripper must have had some knowledge of anatomy and surgical procedures. He went on to surmise that the Ripper may have used a "small amputating knife or a well ground slaughterman's knife, narrow & thin, sharp" and six to eight inches in length.

Sickert didn't need exposure to surgery or internal medicine to know a thing or two about the female pelvic organs. The upper end of the vagina is attached to the uterus, which is distinctly shaped like a lightbulb, and in front of the vagina is the bladder. Assuming the uterus was the trophy Sickert sought, he simply removed it in the dark and took the surrounding tissue with it. This isn't "surgery." It's expediency. It's a frenzied slash and grab in the dark. One can assume he knew the anatomical location of the vagina or various organs. But if he didn't, there were plenty of surgical books available at the time.

As early as 1872 Gray's *Anatomy* was already in its sixth edition, offering detailed diagrams of the "organs of digestion" and "female organs of generation." Sickert had suffered permanent life-altering debilitation from surgeries. He had good reason to have an interest in anatomy, especially the

138

phalaux of ring finger, distinct marking of ring or rings, probably the latter :- on proximal phalaux of same finger. The following parts were missing :- part of belly wall including navel; the womb; the upper part of vagina & greater part of bladder. The Dr gives it as his opinion that the murderer was possessed of anatomical knowledge from the manner of removal of viscera, & that the knife used was not an ordinary knife, but such as a small amputating knife, or a well ground slaughterman's knife, narrow & thin, sharp & blade of six to eight inches in length.

9th Sept. The body was identified as that of Annie Chapman, by John Donovan, 35 Dorset Street, Spitalfields, lodging house keeper, where she had resided & also by her brother Mr Fontin Smith 44 Bartholomew Close E.C.

The

"*...& that the knife used was not even an ordinary knife, but such as a small amputating knife, or a well ground slaughterman's knife, narrow & thin, sharp & blade of six to eight inches in length.*"

Dr. Phillips decided that the Ripper was knowledgeable about anatomy and surgery and used an amputation knife to commit murder.

anatomy of the female genitalia and reproductive organs. I would expect a man of his curiosity, intelligence and obsessiveness to have looked at Gray's. He may have perused Charles Bell's *Illustrations of the Great Operations of Surgery* (1821) with its graphic color plates prepared by Thomas Landseer, brother of the Victorian painter Edwin Landseer, whose work Sickert would have known.

It wouldn't have been hard to get one's hands on Carl Rokitansky's *A Manual of Pathological Anatomy*, volumes 1–4 (1849–54), or George Viner Ellis's *Illustrations of Dissections* with life-size color plates (1867) or James Hope's *Principles and Illustrations of Morbid Anatomy*, with its *Complete Series of Coloured Lithographic Drawings* (1834). Had Sickert any doubt as to the location or anatomical shape of the uterus or any other organ, he had a number of ways to educate himself. He may have taken anatomy classes in art school.

Annie Chapman's intestines were pulled out and tossed aside as the Ripper groped in the dark for her uterus. Trophies or souvenirs bring back memories. They're a catalyst for fantasies. The taking of them is so typical as to be expected in violent psychopathic crimes. Sickert was far too smart to keep any incriminating souvenir where someone could have found it. But he had his secret rooms. One might wonder if experiences from his childhood caused him to be drawn to dreadful places similar to those described in a poem his father wrote:

What an uncanny/eerie feeling when I am within your walls,
those high, naked, pale walls, how terrible they are,
they remind me of the old-fashioned guard rooms . . .

Does not one, here and there, pile up
overcoats and caput, long coats, wintercoats
and does not one carry all kinds of
garbage into the room . . .

In a September 1889 letter, the Ripper jots his return address as "Jack the rippers hole." Sickert could have kept whatever he wanted in his secret hovels. It's impossible to know what he did with his morbid detritus, but body parts would have begun to decompose and stink unless he chemically preserved them. In another letter, the Ripper writes of cutting off a victim's ear and feeding it to a dog. He also mentions frying organs and eating

POLICE NOTICE.

TO THE OCCUPIER.

On the mornings of Friday, 31st August, Saturday 8th, and Sunday, 30th September, 1888, Women were murdered in or near Whitechapel, supposed by some one residing in the immediate neighbourhood. Should you know of any person to whom suspicion is attached, you are earnestly requested to communicate at once with the nearest Police Station.

Metropolitan Police Office,
30th September, 1888.

Printed by M'Corquodale & Co. Limited, " The Armoury," Southwark.

A public statement was issued to Whitechapel residents asking anyone with information about the murders to come forward.

them. Sickert might have been inordinately curious about the female reproductive system that had given birth to his malformed anus or penis or both. He couldn't study organs in the dark while eluding police. Perhaps he took prizes from the slaughter back to his lair and studied them there.

After Annie Chapman's murder the relatives who had avoided her in life made funeral arrangements. At seven o'clock on Friday morning, September 14, a hearse appeared at the Whitechapel mortuary to take her away clandestinely. There was no procession of coaches for fear of drawing attention, and she was buried at Manor Park Cemetery, seven miles northeast of where she was slain. The weather had taken a dramatic turn for the better. The temperature was sixty degrees and the sun shone all day.

During the week following her death, businessmen in the East End formed a vigilance committee chaired by George Lusk, a local builder and contractor and member of the Metropolitan Board of Works. The committee issued the following public statement: "Finding that, in spite of the murders being committed in our midst our police force is inadequate to discover the author or authors of the latest atrocities, we the undersigned have formed ourselves into a committee and intend offering a substantial reward to anyone, citizen or otherwise, who shall give such information as will be the means of bringing the murderer or murderers to justice."

A Member of Parliament offered to donate one hundred pounds to the reward fund, and citizens were willing to help. However, Metropolitan Police documents note that such generous gestures weren't appropriate or supported by the authorities. The practice of offering rewards had been abolished some time ago because all it did was encourage people to "discover" misleading evidence or to manufacture it and "give rise to meddling and gossip without end."

Resentment and unruly behavior rose to a new high in the East End. People caroused at 29 Hanbury Street, gawking, even laughing and joking while the rest of London fell into a "kind of stupor," said *The Times*. The crimes were "beyond the ghastliest efforts of fiction," even worse than Edgar Allan Poe's *Murders in the Rue Morgue*, and "nothing in fact or fiction equals these outrages at once in their horrible nature and in the effect which they have produced upon the popular imagination."

22

THE STREETS UNTIL DAWN

ATTI'S HUNGERFORD PALACE OF VARIETIES was one of the most vulgar music halls in London. It was Sickert's favorite haunt the first eight months of 1888, and he went there several nights a week.

Built into a 250-foot-wide arch underneath the South Eastern Railway near Charing Cross Station, Gatti's could seat six hundred. On some nights as many as a thousand rowdy spectators crowded in for hours of drinking, smoking and sexually charged entertainment. The popular Katie Lawrence shocked polite society by dressing in men's breeches or a loose, short frock that exposed more female flesh than was considered decent at the time. Music hall stars Queenie Lawrence (not related to Katie Lawrence), Emily Lyndale, Kate Harvey and Florence Hayes as "The Patriotic Lady" were regulars when Sickert was making his quick sketches in the flickering gaslights.

Cleavage and exposed thighs were scandalous but nobody seemed to worry much about the exploitation of the female child stars prancing about singing the same racy songs as the adults. Girls as young as eight years old dressed alluringly in costumes and little frocks, inviting pedophilic excitement that became the material for a number of Sickert's paintings. Art historian Anna Robins explains that "among decadent writers, painters, and poets, there was something of a cult for the supposed sweetness and innocence of child music hall performers." In her book *Walter Sickert: Drawings* she provides new insight into his artistic interpretations of the female performers he watched night after night, following them from music hall to music hall. His sketches are a glimpse into his psyche and how he lived his life. He might not mind impetuously giving away a painting or leaving it to rot somewhere. But he wouldn't part with the on-the-spot drawings he made on postcards and other small pieces of cheap paper and sometimes jotted with dates.

To look at these faint pencil sketches in the collections at the Manchester Art Gallery, Walker Art Gallery in Liverpool, Leeds Art Gallery or The Royal Pavilion in Brighton is to slip inside Sickert's mind and emotions. His hasty artistic strokes capture what he saw as he sat in a music hall, gazing at people around him or up on the stage. They're snapshots made through the lens of his own imagination, and while other men leered and egged on the half-naked performers, Sickert sketched dismembered female body parts.

One might argue that these drawings were Sickert's attempt at improving his technique. But when he was sitting in his box or several rows back from the stage and making sketches on his little bits of paper, he was drawing a head severed from its neck. He was depicting arms with no hands; a torso with no arms; plump, chopped-off, naked thighs or a limbless torso with breasts bulging out of a low-cut costume. These sketches might be as close as we'll get to reading his thoughts and understanding how they connect to his penciled images.

A series of nine sheet-mounted Gatti's music hall drawings he made in June of 1888 offer a possible hint of his fantasies. These particular sketches in Brighton were mounted by Sickert himself, the arrangement of them his, and in a particularly disturbing sequence he first depicts a woman wearing a feathered hat as if he were seated behind her. In the next two sketches he turns the faceless female around and forcefully taps or "stabs" her in the chest and neck with his pencil, seventeen times in one sketch, fifteen in the other. Some of these pencil marks are deep enough to almost perforate the paper.

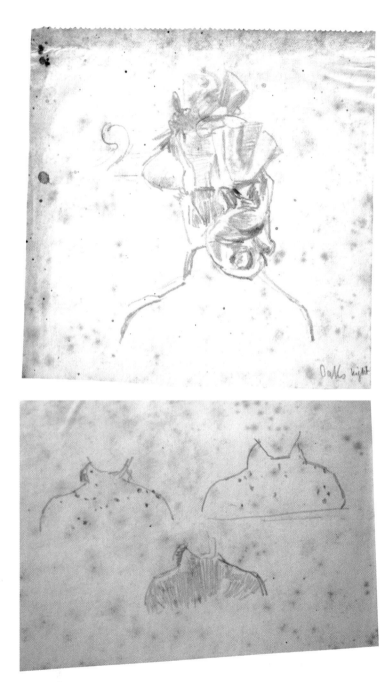

Above: Sickert sketched this woman from behind, not showing her face. *Below:* In this piece, which Sickert displayed next to the previous sketch, he "stabbed" with a pencil into the neck and chest of the woman he drew.

One could argue that Sickert was thinking about new ways to reposition the body in a manner that wasn't stilted or posed. Perhaps he was trying out new methods and impatiently tap-tapping the lead of the pencil on a sketch. He would have seen Degas's pastel nudes, and it could simply be that Sickert was emulating his idol, who had moved far beyond the old way of using draped models in the studio. Degas was experimenting with ways to give the effect of naturalness and movement, and he frequently drew fragments of figures when making studies for his pictures.

Sickert's pencil drawings of limbs and torsos were made while he sat in the audience watching the scantily dressed Queenie Lawrence in her lily-white lingerie or the nine-year-old Little Flossie. But it doesn't seem that the female body parts he depicted in his music hall sketches were routinely used in his studies, pastels, etchings or paintings. These glimpses of his

In Sickert's 1907 painting *Self-Portrait: The Painter in His Studio*, he poses next to a sculpture missing a head and an arm.

imagination might have been significant to him for reasons that had little to do with his art, and curiously he didn't graphically depict male figures or male body parts. There's nothing about his portrayals of males to suggest they're being victimized, with the exception of a pencil drawing titled *He Killed His Father in a Fight*, which depicts a man hacking to death a figure on a bloody bed. The victim may be someone's "father" but the gender is difficult if not impossible to tell.

It's hard for me to comprehend how one can look at Sickert's female torsos, severed heads and limbs and not see them as images from a disturbing imagination. Sketches his artist friend Wilson Steer made at the same time and in some of the same music halls are a startling contrast. When Steer drew a female head, it wasn't missing facial features and didn't seem chopped off at the neck. His sketches of a ballerina's ankles and feet are poised on toe, the calf muscles bunching, and nothing about his sketches looks dead. Sickert's drawn body parts are limp and disconnected, with none of the tension of life, and after he had dashed off these images, he would leave a performance and wander.

Gatti's, the Bedford and other music halls Sickert visited in 1888 were by law supposed to end their performances and sales of liquor no later than half past midnight. If we assume that Sickert stayed until the entertainment ended, he would have been on London's streets on many early mornings. He could wander at will and to his heart's content, staying out all night if he wanted. I don't know if he was an insomniac, but artist Marjorie Lilly recalled in her memoir of Sickert that "he only seemed to relax in odd snatches of sleep during the day." Rarely did he go to bed before midnight and it wasn't unusual for him to "get up again to wander about the streets until dawn."

During the time Ms. Lilly shared a studio and a house with Sickert, she observed that his habit was to wander after the music hall performances. This peripatetic behavior, she adds, continued throughout his life. Whenever "an idea tormented him," he would "thresh round the streets until dawn, lost in meditation." She knew Sickert well until his death in 1942. Theirs was a curious relationship, intimate but with no hint of sexuality, comfortable but off-putting. She seemed intrigued by him, possibly a bit obsessed, and at the same time he unnerved her.

It may very well be that he revealed more of his dark side to Marjorie Lilly than he did to other women who played supportive roles. Or it's possible she was simply more forthcoming with the details. In her book she repeatedly refers to his wanderings, his nocturnal habits, his secrecy. She emphasizes his well-known habit of having as many as three or four studios at the same time, their locations or purposes unknown. She has numerous recollections of his odd preference for dark basements. "Huge, eerie, with winding passages and one black dungeon succeeding another like some horror story by Edgar Allan Poe," she describes.

Sickert's private working life "took him to queer places where he improvised studios and workshops," art dealer Lillian Browse writes a year after his death. As early as 1888, when he was frequenting the music halls, he obsessively rented secret rooms he couldn't afford. "I am taking new rooms," he would tell his friends. In 1911 he writes, "I have taken on a tiny, odd, sinister little home at £45 a year close by here." The address was 60 Harrington Street NW, and apparently he planned to use the "little home" as a "studio."

Sickert would accumulate studios and then abandon them after a short while. It was well known among his acquaintances that these hidden rat holes were located on mean streets. William Rothenstein wrote of Sickert's taste "for the dingy lodging-house atmosphere." Rothenstein says that Sickert was a "genius" at ferreting out the gloomiest and most off-putting rooms to work in, a predilection that baffled those who knew him. He describes Sickert as an "aristocrat by nature" who "had cultivated a strange taste for life below the stairs."

Art critic and biographer Denys Sutton writes that "Sickert's restlessness was a dominating feature of his character." He always had "studios elsewhere, for at all times he cherished his freedom." Sutton says that Sickert often dined out alone, and that after he married Ellen he would go by himself to the music halls or get up in the middle of a dinner in his own home to head out to a performance. Then he would begin another one of his long walks, perhaps retreating to one of his secret rooms. He might meander into the slums of the East End, traveling the dark streets alone with a small parcel or a Gladstone bag in hand, presumably to hold his art supplies.

According to Sutton, during one of these ambles Sickert was dressed in a loud checked suit and came upon several girls on Copenhagen Street about a mile northwest of Shoreditch. The girls scattered in terror, screaming, "Jack the Ripper! Jack the Ripper!" In a somewhat different account, Sickert told his friends that it was he who called out, "Jack the Ripper, Jack the Ripper." Copenhagen Street was very close to Collins's Music Hall, which was described by the *Islington Gazette* on October 2, 1888, as offering an "Unprecedented Array of Talent." It's a certainty Sickert attended performances at the Collins's on September 28, October 5 and October 8, 1888. This is based on his dated sketches held in a private collection and mentioned in Wendy Baron's 2006 *Sickert: Paintings & Drawings*. Despite this readily accessible information, biographer Matthew Sturgis is firm in his claim that Sickert was in France during the summer and fall when the Ripper crimes began.

Sturgis states that the only sketch for this period was of "the music hall at Hammersmith on 4 August 1888." As is the case with a number of his claims, it isn't true. I have to wonder if he looked at the previously mentioned 2006 work by Wendy Baron, "the doyenne of Sickert studies," in Sturgis's words, or visited the archival sources that hold Sickert music hall sketches. It's hard for me to imagine that Sturgis wasn't aware that Sickert was in and out of London during the summer and fall of 1888.

In addition to the dates previously mentioned, sketches at the Walker and Leeds Art Galleries also definitively place him at music halls on the following dates in 1888: July 26, July 30 and 31, August 1, August 4 and 5 and October 4. On other sketches of what appear to be the same period, he simply jotted the month and day but no year, and while they may have been made in 1888, I don't include them if I'm not sure based on his own handwritten notes.

In fact many of his sketches have no dates, and we also can't assume every sketch he made is accounted for. He may have been in London more frequently than his dated sketches indicate, and that seems to have been Whistler's assumption on September 22, 1888, while he was in France on his honeymoon. He writes his sister-in-law, Helen Euphrosyne Whistler, who was in London at the time, and reminds her to keep his whereabouts a secret, especially from "followers or pupils." He then goes on to propose a plot to her, a little "treachery" that involves Walter Sickert. Whistler encourages her to "ask the Sickerts down to dinner." Clearly Whistler thought Sickert was in London.

What remains intriguing about Sickert's music hall sketches is why he made them at all or dated and kept them. As art historian Anna Robins said to me in December 2013, most of the sketches are hastily drawn. But they were important enough that he held on to them. As I've continued to mention, when I was searching archives for Sickert documents I found hundreds of letters and papers written by him but virtually nothing written to him. Clearly the correspondence once existed. Did letters from friends, family, colleagues and even mentors such as Whistler and Degas mean so little to Sickert that he simply threw them away? Possibly, and it's also possible he kept his music hall sketches for more than artistic reasons.

In the late 1800s there were few inciting props available to violent psychopaths. Today's rapist, pedophile or murderer has plenty to choose from, and photographs and audio and video recordings of torture and murder aren't uncommon. Violent pornography found in magazines, movies, books, computer software and on Internet sites is typical. These days there's plenty of fodder for violent fantasies, but not so in the Victorian era. Sickert's props would have been souvenirs or trophies from the victim. They would have been paintings and drawings, and the live entertainment of the theater and the music halls. It also would be expected that he would make dry runs.

"I told her I was Jack the Ripper and I took my hat off," the Ripper writes on November 19, 1888. Three days later he says that he's in Liverpool and "met a young woman in Scotland Road. . . . I smiled at her and she calls out Jack the ripper. She dident know how right she was." About this same time an article appeared in the *Weekly Dispatch* reporting that an elderly woman was sitting in Liverpool's Sheil Park when a "respectable looking man dressed in a black coat, light trousers, and a soft felt hat" pulled out a long thin knife. He said he planned to kill as many women in Liverpool as he could. He intended to send the ears of the first victim to the editor of the newspaper.

Psychopathic killers often try out their MO before going through with the plan. Practice makes perfect, and the killer gets a thrill from the near-strike. The pulse picks up. Adrenaline surges. He will continue to go through the ritual, each time getting closer to actualizing the attack. Violent offenders have been known to install emergency grille lights or attach magnetic bubble lights to the roofs of their cars. They pull over women drivers multiple times before actually going through with abduction and murder.

Jack the Ripper very likely went through dry runs and other rituals before he killed. After a while these events aren't just about practice and instant gratification. They fuel violent fantasies. They may involve more than merely stalking a victim, especially if the assailant is creative and a peripatetic, a nocturnal predator with a disciplined mind capable of choreographing events in a way that ensures he can evade detection or capture. A search of newspapers during the fall of 1888, when the Ripper was foremost on the public's mind, shows that a number of strange events were occurring in various parts of England.

At approximately ten o'clock on the night of September 14, a man entered London's Tower Subway and approached the caretaker. "Have you caught any of the Whitechapel murderers yet?" the man asked as he pulled out a foot-long knife that had a curved blade. He then fled, yanking off "false whiskers" as he was pursued by the caretaker, who lost sight of him at Tooley Street. The description the caretaker gave the police was of a man five foot three with dark hair, a dark complexion and a mustache. He was about thirty years old and was wearing a black suit that looked new, a light overcoat and a dark double-peaked cloth cap.

"I have got a jolly lot of false whiskers & mustaches," the Ripper writes on November 27. On September 11 of the following year, an anonymous writer teases the police, "I ware black wiskers all over my face."

After the Tower Bridge was completed in 1894, the Tower Subway was closed to pedestrians and turned into a gas main. But in 1888 it was a hellish cast-iron tube seven feet in diameter and 1,340 feet long. It began at the south side of Great Tower Hill at the Tower of London, ran under the Thames and surfaced at Pickle Herring Stairs on the south bank of the river. If what the caretaker told police was accurate, he chased the man through the tunnel to Pickle Herring Street, then to Vine Street, which intersected with Tooley Street.

The Tower of London is about half a mile south of Whitechapel, and the subway was most unpleasant. It's hard to imagine that people routinely used it to cross the river, especially if one were claustrophobic or fearful of traveling through a dirty, gloomy tube underwater. To this day it's an eerie thing to imagine as one watches the Thames seeping on the muddy shore in the area where the tunnel once was. It's a wonder the tunnel didn't spring a terrible leak or suffer some other catastrophe, and the idea of a foot pursuit going on in such a confined, gloomy space is bizarre if not inconceivable— or would have been to the police.

No doubt they considered the man with the false whiskers a kook. Yet this unseemly prankster in disguise was rational enough to pick a deserted, poorly lit place, and it's unlikely he viewed the caretaker as one who could physically overtake him. It seems the knife-wielding fiend had every intention of causing a stir and no intention of being caught—Friday, September 14, was also the day that Annie Chapman was buried.

Three days later on September 17, the Metropolitan Police may have received the first letter signed "Jack the Ripper."

> *Dear Boss,*
>
> *So now they say I am a Yid when will they lern Dear old Boss? You an me know the truth don't we. Lusk can look forever he'll never find me but I am rite under his nose all the time. I watch them looking for me an it gives me fits ha ha. I love my work an I shant stop untill I get buckled and even then watch out for your old pal Jacky*
>
> *Catch me if you can*

Peter McClelland, a noncommissioned Army officer, discovered the letter in 1988 when he happened upon an unopened card folder at The National Archives next to non-Ripper-related correspondence. Inside the folder was this September 17 letter. Because of its illogical location and the fact that it had never been seen before, it's been regarded by some as a modern hoax, and in November of 2007, I was given permission once again to see if science might have answers for us.

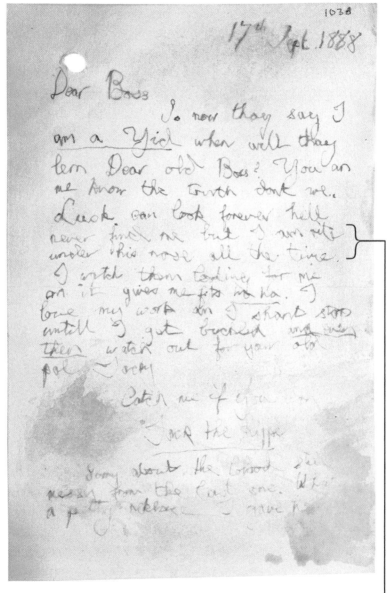

In what is possibly the first letter sent to the police signed "Jack the Ripper," the Ripper taunts that he is "rite under his nose."

I brought a forensic light source expert to London and recruited the assistance of Peter Bower. While Paul Begg, Keith Skinner, Peter McClelland and others observed, we examined the September 17 letter. While we couldn't prove Jack the Ripper wrote what would be the earliest known document introducing his name, we did discover a number of findings that if nothing else are grist for continued conversation and speculation. The paper the letter is written on is of the period, Bower determined, and the language and erratic handwriting appear to be deliberately disguised. This is consistent with other Ripper letters, but what turned out to be the most intriguing discovery is a stain on the paper. What the Ripper claims is blood faintly fluoresced under a forensic light, and blood doesn't fluoresce white or whitish. But seminal fluid does. I described this in my journal at the time: "Sept. 17 fluor like semen."

It can't be shown irrefutably that the letter is authentic. However, I can state with confidence that if it's not, then someone quite clever and well informed went to a lot of trouble. This person would have had to find paper of the period and imitate the style and language of a Ripper communication in a manner that fit the timeline of the crimes. Finally this hoaxer would then have to fake a bloodstain using a body fluid or some other substance unusual enough to fluoresce under a forensic light source. Another detail that adds credence to the authenticity of the letter is that the Ripper's name was known by the public in September, certainly by the end of the month. This supports the likelihood that there were early communications that introduced the Ripper by name.

As is true of many documents in this case, these letters could have disappeared over the years. Unquestionably, by September 30, when Elizabeth Stride was murdered, the now notorious nickname of the Whitechapel fiend was known. A Swedish church pastor named Johannis Palmer mentioned in a diary entry he made at the time: "In the morning at 1 a.m. Elizabeth Gustafsdotter Stride was murdered in Berner St. She had often received assistance from the Church. (Murdered by Jack the Ripper?)"

In the grand scheme of things, the September 17 letter isn't hugely important. I mention it because it must be awful to discover an historic document and then have some people suspect you faked it and planted

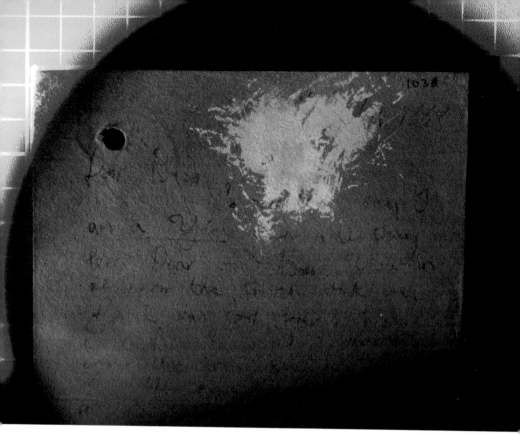

A letter dated September 17, 1888, has a spot that fluoresces white under a forensic light. The spot is not blood, as the Ripper claims. Rather, it fluoresces very much like semen.

it in a drawer. To me it's not logical that Peter McClelland would have done such a thing. If he were guilty of going to so much trouble, why would he encourage a scientific examination and show up to witness it? What if Bower had determined the letter was a modern fake while McClelland looked on surrounded by a host of witnesses inside The National Archives? I believe the September 17 letter is genuine, and at the time it was received the taunts, teases and odd events were escalating. The media was getting frenzied. Rumors were becoming more sensational and inspiring panic.

One news story making the rounds was that an American had contacted a subcurator of a medical school in hopes of buying human uteri for twenty pounds each. The would-be purchaser wanted the organs preserved in glycerin to keep them pliable, planning to send them out with a journal article he'd written. The request was refused. The "American" wasn't identified and no further information about him was given but the story gave rise to a new possibility. The Ripper was killing women to sell their organs, and the stealing of Annie Chapman's rings was a "veil" to hide the real motive of procuring her uterus.

Murders outside London also were hitting the news. But the police didn't seriously entertain the idea that the Ripper might kill anywhere but in the East End. On Saturday, September 22, there was another Ripper-like crime in Birtley, Durham, the coal-mining country near Newcastle upon Tyne. Twenty-six-year-old Jane Beetmore was last seen alive by friends at 8:00 p.m., her body found the following morning, Sunday, September 23, in a gutter near Guston Colliery Railway. The left side of her neck had been cut through to the vertebrae. A gash on the right side of her face had laid open her lower jaw to the bone, and her bowels protruded from her mutilated abdomen.

The striking similarities between her murder and those in London's East End prompted Scotland Yard to send Dr. George Bagster Phillips and an inspector to meet with Durham police officials. They decided the Ripper wasn't responsible. Jane Beetmore's "sweetheart," William Waddle, eventually was charged with her murder although the accusation, indictment and conviction were "not supported by any tangible evidence," as it was reported in the news. Waddle, characterized as dull witted, was hanged December 19, 1888.

We'll probably never know if he was guilty or innocent. But in an anonymous letter to the City of London Police dated November 15, 1888, the writer offers this suggestion: "Look at the case in County Durham . . . twas made to appear as if it was Jack the Ripper." Was it the Ripper who sent this letter? If so, was he telling the truth or taunting? Of course critics of my work on this case continue to say Sickert wasn't playing pranks or writing letters or killing anyone because he wasn't in England. But he was. As I've pointed out, the dates Sickert wrote on his own music hall sketches place him in London on at least some occasions during June, July, August, September and October. However, it's true that in the main his whereabouts are a mystery and likely always will be. Certainly he was in France some of the summer and fall of 1888. But just how often and for how long on any visit can't be known with certainty.

In a letter dated September 21, 1888, Ellen Sickert writes to her brother-in-law Dick Fisher that her husband was with "his people in Normandy for a few weeks." Between August 19 and September 17 it would seem he was in Saint Valery en Caux. What's perplexing about this, though, is Whistler's letter dated one day after Ellen's, on September 22. Why does he assume Ellen and Walter are in London? Maybe the answer is simple. Whistler didn't know where Sickert was. Maybe Ellen didn't either and thought he was in Normandy.

Based on her September 21 letter she was in Ireland with her sister Janie, and Whistler didn't seem aware of that necessarily, not that one might expect him to keep up with Ellen's activities. But he would have known Sickert's patterns all too well, and historically they did include his spending the summer months in France. So why would Whistler suppose Sickert was in London in late September? He must have had a reason. But one thing is certain. Wherever Sickert was, he and Ellen weren't together or writing to each other, it seems, making it all the more difficult to know where he was and what he was doing.

On August 19, Sickert's mother wrote to her friend Mary Adams that he had been in Normandy for a visit. She again mentioned his being there in a letter dated September 6 that she wrote to her friend Pennie Muller. Artist Jacques-Émile Blanche wrote of having lunch with Sickert in St. Valery en Caux, but it's not clear exactly when this might have been. The letter was dated September 18, 1888, after the fact, possibly by an archivist. Maybe the date is accurate, maybe it's not. Letters Sickert wrote to Blanche in the autumn of 1888 appear to have been written in London on Sickert's 54 Broadhurst Gardens stationery, and apparently he didn't use this when he was abroad.

It's impossible to know for a fact exactly how long Sickert was in France, and more importantly if he was there every day during a pre-scribed period of time or if he came and went. What we can trust is that he was in London at Collins's Music Hall on September 28, the date he jotted on a sketch he made of an artist onstage. He was there again on October 5 drawing the studies of a girl he called "May." The police didn't seem to consider that the Ripper was manipulating the machinery behind the scenes, that he was doing far more than committing crimes against individuals. He was creating a massive spectacle that was grabbing the attention of the world.

The Ripper's violent appetite had been whetted and he craved "blood, blood, blood," he writes. He craved drama. He had an insatiable appetite for enthralling his audience. As Henry Irving once said to an unresponsive house, "Ladies and gentlemen, if you don't applaud, I can't act!" Perhaps the applause was too faint, and several more events happened in quick succession. On September 24, the police received the taunting letter with the killer's "name" and "address" blacked out with heavily inked rectangles and coffins.

The next day the Ripper writes another letter, but this time he makes sure someone paid attention by mailing his murderous missive to the Central News Agency. "Dear Boss, I keep on hearing the police have caught me but they won't fix me just yet," he writes in red ink. His spelling and grammar are correct, his writing as neat as a clerk's.

In August, the compulsive letter writer Sickert sent a note to Blanche apologizing for not "writing for so long. I have been very hard at work, and I find it very difficult to find 5 minutes to write a letter." There's no reason to believe Sickert's "work" was related to his art. It doesn't seem his productivity was at its usual high from August 1888 through the rest of the year. Paintings circa 1888 are few, and there's no guarantee that *circa* didn't mean a year or two earlier or later. I found only one article written by Sickert in 1888. It was published in the spring. If he was constantly on the move and writing hundreds of letters he mailed from all over it might explain a slump in artistic and literary output.

In the late nineteenth century, passports, visas and other forms of identification weren't required to travel on the Continent unless it was to enter Germany from France. There's no mention of Sickert having any form of "picture identification" until World War I when he and his second wife, Christine, were issued laissez-passers to show guards at tunnels, railway crossings and other strategic places as they traveled about France. Entering France from England was an easy, friendly transition and remained so during the years Sickert traveled to and fro.

Crossing the English Channel in the late 1800s could take as little as three and a half hours in good weather. One could travel by express train and "fast" steamer seven days a week, twice daily, with the trains leaving Victoria Station at 10:30 in the morning or London Bridge at 10:45. The steamer sailed out of Newhaven at 12:45 p.m. and arrived in Dieppe no later than dinnertime. These vessels routinely held more than seven hundred passengers, indicating the commute was common. It would have been easy to get lost in the crowd.

A single one-way first-class ticket to Dieppe was twenty-four shillings, second class was seventeen, and the Express Tidal Service included trains from Dieppe straight through to Rouen and Paris. Once in Dieppe, if Sickert's final destination was St. Valery en Caux, that was an additional twenty-some miles. This may have been manageable by bicycle, as suggested in his mother's letter of August 19, 1888. She describes the roads as "Quite dry and hard, no mud, no holes, you could run over all France in no time." She mentions that the roads were excellent for "bi & tri cycles!"

Someone high on adrenaline after committing a murder is quite motivated to cover his tracks and create alibis, and violent offenders are known to move around quickly, stealthily. They will go to great lengths to do so, and Sickert's disappearing acts were legendary among those close to him. Maybe he sailed back and forth from England to Dieppe while the Ripper's earliest crimes were reaching a crescendo of panic in 1888. Maybe his travels to France were to cool off. French death and crime statistics for the Victorian era don't seem to have survived, and I was unable to find records of homicides that might resemble the Ripper's crimes.

When I visited Dieppe's narrow old streets and passageways, its rocky shore and soaring cliffs that sheer off into the Channel, I tried to imagine the small seaside village as a killing ground. It didn't seem the sort of place where one could be anonymous and easily vanish after committing frenzied, mutilating murder. Perhaps Sickert's childhood getaway in France was a safe haven, a refuge. It may be that England brought out the worst in him.

23

A SHINY
BLACK BAG

THE SUN DIDN'T SHOW ITSELF on Saturday, September 29, and a persistent cold rain chilled the night as *Dr. Jekyll and Mr. Hyde* ended its long and controversial run at the Lyceum. Citizens were blaming the frightening duality play for influencing the Ripper, and a tip in yet another letter from an anonymous concerned citizen already had resulted in American actor Richard Mansfield being questioned by the police.

Hyde was linked to the Ripper, and almost a month earlier on September 1, an article in *The Evening News* stated: "Certain is it that beings, outwardly human, one such as was suggested to the police by either the performance or perusal of *Dr. Jekyll and Mr. Hyde*, do exist." A week later (September 8) the *East London Advertiser* carried the following: "If, as we imagine, there be a murderous lunatic concealed in the slums of Whitechapel, who issues forth at night like another Hyde, to prey upon the defenceless women of the *unfortunate* class, we have little doubt that he will be captured."

That same day the *Pall Mall Gazette* published its own version of this snowballing rumor: "There certainly seems to be a tolerably realistic impersonification of Mr. Hyde at large in Whitechapel." Later it would be suggested by another concerned citizen who signed his letter to the editor

G.C.: ". . . Let detectives consider how Mr. Hyde would have acted—for there may be a system in the demonic actions of a madman in following the pattern set before him." Eventually these sensational speculations made their way across the Atlantic, and New York's *Ogdensburg Journal* would report on October 10: "This theory is that the horrible crimes which have so disturbed the city [London] and interested the entire world are the result of a case in real life of *Dr. Jekyll and Mr. Hyde.* Furthermore, the detectives believe that the existence of such a case is directly attributable to the excitement and morbid reflections caused by a mind dwelling upon the circumstances detailed in the story and play just named."

Oddly, the article went on to say that the police were focusing their surveillance on a man who lived in Grosvenor Square, and maybe it's nothing more than a coincidence that at the time Sir. William Gull lived just off Grosvenor Square, at 74 Brook Street. As a formal journalist I have to wonder about the source of all these tips and other information. Who was supplying such details to the press? More anonymous concerned citizens? Perhaps ones who wished to cast a shadow of suspicion over the Queen's physician, a famous actor—or even Whistler himself, who also would be linked to the Ripper's atrocities by the end of the year?

By the end of September 1888, the stage certainly was set for more horror and uproar to come. The media was increasingly frenzied, and the Great Metropolis was beginning to feel terrorized. But citizens concerned and otherwise had no idea that the worst had yet to come, far from it, and it seems fitting that on the last Saturday of the month it was reported that the "great excesses of sunshine were at an end." London's chilly gloom returned, and on the night of September 28, Sickert ventured out to Collins's Music Hall on Islington Green, based on his own handwritten notes on sketches he made and dated.

Several miles away in the East End, the Ripper's next known victim, Elizabeth Stride, was concerned about earning enough money for drinks and a bed for the night. She'd only recently moved out of a lodging house on Dorset Street in Spitalfields where she'd been living with Michael Kidney, a waterside laborer. Long Liz, as her friends called her, had left Kidney before. She carried her few belongings with her this time but there was no reason to assume she was gone for good. Kidney would testify at her inquest that now and then she wanted her freedom and an opportunity to indulge her "drinking habits" but after a spell of wandering off she always came back, he said.

Elizabeth's maiden name was Gustafsdotter, and she would have turned forty-five on November 27. She'd led most people to believe she was about ten years younger than that. Her lies seem a pitiful attempt to weave a brighter, more dramatic tale than the truth of her depressing, desperate life. Born in Torslanda near Göteborg, Sweden, she was the daughter of a farmer. Some said she spoke fluent English without a trace of an accent. Others claimed she didn't properly form her words and sounded like a foreigner.

Elizabeth often told people she came to London as a young lady to "see the country," and it was just one more of her fabrications. The earliest record I could find of her living in London was in the Swedish Church register that listed her name in 1866. Three years later, she married John Thomas Stride, and together they ran a coffee shop in Poplar. By 1879 their marriage was in shambles and she was appealing to the Swedish Church for financial support.

Elizabeth was five foot two or four according to people who went to the mortuary to figure out who she was. Her complexion was "pale." Others described it as "dark." Her hair was "dark brown and curly." It was "black," according to someone else. A policeman who would view Elizabeth in the poorly lit mortuary would decide that her eyes were "gray." Some of these descriptions are misleading for the simple reason that police understood very little about postmortem artifacts and other changes related to a medicolegal examination.

In Elizabeth's mortuary photograph her hair looks darker because it was wet and stringy from having been rinsed. Her face was pale because she was dead and had lost virtually all of her blood. Her eyes may once have been bright blue but not by the time the policeman lifted a lid to check. After death the conjunctiva of the eye begins to dry and cloud. Most people who have been dead for a while appear to have gray or grayish-blue eyes unless their irises were very dark. After her autopsy, Elizabeth was dressed in the same clothing she was wearing when she was murdered, and she was placed in a shell that was stood up against a wall

Elizabeth Stride was the alleged fourth victim of Jack the Ripper, found dead in the early hours of Sunday, September 30, 1888.

to be photographed. Barely visible in the shadow of her tucked-in chin is the cut made by her killer's knife, jaggedly trailing off inches below the right side of her neck. Thin with good features and a mouth that might have been sensuous had she not lost her upper front teeth, Elizabeth may have been a beauty in her youth.

During her inquest, truths about her began to emerge. She'd left Sweden to take a "situation" with a gentleman who lived near Hyde Park. It's not known how long that "situation" lasted but at some point after it ended she lived with a policeman. Everyone who knew her in the local lodging houses she frequented had heard the tragic tale that her husband, John Stride, drowned when the *Princess Alice* sank after a steam collier ran it down. Elizabeth actually had different versions of this tale depending on who was listening.

Her husband and two of her nine children had drowned when the *Princess Alice* sank. Or her husband and all of her children drowned. Elizabeth somehow survived the shipwreck that killed 640 people, and according to her while she was struggling for her life another panicking passenger kicked her in the mouth causing the "deformity" to it. Elizabeth told everyone that the entire roof of her mouth was gone but her autopsy revealed nothing wrong with her hard or soft palates. The only deformity was her missing front teeth, which must have been a source of shame for her.

Records at the Poplar and Stepney Sick Asylum showed that her husband died there on October 24, 1884. He didn't drown in a shipwreck and neither did any of their children—if there were any children. Perhaps Elizabeth felt it necessary to tell falsehoods about a past that was painful and humiliating and did nothing but cause trouble. Or maybe her confabulations were all about money. A fund had been set aside for the survivors of the *Princess Alice*, and when the clergy of the Swedish Church discovered that her husband didn't die in the shipwreck, they ceased any financial assistance. One way or another Elizabeth had to be supported by a man. Otherwise all she had was what she made from sewing, cleaning and prostitution, and of late she'd been spending her nights at a lodging house at 32 Flower and Dean Street where the deputy, a widow named Elizabeth Tanner, knew her fairly well.

During the inquest Mrs. Tanner testified that Elizabeth had been living with Michael Kidney. On Thursday, September 27, she'd walked out on him with nothing but a few ragged clothes and a hymnbook. That night and the next she stayed in Mrs. Tanner's lodging house. On the early evening of Saturday, September 29, Elizabeth earned sixpence by cleaning two of the lodging-house rooms, and afterward she and Mrs. Tanner had a drink at the Queen's Head public house on Commercial Street. Between seven and eight Elizabeth was in the kitchen, where she handed a piece of velvet to her friend Catherine Lane. "Please keep it safe for me," Elizabeth said, and she added that she was going out for a while.

She was dressed in two petticoats made of a cheap material resembling sacking, a white chemise, white cotton stockings, a black velveteen bodice, a black skirt and a black jacket trimmed with fur. Around her neck was a colorful striped silk handkerchief, and she wore a small black crêpe bonnet. In her pockets were two handkerchiefs, a skein of black worsted darning yarn and a brass thimble. Before she left the lodging-house kitchen, she asked Charles Preston, a barber, if she could borrow his clothes brush to tidy up a bit. She didn't tell anyone where she was headed but proudly showed off her six newly earned pennies as she headed out into the dark, wet night.

Berner Street was a narrow thoroughfare of small, crowded dwellings occupied by Polish and German tailors, shoemakers, cigarette makers and other impoverished people who worked out of their homes.

It was also the location of the International Working Men's Educational Club, which had approximately eighty-five members, most of them Eastern European Jewish socialists. The only requirement for joining was to support socialist principles, and the club met every Saturday night at 8:30 to discuss various topics.

They always closed with a social time of singing and dancing, and it wasn't unusual for people to linger until one o'clock in the morning. On this particular Saturday night almost a hundred people attended a lecture and debate at 40 Berner Street. The event was at a high pitch by the time

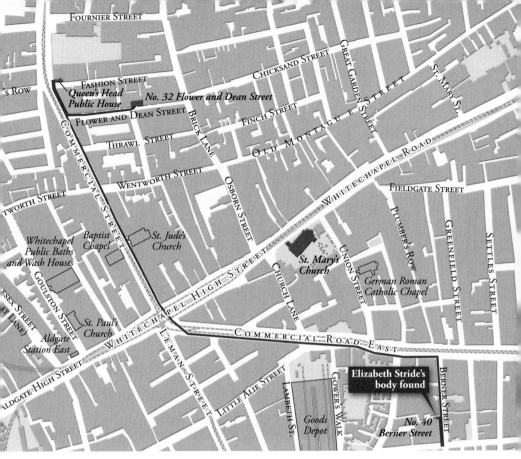

Elizabeth Stride was killed in an approximately fifteen-minute window in the early hours of Sept. 30, 1888. Israel Schwartz saw a man knock her to the ground around 12:45 a.m., and at 1:00 a.m. Louis Diemschutz found her body in the courtyard of 40 Berner Street.

Elizabeth Stride set out in that direction. Her first client of the evening as far as anyone seems to know was a man she was observed talking to on Berner Street very close to where a laborer named William Marshall lived. This was about 11:00 p.m.

Marshall later testified that he didn't get a good look at the man's face but described him as being dressed in a small black coat, dark trousers and possibly a sailor's cap. He wore no gloves and was clean-shaven. He and Elizabeth were kissing, and Marshall said he overheard the man tease, "You would say anything but your prayers." She laughed, neither of them appearing to be intoxicated, Marshall recalled, and they walked off in the direction of the International Working Men's Educational Club clubhouse.

Soon after, another local resident named James Brown saw a woman he later identified as Elizabeth Stride leaning against a wall, talking with a man at the corner of Fairclough and Berner Streets. The man wore a long overcoat and was approximately five foot seven. At 12:35 a.m., Police Constable William Smith, 452 H Division, whose beat that night included Berner Street, noticed a woman he later identified as Elizabeth Stride, and it caught his eye that she was wearing a flower on her coat. The man she was with carried a newspaper-wrapped package that was eighteen inches long and six or eight inches wide. He was five foot seven, Smith recalled, and was dressed in a hard felt deerstalker, a dark overcoat and dark trousers. Smith thought the man seemed respectable enough, about twenty-eight years old and clean-shaven.

Smith continued his beat, and possibly ten minutes later a man named Israel Schwartz entered Berner Street from Commercial Road. He noticed a woman he identified as Stride standing outside the gates of the club with a man who seemed tipsy. Schwartz would later claim he observed this man assault Elizabeth, throwing her to the ground. Then Schwartz hurried along his way to avoid the altercation, looking back as the man antagonized another man by calling him "Lipski," presumably an anti-Semitic slur that may have referenced a Polish immigrant named Israel Lipski, a convicted murderer who had been hanged the year before.

At 1:00 a.m. Louis Diemschutz was driving his costermonger's barrow to 40 Berner Street. The manager of the socialist club, he lived there and was surprised when he turned into the courtyard to find the gates open. Usually they were closed after 9:00 p.m., and as he passed through, his pony suddenly shied to the left. It was too dark to see much but Diemschutz made out a form on the ground near the wall. He poked it with his whip, expecting to find garbage.

Climbing down he struggled to light a match in the wind and was startled by the dimly lit shape of a woman either drunk or dead. Diemschutz ran inside the clubhouse and returned with a candle, not realizing when he'd turned his pony and barrow into the courtyard he'd likely interrupted Jack the Ripper. Elizabeth's throat had been slashed, possibly just minutes ago. Blood flowed from her neck toward the clubhouse door, and the top buttons of her jacket were undone, exposing her chemise and stays.

She was on her left side, her face toward the wall, her dress wet from recent hard rains that had soaked the ground. In her left hand was a paper packet of cachous or sweets used to freshen the breath, and mysteriously a red rose was pinned to her breast. By now Police Constable William Smith's beat had gone full circle. When he reached 40 Berner Street again he must have been shocked to find that a crowd was gathering outside the clubhouse gates. People were screaming "Police!" and "Murder!"

Smith later testified at the inquest that his patrol had taken no more than a mere twenty-five minutes, and during that brief time, while some thirty members of the club lingered inside, the killer must have struck. The windows were open and the club members were singing festive songs in Russian and German. No one heard a scream or any other call of distress. But Elizabeth Stride probably didn't make a sound that anyone but her killer could hear.

Police Surgeon Dr. George Bagster Phillips arrived at the scene shortly after 1:00 a.m. and instantly decided that since no weapon was found, the woman hadn't committed suicide. She must have been murdered. From there he went on to baselessly deduce that the killer had applied pressure to her shoulders with his hands and lowered her to the ground before cutting her throat from the front. In death, she continued to hold the cachous between the thumb and forefinger of her left hand, and when the doctor removed the packet some of the sweets spilled.

Her right hand rested on her chest and was uninjured but "smeared with blood," and this was perplexing, Dr. Phillips later testified. He offered that perhaps the killer deliberately wiped blood on her hand but it would be an odd thing to do. It didn't seem to occur to Dr. Phillips that it's a reflex to clutch a wound if a conscious person is hemorrhaging, and when Elizabeth's throat was cut she would have grabbed her neck. It also makes no sense to assume that she was pushed to the ground before she was killed. If she had been, chances are she would have struggled and dropped the packet of sweets.

It's hard to fathom that the man who was seen assaulting her earlier is the one who killed her. Would Jack the Ripper attack a victim in front of witnesses? It's also unlikely that Elizabeth's killer cut her throat from the front, which usually results in several small incisions due to the awkward angle. It's much easier to attack from the rear. Those incisions typically are long, severing major blood vessels and cutting through tissue and cartilage all the way to the bone. I doubt Elizabeth Stride had a chance to resist the person who ultimately killed her. I doubt she knew what hit her.

She may have drifted toward the building on Berner Street because she knew that the club members—most of them there without their girlfriends or wives—would begin heading out around 1:00 a.m. They might be interested in quick sex, and the Ripper may have been watching her from the deep shadows as she conducted business with other men. She may have been shoved around by one of them but it doesn't mean the person who did it was her killer.

The Ripper could have been familiar with the club and shown up there before, possibly even earlier that night. He could have been wearing a false mustache or beard or some other disguise to ensure that he wouldn't be recognized, and he may have had a personal reason to be interested in the International Working Men's Educational Club on the night Stride was murdered. The speaker was prominent libertarian socialist William Morris, an artist, author and publisher who led the Arts and Crafts movement. Morris was close friends with book designer and binder Thomas James Cobden-Sanderson, who was married to Ellen's sister Annie. Sickert knew Morris and was no fan of his philosophies. Sickert also was fluent in German and would have understood the debate that had been going on for hours.

Maybe he was in the crowd that night. It would have been in keeping with his character to participate before slipping out close to 1:00 a.m. as the singing began. Or maybe he never stepped inside the club at all, and had been watching Elizabeth Stride since she left the lodging house. Whatever he did, killing her may not have been as difficult as one might suppose. If a violent offender is sober, intelligent, logical, speaks several languages, is an actor, has hiding places and doesn't live in the area but knows it extremely well, then it really isn't so mind-boggling to imagine him getting away with murder in unlighted slums. The Ripper may have spoken to Elizabeth Stride right before he killed her. Or perhaps he had encountered her earlier, when she was spotted with the clean-shaven man who may have lingered in the shadows to cut her throat. There was never an explanation for her single red rose or where she got the sweets.

The Ripper had ample time to escape when Louis Diemschutz hurried inside the building for a candle, and members of the club rushed outside to look. Shortly before the commotion began, a woman living several doors down at 36 Berner Street stepped outside and noticed a young man she identified as Leon Goldstein walking quickly toward Commercial Road. He glanced up at the lighted windows of the clubhouse, the woman later testified. He was carrying a shiny black Gladstone case, popular in those days and similar in appearance to a medical bag.

Whether the identification was accurate or not it's interesting to point out that Marjorie Lilly recalled in her written recollections of Sickert that he owned a Gladstone bag "to which he was much attached." On one occasion in the winter of 1918, while they were painting in his studio, he suddenly decided they should go to Petticoat Lane, and he went into the basement to fetch the bag. She recalls that painted on it in bright white numbers and letters was "The Shrubbery, 81 Camden Road," and she had no clue as to what this might have meant to him.

She certainly didn't understand the "Shrubbery" part of the address since there was no shrubbery in the patchy front yard, and he didn't offer her an explanation for his bizarre behavior. He was fifty-eight years old at the time and anything but senile, but now and then he acted strangely. Ms. Lilly recalls being unnerved when he carried his Gladstone bag out the door, taking her and another woman on a frightening excursion into Whitechapel during a thick, acrid fog. They ended up on Petticoat Lane, and Ms. Lilly watched in astonishment as Sickert and his black bag disappeared in fog that "exceeded our worst fears." It was almost as dark as night, she writes, as they chased Sickert "up and down endless side streets until we were exhausted." She describes him staring at poor wretches huddled on steps leading into their slums, and joyfully exclaiming, "Such a beautiful head! What a *beard*. A perfect Rembrandt." He couldn't be dissuaded from an adventure that took him within blocks of where the Ripper's victims had been murdered thirty years earlier.

In 1914, when World War I began and London was dark with lights extinguished and blinds drawn, Sickert writes in a letter, "Such interesting streets lit as they were 20 years ago when everything was Rembrandt." He

The "chameleon" Sickert in middle age, pictured outside a studio he rented on Camden Road.

had just walked home "by bye-ways" through Islington at night. He adds, "I wish the fear of Zeppelins would continue for ever so far as the lighting goes." Almost ninety years later in 2001, I questioned Sickert's nephew John Lessore about Ms. Lilly's story. He told me he wasn't aware of anyone in the family knowing about a Gladstone bag that might have belonged to Walter Sickert, who at the end of his life was married to Thérèse Lessore, the sister of John Lessore's father.

I tried hard to track down that bag. If it had been used to carry bloody knives or body parts, DNA may have come up with some interesting findings. There's also a possible explanation (granted, a remote one) for why Sickert painted "The Shrubbery" on his bag. It may have been another shard of a fantasy, a relived moment that he could have recalled from long-ago news stories. During the Ripper murders, the police found a bloody knife "in shrubbery" close to where Sickert's mother lived.

In fact bloody knives began to turn up in several places as if left deliberately to excite police and neighbors. On the Monday night after Elizabeth Stride's murder, Thomas Coram, a laborer in a coconut-fiber factory, was leaving a friend's house in Whitechapel when he noticed a knife at the bottom of steps leading into a laundry. The blade was a foot long with a blunted tip, and the black handle was six inches long and wrapped in a bloody white handkerchief that had been tied in place with string. Coram claimed he didn't touch the knife but immediately showed it to a local constable, who later testified that it was in the exact spot where he'd stood not an hour earlier. The constable described the knife as "smothered" with dried blood, and the sort a baker or chef might use. Sickert was an excellent cook. He often dressed as a chef when he entertained his friends.

While police were interrogating the members of the International Working Men's Educational Club who had been singing inside the building when Elizabeth Stride was murdered, Jack the Ripper was making his way toward Mitre Square. Catherine Eddowes was headed there after being released from jail. If the Ripper took the direct route of Commercial Road and followed it west, he could turn left on Aldgate High Street and enter the City of London. His next crime scene was but a fifteen-minute walk from his last one.

24

THESE
CHARACTERS
ABOUT

CATHERINE EDDOWES spent the Friday night of September 28 in a casual ward north of Whitechapel Road. She didn't have fourpence to pay for her half of John Kelly's bed.

It had been seven or eight years now that she'd been living with him in the lodging house at 55 Flower and Dean Street in Spitalfields. Before that she was with Thomas Conway, the father of her two boys, ages fifteen and twenty, and a daughter named Annie Phillips, twenty-three and married to a lampblack packer. The sons lived with Conway, who'd left Catherine because of her drinking habits. She'd not seen him or her children in years and this was by design. In the past when she'd come around, she was always in need of money. Although she and Conway were never married, he'd bought and paid for her, she used to say, and his initials were tattooed in blue ink on her left forearm.

Catherine Eddowes was forty-three years old and very thin. Hardship and drink had given her a pinched look. But she may have been attractive once with her high cheekbones, dark eyes, and black hair. She and Kelly took one day at a time, holding themselves together mostly by hawking cheap items on the streets. Now and then she cleaned houses. September was harvest season and she and John Kelly had only just gotten back the day before from weeks of "hopping" with thousands of other people who'd fled London for migrant work. Catherine and Kelly had escaped the East End to roam the farming districts of Kent, gathering hops used in the brewing of beer. It was a yearly adventure that was considered a holiday far away from smog and filth, staying in barns and eating well. Usually they earned as much as a shilling per bushel, but in 1888 bad weather destroyed the crops. The couple had little work,

Catherine Eddowes, another alleged Ripper victim, lived in a lodging house with her romantic companion, John Kelly.

and when they returned to London they had not a penny between them.

On the last Friday of September Kelly returned to the lodging house at 55 Flower and Dean Street in Spitalfields, and Catherine stayed without him in a free bed at a casual ward. It's not known what she did that night. He later stated at her inquest that she wasn't a woman of the streets, and he wasn't the sort to tolerate her being with another man. Catherine never brought him money in the morning, he added, as if to imply she didn't pick up a pittance here and there through prostitution. He was adamant that she didn't have an addiction to alcohol. She was only occasionally "in the habit of slightly drinking to excess."

They considered themselves man and wife, and were fairly regular in paying the nightly rate of eightpence for their double bed at Flower and Dean Street. It was true they might have a word or two now and then, and some months earlier she'd left him for "a few hours." But Kelly swore under oath that he and Catherine had been getting along just fine of late. He said that on Saturday morning she offered to pawn some of her clothing so they could buy food. Instead he insisted that she pawn boots he'd purchased from an Arthur Pash who owned a chain of shops, and she did for half a crown.

That pawn ticket and another one were safely tucked inside one of Catherine's pockets in hopes she might be able to reclaim their belongings someday soon. She met up with Kelly between ten and eleven in the old clothing market at Houndsditch, a healed gash in the earth that in Roman days had been a moat protecting the city wall. Houndsditch ran between Aldgate High Street and Bishopsgate Within, and bordered the northeast side of the City of London. As Catherine and Kelly spent most of his boot money on food and enjoyed what for them was a hearty breakfast, she moved into the outer limits of her life. In less than fifteen hours Catherine Eddowes would be hacked up, bloodless and cold.

By early afternoon that Saturday she was dressed in what must have been everything she owned. Her black jacket had imitation fur around the collar and the sleeves. Two outer pockets were trimmed in black silk braid and imitation fur. A chintz shirt had a Michaelmas daisy pattern, and she wore three flounces, a brown linsey dress bodice with a black velvet collar and brown metal buttons down the front. Other layers included a gray petticoat, a very old green alpaca skirt, a ragged blue skirt with a red flounce and light twill lining, a white calico chemise, a man's white vest with buttons down the front and two outer pockets.

Her brown ribbed stockings were mended at the feet with white thread, and her right men's lace-up boot had been repaired with red thread. A black straw bonnet was trimmed with black beads and green-and-black velvet, her apron white but very dirty, and tied around her neck were "red gauze silk," according to the coroner's inquest, and a large white handkerchief. Tucked inside her many layers and pockets were another handkerchief, bits and pieces of soap, string, white rag, white coarse linen, blue-and-white skirting, blue ticking and flannel, two black clay pipes, a red leather cigarette case, a comb, pins and needles, a ball of hemp, a thimble, a table knife and a teaspoon. Two mustard tins safely secured a precious stash of sugar and tea she'd bought with Kelly's boot money.

At 2:00 p.m., she told him she was going to Bermondsey in the southeast part of the city. Maybe she could find her daughter, Annie, who used to have a house on King Street. Apparently Catherine didn't know that she hadn't lived there for years. Kelly said he wished Catherine wouldn't go anywhere. "Stay here," he told her. But she was insistent, and when he called out to be careful of the "Knife," a street name for Jack the Ripper, Catherine laughed. Of course she would be careful. She was always careful. She promised to be back in two hours.

Mother and daughter never saw each other that day, and no one seems to know where Catherine went. Perhaps she walked to Bermondsey and was dismayed to find that Annie had moved. Perhaps Catherine was informed that Annie and her husband had left the neighborhood at least two years earlier. Or maybe no one knew whom Catherine was talking about. It's also possible she didn't intend to go to Bermondsey at all and just wanted an excuse to earn pennies for gin. She may have been all too aware that no one in her family wanted anything to do with an alcohol-addicted, immoral woman who belonged in the dustbin. Whatever she was thinking, Catherine didn't return to Kelly by four o'clock as she'd promised.

Instead she got drunk and was locked up at Bishopsgate Police Station, just north of Houndsditch where Kelly had seen her last while they were eating and drinking away his boot money. When word reached him that she was in jail, he figured she was safe enough and went to bed. At the inquest he would admit that she'd been locked up before. But as was said of the other Ripper victims, she was a "sober, quiet" woman who got jolly and liked to sing when she had one drink too many, which of course was rare. None of the Ripper's victims were addicted to alcohol, friends swore from the witness stand.

In Catherine Eddowes's time, alcoholism was not considered a disease. "Habitual drunkenness" afflicted someone "of a weak mind" or "weak intellect" who was destined for the lunatic asylum or jail. Drunkenness was a clear indication that a person was of thin moral fiber, a sinner given to vice, and an imbecile in the making. Denial was just as persistent then as it is now, and euphemisms were plentiful. People got into the drink. They had a drop to drink. They were known to drink. They were the worse for drink, and Catherine was the worse for it on Saturday night. By 8:30 she'd passed out on a footway on Aldgate High Street, and Police Constable George Simmons picked her up and moved her off to the side. He leaned her against shutters but she couldn't stay on her feet. He called for another constable, and they got on either side of her to help her to the Bishopsgate Police Station.

Catherine was too drunk to say where she lived or whether she knew anyone who might come for her. When she was asked her name, she mumbled, "Nothing." At quarter past midnight she was awake and singing to herself inside her jail cell. Constable George Hutt testified at the inquest that he'd been checking on her the past three or four hours, and at approximately 1:00 a.m. she asked him when he was going to let her out. When she was capable of taking care of herself, he answered.

She told him she was fine to leave now and wanted to know what time it was. Too late for her to get "any more drink," he said. "Well, what time is it?" she persisted. He told her "just on one," and she retorted, "I shall get a damned fine hiding when I get home." Constable Hutt unlocked her cell and replied, "And serves you right; you have no right to get drunk." He brought her inside the office for questioning by the station sergeant. She gave a false name and address of "Mary Ann Kelly" of "Fashion Street."

Constable Hutt pushed open swinging doors that led to a passageway. "This way, Missus," he said as he showed her out, telling her to make sure to pull the outer door shut behind her. "Good night, ol' Cock," she said, leaving the door open, and she turned left toward Houndsditch, where she'd promised to meet John Kelly nine hours earlier. It's not known why Catherine headed that way first and then set out to Mitre Square, a fifteen-minute walk from Bishopsgate Police Station. Perhaps she planned to earn a few more pennies, and trouble wasn't likely in the City, at least not the kind of trouble Catherine might have been considering.

The wealthy "square mile" City of London can be traced back to AD 1 when Romans founded it on the banks of the Thames.

It has its own municipal services and government, including its own police force, which today serves a resident population of six thousand, a number that swells to more than a quarter of a million during business hours. Catherine's and Kelly's common lodging house at Flower and Dean Street was outside the City. Since he supposedly was unaware of her late-hours entrepreneurial activities, she may have concluded that it was wise to earn a few pennies in the City and not wander home and get into a row.

Perhaps she simply didn't know what she was doing. She'd been in jail less than four hours. The average person metabolizes approximately one ounce of alcohol or about one beer per hour. Catherine must have had quite a lot on board to be "falling down drunk," and it's possible that when Constable Hutt bid her good night she was still intoxicated. At the very least she was hungover and bleary. She may have suffered from tremors and blank spots in her memory.

The best cure was a little hair of the dog that bit her. She needed another drink and a bed, and could have neither without money. If her man was going to give her hell, it might be best if she slept somewhere else the rest of the night. Whatever she was contemplating, it doesn't appear that reconnecting with Kelly was foremost on her mind when she left the police station. Heading to Mitre Square meant walking in the opposite direction from where he was staying.

Some thirty minutes after Catherine left her jail cell, Joseph Lawende and his friends Joseph Levy and Harry Harris left the Imperial Club at 16 and 17 Duke Street in the City. It was raining, and Lawende was walking at a slightly faster pace than his companions when at the corner of Duke Street and the Church Passage that led to Mitre Square, he noticed a man and a woman together. Lawende would state at the inquest that he saw the man from the back, describing him as taller than the woman and wearing a cap that might have had a peak.

The woman was dressed in a black jacket and a black bonnet, Lawende recalled. When he visited the police station later he identified items of clothing as belonging to the woman he saw at 1:30 a.m., an exact time he based on the clubhouse clock and his own watch. "I doubt whether I should know him again," Lawende said of the man. "I did not hear a word said. They did not either of them appear to be quarreling. They appeared [to be] conversing very quietly—I did not look back to see where they went."

Joseph Levy didn't get a good look at the couple either, but he estimated that the man was perhaps three inches taller than the woman. Levy testified that he commented to his friend Harris, "I don't like going home by myself when I see these characters about." When questioned closely by the coroner

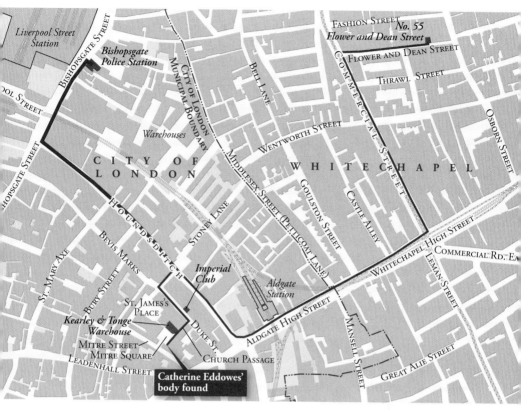

The police picked up Catherine Eddowes for drunkenness on Aldgate High Street and took her to Bishopsgate Police Station. They let her out later that night, and her body was found less than an hour later in Mitre Square at 1:44 a.m., Sept. 30, 1888.

at the inquest, Levy amended his statement. "There was nothing I saw about the man and woman which caused me to fear them," he said.

The Ripper may have struck minutes after Levy and his friends were gone from the square. His attack was fast, frenzied and quiet. A City Police constable and his family were home nearby, and a watchman stationed inside the Kearley & Tonge (wholesale grocers) warehouse was awake and working. No one heard a thing. P. C. Edward Watkins would testify at the inquest that he could walk his beat in twelve to fourteen minutes, and when he passed through the square last at 1:30 a.m. there wasn't the slightest hint of anything out of the ordinary.

Fourteen minutes later, at 1:44 a.m., he shone his bull's-eye lantern into a very dark corner and discovered a woman lying on her back, her face turned to the left, her arms by her sides, her palms up. Her left leg was straight, the other bent, and her clothing was bunched up above her chest. Her exposed abdomen had been cut open from just below the sternum to her genitals, the intestines pulled out and tossed on the ground above her right shoulder. Watkins ran to the Kearley & Tonge warehouse, knocked on the door and pushed it open. The watchman inside was sweeping the steps, completely oblivious to what had just happened.

"For God's sake, mate, come to my assistance," Watkins exclaimed, and the watchman fetched his lamp as an agitated Watkins described "another woman cut up to pieces." The two men hurried out to the southwest corner of Mitre Square, where Catherine's body lay in a pool of blood, and Watkins blasted his whistle and ran. Finding two more constables he yelled to them, "Go down to Mitre Square. There has been another terrible murder!"

Not long after 2:00 a.m. the police surgeon for the City Police, Dr. Gordon Brown, arrived at the scene. He squatted by the body, and near it were three metal buttons, a "common" thimble, and a mustard tin containing two pawn tickets. Based on Dr. Brown's observations about the body's warmth and the complete absence of rigor mortis, he decided that the victim had been dead no longer than half an hour. He saw no bruises, no signs of struggle and no evidence of "recent connection" or sexual intercourse.

He was of the opinion that the intestines had been placed where they were "by design," an observation made before by police and likely too complicated when one considers the circumstances. The Ripper was in a frenzy. It was very dark unless he had some means of illumination such as a candle or a lantern, which would have been extremely risky. He probably was crouched or bent over the lower part of Catherine's body when he slashed and tore through clothing and flesh, and it's likely that he simply tossed the intestines out of the way because it was certain organs he wanted.

It was fortuitous that the City Police Superintendent's son, Frederick William Foster, was an architect. Immediately, he was summoned to sketch the body and the area where it was found, and these drawings at the Royal

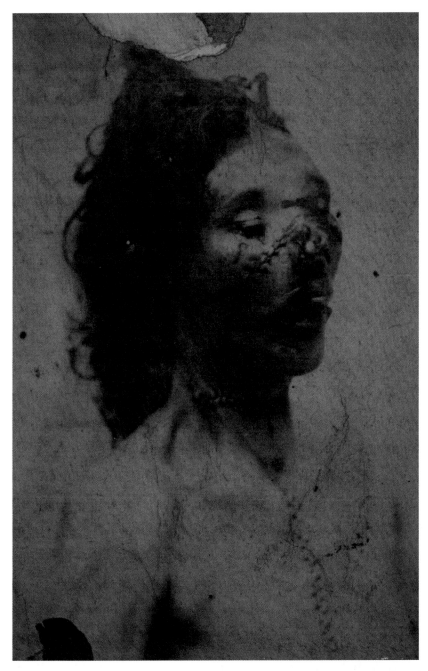

Eddowes was found with her abdomen cut open from sternum to genitals. The City of London had better funding for mortuary facilities than the East End of London, which is why more photos were taken of Eddowes than of the Ripper's other victims.

London Hospital Museum depict a detailed and disturbing sight that's worse than any description at the inquest. Catherine Eddowes's clothing was cut and torn open, blatantly displaying a body cavity that couldn't have been more violated had she already been autopsied. The Ripper slashed open her chest and abdomen to her upper thighs and genitals. He cut through her vagina and across the tops of her thighs as if he were reflecting back or removing tissue in preparation for dismembering her legs at the hip joints.

The disfigurement to her face was shocking. Peculiar deep nicks through both eyes and under them are similar to brushstrokes Sickert used in some of his paintings, most dramatically in *Putana a Casa*, a portrait of a Venetian prostitute he called La Giuseppina. The most severe damage to Catherine's face was to the right side, the same side of Giuseppina's face that has disturbing black brushstrokes reminiscent of mutilation. A morgue photograph of Catherine resembles Giuseppina. Both women had long black hair, high cheekbones and pointed chins.

In another painting titled *Le Journal* (circa 1906), a dark-haired woman has her head thrown back, and her mouth open. She's reading

The son of the City Police Superintendent was immediately summoned to sketch the murder scene.

Above: Sickert's painting *Putana a Casa* ***(left)*** depicts a prostitute with strange black brushstrokes that appear similar to the cuts on Eddowes's face ***(right)***. *Putana a Casa*, 1903–1904 by Walter Sickert, Harvard Art Museums / Fogg Museum, gift of Patricia Cornwell, 2009.90.34 / Imaging Department © President and Fellows of Harvard College. ***Below:*** Sickert's 1906 painting *Le Journal* ***(left)*** features a woman with a tight white necklace, with her head thrown back and her mouth open. It bears a resemblance to the pre-autopsy photo taken of Eddowes with her neck cut open ***(right)***.

a book or journal that she bizarrely holds high above her stricken face. Around her throat is a tight white necklace. "What a pretty necklace I gave her," the Ripper writes on September 17, 1888. Catherine Eddowes's "pretty necklace" is a gaping gash in her throat that is shown in one of the few photographs taken before the autopsy and the suturing of the wounds. If one juxtaposes that photograph with the painting *Le Journal*, the similarities are startling.

Catherine's body was transported by hand ambulance to the mortuary on Golden Lane, and when she was undressed under close police supervision, her left earlobe fell out of her clothing.

25

NIGHT HORRORS

A T 2:30 THAT SUNDAY AFTERNOON, Dr. Brown and his associates performed Catherine Eddowes's postmortem examination.

Other than one small fresh bruise on her left hand, the doctors found no other injuries that might suggest she fought with her assailant. There were no indications she was struck, yoked or thrown to the ground. Her cause of death was a six- or seven-inch cut across her neck that began at her left earlobe and terminated about three inches below her right ear. The incision severed her larynx, vocal cords and the deep structures of her neck and nicked the intervertebral cartilage.

Dr. Brown determined that Catherine had hemorrhaged from her severed left carotid artery. Death "was immediate," and the other mutilations were inflicted postmortem. He believed there was only one weapon, probably a knife, and that it was pointed. Much more could have been said and asked. The autopsy details indicate that the Ripper "cut" through Catherine's clothing, and considering the many layers she was wearing, this poses questions and difficulties. Not just any type of cutting instrument could have been used, no matter how old and rotted the fabrics might have been.

During my early days in this investigation, I experimented with a variety of nineteenth-century knives, daggers and straight razors, trying them out on large, raw rump roasts that I hollowed out and filled with cow and pig organs I got from the grocery store. I dressed my unseemly creations in layers of old cotton, wool and linen. I discovered that cutting through many layers of fabric and tissue with a folding straight razor or a long curved blade is tricky and impractical. The weapon that worked best was a six-inch dagger with a scored handle and a guard that prevents the hand from slipping.

We can't know for a fact that Jack the Ripper ever used a dagger. Just as an artist uses different brushes he may have used a variety of knives depending on whether he was slashing a throat or face, disemboweling or dismembering. Many Ripper letters include drawings of knives, most of them daggerlike. I suspect the Ripper didn't actually cut through the

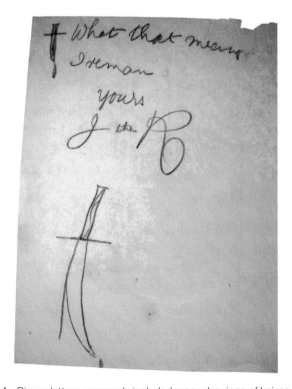

Above and right: Ripper letters commonly included many drawings of knives.

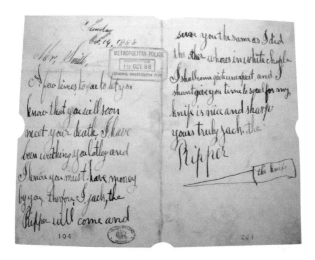

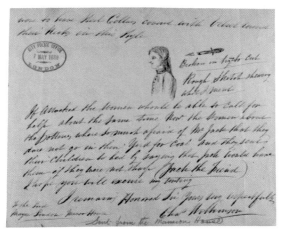

clothing but rather stabbed through layers and tore them open, exposing the abdomen and genitals.

A proper examination of what Catherine had on when she was killed would answer the question. But that's not possible since none of the Ripper victims' personal effects were kept by the police. There are no garments or items that provably belonged to any of the victims, and at the time of the murders, little importance was placed on whether the killer cut clothing, tore it or simply moved it out of the way. There was no such thing as using case data to psychologically interpret the rituals or signature of a violent psychopath's crimes.

The MO or method of operation was grossly misinterpreted if it was considered at all, and explanations offered were little more than guesses that indicate a profound misunderstanding of the physics of dying. Based on blood patterns, it was concluded that the Ripper's victims couldn't have been standing when the killer severed their carotid arteries. There's no empirical evidence for such an assumption, and a proper understanding of the injuries strongly indicates otherwise. The incisions to Elizabeth Stride's and Catherine Eddowes's necks are consistent with the women being attacked from behind. But in 1888 little was known about how blood drips, flies, sprays, spurts and spatters according to the laws of physics. No one working the Ripper cases was spending his time researching how far or high blood arcs when an upright person's carotid artery is cut. There was no consideration or comprehension of the cast-off pattern caused by the repeated swinging or stabbing motions of a bloody weapon.

Doctors who responded to the crime scenes didn't seem to consider that perhaps Jack the Ripper simultaneously cut a victim's throat and pulled her backward to the ground as arterial blood spurted out of her neck. As she was hemorrhaging to death and aspirating her blood, he moved around to begin cutting and tearing through her clothing. He began mutilating her lower body, and in Catherine Eddowes's homicide also her face. The attack may have lasted only minutes.

Although the City of London would come no closer to capturing the Ripper, at least it was better equipped to handle his carnage. Catherine's records are surprisingly well preserved, revealing that the examination of her body was very thorough and professional for that era. The City Police

had certain advantages, including a substantially smaller, wealthier jurisdiction to control. They had a suitable mortuary and access to superb medical men. Every possible effort was made to work her murder properly,
and it wasn't the fault of those involved that little was known or correctly
understood about forensics. There were no such things as crime labs or
training programs for pathologists and crime scene investigators.

After Catherine was transported to the City mortuary on Golden Lane,
the police assigned an inspector whose only responsibility was to look after
her body, clothing and personal effects. When Dr. Brown performed the
autopsy, he was assisted by the Metropolitan Police Surgeon Dr. George
Bagster Phillips and an additional physician. If one assumes that she was
the first victim whose clothing was "cut off" instead of pushed out of the
way, what this would tell us today is the Ripper's MO was rapidly evolving.
His sexual violence, confidence and need to shock were escalating. He'd
butchered his most recent victim in the middle of a sidewalk and left her
almost nude with legs splayed. The blood flowing out of her severed carotid
artery seeped under her and left an outline of her body that was visible
to passersby and the curious the next day. The Ripper struck practically
within view of a watchman, a sleeping constable who lived on the square,
and a City officer whose beat took him past the murder scene every twelve
to fourteen minutes.

The damage the Ripper inflicted on Catherine's body required no surgical skill. He simply slashed like mad, the mutilation to her face quick and
forceful, slicing through her lips to the underlying gums. The cut to the
bridge of her nose extended down to the angle of her left jaw and laid open
her cheek to the bone, the tip of the nose completely severed. Two other
cuts to the cheeks peeled up the skin in triangular flaps, and the damage to
her abdomen, genitalia and internal organs was just as brutal. The incisions
that laid her open were jagged and mixed with stabbing injuries. Her left
kidney and half of her uterus were missing, and she'd suffered wounds to
her pancreas and spleen.

A stabbing cut to her vagina extended through her rectum, and hacks
to her right thigh were so deep they severed ligaments. There was nothing
careful or even purposeful about her injuries. The intention was mutilation, and the Ripper could have inflicted his sloppy, frenzied damage to

her body in less than ten minutes, maybe in as few as five. His violence and brazenness were in overdrive. It was requiring more daring and savagery to achieve the same thrill, and it wouldn't be surprising if he returned to Mitre Square to observe the throngs of people gawking at his latest victim's bloody outline on the pavers. In a Sickert painting titled *The Fair, Dieppe* (circa 1902), he depicts a mob of people from the rear, as if we're looking through the eyes of an observer standing some distance back. Were it not for what appears to be a carousel tent intruding into the painting from the right, there would be no reason to think the scene has anything to do with

Sickert's painting titled *The Fair, Dieppe* depicts a crowd of people eagerly watching a spectacle that is not visible to the viewer.

a fair. The people don't necessarily seem interested in the carousel but in activity occurring in the direction of tenement or row houses.

A fair or carnival is exactly what the Ripper's crime scenes had become by the end of September 1888. Boys hawked special editions of newspapers, vendors arrived with carts, and neighbors sold tickets for a better view. The International Working Men's Educational Club on Berner Street raised money to print its socialist tracts by charging admission to enter the yard where Elizabeth Stride was killed. For a penny one could purchase "A Thrilling Romance" about the Whitechapel murders that promised "all details connected with these Diabolical Crimes, and faithfully pictures the Night Horrors of this portion of the Great City."

No footprints were found at any of the Ripper's crime scenes, according to the extant documentation. It's almost impossible to imagine he didn't step in blood when pints of it were spurting and flowing.

But bloody footprints wouldn't necessarily have been visible without the aid of forensic alternate light sources and chemicals. Trace evidence would have been missed and one can be certain that the Ripper left hairs, fibers and other microscopic materials at the scene and on his victims. He carried trace evidence away with him on his person, footwear and clothing. His victims would have been a forensic nightmare because of the contamination and mixture of evidence including fibers and other debris and DNA from multiple clients.

But there would have been something worth collecting. Unusual evidence may have been discovered. Cosmetics worn by a killer are easily transferred to a victim, and had Sickert applied greasepaint to darken his skin or temporarily dyed his hair or been wearing adhesives for false mustaches and beards, traces of them could have been detected. Today's forensic scientists would use microscopes, chemical analysis and spectrophotofluorometric methods that could identify the actual brand or trade name of a makeup, glue or other materials and media. A residue of paints from Sickert's studios wouldn't have eluded the scanning electron microscope, the ion microprobe, the X-ray diffractometer or thin-layer chromatography, to mention a few of the resources available today. Tempera paint on a Sickert painting lit up a neon blue when scientists in Virginia examined it with a nondestructive alternate light source. If Sickert had transferred a microscopic paint residue from his clothing or hands to a victim, today's investigators would find it. Chemical or elemental analysis would follow.

Had it been possible in the Victorian era to detect an artist's paints adhering to a victim's blood, the police might not have been so quick to assume Jack the Ripper was a butcher, a lunatic Pole or Russian Jew or an insane medical student. The presence of microscopic residues consistent with cosmetics or adhesives would have raised significant questions. Stray knives turning up would have given answers instead of only posing questions. A preliminary quick-and-easy chemical test could have determined whether the dried reddish material on the blades was blood instead of rust or some other substance. Precipitin tests that react to antibodies would have determined whether the blood was human, and DNA would either match a victim's genetic profile or not. It's possible that fingerprints and the killer's DNA could have been found on a knife.

Hairs could be compared or analyzed. Tool marks imparted by a blade to cartilage or bone could have been compared to any weapon recovered. Today all possibilities would be exhausted. But what we can't account for is how much the Ripper would know were he committing his murders now. I continue to point out that Sickert was described by acquaintances as having a scientific mind. He was known for his memory, and his paintings and etchings demonstrate considerable technical skill. Some of his drawings were made in a tradesman's daybook that had columns for pounds, shillings, and pence. On the backs of other sketches are mathematical scribbles, perhaps from Sickert's calculating the prices of things. Similar scribbles are on a scrap of lined paper the Ripper wrote a letter on. Apparently he was figuring out the price of coal.

Sickert made careful preparations for his paintings, and he premeditated his crimes. Were he committing his murders now, he'd be sure to know quite a lot about modern criminalistics. I have no doubt he would have known what was available in 1888, which was little more than handwriting comparison, identification by physical features, and "finger marks."

He likely would have been aware of sexually transmitted diseases and may have exposed himself to his victims' body fluids as little as possible.

Sickert acquaintances recalled in their written anecdotes that he had a fetish about hygiene and was continually washing his hands. He would immediately wash his hair and face if he accidentally put on another person's hat. Maybe his phobia was real or maybe such stories are simply more of his histrionics. But he would have been well aware that blood splashed into his face or transferred from his hands to his eyes or mouth or an open wound could cause him a serious problem. Years later he would worry that he had a sexually transmitted disease. It turned out to be gout.

He may have worn gloves when he killed and then removed his bloody clothing as quickly as he could. He may have worn rubber-soled boots that were quiet on the street and easy to clean. He could have carried weapons, changes of clothing and disguises in a Gladstone bag. "Togs 8 suits, many hats I wear," the Ripper writes in an eighty-one-line poem he sent the "Superintendent of Great Scotland Yard" on November 8, 1889. "The man is keen: quick, and leaves no trace—" His objective is to "destroy the filthy hideous whores of the night; Dejected, lost, cast down, ragged . . . and thin, Frequenters of Theatres, Music-halls and drinkers of Hellish gin."

Sickert was well known for his theatrical attire and alterations of his physical appearance. In a collection of Florence Pash–Walter Sickert letters edited by Violet Overton Fuller there's a story of a London merchant named Louis Cornelissen, whose art supply shop Sickert and Whistler frequented. Ms. Fuller writes that "Mr. Louis remembers his [Sickert] coming to the shop in various disguises, sometimes clean shaven, sometimes with a beard, sometimes a real 'Piccadilly swell', sometimes an old tramp or country farmer. At times he was quite unrecognizable, but Mr. Louis always knew by his voice, which was very cultured and agreeably pitched."

An actor, a brilliant artist and master of disguise would script and choreograph his crimes in a way that is frightening to consider. Sickert's mathematical logic, his mockery and imagination would have been quite the combination, and may suggest an explanation for an odd story that ran in the *Daily Telegraph* and the *Weekly Dispatch* on Saturday, September 1, 1888. A dairyman reported to police that within hours of Mary Ann Nichols's murder, a stranger appeared at his shop on Little Turner Street

Sickert created this self-portrait. A shopkeeper described him as often dressing in "various disguises."

off Commercial Road. The man carried a shiny black bag and asked to buy a penny's worth of milk that he drank in "one gulp."

Next he asked to borrow the shed, and while he was inside it the dairyman noticed a flash of white. He went to investigate and caught this person covering his trousers with a "pair of white overalls such as engineers wear." Then he snatched out a white jacket, and as he hastily pulled it over his black cutaway, he said, "It's a dreadful murder, isn't it?" He grabbed his black bag and rushed into the street, exclaiming, "I think I have a clue!"

The dairyman described his uninvited visitor as about twenty-eight years old with a ruddy complexion, three days' growth of beard, dark hair and large staring eyes. He had the general appearance of a "clerk" or "student," and I find it interesting that Sickert wore white coveralls when he worked in his studios. He didn't want to get paint on his clothes. Maybe he didn't want to get blood on them either when he destroyed his victims in much the same way he would destroy a painting if it wasn't up to par.

Sickert was known for slashing to tatters unworthy or failed works of art, and according to writer Osbert Sitwell, on one occasion Sickert instructed his wife Ellen to go out and buy two long sharp knives with curved blades like the ones she used for pruning. He needed them to cut up paintings Whistler supposedly was discontented with. Symbolically, an artist destroying a painting could be viewed as analogous to a killer destroying the face and body of a victim. The destruction could be an effort to eradicate what causes frustration and rage or an attempt to ruin what one can't possess, whether it is artistic perfection or the object of lust. As I've pointed out, not all serial killers sexually assault their victims. For some of these offenders the violent acts themselves are what arouse and become a compulsion.

Night after night, Sickert watched sexually provocative performances at music halls. During much of his career he would sketch nude female models. He spent time behind locked studio doors, staring, posing, possibly touching but perhaps never consummating except through a pencil, a brush and a palette knife. If he was capable of sexual desire but incapable of gratifying it, his frustration must have been agonizing and enraging. A young art student named Cicely Hey recalls that in the early 1920s, while he was painting portraits of her, he sat next to her on the studio sofa one day. Without warning or explanation he started screaming.

Sickert titled this portrait of Cicely Hey *Death and the Maiden*.

He ominously titled one of her portraits *Death and the Maiden*. At some point between the early 1920s and when he died in 1942, he gave her the painting he titled *Jack the Ripper's Bedroom*. In a letter to art critic John Russell dated September 30, 1958, Cicely Hey explains that Sickert told her Jack the Ripper was a veterinary student who had stayed in a room at Mornington Crescent, where Sickert was living at the time. In her will she left one of her portraits and *Jack the Ripper's Bedroom* to the City Art

Gallery in Manchester, and on September 2, 1980, Keeper of Fine Art Julian Treuherz writes the following to Sickert expert and art historian Wendy Baron:

> *We have just received a bequest of two oil paintings by Sickert from Mrs. Tatlock, nee Cicely Hey. They are Jack the Ripper's Bedroom, oil on canvas, 20 x 16", and Portrait of Cicely Hey, oil on canvas 24 X 20". . . . I imagine you know them, and I wonder if you have any comments on them. Jack the Ripper's Bedroom seems to be similar to your catalogue numbers 213 and 259, Mornington Crescent Nude, 1906–7.*

Sickert's *Jack the Ripper's Bedroom* depicts a room at 6 Mornington Crescent.

On October 12, 1980, Dr. Baron thanks Mr. Treuherz for his letter and photographs of these two paintings. She confirms that the interior of *Jack the Ripper's Bedroom* was 6 Mornington Crescent, where Walter Sickert claimed Jack the Ripper had lodged in the 1880s. It was the same address where Sickert lived from 1905 to 1907.

26

A GREAT JOKE

A T 3:00 A.M. ON SEPTEMBER 30, Metropolitan Police Constable Alfred Long was patrolling Goulston Street in Whitechapel. He'd just been reassigned to H Division because of the Ripper murders, and he wasn't very familiar with the area.

Long walked past several dark buildings occupied by Jews, directing his bull's-eye lantern into the shadows, listening for any unusual sounds. The bleary light illuminated a gloomy passageway leading inside a building, then a porch where a filthy piece of dark-stained fabric was on the ground. Above it written in white chalk on the black dado of the wall was:

The Juwes are
The men That
Will not
be Blamed
for nothing.

Long picked up what appeared to be a piece of an apron partially wet with blood, and he immediately searched the staircases of 100–119. He got out his notebook, copied the chalk writing and rushed to the Commercial Street Police Station. It was more important that he report what he'd discovered than knock on doors, he decided, and he didn't have a partner to assist him. He may have been scared. Some forty minutes earlier he'd patrolled that same passageway on Goulston Street, shining his lantern into the porch, and the piece of apron wasn't there then. He also would testify at the inquest that he didn't know for a fact if the chalk message on the wall was "very recently written."

Perhaps the ethnic slur had been there for a while and it was simply a coincidence that the bit of bloody apron was directly below it—but that's not likely considering the neighborhood. It wouldn't make sense for a slur about Jews to be left in the passageway of a building occupied by them. The residents would have eradicated the offensive words earlier, the police decided, and probably they were right. The accepted view has always been that the Ripper wrote those bigoted words right after he murdered Catherine Eddowes, and this is yet one more source of controversy in the Ripper case.

The message presumably dashed off by him was in a legible hand, and I found two versions of it in the Metropolitan Police files at The National Archives. Long was fastidious. The two copies he made in his notebook are almost identical, suggesting they may closely resemble what he saw in chalk. His facsimiles show similarities to some characteristics of Sickert's hand-writing. The uppercase *T*'s closely resemble ones in the Ripper letter of September 25. But it's treacherous to compare writing that's a "copy," no matter how carefully it was made, and such an analysis would never hold up in court.

The bull's-eye lantern Constable Alfred Long was carrying when he discovered the chalk message on Goulston Street.

Ripper experts and enthusiasts have always been intent on decoding the writing on the wall. Why was *Jews* spelled *Juwes*? Perhaps the slur was nothing more than a scribble intended to create the very stir it has. The Ripper liked to write. He made sure his presence was known. So did Sickert, who had a habit of scrawling notes in chalk on the dark walls of his studios. Unfortunately, there's no photograph of the writing on the wall in Catherine Eddowes's case because Charles Warren ordered that it be removed immediately. The sun would rise soon and the Jewish community would see the chalky insult. All hell would break loose.

As his policemen anxiously waited for the cumbersome wooden camera, they sent word to Warren suggesting that the first line containing the word *Juwes* could be scrubbed off. Then the rest of the writing could be photographed for handwriting comparison. Absolutely not, Warren fired back. Eradicate the writing *right now*. Day was breaking. People were stirring about, and soon thousands of them would be headed to the Petticoat Lane street market just around the corner from the building where the slur was written. The camera hadn't arrived, and the writing was rubbed out.

It seemed likely that the piece of apron Constable Long found came from the dirty white apron Catherine Eddowes was wearing over her clothing. But Dr. Gordon Brown said he couldn't possibly know if the blood on it was human even though St. Bartholomew's, the oldest hospital in London with one of the finest medical schools, was right there in the City. Dr. Brown could have submitted the bloody piece of apron to a microscopist. But he didn't. At least he thought to tie off both ends of Catherine's stomach and submit it for chemical analysis in the event narcotics were present. They weren't. The Ripper wasn't drugging his victims first to incapacitate them.

The police decided the killer had cut off the bit of apron so he could wipe blood and fecal matter off his hands. For some reason he hung on to the soiled fabric as he left the City and retraced his steps back toward Whitechapel. He ducked into the entrance of the building on Goulston Street to write the ugly words on the wall, and then thought to discard the piece of soiled apron. Or more likely he left it deliberately as a clue, another taunt that linked the ethnic slur to the murder he'd just committed.

The bit of bloody apron wasn't viewed as part of the Ripper's deliberate game, and his visit to Goulston Street wasn't interpreted as more of his ongoing mockery of authority. It's a wonder the police didn't ask why the killer was carrying around chalk. Did people of the East End routinely carry chalk or even own it? A tailor or schoolchildren might. Perhaps it should have been considered that if the Ripper brought a stick of chalk with him when he set out that night, then perhaps he planned to write the bigoted message or something like it on a wall after he committed murder.

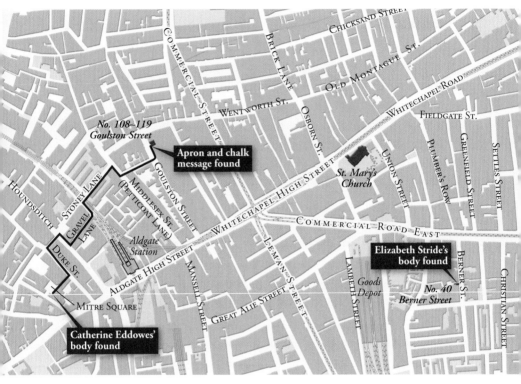

A cryptic message attributed to the Ripper was discovered in Goulston Street soon after the murder of Catherine Eddowes in Mitre Square, reading "The Juwes are The men That Will not be Blamed for nothing."

Maybe he was someone who carried chalk and pencils and paper on his person as a matter of routine.

For the Ripper to backtrack from Mitre Square to Goulston Street involved his virtually returning to Elizabeth Stride's crime scene. Quite likely this route took him from the Church Passage out of Mitre Square and to Houndsditch, Gravel Lane, Stoney Lane and across Petticoat Lane, where Sickert would take Marjorie Lilly and her friend on an unnerving sojourn in the fog many years later. The police were baffled that the murderer would be this bold. There were constables and detectives all over the place. The law-enforcement community would have been better served had it spent more energy analyzing the killer's outrageous backtrack and his piece of chalk instead of getting stuck on the meaning of *Juwes*.

For the likes of Walter Sickert it would have been another big "ha ha" to head back to the scene of Elizabeth Stride's murder, and he might have been so bold as to ask a constable what was going on. In the same 1889 poem about his many disguises, the Ripper boasts: "I spoke to a policeman who saw the sight, And informed me it was done by a Knacker in the night. . . . I told the man you should try and catch him; Say another word old Chap I'll run you in. One night hard gone I did a policeman meet— Treated and walked with him down High St."

Old Chap? If the policeman really said such a thing to Jack the Ripper, this might hint of a disguise. The 1889 poem was "filed with the others." No significant attention was paid to the distinctive form of printing or the clever rhymes, which clearly aren't the work of an illiterate, ignorant or deranged person. The reference to theaters and music halls as places where the Ripper spots "whores" should have been another clue. Perhaps an undercover man or two should have begun frequenting such places. Sickert spent many of his nights at theaters and music halls. Lunatics and impoverished butchers and East End ruffians probably didn't.

In the 1889 poem, the Ripper also admits he reads the "papers" and takes great exception to being called "insane." He says, "I always do my work alone," contradicting the much-publicized theory that the Ripper might have an accomplice. He claims he doesn't "smoke, swill, or touch gin." "Swill" was street slang for excessive drinking, which Sickert didn't engage in at this stage in his life. If he drank at all, he wasn't likely to touch rotgut gin. He didn't smoke cigarettes but was fond of cigars and became rather much addicted to them in later years. "Altho, self taught," the Ripper says, "I can write and spell." As I've mentioned, Sickert supposedly taught himself to read and write.

The poem is difficult to decipher in places. *Knacker* might be used twice or might be *Knocker* in one of the lines. "Knacker" was street slang for a horse slaughterer. "Knocker" was someone finely or showily dressed, or it could refer to men who were human alarm clocks, charging a fee for knocking on windows and doors to wake people up. Sickert was no horse slaughterer but the police publicly theorized that the Ripper might be one. Sickert's greatest gift wasn't poetry but this didn't deter him from jotting a rhyme or two in letters or singing silly original lyrics he set to music hall tunes. "I have composed a poem to Ethel," he writes in later years, when his friend Ethel Sands was volunteering for the Red Cross:

With your syringe on your shoulder
And your thermometer by your side
You'll be curing some young officer
And making him your pride

In another letter he jots a verse about the "incessant sopping drizzle" in Normandy:

It can't go on for ever
It would if it could
But there is no use talking
For it couldn't if it would

In a Ripper letter sent in October 1896 to the Commercial Street Police Station in Whitechapel, the writer mockingly quotes, "'The Jewes are people that are blamed for nothing' Ha Ha have you heard this before."

During Catherine Eddowes's inquest, the spelling of *Jews* was a point of heated discussion. The coroner repeatedly questioned police whether the word on the wall was *Juwes* or *Jewes*. Even though the Ripper was presumed dead by 1896, according to Chief Constable Melville Macnaghten, the letter I just mentioned concerned the police enough to result in a flurry of memorandums written around the time Sickert had returned to London from Venice. "I beg to submit attached letter received per post 14th inst. signed Jack the Ripper stating that writer has just returned from abroad and means to go on again when he gets the chance," Detective Inspector George Payne writes in his special report from the Commercial Street station. "The letter appears similar to those received by police during the series of murders in the district in 1888 and 1889."

A telegram was sent to all divisions requesting that police keep a "sharp lookout," but at the same time to keep the information quiet.

"Writer in sending the letter no doubt considers it a great joke at the expense of the police." On October 18, 1896, Chief Inspector Henry Moore writes in a Central Officer's Special Report that he'd compared the recent letter with old Jack the Ripper letters. He "failed to find any similarity of handwriting in any of them, with the exception of the two well remembered communications which were sent to the 'Central News' Office; one a letter, dated 25th Sept./88 and the other a postcard, bearing the postmark 1st Oct./88."

The chief inspector goes on to note "many similarities in the formation of letters. For instance the y's, t's and w's are very much the same. Then there are several words which appear in both documents." But in the end he decides, "I beg to observe that I do not attach any importance to this communication." CID Superintendent Donald Swanson agreed. In his opinion "the handwritings are not the same," he jots on Henry Moore's report. "I beg that the letter may be put with other similar letters. Its circulation is to be regretted."

The letter of 1896 was given no credibility by police and wasn't published in the newspapers. The Ripper was banished, exorcised. He no longer existed. Maybe he'd never existed but was just some lunatic who killed a few prostitutes, and all of those letters were from crackpots. Ironically Jack the Ripper became a "Mr. Nobody," at least to the police, who likely were eager to believe the Ripper wasn't killing anymore. It was convenient to live in denial, and it wasn't understood that serial killers don't typically suddenly start and stop.

The Ripper was no exception, and as is true of other violent sexual predators he may not have restricted his murders to one location, especially if it were heavily patrolled by police—especially if thousands of anxious citizens were looking for him. It would have been risky to write letters laying claim to every murder he committed. He had a compulsion to kill but didn't want to be caught, and while on the lam or traveling about, he would have chanced upon other opportunities. If he acted on them he may not have bragged about his every slaughter. I can't definitively prove the Ripper killed more victims than the five, six or seven generally agreed upon. But there were other violent deaths that merit a review, one of them eleven months after the 1896 Ripper letter that the police concluded wasn't written by him.

Twenty-year-old Emma Johnson was a domestic servant who set out alone on the early evening of Wednesday, September 15, to walk home after visiting friends near Windsor, about twenty miles west of London. She vanished, and the following day, two women picking blackberries close to Maidenhead Road discovered two muddy petticoats, a bloody chemise and a black coat in a ditch under shrubbery. On Friday, September 17, the Berkshire police were notified of Emma's disappearance and organized a search. The clothing was identified as hers. Two days later on Sunday a laborer found a skirt, a bodice, a collar and a pair of cuffs in the same area of the field where the other bloody clothing had been discovered. Emma's mother located a pair of her daughter's stays on the banks of a stagnant inlet of the Thames, and nearby were the imprint of a woman's boot and scrape marks in the dirt, apparently made by someone dragging a heavy object toward the murky water.

Police searched the inlet, and fifteen feet offshore a muddy, slimy, naked body emerged. It was identified by the Johnsons as their daughter, and a doctor conducted an examination at the family home. He concluded that Emma was grabbed by the right arm and received a blow to the head that would have rendered her insensible before the killer cut her throat. At some point her clothing was removed, then the killer dragged her body to the inlet and shoved or threw it into the water. Maidenhead Road was a well-known spot for romantic couples to frequent at night, and the murder was never solved.

There's no evidence it was committed by Jack the Ripper but it's noteworthy that in September there were events at the Ascot Racecourse in Windsor, and Sickert was fond of the Ascot and had been there before. I don't know where he was when Emma Johnson was savagely slain, but he wasn't with Ellen. She was in France, the two of them having separated the year before. She wasn't there to take care of his every selfish need, and by 1897 he had lost his safe base and was burning bridges. Sickert was under tremendous stress.

He was being sued for libel after publishing an article in the *Saturday Review* that claimed artist Joseph Pennell's prints made by transfer lithography weren't true lithography. Whistler used the same lithographic process—as did Sickert—and Pennell's attorney, the flamboyant George

In this never-before-published letter from Janie Cobden to her sister Ellen Sickert, Janie quotes Whistler describing Sickert as having a "treacherous side to his character." Around the same time, another artist sued Sickert for libel and Whistler appeared as a witness for the prosecution, signaling a final break between the master and apprentice.

Lewis, convinced the obstreperous peacock Whistler to appear as a witness in the case. In an October 1896 letter to Ellen from her sister Janie, the master was quoted as saying that he believed Sickert's arrow was really aimed at him, not Pennell.

Sickert had a "treacherous side to his character," Whistler tells Janie. "Walter will do anything, throw anyone over for the object of the moment." Sickert lost the lawsuit. But perhaps the greater sting was when Whistler testified from the witness stand that his former pupil was an unimportant and irresponsible man. Whistler had nothing but contempt for him, and in an April 6, 1897, telegram to his sister-in-law Rosalind Birnie Phillip, Whistler gleefully writes, "ENEMY MET AND DESTROYED . . . SICKERT IN AMBULANCE." Weeks later Whistler writes to his half sister, Deborah Delano Haden, that as for the "miserable" Irish novelist and art critic George Moore "of course I have destroyed him forever and for that matter Walter Sickert too!"

27

A SOCIAL
DISEASE

AT THE MORTUARY on Golden Lane, Catherine Eddowes's naked body was displayed upright against the wall, hung by a nail like a ripped-up painting.

In her postmortem photographs railroad tracks of sutured twine snake down from her diaphragm to her right thigh, where they loop back up, closing the flap the Ripper had cut to remove her organs. She literally was gutted; the damage is so severe it's difficult to tell the Ripper's incisions from those made during the autopsy.

One can only imagine the shock and disgust of the male jurors and Coroner Samuel Frederick Langham, Esquire, as they filed in to look at her ghastly mutilations. On October 4, 1888,

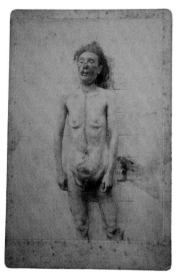

The coroner stitched up Catherine Eddowes's body where it had been slashed open by the Ripper.

they returned what was becoming a familiar verdict: "Wilful murder by some person unknown." The public outcry was approaching hysteria. Two women had been slaughtered within an hour of each other, and the police still hadn't a clue.

Letters from the public warned, "The condition of the lowest classes is most fraught with danger to all other classes." Londoners in better neighborhoods were beginning to fear for their lives. Perhaps they ought to raise a fund for the poor to "offer them a chance to forsake their evil lives." An "agency" should be formed, and letters to *The Times* suggested that if the upper class could civilize the lower class there would be no more of this violence.

But overpopulation and the class system had deeply rooted problems that couldn't be remedied by simply tearing down slums or forming "agencies." The advocacy of birth control was considered blasphemous, and intractable poverty abounded more than empathy did. While the public wanted the Ripper caught, not everyone held his victims blameless or considered their murders a loss to society. The people of the dustbin were trash and would always be trash, many people thought, and to be lulled into such a mind-set was a dangerous trap.

While it's true that serious social problems existed in Victorian England, that's not why prostitutes and possibly others were dying at the Ripper's hands. Serial murder isn't a social disease, and the poor and disadvantaged may not have been familiar with the word *psychopath*. But they knew they were being terrorized by one, and the police investigation went into high gear in the East End. Scores of plainclothes detectives began lurking in the shadow, and their disguises and demeanor fooled no one.

Some officers and reporters began wearing rubber-soled boots, and they must have frightened each other as they quietly crossed paths in the dark trying to catch the Ripper. But they weren't looking in the right places. They didn't seem aware that the violence was escalating as his MO evolved, and the body count was higher than was being reported. In fact the Ripper had committed another mutilating murder weeks earlier that the police had decided not to attribute to him. If they had, they might have begun to get a better sense of the diabolical mind they were up against.

Punch mocks the police for being unable to catch the one responsible for the string of murders.

They might have realized that Jack the Ripper was hell-bent on playing mocking and sadistic games with them, and this would suggest he was far more intelligent, resourceful and cunning than the police believed. He was no primitive brute. He wasn't some insane, illiterate or ignorant immigrant. The violent antisocial acts the Ripper engineered were carefully calculated

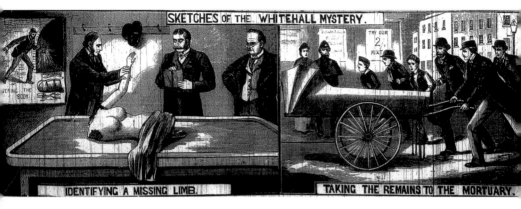

Two days after the double murder of Stride and Eddowes, the decomposing torso of a woman was found in the construction site of Scotland Yard's new headquarters.

and planned as his contempt toward government and law enforcement fomented, as his need to degrade and shock intensified. The police seemed clueless that for the Ripper this was personal. Like a nasty little boy with a stick, he was poking them but good, goading and taunting.

On Tuesday, October 2, two days after the murders of Elizabeth Stride and Catherine Eddowes, a decomposing female torso was discovered in the foundations of Scotland Yard's new headquarters under construction on the Embankment near Whitehall. Weeks earlier on September 11, a severed female arm had turned up nearby in Pimlico, alarming a Mrs. Potter whose feeble-minded seventeen-year-old daughter had been missing for three days. She went to the police, only to be reminded that they had little power of intervention in the cases of missing teenagers, especially the likes of Emma Potter, who'd been in and out of workhouses and infirmaries. She was nothing but a nuisance, and her disappearances were nothing new.

But it was different this time. A body part had turned up as the Ripper continued his gruesome crimes, and Mrs. Potter feared the worst. But as fate would have it, her increasingly frantic pleas to the police were rewarded by a benevolent fate when a constable found Emma wandering about alive and well. Nonetheless, the story had made it into the press, and reporters were paying attention to a different possibility. Was the Whitechapel fiend up to other horrors? Was he dragging victims off to his hellhole and chopping them up? The police said no. Dismemberment was an entirely different MO, it was assumed at the time, and Scotland Yard and its medical men weren't inclined to accept that a killer's pattern might evolve and escalate.

They made no connection between the Ripper and the dismembered arm, severed from the shoulder and tied with string. It was discovered on the foreshore of the Thames near the Grosvenor Railway Bridge in Pimlico, less than four miles southwest of Whitechapel and on the same side of the river. A quaint area of neat homes and small gardens, Pimlico was about five miles south of 54 Broadhurst Gardens, and a short walk for the likes of Sickert.

"I went [on] such a walk yesterday about 11 kilom.'s," he writes from Dieppe when he was fifty-four years old. Five miles was no distance at all, not even when he was elderly and his disoriented and bizarre peregrinations were a constant worry to his third wife, to those who looked after him. The area where the severed arm turned up was also barely a mile east of Whistler's studio on Tite Street in Chelsea where Sickert had worked as an apprentice.

It was laborer Frederick Moore's sorry luck to be working outside the gates of Deal Wharf near the railway bridge when he heard excited voices on the shore of the Thames. The tide was low. Several men were talking loudly as they stared at a suspiciously morbid-looking object in the mud. Since no one offered to pick it up, Moore did, and the police were summoned. They carried the decomposing limb to Sloane Street, where a Dr. Neville examined it. He quickly determined it was the right arm of a female, adding that the string tied around it was "in order for it to be carried."

The arm had been "cleanly severed" with a "sharp weapon," and was in the water two or three days before it was found, Dr. Neville decided. He went on to wrongly deduce that it was amputated after death because had the victim still been alive the muscles would have been more "contracted." In the late nineteenth century the notion persisted that the expression on a dead person's face indicated pain or fear as did clenched fists or rigidly bent limbs. It wasn't understood that the body undergoes a variety of changes after death resulting in clenched teeth and fists due to rigor mortis.

For a while the police suspected a medical student must be responsible for leaving the severed limb on the shore of the Thames. It was a prank, a very bad joke, police told journalists, and news about body parts and a torso turning up was kept to a minimum. There had been enough bad publicity in August and September, and readers were beginning to complain that details printed in the newspapers made matters worse. It was "hurting the work of the police," one person wrote to *The Times*. Publicity adds to the "state of panic," which only helps the killer, someone else offered.

Londoners began pointing fingers at the police for being incompetent and an embarrassment. Scotland Yard couldn't bring offenders to justice, and in confidential memorandums police officials worried that "if the perpetrator is not speedily brought to justice, it will not only be humiliating but also an intolerable perpetuation of the danger." The amount of mail sent to Scotland Yard was overwhelming, and Commissioner Charles Warren published a letter in newspapers "thanking" citizens for their interest. He apologized that he simply didn't have time to answer them.

One might expect that a great many letters were being written to newspapers. To sort out crank mail, *The Times* had a policy that a person could choose not to have his or her name and address published, but the information must be included in the original letter. For all practical purposes the policy was worthless. The telephone had been patented only twelve years earlier and wasn't yet a household appliance. The only option was to show up on someone's doorstep, and it's doubtful that a member of the newspaper staff got into a hansom or galloped off on a horse to check out the validity of a name and address.

This was especially unlikely if the individual wasn't listed in the local directory, and not everyone was. My scan of countless newspapers printed in 1888 and 1889 revealed that anonymous letters to the editor were uncommon. Most writers allowed their names, addresses and even their occupations to be published. But as the Ripper crimes began to pick up momentum, there seemed to be an increase in letters to the editor with no attribution beyond initials or cryptic titles. In some instances the names seem Dickensian or mocking.

Days after Annie Chapman's murder, a letter to *The Times* suggested that the police should check on the whereabouts of all cases of "homicidal mania which may have been discharged as 'cured.'" The letter was signed "A Country Doctor." A letter published September 14 and signed "J.F.S." stated that the day before at 10:00 a.m. a man ran into a bakery shop and made off with the till, and an hour later on Hanbury Street someone was robbed, and late that afternoon a seventy-year-old man was attacked on Chicksand Street. The anonymous writer said all of this had happened "within 100 yards of each other and midway between the scenes of the last two horrible murders."

Yet I found no record of any such crimes in the police sections of the newspapers. Most letters to the editor were with attribution and offered sincere suggestions. Members of the clergy wanted more police supervision and better lighting. All slaughterhouses needed to be moved out of Whitechapel because violence to animals and the gore in the streets had a bad effect on ignorant people. The children of these wretched people should be taken away and raised by the government, and wealthy Londoners should buy up the East End slums and demolish them.

The Ripper must have enjoyed the concern and fright he was causing. "If the people here only new who I was they would shiver in their shoes," he writes in a letter mailed from Clapham on November 22, 1889. As an additional "ha ha," he uses the return address of "Punch & Judy St."

Sickert was quite familiar with Punch and Judy. As I've mentioned, his father, Oswald, scripted and illustrated the violent puppet plays. They were wildly popular. Sickert's idol Degas adored them. He wrote about them in his letters, and what was acceptable humor then would be considered offensive today.

Punch beats his infant daughter and throws her out a window. He repeatedly cracks his wife Judy on the head, "fairly splitting it in two." He kicks his doctor and says, "There; don't you feel the physic in your bowels? [Punch thrusts the end of the stick into the Doctor's stomach: the Doctor falls down dead, and Punch, as before, tosses away the body with the end of his staff.] He, he, he! [Laughing.]"

In Oswald Sickert's Punch and Judy script, "Murder and Manslaughter or, The Devil Fooled," the puppets' cruel antics go beyond Punch's spending all the household money on "spirits."

PUNCH, *dances around with the child.*
>   *(hits the child's head against the railing, the child cries)*
>   Oh don't . . . be quiet my boy *(puts him in the corner).*
I will get you something to eat *(exits).*
PUNCH, *returns, examines the child very closely.*
>   Have you already fallen? Be quiet, be quiet *(exits, the child continues*
to cry)
PUNCH, *with porridge and spoon.*
>   Son of my quiet love
>   do not make me stroppy. There, now be quiet.
>   (*Feeds the child porridge non-stop*) there you go,
there you go. Good heavens! . . . don't you want to be quiet? Quiet,
I say! There you go, there's the rest of the porridge.
>   (*Turns the bowl upside down into the child's face!*)
>   Now I have nothing left! *(Shakes it crudely)*
>   You still won't be quiet?
>   . . . *(throws the child out of the box)*

Oswald Sickert was writing Punch and Judy scripts and illustrating them for the magazine *Fliegende Blätter*, and it's hard to imagine Walter wasn't vividly aware of his father's work. Several Ripper letters include Punch and Judy–like figures, as does a guest book signed "Jack the Ripper," possibly in 1889. It's also filled with lewd sketches and doodles and mocking comments (there will be more about this in the next chapter). In Ripper letters, the Judy-like woman is on her back, the man leaning over her and poised to stab her or strike a blow with his raised long dagger or stick. In the guest book, a stick figure of a woman is beating a child.

The Ripper was quite amused by many events he followed in the press. He thrived on the chaos he caused and adored center stage. He wanted to interact with police and journalists, and he did. He reacted to what they wrote, and they reacted to his reactions until it became virtually impossible to tell who

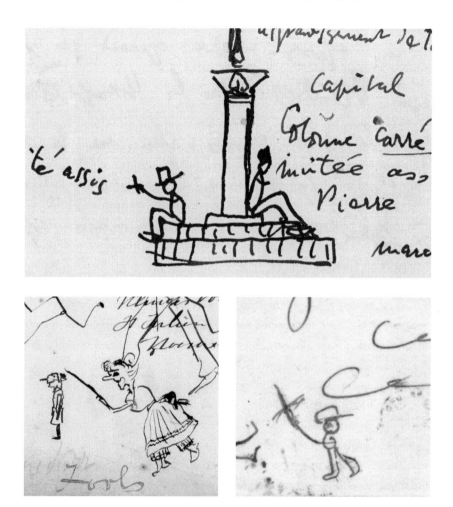

Above: Sickert embellished a letter with two cartoonish figures, possibly inspired by Punch and Judy. *Below left:* A guest book signed "Jack the Ripper" includes a similar type of illustration, with a woman beating a child. *Below right:* Some Ripper letters include drawings of Punch and Judy–like figures.

suggested or did what first. He responded to his audience and it responded back. Ripper letters began to include more personal touches that offer stronger hints of the fantasy relationship he was developing with his adversaries.

This sort of delusional thinking isn't unusual with violent psychopaths. Not only do they believe they have relationships with the victims they stalk, but they bond in a cat-and-mouse way with the investigators who track them.

When these violent offenders are finally apprehended and locked up, they often crave being interviewed by police, psychologists, writers, film producers and criminal justice students. Some of these sadistic killers would talk their incarcerated lives away if their attorneys permitted it.

The problem is that psychopaths aren't known for telling the truth. Virtually every word they say is motivated by the desire to manipulate and their insatiable, egocentric need for attention and admiration. The Ripper wanted to impress his opponents. In his own warped way he wanted to be liked and admired, to be appreciated as brilliant, cunning and amusing. He probably believed that the police enjoyed a few laughs at his funny little games. "Catch me if you can," he repeatedly writes, often signing his letters "your friend."

If the Ripper was offstage too long it may have bothered him. If his audience seemed to forget about him, he dashed off a note to the press. On September 11, 1889, the Ripper writes, "Dear Sir Please will you oblige me by putting this into your paper to let the people of England now [know] that I hum [am] still living and running at large as yet." He also makes numerous references to traveling out of the country. "I intend finishing my work late in August when I shall sail for abroad," the Ripper writes in a letter police received July 20, 1889. Later a bottle washed ashore between Deal and Sandwich, across the Strait of Dover from France.

There appears to be no record of who found the bottle and when, but inside was a scrap of lined paper dated September 2, 1889. Written on it was "S.S. Northumbria Castle Left ship. Am on trail again Jack the Ripper." The area of the southeast coast of England where the bottle was found is very close to Ramsgate, Broadstairs and Folkestone. Sickert painted in Ramsgate. He may have visited there during 1888 and 1889, as it was a very popular resort and he loved sea air and swimming. Numerous times, he traveled by steamer from Folkestone to France, and there was a direct line from nearby Dover to Calais.

Certainly this doesn't prove that Sickert wrote a Ripper note, tucked it inside a bottle and tossed it overboard. But he was familiar with the Kentish coast of England. He liked it enough to live in Broadstairs in the 1930s. From the beginning of this investigation it's been frustrating when one tries to pinpoint the Ripper's locations on a map in hopes of

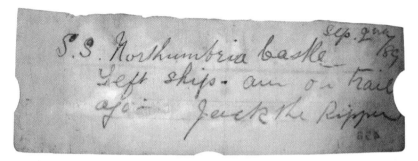

A bottle that washed ashore on the southeast coast of England contained an 1889 letter reading, "Am on trail again." It was signed "Jack the Ripper." The area the letter was found is not far from a resort Sickert was known to frequent.

following him along his tortuous, murderous path. Recently, I asked military and police experts to try their hand at the latest space-age technology, using BAE Systems SOCET GXP, GXP Xplorer, and GXP OnScene software to locate, retrieve and share geospatial data pertinent to the Ripper case. By geotagging all known locations of murders and other possible related events that I've discovered, they created a living satellite map of England. It graphically shows places and other features as they appeared at the time the Ripper was committing his crimes, and a picture really can be worth a thousand words.

One instantly notices a pattern of accessibility to rivers, canals, roads, tunnels, the English Channel and railways. It's easy to connect possible crime scenes and egresses to locales that Sickert would have known well. But that doesn't mean we can trust what we might conclude from this or that we'll ever accurately retrace the Ripper's steps. He was deliberate about what he revealed, and a master of creating illusions.

On November 8, 1888, a Ripper letter mailed from the East End boasts, "I am going to France and start my work there." The next day Mary Kelly would be murdered, and two days after that on the eleventh, a letter from Folkestone arrived, possibly suggesting that the Ripper really was making his way to France. But how could he then write a letter from Kingston upon Hull some two hundred miles north of Folkestone? That letter also is dated November 11, and how could the same person have written both letters during the same twenty-four hours?

A "message in a bottle" from the Ripper was found between the towns of Deal and Sandwich, near Ramsgate, where Walter Sickert traveled to paint.

A possibility is that the Ripper wrote letters in batches. He may have given them the same date and mailed them from different locations. He may have wanted to give the appearance he was in different locations when he wasn't. Or it could be that the dates he wrote are fabricated. A good example is the *A Pirie & Sons* watermarked letters dated November 22, 1888. Supposedly the Ripper mailed one from East London. In another he claims to be in Manchester. In two others that don't appear to have watermarks (one is too torn to tell) he claims to be in North London and in Liverpool.

If one assumes that all of these November 22 letters were written by the same person, and they bear similarities that make this plausible, then how could the Ripper have mailed them from London and Liverpool on the same day? The absence of postmarks precludes knowing with certainty when and where a letter was actually mailed. Unfortunately, after the police recorded dates and locations in their casebooks, many of the envelopes were discarded or lost. The written dates and cities may be deliberately incorrect when they seem to place the Ripper in several different places in one day. But it wasn't impossible for a resourceful, experienced traveler to be in more than one distant location in a twenty-four-hour period.

One could get about fairly rapidly and reliably by train. Some of them were traveling post offices equipped with letter boxes if one wished to post mail while the train was stopped at a station. Possibly the Ripper took advantage of that if he didn't intend to travel anywhere. But the fact is he could have ridden the rails all over the place if he wished to throw the police off his trail, which as it turned out was child's play for him. The trains were an inexpensive and convenient way to get around, and Sickert wasn't likely to be recognized if he chose not to be. He could have disguised himself as an old man or a pauper—as whatever struck his fancy.

Train travel would have been common for him, especially during his acting days, and he would have known fares, timetables and routes. He easily could have calculated how he might get from one place to another, mailing letters along the way. For example, based on the schedules in an 1887 *Bradshaw's Railway Guide*, Sickert could have left Euston Station in London at 6:00 a.m., arriving in Manchester at 11:20 a.m. Changing trains, he would depart at noon to arrive in Liverpool forty-five minutes later.

From Liverpool he could have gone on to Southport on the coast, arriving in an hour and seven minutes, and it's worth noting that in early August 1888, the decomposing body of a nine-year-old boy had been discovered in an unoccupied house there. William Tillyer Rhodes was playing in Hesketh Park and some time later was seen entering the empty house in the company of a man. At the inquest on August 18, the jury returned an open verdict. The cause of death wasn't verified but the police strongly suspected that the boy was murdered. "Any youth I see I will kill," the Ripper writes on November 26, 1888. "I will do the murder in an empty house," the Ripper promises in an undated letter.

Another easy train trip was the one from London to the dramatic coast of Cornwall, a favorite spot for artists to find inspiration. Assuming there were no delays, it would take but a day to reach Lizard Point, the southernmost tip of England, where a guest book at Hill's Hotel, affectionately known as The Lizard, was signed by "Jack the Ripper" and vandalized. A number of Ripper letters were written from Plymouth, which would have been the most convenient destination were one headed to Cornwall, an early haunt of Sickert's, a powerfully evocative one.

In late 1883 and early the following year, he and another art pupil, Mortimer Menpes, had spent time with Whistler painting at St. Ives, one of Cornwall's most popular seaside spots for artists. The Sickert family also had spent several family holidays there. With its majestic cliffs, views of the sea and picturesque harbors, Cornwall would have been a good place for Sickert to tuck himself away when he wanted to rest and hide.

28

A LOVELY SEA SIDE BUSINESS

I N THE SPRING OF 2001, award-winning food writer Michael Raffael was working on a *Food & Travel* feature. He happened to stay at the Rockland Bed & Breakfast, a modest 1950s farmhouse that could sleep seven.

Joan Hill, the woman who owned it, was the only living remnant of The Lizard's distant and illustrious past. Its records and guest books had been in her husband's family for more than 125 years, and it had been hard going of late. Cornwall was in the throes of foot-and-mouth disease. Her farmer son was economically impaired by government restrictions, and the recently widowed Mrs. Hill found her business all but gone as quarantines kept tourists far away from anything with hooves. She may have had a little more time on her hands than usual to visit with an occasional guest.

Michael Raffael recalled that while he was there she began telling him stories about the prosperous days when The Lizard was frequented by artists, writers, actors, Members of Parliament, lords and ladies. Scans through guest books reveal quite the who's who list of luminaries, including writer Henry James, whom Sickert was acquainted with but found boring, and Liberal statesman William Gladstone, a former colleague of Richard Cobden, the father of Sickert's first wife. Artist and critic George Moore stayed at The Lizard, and Sickert was a crony of his and tended to

The Lizard guesthouse in Cornwall is now known as The Top House Inn, pictured here in 2001. A guest book from The Lizard was vandalized by someone whose drawing style bore a strong resemblance to Sickert's sketches and several Ripper letters.

make fun of him. Another guest was artist Fred Hall, a prominent member of the Cornwall-based Newlyn school. In 1888 when Jack the Ripper began his siege, Sickert and his "Whistler gang" were at war with Hall and his compatriots over domination of the New English Art Club.

On this desolate spit of land jutting out into the sea, food and drink were enjoyed with abandon. The rates were reasonable, and trains and horse-drawn carriages made traveling the peninsula convenient if one wished to explore other villages. Visitors came from as nearby as the neighboring town of Penzance or as far away as Australia, South Africa and the United States. They were invited to forget about their cares for a while, to stroll, ride bicycles, sightsee in the bracing air or read in front of the fire.

Sickert could have mingled with interesting people or kept to himself. He could have hiked the cliffs to sketch or simply wandered as was his habit. He knew Lizard Point quite well. In August of 1880, he was in the area with a group of actors, including stars of the day Johnston Forbes-Robertson and Madame Modjeska. They were staying at a rectory in Cadgwith, three miles from Lizard Point. The guest book I'm about to describe makes it all but certain that Sickert visited the hotel, possibly in August 1883 while he was on vacation with his family in Cornwall.

Anna Robins believes this was when "the most significant" entries were made in The Lizard guest book. These include pen-and-ink caricatures that she claims were done by Walter Sickert. Later he returned to The Lizard and vandalized the guest book by adding sexually crude touches to his original artwork and the doodles made by others. He scribbled rude, mean-spirited comments. He made the entry "Jack the Ripper, Whitechapel," as if the murderer had been a guest there. He added other references to the Ripper, and the mocking tone seems to be one heard before in a number of Ripper letters.

Other mocking and crude artistic touches are also disturbingly familiar. Drawings that would appear to have been made in August 1883 and vandalized at a later date include a "caricature in ink of a man in profile with a long bulbous nose." He wears "a top hat, frock coat, breeches, stockings, short boots, and gloves," Anna Robins describes in her detailed report. "He holds an umbrella in his outstretched left arm," and on the same page is a drawing of a "woman in profile with a large beaked nose." She wears a feathered hat, a tightly buttoned jacket and a short skirt with a bustle. "Her pantaloons hang down below her skirt, a sign of a lack of respectability, and her boots are visible."

It's Anna Robins's conclusion that these drawings are supposed to look unsophisticated. They're supposed to appear awkward but in fact they aren't. "The caricature of the profiles, the flowing line of the trouser leg, the schematic circles for the buttons on the jacket of the female figure disguise a skilled hand." She suggests that the drawings were altered after the Ripper murders began, when lewd embellishments were added, such as penciling in a "left breast and nipple."

Overall there is strong artistic evidence that the person who made the drawings in August 1883 was the same individual who vandalized them at some later date. "I believe that this person was Walter Sickert," Anna Robins concludes in the report she wrote after studying The Lizard guest book in 2005 at Harvard's Fogg Museum.

Above: A breast and nipple were added to this sketch of a woman. Her original speech bubble read, "Ain't I lovely." The vandal added a second bubble in pencil: "Only by Jack the Ripper." ***Below:*** Doodles in Ripper letters like this one bear a strong resemblance to the drawings in The Lizard's guestbook.

Sickert's name and the names of his family members and artist colleagues such as Whistler and Mortimer Menpes aren't to be found in the vandalized guest book. But it's obvious that entries have been obliterated or removed. Multiple pages have been cut out, including ones in 1880 when Sickert would have been on Lizard Point with his acting troupe, and names also were rubbed out for December 28, 1883. Sickert was in Cornwall through the autumn and early winter of 1883. In late December he was joined there by Whistler and Menpes, and the three of them remained there through March of 1884.

It was a productive period for Whistler. He painted a number of seascapes and landscapes, his time in Cornwall considered important in his artistic development. His correspondence shows that in early 1884 he was staying at 14 Barnoon Terrace in St. Ives. In January he writes his sister-in-law Helen Euphrosyne Whistler from there, saying that "the work I am doing may make this exile worth while."

Some thirty extant letters he wrote from late December 1883 through January 1884 suggest a vitality and energy, a Whistler who is restless but full of himself. It's obvious he considers his artistic output in St. Ives a turning point, and he writes to sculptor Thomas Waldo Story, "I have plenty of amazing little beauties . . . that will bring golden ducats." Whistler is in high spirits, living "as we like to live while working," and he goes on to say, "I wish you could have been here with us—Walter [Sickert] and the madman [Mortimer Menpes] and I—such a lovely sea side business."

Whistler was exuberant, confident, ready to take the art world by storm, and one is left to wonder what his twenty-three-year-old apprentice, Sickert, was feeling. Maybe this was an idyllic time for him. Maybe the hatred that would poison him later wasn't present yet or was manageable. His early years with his master, particularly their time in Cornwall, might not have been terrible. It would seem that Sickert was still enamored with his master during the years preceding the disenchantment and hostility that would blight the relationship in 1887 and onward.

In a letter Sickert wrote to Whistler in the spring of 1885 he is effusive about the "effect" Whistler and his art had on students and dons at Cambridge University's Fine Art Society, where he had given a lecture in March. "Classically they are amazed not to have found a flaw,"

Sickert writes. "Such style & such familiarity . . . was a thing unlooked for in a man they had always imagined as more or less a rowdy long shore pirate—"

Sickert returned to Cornwall in what I believe was the fall of 1889 and got his hands on the same guest book he had perused and sketched in five or six years earlier. He was the longshore pirate now, only worse, and his seething hatred and rage are evident on pages he ruined. One can imagine his remembering early days that held much promise, of his flipping through The Lizard guest book's pages and coming across the most striking caricature in them—one that Dr. Robins believes Sickert drew. In her report on the guest book she describes a "top-hatted, jowly man with a monocle and a pipe and wind-blown long locks," stating that he "bears more than a passing resemblance to Whistler." A more "youthful chubby-cheeked, snub nosed man in top hat looks like artist Mortimer Menpes." A third man "at the left of the sketch could be Sickert," she concludes.

The face in profile on the left, with curly hair, may be a rendering of Sickert himself. The youthful face in the center with the top hat looks like Mortimer Menpes, Sickert's artistic companion. The man with the pipe on the right resembles James McNeill Whistler.

The Lizard had survived two world wars. The three-hundred-year-old farmhouse was a romantic relic from a long-ago past when the Hills sold it in 1950 and opened the small Rockland B&B. In 2001, Mrs. Hill was telling Michael Raffael the history that had been passed down through the decades, and perhaps because he took the time to listen, she got around to the subject of the old guest book dated from 1877 to July 15, 1888. She dug it out of a cupboard.

After ABC's *Primetime* special on my Ripper investigation had aired, Raffael got in touch with me through my British publisher to tell me about the guest book. He said he'd "spent maybe thirty minutes flicking through it, mostly by myself" when he came across drawings and the name "Jack the Ripper." Based on their position on the page, and the style of handwriting and sepia ink, "I can assure you that the Jack entry was most probably contemporaneous with the book and the other entries around it," Raffael told me, and he would turn out to be both right and wrong about this.

The most significant entries are made in pencil, not ink, and it appears they were added after the guest book was completed. But it's also apparent that the vandalism is indeed of the period, and that Mrs. Hill was completely unaware of what lurked in the pages of a guest book that had been tucked in a cupboard for more than a hundred years. I immediately contacted her, and she verified that the book existed and that Raffael had indeed shown her the Jack the Ripper entries and some drawings. Within days I was on a plane to Cornwall, where as an eerie aside we had what to this day remains an inexplicable encounter at the airport. The moment we disembarked we were confronted by a man in uniform who checked our passports. When we flew from Cornwall to London the next day we were intercepted by customs agents who claimed we had entered England illegally.

Our passports hadn't been stamped. We were informed that there was no such uniformed individual in Cornwall, and the customs agents said they had no idea who we were talking about. It was but one of many unsettling events that occurred during my Jack the Ripper investigation. To recount them makes all of us involved sound a little crazy.

29

A VERY
BAD MAN

WHEN I CHECKED INTO the B&B with my friends and colleagues, we were the only guests. The village was virtually deserted, swept by cold winds blowing up from the English Channel.

I found Mrs. Hill a guileless, shy woman in her early sixties who worried a lot about the happiness of her guests, and cooked breakfasts far too generous for comfort. She told me she'd lived in Cornwall all her life and had never heard of Walter Sickert or James McNeill Whistler. She was only remotely familiar with Jack the Ripper. "I believe I know the name. But I don't know anything about him" except that he was "a very bad man," she said to me.

The sketches Raffael was referring to when he alerted me about the guest book are the ink drawings of a man and a woman on a stroll that Dr. Robins also notes. She believes Sickert drew them in 1883 and then crudely altered them years later by writing "Jack the Ripper" next to the man's big nose. In a balloon coming out his head, he says of the woman in her feathered hat, bodice, bustle and flounces, "Ain't she a beauty though." Her penciled-in response is "Ain't I lovely." In another balloon underneath is the comment "only by Jack the Ripper." An ugly mole has been drawn on the woman's nose, and penciled in under her clothes are

Author Patricia Cornwell reads the The Lizard's guest book dated from 1877 to July 15, 1888.

her naked breasts and legs. The snide inscription "A sweet rustic damsel" was added.

That particular page in the guest book is also filled in with scribbles, comments and allusions to Shakespeare, most of it crude and mean-spirited as if an angry but extremely bright adolescent boy made them. That was as much as I needed to glance at in the guest book, which was musty and falling apart. I bid Mrs. Hill good night. I took the book upstairs to my small, drafty room, where I went through its fragile pages until 3:00 a.m., the space heater on high. The wind howled and the water pounded beyond my window.

The annotations and dozens of doodles and drawings and malicious remarks were astonishing and completely unexpected. I suddenly felt as if Sickert were in my room. While I agree with Anna Robins and believe he wrote and drew these rude comments and art, I will refer to the person responsible as the "vandal." Using lead pencil, and also a violet-colored one and pens, he jotted rude, sarcastic, childish and violent annotations on most of the pages. Sickert's letters and published writings show his delight in using slang, and the guest book is full of it.

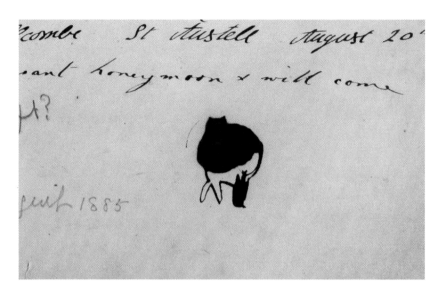

Some drawings in The Lizard's guest book *(above)* bear resemblance to Sickert's sketches *(below)*.

These nasty embellishments seem to have been added by the same arrogant, disparaging individual. Some of the snipes are at guests the vandal seemed to know by reputation or perhaps was acquainted with:

"Fools"

"a big fool"

"wiseass"

"ass"

"Ha! Ha!"

"Dear Dear!"

"Funny"

"O Lord"

"of girls oh fie" (slang when encountering an immoral woman)

"boosed" (boose or slang for mouth)

"garn" (vulgar slang for gal)

"donkey" (slang for penis)

"Dummkopf" (German for blockhead or idiot)

"ta ra ra boom de à" (refrain of a music hall song and the title of a Sickert etching)

"henfool" (seventeenth-century slang for a prostitute or mistress)

"Bosh! Bosh!! Bosh!!!"

"Birdflush" (to flush a wild duck or to seduce a woman)

"Loafers and caulker" (a story that can't be topped)

Under a name with the title "Reverend" the vandal scrawled "3 times married."

After another person's name the vandal jotted "Became a Snob."

The vandal writes snide little ditties on pages filled with guests' cheery comments about what a lovely place The Hill's Hotel (The Lizard) was. How comfortable, how good the food and how modest the rates, guests gushed, and then the vandal chimes in.

"As I fell out/They all fell in/The rest they ran away."

Or

"Rather a queer sort of place."

If a guest had tried his hand at a verse or two, he'd set himself up for a future blasting by the vandal, such as a rhyme by F. E. Marshall from Chester:

Misfortune overtook me here
Still had I little cause to fear
Since Hill's kind care cause my every ill
To disappear—[the vandal added] *after a pill*

The vandal draws a cartoon face and remarks "How Brilliant!!!" After another guest's bad poem, the vandal writes:

A Poet he? It would be rash
To call one so who wrote such trash.
The moon forsooth in all her glory
Had surely touched his upper storey!!

He corrects the spelling and grammar of guests, and this seems to have been a habit of Sickert's. In his annotated copy of actress Ellen Terry's autobiography, he has a good deal to say about her spelling, grammar and diction. He changed and embellished her accounts of events as if he knew her life better than she did.

Another bad poem by a guest at The Lizard ends with "Receive all thanks O hostess *fare.*" The vandal makes the correction "fair" and follows it with three exclamation marks. He turns the *O* into a funny little cartoon with arms and legs. Under it he jots cockney slang, "garn Bill that aint a gal" in response to a guest's mention of having visited the inn with his wife.

"Why do you leave out your *apostrophe?*" the vandal complains, and he includes another cartoon. Turn that page and there is yet another cartoon, this one reminiscent of some of the impish, elfin sketches in the Sickert collection at Islington Libraries. In another entry the vandal has changed the *S*'s into dollar signs for "Sister Helen" of "S. Saviour's Priory London."

Penciled in on the bottom of a page already filled is "Jack the Ripper, Whitechapel." On another page, a guest's London address had been penciled over with "Whitechapel." An exposed circumcised penis has been added to the drawing of a bearded man in a cutaway. There's a Punch and Judy–like doodle of a woman striking a stick figure on the head with a long rod, and scribbled near it are "fools" and "a Cornish wrecker."

Inkblots are turned into figures—just as they were in some Ripper letters. These cryptic shapes are reminiscent of blot-like impressions that may be more than random stains on a wooden partition inside the hovel where the Ripper murdered and mutilated Mary Kelly. (There will be more about this later.) On two other pages, the vandal signs his name as "Baron Ally Sloper," an allusion to a lowlife, sleazy cartoon figure with a big red nose and tattered top hat and a habit of eluding the rent man.

Ally Sloper was very popular with the English lower class, appearing in a periodical and penny dreadfuls between 1867 and 1884, then again in 1916. I suppose adding "Baron" to the name is ironical, a very Sickert-like snipe at English aristocrats. "Tom Thumb and his wife" was added to the guest book next to the date August 1, 1886. He (Charles Sherwood Stratton) obviously didn't sign it—he'd died three years earlier.

A pipe was added to a signed self-portrait of Sickert enemy Fred Hall, and a line was drawn through the fattest part of his protruding belly. "Cow keeper" is a zinger jotted by the name of another Newlyn artist, B. A. Bateman. "We are also seven" is followed by "fat ones." Fred Hall's group of guests at The Lizard included artists Fred Millard and Frank Bramley, and Bateman family friend "Miss Farquhar," who signed the guest book in 1886, possibly on May 1.

Anna Robins points out that in 1889 and 1890 Walter Sickert was further outraged by the Newlyn artists because of their success at the Royal Academy. He conducted "a hostile, personal attack in print on them, which may explain why their names [in The Lizard guest book] incited these rude remarks." Other names the vandal penciled in are social reformers Annie Besant and Charles Bradlaugh, who were in the same circle as Sickert's first wife, Ellen Cobden. As I've mentioned, Sickert sketched Bradlaugh and painted two portraits of him.

The guest book—or "asses book," as the vandal called it—is a miraculous find.

Many of the angry, nasty embellishments are echoed in the sketches and comments Jack the Ripper made in his communications to the police and the press. "Certainly no one could dispute that these [guest book] drawings match the drawings in the Ripper letters," Dr. Robins said, citing as examples the cartoon of the "Pearly King" in a Ripper letter dated November 13, 1888, and what is penciled at the bottom of a page ending with the date July 22, 1886: "20 more & up goes the donkey." In a November 12, 1888, Ripper letter, he writes: "10 more and up goes the sponge."

Dr. Robins reports that some caricatures in the guest book are the same man in different disguises and

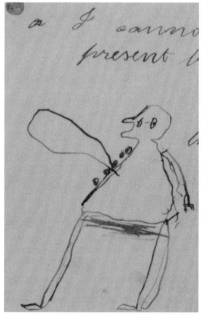

Above right: The "Pearly King" cartoon in one Ripper letter looks very similar to the sketches added into The Lizard's guest book. *Below:* A vandalized sketch in The Lizard's guest book *(left)* uses a similar sketching technique as this drawing in a Jack the Ripper letter *(right)*.

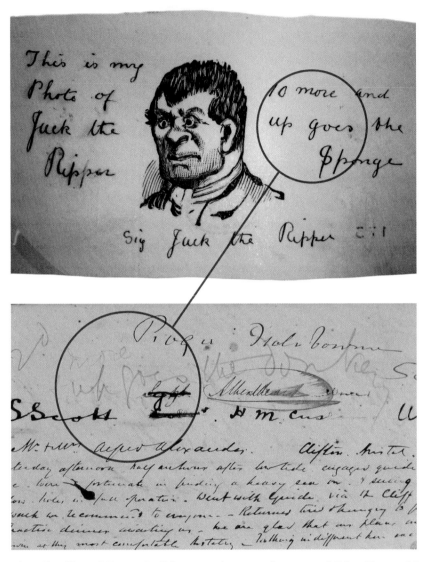

Above: One Ripper letter reads, "10 more and up goes the sponge." ***Below:*** The vandal wrote "20 more & up goes the donkey" in The Lizard's guest book.

costumes, "wearing a frock coat with a large, banded, round top hat, with an oversize handle bar, and a false beard attached to his goatee." Another figure wears a Scottish tam-o'-shanter cap and has "a smaller moustache and a curled goatee." She points out that Sickert made a watercolor-and-ink drawing of a Cornish fieldworker who wears a similar cap. Yet another figure in the guest book has "a clipped goatee." She wonders if these figures might be self-portraits of Sickert in Ripper disguises. "I have got a jolly lot of false whiskers & mustaches in my black bag," the Ripper boasts in a letter dated November 27, 1888.

After I bought the guest book from Mrs. Hill it was studied by a number of experts in addition to Anna Robins. Forensic paper expert Peter Bower examined it and determined that nothing about the paper, writing media and binding are "out of period," and for a while the guest book was at the Tate Archive for further study, then at Harvard's Fogg Museum. As far as we know the name Jack the Ripper didn't appear in public until September of 1888. The last entry in The Lizard guest book is dated some two months earlier, on July 15. The logical resolution to what appears to be a puzzling inconsistency is that the vandalism occurred after the guest book had been closed out and a new one started. This certainly seems obvious when one looks at the pages and notices that the ugly additions are tucked in wherever they might fit between genuine signatures and comments.

A clue about when the vandalism occurred may lurk almost out of view in the guest book's gutter. Faintly penciled in is a cipher that looks like a *W* on top of an *R*, followed by what appears to be an *S* or ampersand and the date "Oct 1889." While the date is very clear, the monogram isn't. It could be another "catch me if you can" but there's reason to suspect the date may be a truthful one. From the beginning, 1889 certainly was proving to be a frustrating year for Sickert.

In the April 27 edition of *The Graphic*, his painting of Collins's Music Hall was described as having "no quality of Art to redeem its essential vulgarity." Then more recently an article in *The Penny Illustrated Paper and Illustrated Times* of October 5, 1889, reported that Sickert and his brother Bernhard had exhibited some of their art at The People's Palace in Whitechapel. The journalist describes Walter as an artist "who has worked so faithfully in the music halls of London." The remark isn't exactly a ringing endorsement. Sickert may have felt trivialized and mistreated. He may have been enraged.

October 1889 may have been a good time for him to flee to the southernmost tip of England. It's probably not a coincidence that weeks earlier, on September 10, another female torso had been found in the East End, this one under a railway arch off Pinchin Street. The story has elements that are all too familiar. A constable's routine beat took him past the very spot, where he noticed nothing unusual. Then less than thirty minutes later he passed by again and discovered a bundle just off the pavement.

The female torso was missing the head and legs. The arms, smooth hands and neat nails indicated the victim hadn't led a terribly hard life. The fabric of what was left of her dress was silk, which the police traced to a manufacturer in Bradford. It was a physician's opinion that she had been dead several days, which is consistent with a bizarre occurrence two nights earlier on September 8. A man dressed as a soldier approached a newspaper carrier outside the offices of the *New York Herald*, where Sickert had just resigned as an art reviewer for its London edition.

The "soldier" exclaimed that there had been another terrible murder and mutilation, and he gave the location as the area off Pinchin Street. The newspaper carrier rushed inside to inform the night editors, who then rode off in a hansom to find the body. There wasn't one. The "soldier" vanished, and on September 10 the torso turned up in that exact spot off Pinchin Street. Draped over a nearby paling was a stained cloth that was the sort women wore during their menstrual periods.

"You had better be carefull How you send those Bloodhounds about the streets because of the single females wearing stained napkins— women smell very strong when they are unwell," the Ripper writes October 10, 1888. "Wrapt in a clean napkin like a lady's dirty valent!" Sickert crudely writes, describing a ham his friend William Rothenstein had sent to him. Once again the Ripper had managed to conceal bodies and body parts and carry them in what must have been heavy bundles. He dropped them virtually at a policeman's feet. "I had to over come great difficulties in bringing the bodies where I hid them," the Ripper writes on October 22, 1888.

The following year, the *Weekly Dispatch* reprinted a story from the London edition of the *New York Herald*, reporting that a landlord claimed to know the "identification" of Jack the Ripper. This article appeared twelve days after the woman's torso was found. In it the landlord, who isn't named, says he was convinced that the Ripper had rented rooms in

"Wrapt in a clean napkin like a lady's dirty valent!"

The unidentified female torso was found with a soiled menstrual napkin draped on a fence nearby. The Ripper letter on the left makes mention of napkins used by women "when they are unwell." Sickert also references menstrual napkins in the letter on the right: "Wrapt in a clean napkin like a lady's dirty valent!"

his house, and that this "lodger" would come in "about four o'clock in the morning," when everyone was asleep. One early morning, the landlord happened to be up when the lodger returned. He was "excited and incoherent in his talk." He claimed he'd been assaulted, his watch stolen, and "he gave the name of a police station" where he had reported the incident.

The landlord checked out the information and was told by police that no such report had been filed. He grew increasingly suspicious when he found the lodger's freshly washed shirt and underclothing draped over chairs. Apparently this suspicious person "had the habit of talking about the women of the street, and wrote 'long rigmaroles'" about them in handwriting resembling "that of letters sent to the police purporting to come from Jack the Ripper," according to the news story. The lodger had "eight suits of clothes, eight pairs of boots, and eight hats." He could speak several languages, and "when he went out he always carried a black bag." He never wore the same hat two nights in a row.

Shortly after the torso was discovered near Pinchin Street, the lodger informed the landlord that he was going abroad and left abruptly. When the landlord went inside the man's rooms, he discovered "bows, feathers and flowers, and other articles which had belonged to the lower class of women." There were three pairs of leather lace-up boots and three pairs of "galoshes" with India rubber soles and American cloth uppers. All were "bespattered with blood."

The Ripper obviously kept up with the news. He would have been aware of the lodger story as it appeared in the London edition of the *New York Herald* or perhaps in some other paper such as the *Weekly Dispatch*. One particularly perplexing Ripper letter is four pages written in rhyming couplets dated November 8, 1889, with the address 30 Bangor Street written at the top. In it the writer makes clear references to the tale told by the landlord:

> *Togs 8 suits, many of hats I wear.*

He denies he was the peculiar lodger who wrote "rigmaroles" about immoral women:

> *Some months hard gone near Finsbury Sqre:*
> *An eccentric man lived with an unmarried pair—*
> *The tale is false there never was a lad,*
> *Who wrote essays on women bad.*

It's hard to believe that Walter Sickert would leave boots or any incriminating belongings in rooms he'd rented unless he wasn't worried about these items being found or wanted them to be. Maybe Sickert had stayed in that lodging house. Maybe he never did. But wittingly or not the Ripper left a wake of suspicion and created more drama. He may have lurked somewhere behind the curtain of the next act that was printed in the *Weekly Dispatch* directly under the story about the "lodger."

A "woman" wrote a letter to the Leman Street Police Station "stating it has been ascertained that a tall, strong woman has for some time" been working in various slaughterhouses "attired as a man." This story gave rise to the theory that the East End victims may have been murdered by a woman. Police searching East End slaughterhouses found no verification that a potential "Jill the Ripper" had been in their midst, and the letter the "woman" wrote the Leman Street Police Station doesn't appear to have survived.

From July 18, 1889 (three days after Sickert resigned from the *New York Herald*), through October 30 at least thirty-seven Ripper letters were sent to the police (based on what I found in The National Archives and London Metropolitan Archives). Seventeen of these letters were dated September. With the exception of three, all supposedly were written from London, which could place the Ripper—or Sickert—in London during the time of the news reports about the "lodger" and the slaughterhouse woman.

From March through mid-July of 1889, Sickert wrote twenty-one articles for the London edition of the *New York Herald*. He likely was in London on September 8. The *Sun* had just interviewed him days earlier at 54 Broadhurst Gardens. His work was to be included in an important impressionistic art exhibition scheduled for December 2 at the Goupil Gallery on New Bond Street, and the reporter went on to quiz him about why he no longer was an art reviewer for the *Herald*. Sickert's printed reply was evasive and perhaps not the whole truth. He claimed he didn't have time to write for the *Herald* anymore, stating that art criticism should be left to people who aren't painters. Yet in March 1890 he was at it again, writing articles for the *Scots Observer, Art Weekly* and *The Whirlwind*, at least sixteen articles for that year.

Maybe it's just another Sickert coincidence that the very day his resignation from the *New York Herald* was publicized in the *Sun*, the mysterious soldier appeared at the *Herald* and announced a murder and mutilation he couldn't have known about unless he was an accomplice or the killer. When the torso was found days later, it was but several miles from Sickert's house. The victim was never identified, and she may not have been a "filthy whore" of doss-houses and the street. She could have been of a higher pecking order, maybe one of those music hall performers Sickert liked to draw. A questionable woman like that could disappear easily enough and never be missed.

Maybe she was someone like music hall star Queenie Lawrence. Sickert must have been a bit upset when he painted her portrait as a gift and her thanks was to complain she wouldn't even use it as a screen to keep the wind out. Queenie Lawrence seemed to fade from public view, possibly by the mid-1890s. I've found no record of what became of her or when she last was seen. But Sickert's models and art students sometimes just slipped away to who knows where. "[O]ne of my art students, a darling who drew worse than anyone I have ever seen & has vanished into the country. Her name?" Sickert writes to his wealthy American friends Ethel Sands and Nan Hudson (circa 1914).

During the Ripper's most intense killing times, he could have lived on the rails. He could have mailed letters from all over. Some lust murderers move about when they're in the throes of their sexually violent addiction, often killing near rest stops and train stations. Bodies and body parts can be scattered for hundreds of miles in trash cans and in the woods or water. Some victims are concealed so well that they will always be missing.

The murderous highs, the risks, the rushes are intoxicating to violent sexual psychopaths. But they don't want to be caught, and neither did the Ripper. Getting out of London now and then would have been smart, especially after the double murder of Elizabeth Stride and Catherine Eddowes. If Sickert murdered and dismembered the woman whose remains were found near Pinchin Street in the fall of 1889, it would make sense that he might have beat a retreat to some faraway safe harbor like Cornwall.

But if his motive in mailing so many letters from so many distant places was to drive the police to distraction and create an uproar? It would seem he misfired and rather much wasted his time. To quote artist and critic D. S. MacColl's words about Sickert: He "over-calculated himself." Jack the Ripper did too. He was so clever that the press and the police didn't believe the letters could be from the murderer. The communications with all their skillful rhyme and art were ignored.

30

IN A HORSE BIN

ARLY ON THE FROSTY MORNING of October 11, 1888, Sir Charles Warren played the role of bad guy with two bloodhounds named Burgho and Barnaby.

The Commissioner of the Metropolitan Police darted behind trees and shrubbery in Hyde Park. He made his getaway as the magnificent pair of tracking dogs lost his scent, and they ended up hunting down several strangers who happened to be out strolling. Four other trials on the misty, cold morning ended just as badly, and this didn't bode well for Warren.

If the hounds couldn't track someone in a relatively deserted park, then turning them loose in the crowded, filthy streets and alleyways of the East End probably wasn't such a good idea. Warren's decision to volunteer for the tracking demonstration turned out to be an unfortunate one. So much for showing Londoners what a great innovation bloodhounds were and how certain it was that they would sniff out that East End fiend at last. Warren's dashing around in the park with his lost hounds was an embarrassment. He would never live it down.

"Dear Boss I hear you have bloodhounds for me now," the Ripper writes October 12, 1888.

Warren's bad decision may have been influenced by yet another peculiar letter published in *The Times* on October 9, two days before his romp in the park:

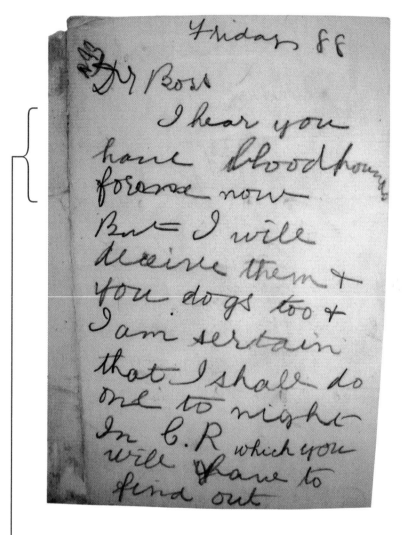

"I hear you have bloodhounds for me now . . ."

When police began experimenting with bloodhounds, the Ripper taunted them.

Sir—Just now, perhaps, my own personal experiences of what bloodhounds can do in the way of tracking criminals may be of interest. Here, then, is an incident to which I was an eye witness.

In 1861 or 1862 (my memory does not enable me to give a more exact date), I was in Dieppe when a little boy was found doubled up in a horse-bin with his throat cut from ear to ear. A couple of bloodhounds were at once put on to the scent. Away they dashed after, for a moment or two, sniffing the ground, hundreds of people, including the keeper and myself, following in their wake.

Nor did the highly-trained animals slacken their pace in the least till they had arrived at the other end of town, when they made a dead stop at the door of a low lodging house, and throwing up their noble heads, gave a deep bay. On the place being entered, the culprit—an old woman—was discovered hiding under a bed.

Let me add that the instinct of a bloodhound when properly trained, for tracking by scent is so marvelous that no one can say positively what difficulties in following a trail it cannot surmount.

Faithfully yours,
Williams [sic] Buchanan
11, Burton St., W.C., October 8.

As is true of other odd letters to the editor, the tone doesn't fit the subject. Mr. Buchanan has the cheerful voice of a raconteur as he relays the horrific account of a boy having his throat cut "from ear to ear," his body stuffed into a "horse-bin."

A search through newspaper records in Dieppe turned up no mention of a child having his throat cut or being murdered by similar means in the early 1860s. This isn't necessarily conclusive. French records at that time were poorly kept. They were lost or destroyed during two world wars. But if there had been such a murder, it's difficult to accept that Dieppe had access to trained bloodhounds available "at once." The huge metropolis of London didn't have trained bloodhounds available in the 1860s or even twenty-eight years later, when Charles Warren had to import the dogs and board them with a veterinary surgeon.

In the eighth century, bloodhounds were known as Flemish hounds. They were prized for their ability to track bears, boar and other animals and flush them out of safe harbor on hunts. It wasn't until the sixteenth century that it became common to use these deep-throated, long-eared hounds to track human beings. The depiction of them as vicious canines used to run down slaves in America's southern states is a complete falsehood as it's not the nature of bloodhounds to be aggressive or have physical contact with their quarry. They don't have a mean fold in their sad, floppy faces. Slave-hunting hounds were usually foxhounds or a mixture of foxhound and Cuban mastiff, which drag a person to the ground or attack.

Training bloodhounds to track criminals is so specialized and painstaking that few are available to assist police even today. Not many of the hounds would have been around in 1861 or 1862 when "Williams Buchanan" claims in what sounds like a Grimm's fairy tale that they tracked the little boy's murderer straight to the house where an old woman was hiding under a bed. "Williams Buchanan" isn't found in the 1888 post office directory. But the 1889 register of electors for St. Pancras South Parliamentary Borough lists a William Buchanan as a voting resident of a dwelling house at 11 Burton Street. In those days, that part of the city wasn't considered dreadful but it wasn't desirable either. The house let for thirty-eight pounds a year. Rooms were rented to a number of people of various occupations, including an apprentice, a printer's warehouseman, a colorman grinder, a cocoa packer, a French polisher, a chair maker and a laundress. William Buchanan wasn't an uncommon name. But I could locate no other records that might identify him beyond an ad that might indicate there was a William Buchanan who sold a hair restorative concoction.

His letter to the editor about the alleged murder in Dieppe shows a literate, creative mind, and the seaside resort was where Sickert had houses and secret rooms for almost half of his life. He may not have used his own name when he rented these secret rooms in Dieppe, London, or elsewhere, and in the late 1880s, identification wasn't required. Cash would do. One might wonder how often Sickert used names other than his own, including those that might belong to real people. Perhaps a person named William

Buchanan really did write the letter to the editor. Apparently he'd written a very similar one to the *Echo* on October 2:

> *Sir—I quite agree with your clever contributor "About Town." Bloodhounds are more likely to discover the terribly-cunning fiend of Whitechapel than are any number of detectives and vigilance committees. . . . Many years ago when I was sojourning at Dieppe, a little boy was found doubled up in a horse-bin, with his throat cut. Immediately a couple of bloodhounds were put on to the scent, and in less than an hour they had tracked the murderer to a low lodging house at the other end of town.*

The author signs his name "William Buchanan, B.A." and lists his address as 11 Burton Street, W.C. A real person or an alias used to rent what former New Scotland Yard investigator John Grieve calls a bolt-hole? Perhaps Mr. Buchanan was who he claimed to be and there really was a murdered seven-year-old boy whose body was dumped in a horse-bin in Dieppe. To date, I've found no evidence of such a crime. It's also a bit too coincidental that within ten weeks of Buchanan's letters to the editor, two boys would be murdered, one of them mutilated and left in a stable.

"I am going to commit 3 more 2 girls and a boy about 7 years old this time I like ripping very much especially women because they don't make a lot of noise," the Ripper writes in a letter he dated November 14, 1888.

Twelve days later, on November 26, eight-year-old Percy Knight Searle was murdered in Havant on England's south coast, approximately eighty miles north of Penzance, Cornwall, and a three-and-a-half-hour train ride from London. Described as a "quiet, sharp and inoffensive lad," Percy was out that evening "between 6 and 7" with another boy named Robert Husband, who later said Percy left him and headed down a road alone. (395) Moments later Robert heard him screaming and saw a "tall man" running away, and Robert found Percy on the ground against palings, barely alive, his throat cut in four places. A porter at the Havant railway station claimed that a man jumped on the 6:55 train to Brighton without buying a ticket. Not realizing a murder had just occurred, the porter didn't pursue him.

*"I am going to commit 3 more 2 girls and a boy about 7
years old this time I like ripping very much especially women
because they don't make a lot of noise"*

In a letter dated November 14, 1888, the Ripper boasts of his plans to kill again, including
"a boy about 7 years old." Twelve days later, eight-year-old Percy Searle was found dead
in Cornwall with his throat cut.

Suspicions focused on Robert Husband when it turned out that a
"bloody" pocketknife recovered near the scene supposedly belonged to his
brother. A medical opinion was offered that the four cuts on Percy's neck
were clumsy and could have been made by a "boy." Robert was charged

with the crime, despite his protests of innocence. The case was never seriously attributed to the Ripper if at all until more than a century later, when on January 31, 1999, *The Independent on Sunday* ran an interesting article with the headline "Did Jack the Ripper Kill a Hampshire School Boy?" In it Gavin Maidment, a senior assistant at Havant Museum, claims to have discovered archives indicating that days before the Percy Searle murder, a magistrate received a letter signed "Yours, Jack the Ripper."

The envelope had a Portsmouth postmark, and the enclosed letter instructed the police not to bother looking for him (Jack the Ripper) in London because "I'm not there." In the article, Maidment echoes my own sentiments: "I'm amazed that this case has not received more publicity over the years and so little is known about it. The Ripper link may be a red herring, but it is possible that he did kill outside London as the letter suggests."

On Thursday, December 20, 1888, another murder occurred in Whitechapel.

According to police, Rose Mylett was about thirty years old. An unfortunate who was "pretty" and "well nourished," she'd been out late the night before, plying her trade. The next morning at 4:15, a constable discovered her body in Clarke's Yard, Poplar High Street, in the East End. He believed she'd been dead only a few minutes, and wrote in his report that her clothing was in place, her hair disarrayed, and a handkerchief was folded around her neck. A postmortem examination revealed that she'd been garroted with moderately thick packing string.

There was "nothing in the shape of a clue," *The Times* reported on December 27, and medical and police officials believe the "deed [was] the work of a skillful hand." A point of medical confusion for the police surgeon was that Rose's mouth was shut and her tongue wasn't protruding. It would seem he didn't understand that in most cases of garroting, the ligature is pulled tightly around the neck and compresses the carotid arteries or jugular veins, cutting off the blood supply to the brain. Unless the larynx (airway) is compressed as it is in manual strangulations or hangings, the tongue doesn't protrude. Garroting bears a similarity to cutting someone's throat. In both cases the victim isn't likely to make much noise and is incapacitated and dead quickly.

One week after Rose Mylett was murdered, a boy disappeared in Bradford, Yorkshire. A theater city on the Henry Irving company's tour, Bradford was four and a half to six hours northwest of London, depending on the number of stops the train made. Thursday morning, December 27, at 6:40, seven-year-old John Gill hopped on the neighborhood milk wagon for a quick ride. At 8:30 he was witnessed playing with other boys, and afterward talking to a man. John didn't come home, and the next day his family posted a notice that he was missing and last seen near Walmer-Villas at 8:30 a.m. He was described as having on a "navy blue top coat (with brass buttons on), midshipman's cap, plaid knickerbocker suit, laced boots, red and white stocking; complexion fair. Home 41, Thorncliffe Road."

The next night, Friday, at 9:00, a butcher's assistant named Joseph Buckle was in the vicinity of stables and a coach house very close to the Gills' home. He would later tell police he noticed nothing out of the ordinary until the next morning, Saturday, when he was up early to yoke his employer's horse for a day of work. As was his usual routine, he cleaned out the stable and was pitching manure into a pit in the yard when he noticed "a heap of something propped up in the corner between the wall and the coach house door." Fetching a light, he discovered that the heap was a dead body, and fled to the bakehouse for help.

John Gill's coat had been tied around him with his braces (suspenders). When several men unwrapped him they made the gory discovery that the boy's severed legs were propped on either side of his body and secured with cord. Both ears had been sliced off. A piece of shirting was tied around his neck and another piece was tied around the stumps of his amputated legs. He'd been stabbed multiple times in his chest, his abdomen slashed open, the organs removed and placed on the ground. His heart was wedged under his chin.

"I shall do another murder on some young youth such as printing lads who work in the City I did write you once before but I don't think you had it I shall do them worse than the women I shall take their hearts," the Ripper had written a month earlier, on November 26, 1888, "and rip them up the same way . . . I will attack on them when they are going home . . . any Youth I see I will kill but you will never kitch me put that in your pipe and smoke it . . ."

John Gill's boots had been removed and stuffed inside his abdominal cavity, according to one news report, and there were other mutilations "too sickening to be described." One might infer these were to the genitals. *The Times* reported that one of the wrappings found with the body "bears the name of W. Mason, Derby Road, Liverpool," a lead that apparently went nowhere. Liverpool was less than four hours away from London by train, and five weeks earlier the Ripper had written a letter claiming to be in Liverpool. Then on December 19, a little more than a week before John Gill's murder, the Ripper sent a letter to *The Times*, also allegedly from Liverpool: "I have come to Liverpool & you will soon hear of me."

Police immediately focused on William Barrett, the dairyman who had given John Gill a ride in the milk wagon two days earlier. But there was no evidence against him beyond his keeping his horse and cart at the stables and coach house where the boy's body was found. Barrett had given him a ride many times in the past and was highly thought of by his neighbors. Police found no bloodstains on the body or the coat wrapped around it, and there was no blood inside the coach house or the stable.

Clearly the murder had occurred elsewhere, and once again the case has the familiar theme of the killer depositing the spoils of his violence almost at the feet of the police. A constable claimed that at 4:30 Saturday morning, while patrolling the area, he tried the coach house doors to make sure they were secure. He'd stood on the "very spot" where John Gill's remains were displayed by the killer not three hours later. In an undated partial letter the Ripper wrote to the Metropolitan Police, he boasts, "I riped up little boy in Bradford." A letter dated January 16, 1889, refers to "my trip to Bradford."

The murders of Percy Searle, John Gill and Rose Mylett were never solved. The notion that Jack the Ripper might have committed any of these crimes didn't seem plausible. Rose's throat wasn't cut, and it wasn't the Ripper's MO to savage little boys, regardless of what was threatened in letters that the police would have considered hoaxes anyway. The scarcity of medicolegal facts revealed in the newspapers and at the inquest makes it difficult to reconstruct John Gill's case. One of the most important unanswered questions is the identity of the man he was last seen talking to (assuming this reported detail is true). If the man was a stranger, then considerable effort should have been made to discover who he was and what he was doing in Bradford. Obviously the boy went off with someone, and this person murdered and mutilated him.

The piece of "shirting" around John's neck is a curious signature on the part of the killer. Most of Jack the Ripper's victims were wearing a scarf, a handkerchief or some other piece of fabric around their necks when their bodies were found. In Rose Mylett's murder a folded handkerchief was draped over her neck. Was this symbolic or simply a coincidence? Sickert had a penchant for neckerchiefs, and his favorite red one was a talisman for him, according to his artist friend Marjorie Lilly. She recalled that the red neckerchief was very important to him when he worked on his Camden Town Murder paintings some twenty years after the Ripper crimes began.

She writes that while "reliving the scene, he would assume the part of a ruffian, knotting the handkerchief loosely around his neck, pulling a cap over his eyes and lighting his lantern." It was commonly known that if a criminal wore a red neckerchief to his execution, it signaled that he had divulged no truths to anyone. He carried his darkest secrets to the grave, and Sickert's red neckerchief was not to be touched by anyone including the housekeeper. She knew to steer clear of it when she saw it "dangling" from the bedpost inside his studio or tied to a doorknob or peg. Ms. Lilly claims that the neckerchief was "so vital to him" because it was what he'd worn "on the nights he was Jack the Ripper."

The details in her book *Sickert: The Painter and His Circle* became public in 1971. Several years later, Joseph Gorman and writers Stephen Knight and Jean Overton Fuller began directly linking Sickert to the Ripper crimes, and Ms. Lilly backed away from some of her published assertions. In an August 15, 1975, letter she wrote to Stephen Knight, she seems unnerved by his sensational book *Jack the Ripper: The Final Solution*, which would be released the following year. As I've pointed out, Knight's conspiracy theory implicates the Royal Family, Sir William Gull and Sickert as having been involved in the Ripper murders.

In her letter, Ms. Lilly reminds Knight that Sickert is considered "the Saviour of British Modern Art." She fears that people in the art world

Sickert wearing one of the handkerchiefs he had a penchant for.

would be "furious" with her if they thought she was disrespecting him. She would appreciate it if Knight would make it clear that she disagrees with his "view" about Sickert "& please play me down whenever you can," she says. She seems especially uncomfortable with her anecdotal information about "the red scarf."

Ms. Lilly wasn't the only member of Sickert's inner circle who knew he was obsessed with murder. In an undated journal essayist and carica-turist Max Beerbohm kept, he describes his acquaintance Walter Sickert as having "two sides." He was the "extreme of refinement" but loved "squa-lor," and had claimed to have "lodged in Jack the Ripper's house." In a letter from Paris dated November 16, 1968, André Dunoyer de Segonzac, a well-known artist with connections to the Bloomsbury group, wrote Sickert biographer Denys Sutton that he'd known Walter Sickert since around 1930. Segonzac had very clear memories of Sickert claiming to have "lived" in Whitechapel in the same house where Jack the Ripper had lived. Sickert had told him "spiritedly about the discreet and edifying life of this monstrous assassin."

Sickert apparently also told his friends a similar story. He'd once stayed in a house where the landlady claimed the Ripper lived during his crimes and that she knew his true identity. He was a sickly veterinary student who was eventually whisked off to an asylum, and the landlady suppos-edly revealed the name, which Sickert claimed to jot down in a copy of Casanova's memoirs. Apparently Sickert did read the book while in Venice in 1903 or 1904. But alas, his copy was destroyed, and despite his photo-graphic memory, it seems he couldn't recall the name.

In an undated letter, Osbert Sitwell writes about this to William Rothenstein:

> I am writing an essay on Sickert, and editing his papers—
> Years ago he told me the story of how he had occupied rooms
> in which previously Jack-the-Ripper (a young vetnerary
> [sic] surgeon) had lived. His landlady had told him the
> name of the murderer but Sickert could not remember it.
> . . . He added "At the time she told me, I was reading
> a volume, in French, of Casanova's memoirs, which Will
> Rothenstein had leant me. I jotted the name down in pencil
> on the margin of one of the pages—and afterwards forgot
> about it, and returned the book to him. . . . One day, ask

Caricature of Max Beerbohm, who said Sickert was the "extreme of refinement" but loved "squalor."

him if he still has it. . . . If he has, that's the name of Jack-the-Ripper!!" . . .

. . . Probably it has long ago been borrowed or stolen? . . . But if not, it wd [*sic*] be very interesting. . . . If you are too busy to remember I shall perfectly understand. Yrs [*sic*] ever Osbert Sitwell

In a biography of Winston Churchill's private secretary Edward Marsh, there is a similar anecdote of what Sickert told Marsh during a dinner: "He [Sickert] told me that it was he who gave Marie Lowndes the idea of *The Lodger*. His landlady had been Jack the Ripper's—and if he hadn't gone to the dinner party where he sat next to her there would have been no novel, no play, no film!" In a diary entry of March 9, 1923, Marie Lowndes offers a different explanation: "*The Lodger* was written by me as a short story after I heard a man telling a woman at a dinner party that his mother had had a butler and a cook who married and kept lodgers. They were convinced that Jack the Ripper had spent the night under their roof."

Helen Lessore, the sister-in-law of Sickert's third wife, Thérèse Lessore, recalled in a 1960 radio interview that Sickert would take her on taxi rides and show her a house where either "Crippen" or "Jack the Ripper" had lived. Andrina Schweder, the sister of Sickert's second wife, Christine Drummond, made a similar comment in an October 20, 1976, letter to Stephen Knight. Ms. Schweder recalled that Sickert was fascinated by Jack the Ripper, the Camden Town murder and Dr. Hawley Crippen. She also claimed that in 1922, Sickert encouraged her eight-year-old daughter to read *The Lodger* by Marie Belloc Lowndes, the story about Jack the Ripper staying in a lodging house.

Sickert's interest in the Crippen case may have been more than morbid curiosity. It's possible he may have encountered the Crippens or been acquainted with them. In the early months of 1910, when the murder of Crippen's wife, Cora, is believed to have occurred, Sickert had a studio at 142 Brecknock Road, about a five-minute walk from the Crippen house at 39 Hilldrop Crescent in Camden Town. Cora Crippen was a former singer with the stage name Belle Elmore and had appeared at Collins's Music Hall. It's entirely possible Sickert had seen her perform.

Hawley Crippen was a homeopathic physician. He was having an affair and money problems. His wife was last seen alive on February 1, 1910, and he claimed they'd had a fight and she left him, possibly running off with another man. New Scotland Yard believed Crippen had poisoned his wife with hyoscine hydrobromide (scopolamine). He was convicted based on sketchy evidence, including pathologist Bernard Spilsbury's testimony that a mark on decomposing tissue was consistent with a scar Cora was believed to have. Crippen continued to protest his innocence and was hanged on November 23, 1910.

Poisoning a spouse in a domestic homicide isn't unheard of, but what Crippen allegedly did with his wife's body is unusual, on the verge of bizarre. The remains discovered in July beneath bricks in the Crippen home's coal cellar were a decomposing horror. The head, limbs, bones and reproductive organs were missing, leaving nothing more of the body than a thigh, flaps of skin and muscle from the lower abdomen in addition to a few articles of clothing and bleached blond hair in curlers. As an interesting footnote, in 2007 forensic scientists in Michigan recently conducted DNA testing on a microscopic sample of Cora Crippen's remains. They concluded that the person in the cellar wasn't her or even a female.

If anyone in Sickert's close circle of friends and fellow artists suspected his obsession with gruesome violence might have manifested itself in actual acts of it, no one talked while he was alive, it seems. Maybe an exception is Florence Pash, assuming the story she told Violet Overton Fuller is true. Some descendants of people who knew Sickert well still aren't talking. During my rewriting of this book, I was forced to paraphrase a surprising amount of information. Some estates in control of copyrights denied me permission to quote from archival documents.

The red neckerchief Marjorie Lilly wrote about—or one like it— purportedly was found among Sickert's belongings after he died. If it still exists, I was unable to locate it. The neckerchief "played a necessary part in the performance of the drawings," Ms. Lilly describes, "spurring him on at crucial moments, becoming so interwoven with the actual working out of his idea that he kept it constantly before his eyes." When he settled in Camden Town after 1905, he began painting some of his most famous and violent works. Ms. Lilly writes that during this era of his life, "he had two fervent crazes . . . crime and the princes of the Church." Crime was "personified by Jack the Ripper, the Church by Anthony Trollope."

Sickert wasn't interested in religion unless he was playing an important biblical role as he did in two of his later works. When he was almost seventy he painted *The Raising of Lazarus*, recruiting a local undertaker to wrap a shroud around the life-size lay figure (manikin) he claimed had been owned by the eighteenth-century artist William Hogarth. The heavily bearded Sickert climbed up a stepladder. He assumed the role of Christ raising Lazarus from the dead while his friend Cicely Hey posed as Lazarus's sister.

Perhaps Sickert's fantasies about having power over life and death were different in his sunset years. He was getting old. He felt bad much of the time. If only he had the power to give life. He already knew he had the power to take it. Testimony at John Gill's inquest indicated the killer slashed open the seven-year-old boy's chest, cut through his ribs, and tore his heart from his body. *Do unto others as was done unto you.* If Sickert murdered John Gill it was because he could.

Perhaps Sickert's own mutilation when he was a boy prevented him from creating life, and he had to mutilate to create art. He was never a normal boy and could never be a normal man, and I don't know of a single instance when he showed physical courage. He victimized people only when he had the advantage. He preyed on people when they were weak even if he'd been on friendly terms in an earlier day. It was all about power. It was all about who had it.

In 1897, after Oscar Wilde emerged from prison, Sickert cruelly shunned him despite the fact that Wilde always had been unfailingly kind and generous to the Sickert family. He'd given Helena a book of poetry, encouraging her to be whatever she wanted to be in life. In 1883, Walter had delivered Whistler's portrait of his mother to the annual Salon exhibition in Paris, and the dashing Wilde generously hosted the young, wide-eyed artist at the Hôtel Voltaire for a week.

When Sickert's father died in 1885, Helena wrote that her mother was "nearly mad with grief" until Oscar Wilde went to see her. Nelly Sickert was receiving no company. But of course she would see him, Wilde declared as he bounded up the stairs. It wasn't very long before she was laughing, and it was a sound Helena thought she would never hear again. The past was the past and meant nothing to Sickert, and he had no loyalty to people no longer of use to him.

Sickert's *The Servant of Abraham*, 1929.

31

THREE KEYS

IN DECEMBER 1907, Ellen Cobden Sickert sent a sealed document to her sister Janie and insisted that it be locked in a safe.

It doesn't appear we'll ever know what Ellen was so secretive about but I doubt it was a will or similar instructions. She wrote all that out later and apparently didn't care who saw it. Those documents along with many of her letters and diaries were donated by the Cobden family to the West Sussex Record Office.

Ellen sent her mysterious sealed letter to Janie three months after the murder of a prostitute named Emily Dimmock about a mile from where her former husband, Sickert, recently had settled in Camden Town. Around this time while Ellen was overseas, she wrote at least two letters to Janie inquiring about "young Woods." Ellen wanted to know what would happen when his case went to trial later that year. In the summer of 1908 she appeared to make a similar reference, writing that the case of "young Woods" was "mentioned" in Parliament.

I've yet to pinpoint exactly who "Woods" was. But it's possible she was referring to the eventual arrest, indictment, trial and acquittal of twenty-eight-year-old Robert Wood, the artist accused of murdering Emily Dimmock. Perhaps Ellen got Wood's name slightly wrong. But her questions about a "trial" were atypical ones for her to ask. She didn't refer to criminal cases in any other correspondence I saw, and her sudden wish to know about "young Woods" is perplexing. It's possible "Woods" isn't Robert Wood, but if he is one must question why Ellen had a personal

These rare drawings from the Robert Wood trial were created for a contemporary newspaper and have not been republished since the time of the trial. There is some evidence that Sickert knew Woods: he may have been a model for some of Sickert's Camden Town paintings, and Sickert's wife may have taken a personal interest in the case in a letter.

interest in the accused murderer. One possible answer is that Sickert knew him, and Ellen was aware of this.

In an essay art historian Wendy Baron wrote for the catalogue *Walter Sickert: The Camden Town Nudes* (2007), she mentions a story told to her by the managing director of the Redfern Gallery, Sir Rex Nan Kivell. Apparently he claimed that "Sickert used Robert Wood . . . as the model for his Camden Town Murder subjects." Baron goes on to say that the "visual evidence" doesn't convince her this is true, and it could be that Nan Kivell simply "had a fine sense of mischief."

I'm not sure what she meant by "visual evidence," and it also strikes me as unusual that a gallery director would make up such a story

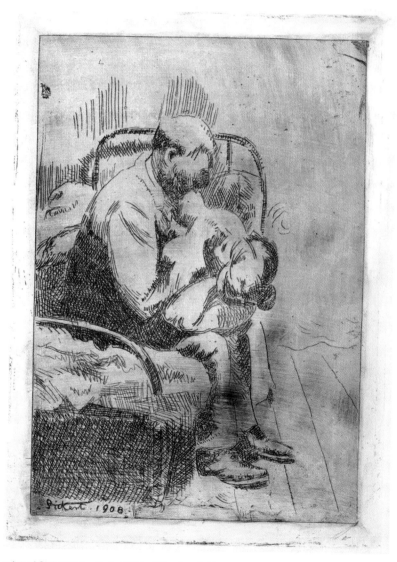

A print of Sickert's *La Belle Gâtée* ("The Spoilt Beauty"), 1908, part of his Camden Town Murders series.

because he had a "sense of mischief." But if Robert Wood was a male model for Sickert, then he knew the young man and possibly quite a lot about him including that Wood's "sweetheart," Ruby Young, was an artist's model who was willing to pose nude and may have been of questionable character. Sickert was painting and sketching nudes at this time, and his taste in female models hadn't changed. He still had a habit of using prostitutes.

Emily Dimmock was a notorious one with venereal disease that periodically required treatment at Lock Hospital on Harrow Road. When the symptoms were fulminating they manifested in eruptions on her face, and based on her mortuary photograph she had these at the time of her murder. Emily was the very sort that Jack the Ripper would have judged as the lowest of the lowest, a filthy, diseased whore that the world was better off without. Sickert held similar views, and Marjorie Lilly recalls once hearing a person defend thieves by preaching that everyone has "a right to exist," and Sickert disagreed, retorting that there are people "who

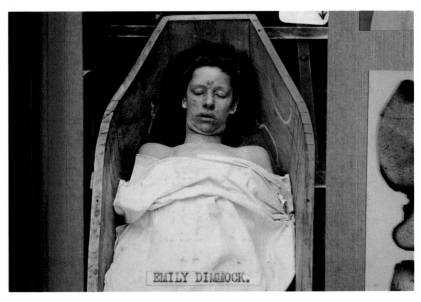

A mortuary photo of Emily Dimmock shows lesions on her face, evidence of a venereal disease that undercut the police's original assumption that she was a "respectable married woman."

have no right to exist!" Certainly the Ripper shared similar sentiments. "As you can see I have done another good thing for Whitechapel," he writes November 12, 1888.

News accounts described Emily Dimmock as twenty-three years old, rather tall, thin and pale with dark-brown hair. She was known for being polite and neatly dressed, and a newspaper sketch depicts her as attractive. When she was found nude in bed with her throat cut on the morning of September 12, 1907, the police at first thought she'd taken her own life. "She was a respectable married woman," the Metropolitan Police report reads, and respectable women were far more likely to commit suicide than to be murdered. That ridiculous assumption changed quickly when the police discovered that Emily had been with many men, most of them sailors. She'd led "an utterly immoral life" and was "known to every prostitute in Euston Rd." The man Emily lived with wasn't her husband, but the two of them had talked about getting married one day.

Bertram John Eugene Shaw was a cook for the Midland Railway, his salary twenty-seven shillings per six-day week. He'd leave for work on a 5:42 p.m. train for Sheffield, where he would spend the night, returning the next morning and arriving back at the St. Pancras Station at 10:40. He was almost always home by 11:30 a.m., and later told police he had no idea that Emily was going out at night and seeing other men. When Shaw first met her, he knew she was a prostitute. But she swore to him she'd changed her ways.

Any money she earned now was through the honest work of dressmaking. She'd been a good woman ever since they began to live together, her days as a prostitute in the past, Shaw told police. He truly may not have known that usually by 8:00 or 8:30 p.m., while he was out of town working for the railway, she could be found at the Rising Sun public house on Euston Road, as witnesses referred to a pub that still exists but is now called the Rocket.

Letters Sickert wrote in 1907 are typically problematic in terms of showing exactly where he was at any precise moment in time. Not only did he rarely date letters but the context isn't always specific as to when he was writing and where he was. It appears that he spent part of the summer of 1907 in Dieppe where he enjoyed a "daily bathe before déjeuner," describing

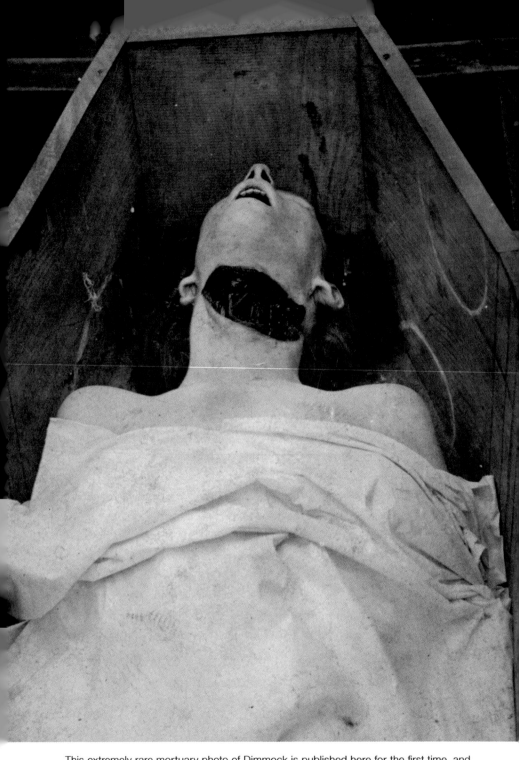

This extremely rare mortuary photo of Dimmock is published here for the first time, and shows the full extent of the wound to her throat.

"big breakers" that one had to be careful diving through. Apparently he was "hard at work" on paintings and drawings.

After returning to England in 1905 and settling in Camden Town, he continued to paint the female nude, and he resumed depicting music halls such as the Mogul Tavern or the Old Middlesex Music Hall on Drury Lane, which wasn't far from where Sickert was living at Mornington Crescent. He went out almost every night and was always in his stall at 8:00 p.m. sharp, he writes in a letter to Jacques-Émile Blanche.

The London summer of 1907 was cool with frequent rains and very little sunshine. Based on a letter Sickert wrote to his American friend Nan Hudson, he was in Camden Town in July. He complains about the weather, wondering how "people who don't work" could tolerate it. Other 1907 letters to Ms. Hudson with "6 Mornington Crescent" at the top of them seem to indicate he was in London. But without envelopes and postmarks or his writing out the date, it's almost impossible to know a timeline and his whereabouts.

I can only offer possibilities based on the absence of documentation to the contrary, and that makes it difficult to do much more than conjecture where Sickert was in the late summer and fall of 1907. It would seem he was in Paris the beginning of October, and planned to attend the Salon d'Automne at the Grand Palais, which opened on the first and ran through the twenty-second. On page 173 of that exhibition's catalogue, there's a listing for *Sickert* of *19 Fitzroy Street, Londres*, and at this time he had at least one studio on Fitzroy Street.

Sickert spent some of the summer of 1907 in Dieppe. He traveled to France often and had a strong affinity for Dieppe in particular, creating many paintings and drawings there.

Certainly there were exhibitions in London that might have appealed to him. The 15th Annual Photographic Salon opened on September 13 at the gallery of the Royal Society of Painters in Water Colours. Sickert had become increasingly interested in photography, which "like other branches of art," said *The Times*, "has proceeded in the direction of impressionism." September would have been a good month to spend in London. Many of his 1907 letters seem to have been written from there, and one of them to Nan Hudson is joltingly odd.

In it he tells the story of a woman who lived below him suddenly rushing into his room at midnight "with her whole head ablaze like a torch, from a celluloid comb." Sickert put out the fire by "shampooing" her hair "with my hands," quickly so that he didn't "burn [himself] at all." He claims the woman wasn't injured but was now "bald." It's a bit difficult to believe that neither of them was burned or that a flaming comb had made her instantly bald, assuming the story is true. Why did he mention this traumatic event only to dismiss it quickly and move on to discuss the New English Art Club?

One might begin to wonder if Sickert was getting more eccentric and histrionic. Or maybe he fabricated the incident for some other reason, possibly to impress Ms. Hudson or to insinuate where he was or wasn't. Nan Hudson and her companion, Ethel Sands, were very close to him, and some of his most revealing letters are the ones he wrote to them. He shared confidences with the couple as much as he was capable of sharing confidences with anyone, and they likely were no threat to him romantically, sexually.

Sickert used them the same way he did everybody else—for money, sympathy and other favors. Manipulating them with his artistic mentoring and encouragement, he shared many details about himself that he didn't divulge to others, in some instances suggesting they "burn" a letter after reading it. Conversely he might encourage them to save it in the event he ever got around to writing a book. In one letter he wrote to Ms. Hudson (circa 1914–1915) he makes a curious comment about Jack the Ripper.

Sickert's handwriting is difficult to transcribe, and there are three possibilities of what he actually wrote: "Answering about Jack the Ripper!" or perhaps "Amusing about Jack the Ripper!" or "Amazing about Jack the Ripper!" In 1914 Sir Melville Macnaghten published his memoirs, *Days of My Years*, which includes the chapter "Laying the Ghost of Jack the Ripper." Perhaps Sickert's Ripper reference was sparked by the publicity about Macnaghten's book. But the comment is strangely out of context in a letter that for the most part is about painting and how much Sickert values his friendship with Ms. Hudson.

It's obvious from other episodes in his life that he had periods of severe depression and paranoia, and he may have had good reason to be feeling that way after Emily Dimmock's murder. Maybe he wanted to make sure that at least someone believed he was home in Camden Town with his flaming neighbor at around the same time a local prostitute had her throat cut. Sickert didn't date the letter about the incendiary comb, and the envelope with its postmark has disappeared. We're likely never to know why he felt inclined to tell such a drama to Nan Hudson. But he had a reason. He always did.

Mornington Crescent was an easy walk from the Rising Sun, and the facts about Sickert's residence or residences at this time are typically confusing and mysterious. In the 1907–1908 St. Pancras Register of Electors there's a listing for an Arthur Ernest Flowers at Number 6 Mornington Crescent. He's cited as renting "Two rooms, top front, and second floor back, furnished for 14 shillings per week." The landlady is noted as Mrs. L. M. Jones of the same address. Sickert's name isn't included in this census. And who was Mr. Flowers?

In a 1911 census of England and Wales there's an Arthur Howard listed at this same 6 Mornington Crescent address. He's the "head" of the family and is further described as thirty-seven and single, his occupation a "tailor's assistant," his birthplace "London, Chelsea." Also listed is Walter Sickert's name in what appears to be his own handwriting. He's described as a fifty-year-old single man, a "teacher of drawing" or "sketching" (the writing is very hard to read) with a postal address of 31 Augustus Street, which is just one more perplexing address.

Pinning Sickert down to precise locations at precise times continues to be difficult if not nearly hopeless. But it's indisputable that in 1907 he had rooms at 6 Mornington Crescent, the same address where he claimed Jack the Ripper had once stayed. A plaque was later placed there in Sickert's honor. For sure he was painting in that rented space in 1907, usually nudes

In a 1914–15 letter to Nan Hudson, Sickert mentions Jack the Ripper, though it's unclear from his handwriting what he says.

on a bed. It was the same setting he used for *Jack the Ripper's Bedroom*, painted from the perspective of someone outside open double doors that lead into a small, murky space. A dark mirror behind an iron bedstead vaguely reflects a man's shape.

The rooming house at 29 St. Paul's Road (now Agar Grove), where Emily Dimmock lived, was but a twenty-minute walk from 6 Mornington

Crescent. She and Shaw had two rooms on the first floor. One was a sitting room, the other a cramped bedroom behind double doors at the back of the house. After Shaw would leave for St. Pancras Station, Emily might clean and sew or go out, and she was described as a cheerful woman who liked to sing to herself.

Sometimes she met customers at the Rising Sun. She might rendezvous with various men at a number of pubs or perhaps show up at the Middlesex Music Hall, which Sickert had painted around 1895. Sometimes her outings took her to the Holborn Empire, home of music hall star Bessie Bellwood, whom Sickert had sketched many times in the late 1880s. Emily also was fond of the Euston Theatre of Varieties, built in 1900 across from St. Pancras Station. It was another place Sickert likely would have known very well.

Emily usually left her rooming house by 8:00 p.m., and when she returned, the couple who owned the house, Mr. and Mrs. Stocks, were asleep. They claimed to know nothing about her "irregular" life, and quite a life it was. Emily was with two, three, four men a night, sometimes standing up in a dark corner of a train station before she might bring the last fellow home and sleep with him. She wasn't in the same desperate straits as the Ripper victims we know about. She didn't live in the slums. She had food, a place to call home and a man who wanted to marry her.

But it would appear she had an insatiable craving for excitement and the attention of men, and the police described her as a woman "of lustful habits." Perhaps lust drove her sexual encounters or it could be what she lusted for was money to buy clothes and pretty little things. She was "greatly charmed" by artwork, and collected penny picture postcards to paste in a scrapbook that was precious to her. The last postcard she'd added to her collection as far as anyone knows came from Robert Wood, an artist employed by London Sand Blast Decorative Glass Works on Gray's Inn Road.

On September 6, while he and Emily were inside the Rising Sun, he'd written a note on the back of the postcard, and this was to become the key piece of evidence against him when he was indicted and tried for her murder. Although police investigations were more sophisticated than they'd been in the late 1800s, that wasn't saying much. Handwriting comparisons in Wood's case weren't made by an expert, for example. They were made by one of Emily's sexual clients, who swore on the witness stand that the handwriting on a postcard and two words on a fragment of charred paper found in her fireplace had been written by the same person.

It seems Emily recently had received a number of postcards—at least four. One was mailed from "a seaside town," and as best a witness could recall, the card read: "Do not be surprised if you hear of a murder being done. You have ruined my life, and I shall do it soon." Emily had given venereal disease to so many men that the police had a long list of former clients angry enough to do her in. She'd been threatened numerous times in the past. Enraged men who had contracted the "disorder" harassed her and threatened to "out" or kill her, but nothing stopped her from continuing her trade no matter how many men she infected. Besides, she remarked to her women friends, it was a man who gave her the disorder in the first place.

Emily was seen with two strangers the week before her murder. One "had a short leg, or hip trouble of some sort," according to Robert Wood's statement to the police. The other was a Frenchman described by a witness as approximately five foot nine, very dark with a short-cut beard, and dressed in a dark coat and striped trousers. He briefly came into the Rising Sun on the night of September 9, leaned over and spoke to her, then left. In police reports and at the inquest there's no other reference to this man. There didn't seem to be any interest in him.

The summer of 1907 ended after thirteen weeks of frequent rains and chilly gloom. *The Times* described the weather as "the coolest experienced since the dismal season of 1888."

On September 11, the last day of Emily Dimmock's life, there was a respite of almost eight hours of sunshine and a light breeze. Early that evening she visited with Mrs. Stocks in the kitchen, saying she had plans she wasn't enthusiastic about. Emily had received a postcard from a man who wanted to meet her at the Eagle near the Camden Road Station at 8:00 p.m. It was signed "Bertie," Robert Wood's nickname. During the trial he would deny having sent it. "I only wrote one of them—the one with

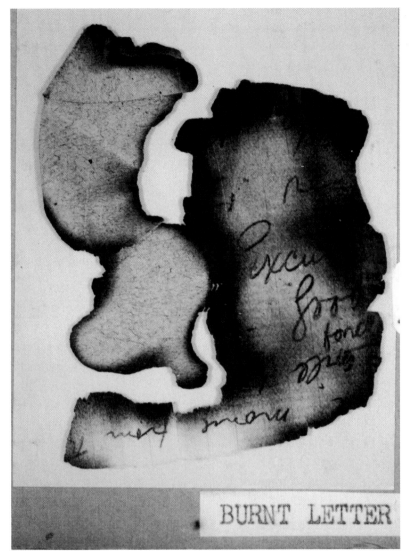

BURNT LETTER

A charred letter was found in Emily Dimmock's fireplace and used to indict Robert Wood for her murder.

the sketch of the rising sun on it," he testified in court. He was befuddled that the handwriting on the charred fragments of paper found in Emily's fireplace was a "good imitation" of his.

When Emily left the rooming house after visiting with Mrs. Stocks in the kitchen, the moon was new, the streets dark. She was in her long dustcoat, with her hair in curling pins, and she didn't plan to stay at the Eagle long. She wasn't eager to go in the least, she explained to acquaintances. It's why she wasn't properly dressed, and she was busy. Shaw's mother was coming to visit from Northampton the next morning, and Emily had been cleaning, doing laundry and getting the house in order. By all appearances it doesn't seem she was expecting to have a client that night. It doesn't seem she headed to the Eagle in search of one. But that doesn't mean she didn't have an encounter.

During the police investigation a cabman claimed to have picked up a man after 1:00 a.m., dropping him off close to Emily's house. A witness said he saw her around midnight walking toward home with a smartly dressed man who didn't resemble Robert Wood. Another witness, Robert McGowan, told police that at around five o'clock the morning of her murder, he noticed a "broad-shouldered" man walking away from Emily's house. He was dressed in a hard felt hat and long overcoat with the collar flipped up. Maybe her killer accompanied her home. But maybe he didn't.

Another explanation of how the killer might have gained access to Emily is her ground-floor back bedroom was accessible by windows and sturdy cast-iron drainpipes. There's no mention in police reports that the windows were locked. Only the bedroom double door, the sitting-room door and the front door of the house were locked the next morning when Emily's body was found. Her three keys to those doors were missing when police and Shaw searched the rooms. It's possible someone climbed into her bedroom while she was asleep, although it would have been risky. She didn't live alone in the house. She might have heard the intruder and screamed.

Bertram Shaw arrived home from the train station on the morning of September 12 and discovered his mother waiting in the hallway, unable to get into her son's rooms. Trying the outer door, he was baffled and alarmed to find it locked, and he wondered if Emily might have gone out to meet his mother at the train station. Maybe the two women had missed each other. He was getting increasingly uneasy and asked the landlady, Mrs. Stocks, for a key, and unlocking the outer door, he discovered the double doors also were locked. He broke in and flung back the covers from Emily's naked body on the blood-soaked bed. Then he ran for the police.

Some twenty-five minutes later, Constable Thomas Killion arrived and determined by touching Emily's cold shoulder that she'd been dead for hours. Immediately he sent for police divisional surgeon Dr. John Thompson, who reached the scene around 1:00 p.m. Based on the coldness of the body and the advanced stage of rigor mortis, he concluded that Emily had been dead seven or eight hours. This would place her time of death at 6:00 or 7:00 a.m., which seems unlikely. The sun rose at 5:30, and by 6:00 or 7:00 people were stirring, many on their way to work.

The position of Emily Dimmock's body was "natural," police said, as if she'd been murdered in her sleep. But the description in reports doesn't sound natural at all. She was facedown, her left arm bent at an angle and across her back, her hand bloody, and her right arm was extended in front of her and on the pillow. There wasn't sufficient space between the head-board and the wall for the killer to attack her from behind. It's possible he had her lie facedown for sex, then straddled her, slashing her throat to the spine in a left-to-right sweep of the knife that cut the bed ticking and nicked her right elbow. Or maybe the attack was an ambush in the dark, and he pinned her to the bed and killed her.

Dr. Thompson decided at the scene that Emily's throat had been cut with a very sharp instrument. The incision is mostly to the center of the neck and doesn't extend from ear to ear, possibly due to the cramped space the killer had to work in, and it's difficult to determine whether she was cut while facedown or faceup. A careful study of her dead house photograph shows what appears to be a single very deep slash to the front of her neck, and there was no indication I found that she put up a struggle.

After the murder it appeared her assailant cleaned himself using a pink petticoat that had soaked up all the bloody water in the hand-wash basin. During the inquest, police remarked that no discernible fingerprints were found, only a few smudges inside the ransacked room where drawers had been pulled out of the dresser, the contents rummaged through and scattered on the floor. Emily's scrapbook was open on a chair, and some of the postcards had been removed from it.

Her homicide didn't instantly resurrect the Ripper panic. But it may have been alluded to by Robert Wood's attorney, Marshall Hall, when he asked the jury, "Was it more probable that [the murder] was the work of some maniac, such as terrorized London some years ago?" Judge William Grantham was astute enough to describe Emily's homicide as the work of a man who "must have been almost adept at that terrible art. . . . No doubt this crime was committed by a man who was leading a double life—a man whom nobody would imagine for a moment would be a murderer—a man who would pass in his particular society without anybody suspecting that he was a murderer."

After what the judge called the most remarkable trial of the century, Robert Wood was acquitted. The case was never solved. There were no Ripper-type letters to the press or the police. But curiously, soon after the homicide a reporter for the *Morning Leader*, Harold Ashton, went to the police and showed them photographs of four postcards sent to the newspaper's editor. It isn't clear from the police report who sent these postcards signed "A.C.C.," and Ashton inquired if the police were aware that the writer of the postcards might be a "racing man." The reporter was suspicious of the communications, and he went on to point out the following:

- A postmark dated January 2, 1907, London, was the first day of racing after "a spell of wintry weather." The race that day was at Gatwick.

- A second postcard was dated August 9, 1907, Brighton. The races there were held on the sixth, seventh and eighth, and at Lewes on the ninth and tenth of that month. The reporter said that many people who attended the races at Lewes "go to Brighton to stay."

- A third postcard was dated August 19, 1907, Windsor. The races were held at the Royal Windsor Racecourse on Friday and Saturday, the sixteenth and seventeenth of that month. The weather was pleasant, the crowds large, the racecourse very close to Ascot, which Sickert was familiar with. Both the Royal Windsor and the Ascot racecourses were easily accessible by regular excursion train, the trip from London quick and easy.

- The fourth postcard was dated September 9, two days before Emily's murder and one day before the Doncaster autumn race in Yorkshire. Strangely, Ashton pointed out, it was a French postcard that appeared to have been purchased in Chantilly, where a race had been held the week before the Doncaster autumn race.

According to this rather confusing police report, Ashton said he believed "the post card may have been purchased in France, possibly at Chantilly, then brought over and posted with English stamps at Doncaster"—as if to imply that it had been mailed from Doncaster during the races. Had the sender attended all of the Doncaster autumn races, it's unlikely he would have been in Camden Town at the time of Emily's murder the late night of September 11 or early morning of the twelfth. The Doncaster races were held on the tenth, eleventh, twelfth and thirteenth of September, and Yorkshire is about 150 miles from London.

Ashton was asked to withhold this information from his newspaper, and he did. On September 30, Inspector Arthur John Hailstone jotted on his report that the police thought Ashton was correct about the dates of the races. But the reporter was "quite wrong" about the postmark of the fourth postcard. "It is clearly marked London NW." Apparently it didn't strike Inspector Hailstone as somewhat odd that a French postcard apparently written two days before Emily Dimmock's murder was, for some reason, mailed in London to a London newspaper. I don't know if "A.C.C." were the initials of an anonymous sender or meant something else. But it seems the police should have pursued or at least questioned why an anonymous "racing man" would have sent these postcards to a newspaper at all.

It might have occurred to Inspector Hailstone that what this person had accomplished was to offer the alibi of attending horse races, specifically at Doncaster, on the date the much-publicized murder of Emily Dimmock occurred. Perhaps by now, Sickert was more obsessed with machinations and misdirects than he was with taunting the police through "catch me if you can" letters. Maybe he enjoyed setting up other people to be blamed and punished for his crimes. At this later stage in life it would be unusual to continue maniacal killing sprees that required tremendous energy and obsessive focus. He was forty-seven years old, and very busy, well-known and admired. But perhaps he still needed a fix, a transfusion of violent energy to inspire what would become his most famous series, the Camden Town Murders.

These paintings depict a limp nude woman sprawled on an iron bedstead next to a clothed man. During this artistic period it was Sickert's habit to keep an iron bedstead in any studio he was using. He'd pose models on it. Sometimes he lewdly posed himself with his wooden lay figure (manikin) to entertain whomever he'd invited over for tea and cakes. On one such occasion, when guests arrived at his dimly lit Camden Town studio they discovered him on the bedstead acting out a lewd scene as he made jests about Emily Dimmock's recent murder. No one seemed to think much about that display or anything else he did. After all, he was Sickert. When he referenced the Camden Town murder in the titles of these works, he was simply viewed as a respected artist who had chosen a theme.

It wouldn't be until many years later that a detail would link him to the actual crime. On November 29, 1937, the *Evening Standard* printed a short article about Sickert's Camden Town Murder paintings, and stated, "Sickert, who was living in Camden Town, was permitted to enter the house where the murder was committed and did several sketches of the murdered woman's body."

True? If so, was it another Sickert coincidence that he just happened to be wandering along St. Paul's Road when he noticed a swarm of police and decided to see what all the excitement was about? If he was the killer and had no idea when the body would be found, he would have had to case the area for many hours to ensure he didn't miss the show. This placed him at risk for being noticed, and a simple solution is suggested by the missing three keys.

How clever if Sickert locked the doors behind him as he left the house, taking the keys with him. This would all but ensure that Emily's body wouldn't be discovered before Shaw came home at 11:30 a.m. Had Sickert been stalking her, he certainly would know when Shaw left the house for work. He would know when Shaw returned, and one may presume that the landlady wasn't going to enter a locked room. This rather much guaranteed what time the body would be discovered. Or the keys might have been a

The Camden Town Murder, or *What Shall We Do For the Rent?* by Sickert shows a clothed man next to the woman he's just murdered. Sickert created several paintings and drawings inspired by Emily Dimmock's death; the series is known as the Camden Town Murders.

souvenir, or there's some other explanation for why they were missing from the scene.

Whatever the truth, it wouldn't seem the police found it suspicious when the local, charming, well-known artist Walter Sickert happened by with a pencil and sketching paper. But they might have thought twice if he'd been spotted in the area for many hours, watching and waiting. It's been established that it wasn't out of character for Sickert to sketch dead bodies, and in later years during World War I he was obsessed with wounded and dying soldiers. He loved their uniforms and weapons, and he collected piles of them. He would cultivate close relations with people at the Red Cross, asking them to let him know when their patients no longer needed their personal effects. "I have got a capital fellow," he writes to Nan Hudson in the fall of 1914. "The ideal noble & somewhat beefy young Briton." Sickert adds that he'd already "drawn him alive & dead."

I found no other mention of "young Woods" or any other explanation for Ellen Sickert's mysterious comments to her sister Janie. After the Camden Town murder and its sensational trial, Ellen's mental and physical health began to deteriorate. She spent most of her time away

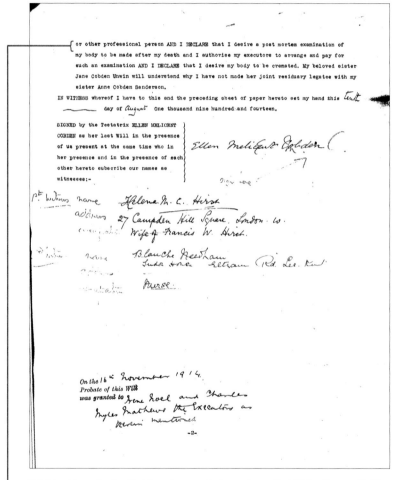

Published here for the first time is a mysterious clause that Sickert's ex-wife Ellen Cobden added to her will. She requested a "post mortem examination" of her body, even though she knew she was dying of cancer. The will was drawn up with no bequest to Sickert in 1914, a year after Ellen finally cut off all contact with Sickert.

from London, seeing her former husband occasionally, helping him as best she could, until she severed their relationship for good in 1913. The following year she executed her will, and in it there's no reference to Sickert. She no longer referred to herself as Ellen Sickert but had returned to using her family name of Cobden. But what strikes me as almost inexplicable is her declaration that upon her death she wanted a "post mortem examination of my body and I authorize my executors to arrange and pay for such an examination."

Ellen was an intelligent, progressive woman, and certainly she would have understood what she was asking for and what it involved. She was dying from cancer of the uterus, and it wouldn't seem to make sense that she would request an autopsy. What questions did she want answered that might prompt her to insist on such an invasive procedure? Unless she feared she might not live long enough to die of natural causes, and considering who she'd been married to, that might be the answer.

32

THE DARKEST
DAY OF THE
DARKEST NIGHT

SICKERT'S ROLES CHANGED like light and shadow in his art. He believed that a shape shouldn't have lines because nature doesn't, and forms reveal themselves in tones, shades and the way light holds them. His life had no lines or boundaries and his character changed with every tilt and touch of his enigmatic moods and hidden purposes.

Those who knew him accepted that *being Sickert* meant being the "chameleon," the "poseur." He was Sickert in the loud checked coat walking all hours through London's foreboding alleyways and streets. He was Sickert the farmer or country squire or tramp. He was the bespectacled masher in the bowler hat or the dandy in a black tie. He was the eccentric wearing bedroom slippers to meet the train. He was Jack the Ripper with a cap pulled low over his eyes and a red scarf around his neck, working in the gloom of a studio illuminated by the feeble glow from a bull's-eye lantern.

Victorian writer and critic Clive Bell's relationship with Sickert was one of mutual love-hate, and Bell quipped that on any given day Sickert might be John Bull, Voltaire, the Archbishop of Canterbury, the pope, a cook, a dandy, a swell, a bookmaker or a solicitor. Bell believed that Sickert wasn't the scholar he was reputed to be. He appeared to "know a

A 1935 photo of Sickert taken by his longtime friend, the artist Jacques-Émile Blanche. Even as he grew older, Sickert didn't lose his taste for rakishly tilted hats or checkered suits.

great deal more than he did" even if he was the greatest British painter since Constable, Bell observed. One "could never feel sure that their Sickert was Sickert's Sickert, or that Sickert's Sickert corresponded with any ultimate reality."

He was a man of "no standards," and in Bell's words Sickert didn't feel "possessively and affectionately about anything which was not part of himself." Ellen had been part of Sickert's self because she was his possession. He had use for her, and couldn't respect much less cherish her as a separate human being. All people and all things were entities for him to objectify, and this is very much in keeping with how violent psychopaths in general regard their victims.

Sickert glowers at the camera, his head freshly shaved in an aggressive, unfashionable style.

In the early fall of 1888, Ellen and Janie were in Ireland when Elizabeth Stride and Catherine Eddowes were murdered. Ellen and her sister hadn't returned to London yet when George Lusk, the head of the East End Vigilance Committee, received a partial human kidney by post on October 16. Almost two weeks later, Dr. Thomas Openshaw received the letter written to him on *A Pirie & Sons* watermarked paper that was signed "Jack the ripper." As I described earlier, the envelope from this letter rendered the single-donor DNA profile, components of which were found in other Ripper and Sickert communications.

Dr. Openshaw taught anatomy to artists and was the curator of the pathology museum of the London Hospital. In the letter to him the Ripper writes: "Old boss you was rite it was the left kidny . . . i wil be on the job soon and will send you another bit of innerds." The partial kidney was suspected of being Catherine Eddowes's. It probably was unless the Ripper managed to get half of a human kidney from somewhere else. According to Royal London Hospital archivist Jonathan Evans, the organ was anatomically preserved as a pathological specimen until it became so disintegrated that the hospital disposed of it in the 1950s—ironically about the time Watson and Crick discovered the double helix structure of DNA.

In centuries past, bodies and body parts were preserved in "spirits" or alcoholic beverages such as wine. Formaldehyde had been discovered in the mid-1800s but wasn't being used as a tissue fixative during the Ripper's time, and that's a shame. Had the kidney been preserved long enough to attempt DNA analysis, perhaps it could have been proven that the kidney really was Eddowes's. That would remove most doubt about the Ripper himself writing at least some of these vile communications. Anything that linked an actual murder to a letter would argue against these taunts being nothing but a hoax.

Proving the partial kidney came from Eddowes would have verified that the sender obviously had committed her murder or been involved in it, and this person knew enough to preserve the partial organ in "spirits," probably wine. While there could be other explanations for attempting to preserve human flesh, it may be that Jack the Ripper wasn't new to experimenting with postmortem tissue preservation. The likely truth is he had done this before and would do it again in the privacy of one of his secret hovels.

George Lusk's morbid gift arrived inside a three-inch square cardboard box wrapped in brown paper. Accompanying it was the infamous "From Hell" letter dated October 16. At first it was suggested that the kidney was from a dog, and as the marinated mystery began making the rounds it ended up in the care of medical experts such as Dr. Openshaw. He believed the organ was the anterior of a left human kidney, and Dr. Gordon Brown wrote in his report that the kidney remaining in Eddowes's body showed signs of Bright's disease. Apparently so did the partial kidney, claimed Dr. Henry Sutton, a senior surgeon at the London Hospital.

What's unmistakable in retrospect is the police took the ghoulish package seriously. They sought a variety of professional opinions. They photographed the accompanying letter and published it in the press:

From hell

Mr Lusk
Sor [Sir?]

I send you half the
Kidne I took from one women
prasarved it for you tother piece I
fried and ate it was very nise I
may send you the bloody knif that
took it out if you only wate a whil
longer

> *signed Catch me when*
> *you can*
> *Mishter Lusk.*

The letter and original photograph of it vanished from the City of London Police Museum, possibly in the 1960s. Fortunately a copy was discovered in the basement of the Royal London Hospital, otherwise we might not have a record of it. The letter is extremely important if one accepts that the partial kidney accompanying it was Catherine Eddowes's.

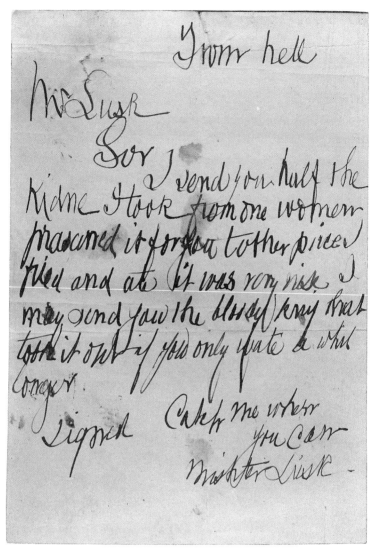

This letter, along with part of a human kidney believed to be that of Catherine Eddowes, was sent to the head of the East End Vigilance Committee, George Lusk, in October 1888.

This not only would have been sufficient proof that the writer of the letter was indeed Jack the Ripper, but it also mentions cannibalism, yet another violent psychopathic trait that rarely if ever is mentioned in the same breath as this case.

The Ripper may have fancied himself uniquely brilliant and civilized, but he actually belongs to a club of deranged offenders who have committed similar atrocities that include sexual murder, mutilation and consuming human flesh. Albert Fish is perhaps one of the most shocking examples in the annals of criminal classification. In 1928, he lured ten-year-old Grace Budd to an empty house in Westchester, New York, where he cut up her body and ate it in a stew that included vegetables and potatoes. Forensic psychologist Louis Schlesinger suggests that during the six years the case went unsolved, Fish "probably fantasized about the crime many times." His compulsive need for sadistic sexual gratification then prompted him to write a graphic letter to the victim's mother. "How sweet and tender her little ass was, roasted in the oven. It took me nine days to eat her entire body. I did not fuck her tho I could had I wished."

Dr. Schlesinger repeatedly makes the point in his lectures and writings that these types of homicides, including Jack the Ripper's, are a compulsion. The killer William Heirens, who terrorized Chicago in 1946, would write in lipstick on the mirror of one of his victim's homes, "For Heaven sakes catch me before I kill more, I cannot control myself." After his apprehension, he reported that when he attempted to resist the compulsion he developed headaches and sweated profusely. Maybe he could resist for about two hours before he had to give in.

In Robert Louis Stevenson's brilliant novella *The Strange Case of Dr. Jekyll and Mr. Hyde*, we find a graphic depiction of a psychopath overcome by his compulsions. Dr. Jekyll's characteristics when he transforms himself into Mr. Hyde eerily parallel the Ripper side of Sickert: inexplicable disappearances, different styles of handwriting, fog, disguises, secret dwellings where changes of clothing are kept, disguised build, height and walk. Stevenson writes that the good man Dr. Jekyll is in "bondage" to the mysterious Mr. Hyde, who is "a spirit of enduring evil."

After Hyde commits murder, he escapes through the dark streets, euphoric from his bloody deed and already fantasizing about the next one. Dr. Jekyll's evil side is the "animal" that lives within him and feels no fear and relishes danger, and it's in this "second character" of Hyde when Dr. Jekyll's mind becomes most nimble, his faculties "sharpened to a point." As the beloved doctor transforms himself into the monster, he is overwhelmed by rage and a lust to torture and murder whomever he happens upon and can overpower. "That child of hell had nothing human," Stevenson writes. Neither did Sickert when his child of hell replaced his paintbrush with a blade.

The Ripper was nimble and focused. He was overwhelmed by a lust to murder and mutilate. He craved flesh and blood, and when he claimed to have fried and eaten a portion of Catherine Eddowes's kidney, he may have been telling the truth.

It's possible Walter Sickert wasn't taunting or simply trying to shock when he made a similar allusion to Lady Jean Hamilton, a close associate of the Churchills. During "many happy hours with the charismatic Sickert," she recounts in her biography, ". . . he tells me none of the brutal facts of life bother him at all." She claims that during a social visit he told her that he "would not mind having to kill and eat raw flesh."

This struck her as incredible because of "his face," a reference that likely alludes to the usual assumption that someone handsome would be revolted by the basest, most primitive aspects of human nature. Such assumptions are ridiculous. Attractiveness has nothing to do with a person's capacity for barbaric violence or perversion. Serial murderer Jeffrey Dahmer was handsome and a cannibal. While there's no real proof the good-looking former law student Ted Bundy engaged in cannibalism, he was known to have sex with his dead victims even as their bodies were decomposing. Some of what these offenders do is also intended to terrorize and shock.

After Catherine Eddowes was murdered and ripped open, her killer achieved the desired effect. Londoners were looking on in stunned horror. If Ellen Sickert was keeping up with the frightening news at home, she would have known about the kidney sent to George Lusk. She would have known about the double murder that occurred within a week of her leaving for Ireland. She may have heard of "human bones" wrapped in a parcel in a Peckham gutter or the parcel containing a decomposing female arm found in the garden of a school for the blind on Lambeth Road. Ellen could have heard the news about a female torso discovered at the construction site of the new Scotland Yard building on the Monday morning of October 1, 1888.

A carpenter named Frederick Wildbore was reaching for the basket of tools tucked inside a dark recess of the dug-out earth when he noticed a bundle wrapped in old cloth and tied with string. He would testify at the inquest that no one touched it at first, and it wasn't until the following afternoon that bricklayer George Budden dragged out the bundle, deciding at a glance that it "was old bacon, or something like that." Budden described the labyrinthine foundation where the package was discovered as "a very dark place . . . always as dark as the darkest night in the day."

The headless, limbless female body was transported to the mortuary on Millbank Street and had little to say to Dr. Neville or the police. They couldn't seem to agree about the arm found in Pimlico weeks earlier, on September 11, but Dr. Neville was certain it was from this torso. The hand was rough, the fingernails unkempt like those of a woman whose life was hard, he decided. Yet when Dr. Thomas Bond was summoned to assist in the examination, it was his observation that the hand was soft with well-shaped nails. In fact, the limb would have been dirty, possibly abraded, and the fingernails would have been caked with mud from the muck of low tide. But perhaps when it was cleaned up it took on a higher social status.

Both Dr. Neville and Dr. Bond estimated the torso was that of a woman about twenty-six years old and about five foot seven or eight. They may have been off base about the height, and their estimate that she'd died five weeks earlier wasn't much better than a guess. The doctors simply didn't have the scientific means to estimate age and height or to judge time of death by decomposition. They knew little about anthropology. They knew nothing about forensic entomology, the interpretation of insect development as a marker for time of death. Maggots were teeming over the torso, and in today's autopsy room they would have had something to say about how long the body had been where it was found.

The autopsy revealed pale, bloodless organs that indicated hemorrhage, which was consistent with the woman's throat being cut before dismemberment, Dr. Thomas Bond testified at the inquest. The remains were those of a "well nourished" woman with "breasts that were large and prominent," and at some point she'd suffered from severe pleurisy in one lung. Her uterus was missing, her pelvis and legs sawn off at the fourth lumbar, and the arms removed at the shoulder joints by several oblique cuts. She'd been decapitated by several incisions below the larynx, and Dr. Bond said that the torso had been skillfully wrapped, the flesh bearing "clearly defined marks" where it had been bound with string.

Beneath the wrapping and adhering to the skin were fragments of newspaper from a *Daily Chronicle*. There also was a blood-saturated section of the August 24, 1888, edition of the *Echo*, a daily paper that cost a halfpenny. Sickert was a news addict, and the *Echo* was a liberal paper that published numerous articles about him throughout his life.

Curious about what might have been in the August 24 *Echo*, I found a copy. On page 4 was the "Notes & Queries" section, and of the eighteen "Answers" published that day, five of them were signed "W.S.":

> *Answer One (3580): OSTEND.—I would not advise "W. B." to choose Ostend for a fortnight's holiday; he will be tired of it in two days. It is a show place for dresses, &c., and very expensive. The country around is flat and uninteresting; besides, the roads are all paved with granite. To an English tourist I can recommend the "Yellow House" or "Maison Jaune," which is kept by an Englishman, close by the railway station or steamboat pier; also the Hotel du Nord. Both are reasonable, but avoid grand hotels. The sands are lovely. No knowledge of French is required.—W.S.*

> *Answer Two (3686): POPULAR OPERAS.—The popularity of Trovatore is naturally due to the sweetness of the music and the taking airs. It is not generally accepted as a "high class" music—indeed, I have frequently heard "professional" musicians call it not music at all. For myself, I prefer it to any other opera, except Don Juan.—W.S.*

> *Answer Three (3612): PASSPORTS.—I am afraid "An Unfortunate Pole" will have to confine his attention to those*

countries where no passports are required of which latter there are plenty, and are, besides more pleasant to travel in. I once met a countryman of his who traveled with a borrowed passport; he was caught at it and sent to quod [street slang for prison], where he remained some time.—W.S.

Answer Four (3623): CHANGE OF NAME.—All "Jones" has to do is to take a paint brush, obliterate "Jones" and substitute "Brown." Of course this will not relieve him from any liabilities as "Jones." He will simply be "Jones" trading under the name of "Brown."—W.S.

Answer Five (3627): LETTERS OF NATURALISATION.—In order to obtain these, a foreigner must have resided either five consecutive years, or at least five within the last eight years, in the United Kingdom; and he must also make a declaration that he intends to reside permanently therein. Strict proofs of this will be required from four British-born householders.—W.S.

While it certainly can't be proven that W.S. is Walter Sickert, he would have been very familiar with the *Echo*. To offer answers by using the original query number implies that W.S. probably was an avid reader of the paper, and sending in five answers to queries is compulsive. It's in keeping with Sickert's prolific writing and the stunning number of Ripper letters received by the police and press.

Newsprint is a leitmotif that shows up repeatedly in Sickert's life and in the Ripper's game playing. One Ripper letter to a police magistrate was written in an exquisite calligraphy on a section of *The Star* newspaper dated December 4, 1888. The torn-out section of paper includes the notice of an etching exhibition. On the verso is a subheadline, "Nobody's Child."

Walter Sickert was never sure who he was or where he was from. He was "No Englishman," to quote the signatory of another Ripper letter. As a young actor he was "Mr. Nemo" (Mr. Nobody), and in a telegram the Ripper sent to the police (no date, but possibly the late fall of

1888), the Ripper crosses out "Mr. Nobody" as the sender and writes in "Jack the ripper" instead. Sickert wasn't French but considered himself a French painter. He once wrote that he intended to become a French citizen (he never did). In another letter he states that in his heart he will always be German.

Most Ripper letters mailed October 20 through November 10, 1888, were postmarked London, and it's more than a possibility that Sickert was in London prior to October 22, to attend an early showing of the first pastel exhibition at the Grosvenor Gallery. In letters he wrote to Blanche, Sickert references the New English Art Club's election of new members. There are many indications including dates on his music hall sketches that show he was in London at least some of the autumn and early winter, and possibly until the end of the year.

It can't be proven where he was on August 24, 1888, the date of the *Echo* newsprint found adhering to the torso recovered at the construction site of the new Scotland Yard headquarters. Letters his mother wrote

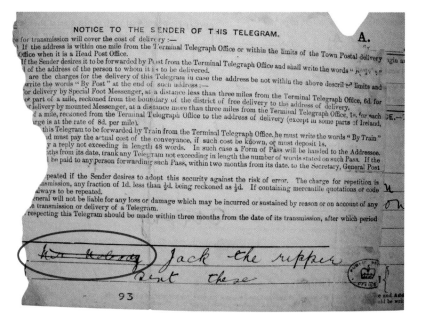

A telegram sent to the police features "Mr. Nobody" crossed out and corrected to read "Jack the Ripper." Sickert's stage name was "Mr. Nemo"—*Nemo* is Latin for "nobody."

suggest he might have been in France, but we can't know for certain when letters to an editor were submitted to the *Echo*, and it's also unclear exactly when the unidentified, dismembered woman was murdered. More to the point, Sickert's whereabouts will always be questionable. In a letter Whistler wrote to Charles James Whistler Hanson in September of 1888, he asks, "Where are the Sickerts?" More to the point, where was Walter?

His only "diary," it seems, was his music hall sketches, typically dashed out on low-grade paper from pads, cashbooks and notebooks probably bought at local news agents rather than stationers. Except for these dated drawings that are snapshots of what he was seeing and recording in real time, one can make only inferences based on the correspondence of others who mention having encountered him or hearing he was visiting.

Ellen returned home to 54 Broadhurst Gardens toward the end of October 1888. Immediately she came down with a terrible case of the flu that lingered and sapped her health well into November. I could find no record of her spending time with her husband or whether she knew where he was from one day to the next. I don't know if she was frightened by the violent atrocities happening a mere six miles from her home, but it's hard to imagine she wasn't aware of them. People in Sickert's circle were. The fourteen-year-old son of his mother's best friend, Penelope "Pennie" Muller, wrote in the fall of 1888:

> *I supposed you have heard all about the other two women who were murdered in Whitechapel in the same manner, there is now nearly £2000 reward. . . . It's quite time something was done now. To let a man murder six women with impunity is rascally and I'm more than half inclined to turn Liberal or Radical if the present Government goes on in such a feeble manner.*

The Great Metropolis was terrorized and the worst was yet to come.

33

SWEET VIOLETS

MARY KELLY wasn't photographed in life as far as I know. But by all accounts she was a handsome, gregarious woman with the hourglass figure coveted in that era.

Her education, fine dress and manner were atypical of other unfortunates who trolled the East End district of Spitalfields, where she lived in No. 13 Miller's Court, an area of the city described by social reformer Charles Booth as teeming with thieves, prostitutes and bullies. Mary's landlord, John McCarthy, rented rooms to the very poor for approximately twenty-two pence a week, his chandler's shop (grocery) next door at 27 Dorset Street.

Miller's Court was accessed by an arched passage that was some twenty-six feet long and not quite three feet wide. Three public toilets were at one end of the court, and at the other were the single-room dwellings and possibly one gas lamp. Mary's ground-floor room was located at the back of the house. It was twelve square feet, and various descriptions of what the police found after her murder depict a cramped space with a small cupboard containing broken crockery and empty ginger beer bottles.

Opposite the door was an alcove, and next to it a fireplace that had a kettle. Hanging above the mantel was the only decoration in the room, a print called *The Fisherman's Widow*. The furnishings were a table, a chair

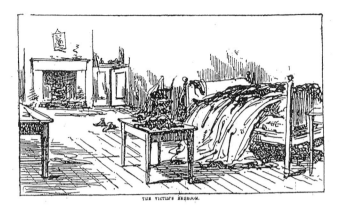

A drawing of Mary Kelly's room, located at the back of the house at No. 13 Miller's Court.

and a tin bath under a wooden bedstead that was flush against a wooden partition or wall. Opposite this were two curtained windows very close together, and one of them had shattered weeks earlier when Mary got drunk and fought with her man, Joseph Barnett, a market porter. Next she lost her key, and the only way she and Barnett could access her hovel was to reach through the broken windowpane and release the spring lock of the door.

Their last big row was ten days before her murder, the cause of the fight a woman named Maria Harvey, who'd begun sleeping with Mary on Monday and Tuesday nights. Barnett wouldn't put up with it. He moved out, leaving Mary to somehow pay off the one pound, nine shillings owed in rent. The two of them patched up their relationship, and now and then he dropped by and gave her a little money.

By some accounts, Maria Harvey last saw Mary alive the early evening of Thursday, November 8, when she dropped by for a visit. Maria wanted to know if it would be all right to leave some dirty laundry inside the room: two cotton shirts, a little boy's shirt, a black overcoat, a black crêpe bonnet with black satin strings, a little girl's white petticoat, and also a pawn ticket for a gray shawl. Maria promised to retrieve the items later, and at some point during their chat Barnett showed up unexpectedly. "Well, Mary Jane," Maria said on her way out, "I shall not see you this evening again." It was the last time she would ever see Mary Kelly alive.

Very little is known about her. Most of the information we have comes from Joseph Barnett, and isn't necessarily factual. As the stories go, she was born in Limerick, the daughter of John Kelly, an Irish ironworker. She had six brothers who lived at home, a brother in the army, and a sister who worked in the markets. The family had moved to Caernarvonshire, Wales, when Mary was young, and at sixteen she married a collier named Davis. Two or three years later, he was killed in an explosion and she left for Cardiff to live with a cousin. It was at this time that she began to drift into alcohol and prostitution. At one point she was treated for venereal disease.

For a while she was a prostitute in the West End, where gentlemen knew how to reward a pretty woman for her favors. One such man took her to France. She stayed only ten days, explaining to her London friends that life on the Continent didn't suit her. For a while she lived on Ratcliff Highway, then on Pennington Street before moving in with a man near Stepney Gasworks, and next a plasterer in Bethnal Green. At her inquest, Joseph Barnett would testify he wasn't certain how many men she'd lived with or for how long.

The pretty Mary Kelly had caught his eye on Good Friday the year before, and he'd treated her to a drink. Within days they decided to live together, and eight months later he rented room No. 13 in Miller's Court at 26 Dorset Street. Occasionally she got letters from her mother in Ireland, and unlike many unfortunates, Mary was literate. But when the East End murders began, she would ask Barnett to read news accounts of them to her. Perhaps the details of the slayings were too unnerving for her to take in alone and in the quiet of her own imagination. She may not have known Martha Tabram, Mary Ann Nichols, Annie Chapman, Elizabeth Stride or Catherine Eddowes but there's a good chance she'd seen them on the street or in a public house at some point. She would have been aware of what happened to them. She would have been mindful of the mounting public panic and police presence.

Joseph Barnett would testify at Mary's inquest that his life with her wasn't a bad one. He finally moved out, "Because she had a person who was a prostitute whom she took in and I objected to her doing so, that was the only reason, not because I was out of work. I left her on the 30th October between 5 & 6 p.m." He claimed the two of them remained on "friendly terms," and the last time he saw her alive was Thursday night, November 8, between 7:30 and 7:45. During their brief encounter he told her he was sorry he had no money to spare. "We did not drink together," he testified. "She was quite sober, she was as long as she was with me of sober habits" and only got drunk now and then.

Despite the murders happening in close proximity to her rooming house, Mary continued walking the streets at night after Barnett moved out. She had no other way to earn money. She needed her drinks, and she was about to get evicted with no prospect of another decent man to take her in. Mary was becoming desperate. Not so long ago she was an upscale prostitute, but during the past year she'd been sliding down deeper into the bottomless pit of poverty, alcoholism and despair. Soon enough she would lose her looks. It didn't seem to occur to her she might lose her life.

Mary was spotted several times that Thursday night as the temperature dipped into the low forties.

On Commercial Street she was witnessed to be quite drunk, and at 10:00 p.m. she was seen on Dorset Street. The times cited by witnesses aren't to be trusted, and there's no certainty that when a person saw "Mary Kelly" it was really Mary Kelly. One person considered a reliable witness was George Hutchinson, a former laborer and groom currently unemployed and living at the Victoria Home on Commercial Street.

On November 12 he would appear at the H Division station and tell police that three days earlier at 2:00 a.m. he talked to Mary Kelly near Flower and Dean Street. She asked him to lend her a sixpence, and he replied that he'd spent what he had. Hutchinson went on to say that Mary told him, "I must go and find some money," then she walked toward Thrawl Street as a man headed in her direction. He "tapped her on the shoulder and said something." Both of them "burst out laughing," Hutchinson recalled, adding that the man carried "a kind of a small parcel in his left hand with a kind of strap around it."

During the investigation of the Ripper's murders and others that seem chillingly similar, there were numerous references to packages wrapped in paper, to parcels, to body parts tied with string or a torso with bits of newspaper adhering to it. Sickert often used newspaper and string to wrap his drawings. In August 1923, he wrote a note to his artist friend Cicely Hey after dropping off a portfolio of his work while she was out. He said he told the housekeeper that the drawings were important and to place them in Cicely's room on her bed. He described the portfolio as "wrapped in newspaper and tied with string."

George Hutchinson was leaning against a lamp in front of the Queen's Head public house when Mary Kelly had her encounter with the man carrying the parcel. According to the police report, she said "alright" to him and he replied, "You will be alright for what I have told you" as he placed his right arm around her shoulder. The two of them walked past Hutchinson, and he later told police that the man "hung down his head with his hat over his eyes." When Hutchinson stooped down to get a better look at him, "he looked at me stern." Hutchinson told police he followed the couple for several minutes and overheard the man say something else to Mary, who answered, "Alright my dear come along you will be comfortable." He "gave her a kiss," and she mentioned to him she'd lost her handkerchief. The man produced his, "a red one," and gave it to her. (446)

They entered Miller's Court with Hutchinson following until he lost sight of them. He told police he waited for three-quarters of an hour to see if they would come back, and when they didn't, he left. His description to the police was remarkably detailed, and it was later conjectured that he might have paid close attention because he had robbery in mind. The man Mary disappeared with looked like he might have money. Hutchinson described him as "respectable in appearance," about thirty-five or thirty-six, possibly five foot six with a pale complexion, dark eyes and eyelashes, and a slight mustache twisted up at the ends. His hair was dark, very curly. He was dressed in a long dark coat with collar and cuffs trimmed in astrakhan, and a dark jacket with a light waistcoat, dark trousers, a dark felt hat "turned down in the middle." He had on boots, and gaiters with white buttons. On his black tie was a horseshoe pin, and he wore a thick gold chain.

In a report Inspector Frederick Abberline made on November 12, the day of Mary Kelly's inquest, he referred to Hutchinson's statements as "important" and "true." Abberline noted that Hutchinson said he'd known

Mary Kelly for approximately three years, occasionally gave her "shillings," and that "he was surprised to see a man so well dressed in her company which caused him to watch them." Hutchinson claimed he could identify this man if he saw him again, and Abberline arranged for several officers to accompany him around Spitalfields. Apparently Hutchinson didn't spot the well-dressed man, although there were several arrests made "on suspicion of being connected with the recent murder," Abberline reported. "But the various persons detained have been able to satisfactorily account for their movements and were released."

If the account Hutchinson gave is accurate it would place Mary Kelly's death at some point after 2:00 a.m. It may be that the well-dressed man with a red handkerchief and a parcel of some sort was Jack the Ripper, who after the murder escaped the area without encountering Hutchinson. It's also possible the Ripper had changed his appearance by the time he left Miller's Court and wouldn't look familiar to anyone he came across. There was evidence of clothing and possibly other items burned in Mary Kelly's fireplace. Maybe what was consumed by flames wasn't just the dirty laundry Maria Harvey had dropped by during her visit. Maybe the Ripper was dressed one way when he made his entrance and another when he exited.

The well-dressed man with Mary wasn't the only sighting after midnight on November 9. If witness reports are to be believed, she was quite intoxicated by the time she met the respectable man with the red handkerchief and disappeared with him. Several hours prior to that, Mary Ann Cox of No. 5 Miller's Court spotted Mary Kelly on Dorset Street with a man carrying a quart of beer. Mary Ann testified at the inquest that the man was shabbily dressed, approximately thirty-six years old, about five foot five with a blotchy complexion and small side-whiskers and a thick carroty mustache. Mary Kelly was so drunk she was almost incoherent, and when she and the man entered No. 13, she began singing the poignant Irish song "Sweet Violets."

"A violet I plucked from my mother's grave when a boy," she sang, and the light of a candle could be seen through her curtains. At 1:00 a.m., she was "still singing in her room" when Mary Ann went out again, returning at around 3:00 a.m. At that time, Mary Kelly's room was dark and

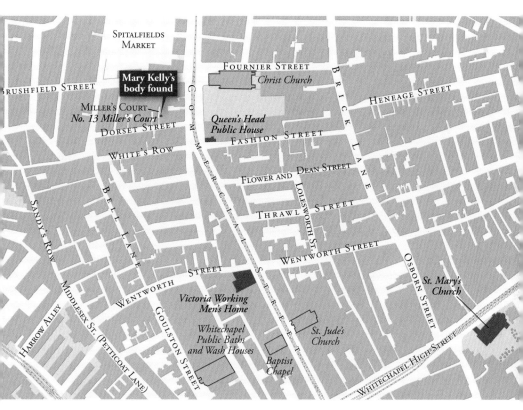

Mary Kelly's body was found on her own bed at 13 Miller's Court at 10:45 a.m., Nov. 9, 1888. Two neighbors recalled hearing screams of "murder" at 3:30 or 4:00 a.m., but they did not investigate.

silent, and Mary Ann went to bed with her clothes on as a hard, cold rain splashed the courtyard and streets. Unable to sleep, she heard men entering and leaving the building as late as a quarter of six.

Another neighbor was Elizabeth Prater in No. 20, directly above Mary Kelly's room. She testified at the inquest that when she went upstairs at close to 1:30 a.m. she didn't see any light through the "partition," which likely was the wooden wall between the stairs and Mary's room. But Elizabeth also confessed she'd "had something to drink." So it's possible that when she returned to Miller's Court it was later than she remembered. She testified that she secured her door for the night by wedging two tables against it. She went to bed, sleeping soundly until

A rare photograph of Miller's Court, showing the window of Mary Kelly's room.

her black kitten, Diddles, walked across her neck, waking her up at the same moment she heard "screams of murder about two or three times in a female voice." She recalled the time was 3:30 or 4:00 a.m., close to when another resident of Miller's Court, Sarah Lewis, also heard a scream of "murder."

Much later that cold, wet Friday, John McCarthy was working hard in his chandler's shop and trying to figure out what to do about Mary Kelly. She was behind in her rent. His patience had run out. "Go to number 13 and try and get some rent," he told his assistant, Thomas Bowyer. It was around 10:45 a.m. when Bowyer walked over to Mary Kelly's room and knocked on the door. He got no response. Next he tugged on the handle but the door was locked. Pushing the curtains aside, he looked through the broken window and saw Mary Kelly's bloody, mauled body on the bed. He ran back to fetch McCarthy, both of them hurrying to her room and peering through the window at the carnage inside. "It looked more like the work of a devil than a man," McCarthy would later recount at the inquest. "I had heard about the Whitechapel murders but I swear to God I had never expected to see such a sight as this."

Bowyer ran to find the police, and an H Division inspector hurried to the scene and sent for Police Surgeon Dr. George Bagster Phillips. When he arrived at 11:15, he looked through "the lower broken pane and satisfied myself that the mutilated corpse lying on the bed was not in need of any immediate attention from me."

By now Scotland Yard had been wired about the murder. Inspectors were arriving, and Abberline ordered that no one could come into the courtyard or leave it without police authorization. Commissioner Charles Warren decided that no one should enter the room because the blood-hounds were coming. But they weren't, and Warren would resign from Scotland Yard by the end of the day.

34

SHAPES ON THE WALL

AT APPROXIMATELY 1:30 P.M., the door to No. 13 was broken open. It knocked against a table close to the side of the bedstead that was flush against the wooden partition or wall.

Mary Kelly's body was two-thirds of the way across the bed, and it was Dr. Phillips's observation that her body had been moved after she was killed. He noted a "large quantity of blood" under the bedstead and saturating the pillow, the sheet and the corner nearest the partition. Based on this he decided that Mary's right carotid artery was severed while she was "lying at the right side of the bedstead and her head & neck in the top right hand corner."

I'm not sure why he deduced that only her right carotid was severed. She was almost decapitated. The severity of the damage the Ripper inflicted upon her would have made it difficult to know which cuts and hacks might have been first. Dr. Phillips's observations and opinions are ambiguous but his descriptions indicate Mary was faceup on the bedstead when she was attacked. Then the Ripper must have straddled or leaned over her when he cut her throat. How much he repositioned her body after that is anybody's guess. The more important question is how he got into her room.

It's assumed that the Ripper was a client Mary met the early morning of her murder, or perhaps he was someone she knew and invited to her bed.

But it's possible she never saw her assailant when he struck. The Ripper may have opened her door the same way she and Barnett did, by reaching through the broken windowpane and released the spring lock. This could explain why she was in her chemise, and her neatly folded clothing was on a chair. Perhaps after several clients and much alcohol she'd gone to bed. If the Ripper was watching and stalking, he would have known about her routine of letting herself into her room without a key.

If he was the well-dressed man with the red handkerchief she was spotted with at 2:00 a.m., it's also possible the two of them entered her room by reaching through the broken windowpane. Maybe he left her alive. Maybe that was his MO, his dry run, his violent sexual foreplay. He would encounter a victim and leave her unharmed, perhaps with a rose pinned to her coat. Then a short time later he would strike from the dark in a murderous ambush the victim never saw coming. Perhaps after Mary Kelly was asleep, the Ripper returned to her room and let himself in. It might explain the cries of "murder!" heard between 3:30 and 4:00 a.m.

She may have been startled out of a drunken sleep when he suddenly was on top of her. If no candle was burning and the fire was out, her room would have been quite dark, and one wonders how he could see what he was doing. It's not beyond reason that the Ripper might have had some means of illumination when he needed it. Sickert was known to paint in the wan glow of a bull's-eye lantern. It's also possible that people used to very dark conditions were more accustomed to adapting to them than we are today. Whatever happened, it's apparent the Ripper spent some time with Mary Kelly after she was dead, her injuries so mutilating that when Joseph Barnett viewed the body at the Shoreditch Mortuary he barely identified her by an ear and her eyes. Her face had been slashed and defleshed down to the skull, her lips cut through to the gums in strange vertical lines similar to what was done to Catherine Eddowes.

Mary's gory visage framed by her long dark hair was turned toward the windows, and it was certain to horrify whoever found her first. Her incised arms gracefully rested on her ripped-open and flayed torso, her bent legs spread-eagle, displaying the mass of bloody pulp where her genitals had been. One amputated breast was under her head, the other under her right foot, and her liver was between her feet.

Her intestines were on one side of her gutted body, her spleen on the other, and flaps of flesh removed from her abdomen and thighs were heaped on the table by the bed.

Incisions on the front of her neck "showed distinct ecchymosis [bruising]," meaning she still had a blood pressure when those injuries were inflicted. This suggests they were inflicted first, and that she was faceup. Defense injuries inflicted when she attempted to ward off slashes or stabs include jagged wounds to both arms and forearms, a "superficial incision" approximately one inch long on her right thumb and abrasions on the back of her right hand. She resisted the Ripper as best she could, and she must have known she was about to die.

Abberline searched the room, and he would testify that burned clothing in the fireplace indicated the killer had continued to stoke the flames, presumably "for the purpose of light." There was only "one piece of candle," which was described in news accounts at the time as a halfpenny candle someone had placed on top of a broken wineglass. Nearby was a crust of bread on a plate. The heat of the fire was so intense that it melted the spout of the kettle, Abberline reported, although one wonders how he knew exactly when the kettle might have melted. It could have happened earlier.

One also wonders how a fire could burn so brightly and not have been noticed in the courtyard through the cheap curtains. Someone might have worried that the room was ablaze. Or maybe the fire the Ripper continued to stoke was a low, steady one. He needed light as he used a sharp blade or blades to remove organs and body parts and flay to the bone, and there may have been other work he was busily engaged in during all this. It would have been difficult for him to stand up the entire time he dissected Mary's right thigh to the femur. If one studies the existing scene photographs, it appears logical that at some point he situated himself near the foot of the bed between her bent, splayed legs. In this position the Ripper would have been presented with the "partition" or wooden wall, and it becomes quite intriguing when photographic images are forensically processed, as one of them was in 2001 by documents expert Chuck Pruitt. At the time, none of us noticed the subtle blotchy shapes on the wood. The question is what are they and what do they mean?

In late August 2012, I was researching a possible TV show about the Mary Kelly crime scene when I looked closely at Pruitt's forensically processed photograph. I was more interested in the room than the body because a set needed to be built for what I had in mind, and what I'd clearly missed eleven years earlier startled and baffled me. It was the first thing I saw, a shape midway up the wall behind Mary Kelly's body, directly above her incised left knee. It looks like a cartoonish smiling face, possibly male with a shock of parted hair. Next to it is another cartoonish figure that might resemble a baby.

Farther up the wall there appears to be a carved cross or cracks shaped like one, and then another face-like shape, what could be construed as a boy with a mop of dark hair, an ear, the white of an eye, a pupil and a smile. There may be other odd images, and I include various versions of forensically processed scene photographs so readers can take a look for themselves. There may well be nothing to see beyond old, dirty wood. But it's important I report a finding that has been noticed by a number of people, and this isn't the only example of odd shapes in the background of Sickert's work.

In his famous painting *Minnie Cunningham at the Old Bedford* that I saw at the Tate Britain in the spring of 2015 there's what appears to be a male face-like shape in the murky dark background. Typical of Sickert, the image is there but then again we aren't so sure. When five of us were looking at this painting we saw the "face" instantly and at the same time, and such discoveries aren't uncommon with Sickert. But they are maddeningly inconclusive. In fact they ask more questions than they answer. Chuck Pruitt was able to verify his results from 2001 by reviewing his original disks of the forensic image processing he did at the time in his Virginia crime lab. In the fall of 2012, he was able to reproduce these images by using the latest software on three different high-resolution photographs of the originals held by The National Archives and New Scotland Yard's Crime Museum. In addition, he processed the copy of a Mary Kelly photograph from Lacassagne's 1899 book.

Repeated forensic processing of the photographs taken on November 9, 1888, consistently produced what appear to be cryptic images on the wall, although the cartoonish man isn't as sharply outlined as it is in the

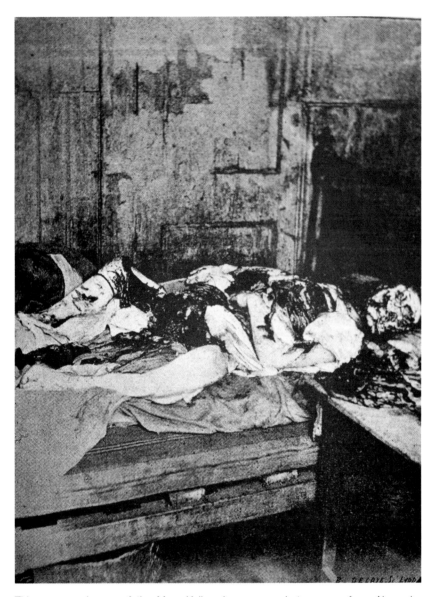

This processed copy of the Mary Kelly crime scene photo comes from Alexandre Lacassagne's *Vacher l'éventreur et les crimes sadiques* (1899), which Sickert could have read in the original French.

photograph Pruitt worked on in 2001. At that time he was using different forensic software, and the original photographs were in better shape than they were when we got new copies of them in 2012. Unfortunately and ironically, the original publication of this book caused much interest in the original Ripper documents and photographs, and subsequent exposure to light hasn't been their friend.

I'm quick to point out that as is true of Rorschach inkblots, what an image looks like is up to the beholder. Configurations of clouds and imprints on walls or a shroud or curiosities in famous paintings become the Virgin Mary or Jesus or a secret code left by da Vinci. Nonetheless, it's difficult to accept that oddities in different crime scene photographs processed multiple times with different software are artifacts. The shapes might be stains on the wood partition inside Mary Kelly's room, and they might mean nothing. But one wonders if the wall across from the windows and door in room No. 13 was turned into a gory mural. Were these shapes made with Mary Kelly's blood or perhaps a dilution of it? We may never know.

I've found no reference to unusual images on Mary Kelly's partition or wall. But then I've also found no references to the conspicuous artwork in the Ripper letters. It's plausible that when Abberline and others searched her crime scene they weren't scrutinizing brownish shapes that at a glance might seem to be water stains or some other dirty discolorations in a poor person's hovel. The police weren't looking for an artist who might have signed his work.

The extreme gore of that scene likely was distracting to all who entered or peered through the windows, and the objective for the police was to see if the killer left "clues" or evidence. Of particular interest was what was in the fireplace.

It would seem that all of Maria Harvey's dirty laundry had been burned except for the black overcoat. This is what she told police, and it seems that Mary Kelly's clothing had been spared. It was still neatly folded on the chair. It seems she'd stripped down to her chemise before the Ripper slashed her throat and cut and hacked into her body, laying it wide open and mutilating her face and genitalia. The Ripper removed every organ except her brain. He defleshed her right thigh down to its gleaming white femur, and the dark line just below the knee suggests he may have been in the process of dismemberment or more defleshing when for some reason he stopped.

Perhaps the fire had burned down or the candle went out. Maybe it was dawn or getting close and it was time for him to make his getaway. When Dr. Thomas Bond arrived at the scene at 2:00 p.m., he determined that rigor mortis had set in by then and was continuing

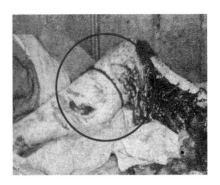

The Ripper made a dark incision below Kelly's knee.

to advance. He admitted he couldn't give an exact time of death, but the body was cold. Based on those observations and the presence of partially digested food in Mary's ripped-open stomach and scattered over her intestines, he estimated she'd been dead twelve hours.

If Dr. Bond was correct in saying that rigor mortis was still in the process of forming when he began to examine the body by 2:00 p.m., then it's possible that Mary hadn't been dead as long as he believed. Her body would have cooled quickly because it was drained of blood, and she was slender. Her body cavity was exposed, and she was barely covered by what was left of a chemise in a room where the fire had gone out. Cool temperatures delay the onset of rigor mortis, and this could explain why it was still forming. But without more detail it's impossible to say.

If witnesses are to be believed, Mary Kelly was still alive and on the street twelve hours earlier at 2:00 a.m. Of course the times given to police and at the inquest can't be considered reliable. They were based on area church clocks, on changes of light, on when the East End was silent or beginning to stir. Such details were noted by people not necessarily sober or paying attention. It may be that the most reliable witness to time of death in Mary Kelly's murder is the kitten, Diddles, that began walking over Elizabeth Prater at around 3:30 or 4:00 a.m. Cats have extraordinarily good hearing, and Diddles may have been disturbed by sounds directly below. It may have sensed the pheromones secreted by people who are terrified and panicking or frenzied. About the time the kitten began restlessly stirring, Elizabeth heard someone cry "murder!"

Had Mary Kelly been intoxicated and asleep, she wouldn't have anticipated what was about to happen to her. But she would have felt a spike of terror when she realized a violent presence or felt the beginning of the Ripper's attack. She could have lived for as long as several minutes as she hemorrhaged and he began destroying her body. We don't know what parts of her he ripped first or if she felt the cuts and hacks as blood loss caused her to shiver into shock. Her teeth might have begun to chatter. She may have drowned as she inhaled blood through her severed windpipe.

"The air passage was cut through at the lower part of the larynx through the cricoid cartilage," reads page 16 of autopsy details provided by Dr. Bond in his report dated 10 November 1888 to Assistant Commissioner Robert Anderson.

She couldn't have screamed or uttered a word.

"Both breasts were removed by more or less circular incisions, the muscles down to the ribs being attached to the breasts."

This would require a sharp, strong knife with a blade that wasn't so long as to make the weapon unwieldy. A dissecting knife has a four- to six-inch blade and a handle with a good grip. But a common knife available to the Ripper would have been the kukri with its unique curved blade that's sturdy enough for chopping vines, branches or even small trees. When Queen Victoria was the empress of India, many British soldiers wore kukris, and an abundance of the vicious weapons found their way into the English market.

On October 21, 1888, this same class of knife was discovered bloody and in shrubbery near a house in Chelsea where Sickert's mother was living at the time. In a letter dated two days earlier on October 19, Jack the Ripper confesses that he "felt rather down hearted over my knife which I lost comming [sic] here must get one tonight." The bloody knife discovered near Nelly Sickert's house was a kukri. It's not a stabbing knife but it's perfectly suited to cut throats, to decapitate and to sever limbs.

It's possible that the Ripper used more than one type of cutting instrument. He might have arrived with a parcel or a Gladstone bag that held more than one weapon in addition to other supplies he might need such as chalk or a paintbrush or newspaper to wrap body parts. There's no mention by Abberline whether a red handkerchief was found at the scene. Either it wasn't listed, was burned or the "respectable looking" man who gave it to Mary had it with him when he left. If it wasn't the Ripper's to begin with, maybe he took it.

"The skin & tissues of the abdomen . . . were removed in three large places. . . . The right thigh was denuded in point to the bone. . . . The lower part of the [right] lung was broken and torn away. . . . The Pericardium was open below & the heart absent."

These autopsy details come from pages 16 and 18 of the report provided by Dr. Bond, and as I've mentioned, they seem to be the only pages from any of the autopsy details that survived. The loss of these documents is a true calamity. The medical details that would tell us the most aren't as clearly defined in the inquests as they would be in autopsy reports. It wasn't mentioned in Mary Kelly's published inquest, for example, that her heart was missing. That was a detail the police, the doctors and the coroner thought the public didn't need to know.

The postmortem examination was held at the Shoreditch Mortuary and lasted six and a half hours. The most experienced forensic medical men were present: Dr. Thomas Bond of Westminster, Dr. Gordon Brown of the City, a Dr. Duke from Spitalfields, Dr. Phillips and an assistant. Accounts say that the men wouldn't complete their examination until every organ had been accounted for. Some reports suggest that no organs were missing, but that isn't true. The Ripper took Mary Kelly's heart and possibly portions of her genitals and uterus.

The inquest began and ended at Shoreditch Town Hall on November 12. Dr. Phillips had barely begun describing the crime scene when Dr. Roderick Macdonald, the coroner for North East Middlesex, said that no further particulars were needed at that time. The jurors had viewed Mary Kelly's body at the mortuary. They could reconvene and hear more later unless they were prepared to reach a verdict now. They were. They'd seen and heard quite enough. "Wilful murder against some person unknown," they decided.

Soon after this latest atrocity, the media attention grew tepid. It was as if the Ripper case was closed. Even as his letters continued to arrive they were filed "with the others" and weren't printed in respectable newspapers. Then on December 1, 1888, a curious story appeared in the United

States, published in the *Atlanta Constitution:* "Artist Whistler, the eccentric American who is one of London's celebrities, is painting a horrible picture of one of the Whitechapel victims as her mutilated body appeared when it was discovered."

Five days later another American paper, the *Frederick News* ran the same story: "It is said that Whistler, the celebrated artist, is at work on a picture representing one of the victims of the Whitechapel murder as she was found mutilated and bleeding. 'Realism in art' is what such indecencies are called, but the term is frequently synonymous with the apotheosis of disgusting naked filth."

There appears to be no source cited for this printed rumor about Whistler. But it has no basis in truth as far as I can tell. I've yet to unearth a shred of evidence that might suggest he ever intended to paint such a thing or even knew what had appeared in the American press. At the time the Ripper's murders began, Whistler was honeymooning in France, and a search through his correspondence reveals nothing that might tell us he was interested or even mindful of the brutal crimes. Who was the source of the story? Why would Whistler's name come up at all in the context of Jack the Ripper?

Did someone who had Whistler on his mind write at least one letter to an American newspaper? (The story was reprinted in at least a dozen US newspapers in December 1888.) Perhaps Walter Sickert wasn't happy about being dismissed and abandoned by his master, and by the time the stories began to appear, Sickert felt compelled to send a letter to Whistler's new wife instead of trying to write the master directly because "Jimmy might not read."

It makes sense that the histrionic Ripper wouldn't have been pleased when the media in London began to quiet down. Maybe he was sending letters all over the place, and for the most part they were ignored or dismissed as crank communications. The Ripper may have taken it as an affront that subsequent murders didn't create an uproar, and if a new case was suspected to be his it didn't make headlines anymore. Jack the Ripper wasn't getting credit even as death, mutilation and his violent taunts continued. In June 1889 more dismembered female remains were found in London, and as usual they were never identified. The next month on July

16 an unfortunate named Alice McKenzie went out to the Cambridge Music Hall in the East End where she was overheard by a blind boy to ask a man to treat her to a drink. At close to 1:00 a.m., her body was found in Castle Alley, Whitechapel. Her throat was cut, her clothing pushed up to display severe mutilation to her abdomen.

Dr. Thomas Bond performed the autopsy and concluded, "I am of the opinion that the murder was performed by the same person who committed the former series of Whitechapel murders." The case was never solved, and little public mention was made of it or the Ripper. Three weeks later, on August 6, an eight-year-old girl named Caroline Winter was murdered in Seaham Harbour, on England's northeast coast, not far from Newcastle upon Tyne. Her skull was bashed in, her body "bearing other terrible injuries," and she was dumped in a pool of water near a sewer. She was last seen playing with a friend who told police that Caroline was talking to a man with black hair, a black mustache, and dressed in a shabby gray suit. He offered her a shilling to go somewhere with him.

The female torso found in the railway arch off Pinchin Street on September 10, 1889, was quickly dismissed as well. There was no evidence the victim's death was caused by a slashed throat, officials decided. Of course that would have been difficult if not impossible to determine since she was decapitated and her head was missing. She showed no sign of mutilation—despite an incision down the front of her torso. But that was easily explained away: "The inner coating of the bowel is hardly touched and the termination of the cut towards the vagina looks almost as if the knife had slipped, and as if this portion of the wound had been accidental." If the killer had been "the previous frenzied murderer we may be tolerably sure that he would

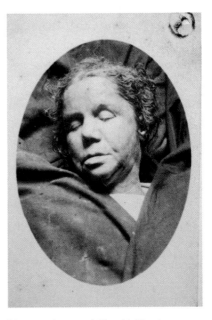

Mortuary image of Alice McKenzie.

have continued his hideous work in the way which he previously adopted" was the official conclusion. The case was never solved.

On December 13, 1889, at the Middlesbrough docks, also on England's northeast coast just south of Seaham Harbour, more decomposing human remains were found. They included a woman's right hand that was missing two joints of the little finger. "I am trying my hand at disjointing," the Ripper writes in a letter dated December 4, 1888, "and if can manage it will send you a finger."

On February 13, 1891, the body of a prostitute named Frances Coles was found in Swallow Gardens, Whitechapel. Her throat was cut. She was approximately twenty-six years old and "of drunken habits," according to police reports. Dr. George Bagster Phillips performed the postmortem examination and was of the opinion that the body wasn't mutilated and there was no connection "with the series of previous murders." Her homicide also went unsolved.

Another case involving dismembered female body parts discovered in London occurred in June 1902. Various news sources described the body as crudely sawn into pieces, the hands and feet missing, the head "boiled" to make identification impossible. It's important to note that in 1892, British anthropologist Sir Francis Galton had published the first book showing the unique characteristics of fingerprints. By 1901 Sir Edward Henry had developed the first system of classifying them for purposes of identification.

Criminals keeping up with these innovations knew they had to be more careful. But the advent of forensic science wasn't going to intimidate and stop the likes of Jack the Ripper, and there's no good reason to think he didn't continue to kill. But it didn't seem to matter. After Mary Kelly's butchery this fiend "from hell" began to fade into a nightmare from Victorian London's past. He was probably that sexually insane young "doctor" who was really a barrister and drowned himself in the Thames. He could have been a lunatic barber or better yet a lunatic Jew who was now safely locked up in an asylum. What a relief to make such assumptions, and after 1896 it seems the Ripper letters stopped. Maybe there were more of them and they were lost or pitched in the rubbish bin.

35

FURTHER FROM THE GRAVE

S ICKERT'S FRACTURED PIECES AND PERSONAS seemed to go AWOL in 1899. He withdrew across the English Channel to live very much like the paupers he terrorized.

"I arise from dreams & go in my nightshirt & wipe up the floor for fear of the ceilings," he writes to Jacques-Émile Blanche, adding that he needed to move a mattress to "catch the drips." In between killings, artistic output and getting divorced, Sickert drifted about in Dieppe and Venice, his living conditions described by friends as shockingly appalling. He subsisted in filth and chaos. He was a slob and he stank. In a fit of paranoia he told Blanche that Ellen and Whistler had conspired to ruin his life, and Sickert feared that someone might poison him. He became increasingly reclusive, depressed and morbid, pondering that perhaps people find the past "so touching and interesting" because it's "further from the grave."

Psychopathic killers can sink into deep depression after murderous sprees. For one who had exercised seemingly perfect control, Sickert may have found himself completely out of it with nothing left of his life. He ignored and avoided his friends, and would disappear from society without warning or reason. His demented violent compulsions had completely dominated his life, and he no longer had a caretaker, a home or money. "I am not well—don't know what is the matter with me," he writes Nan

Hudson in 1910. "My nerves are shaken." By the time Sickert was fifty, he'd begun to self-destruct like an overloaded circuit without a breaker.

When Ted Bundy decompensated, his crimes escalated from spree killings to the orgy of the crazed multiple butcheries he committed in a Florida sorority house. He was completely haywire and didn't live in a world that would let him get away with it. Sickert lived in a world that would. He wasn't pitted against sophisticated law enforcement and forensic science. He had people like Ellen to protect him no matter what they suspected or even knew for a fact—and no matter how badly he'd treated them.

Sickert's inner circle of art-minded friends witnessed his violently charged, bizarre behavior and looked the other way. Marjorie Lilly was one of them, and she later would seem to regret the incriminating anecdotes she'd written about him, wishing to play them down or retract them altogether. Sickert traversed the surface of life as a respectable, intellectual gentleman. He was on his way to becoming a master, and artists are forgiven for not having a structured or "normal" way of going about their affairs. They're forgiven for being a little peculiar or a bit deranged. It's not unusual if they're egocentric and selfish or in Sickert's case completely devoid of empathy.

He felt nothing for anyone including Ellen, the classic victim, an emotionally used and abused woman who was an enabler, a caretaker. The stigma of divorce was worse for her than for him, and she felt like a failure. She tormented herself with the fear that she'd betrayed her esteemed late father and was a burden to those she loved. She had no peace, only regrets, while Sickert seemed unrepentant about anything he'd done to anyone. Psychopaths don't accept consequences. The only thing they're sorry for is the misfortune they bring upon themselves and blame on others.

"Divorce granted yesterday, thank God!" Sickert crowed to Blanche in 1899, going on to compare it to having "a thumb screw" removed. Sickert didn't feel grief over the loss of Ellen but was relieved to have one set of complications out of his life. Yet he felt more destabilized than before. Ellen had given him a sense of identity, their marriage a safe base in the endless game of tag he played. He found himself alone backstage in a dark, cold place, damned to a life that wouldn't allow physical or emotional intimacy. "At least you *feel*!" he once exclaimed to Blanche.

Sickert's genetic aberrations and childhood traumas had found his fissures and chiseled him into contradictory and disconnected pieces. One part of him would give painting lessons to Winston Churchill while another would write a letter to the press in 1937, praising Adolf Hitler's art. Sickert was kind to his weak alcoholic brother Bernhard yet thought nothing of appearing at the Red Cross hospital to sketch soldiers suffering and dying. Then he'd ask for their uniforms since they wouldn't be needing them anymore.

Sickert could praise a fledgling artist and be very generous with his time and instruction, then criticize Cézanne and Van Gogh and write an article in the *Saturday Review* that defamed the career of Joseph Pennell. Sickert played the role of a ladies' man but called women "bitches"—or in Ripper letters, "cunts." He wrote them off as a lower order of life. He murdered and mutilated them, and further degraded and violated them in his art. The complexities of Sickert and his multiple characters may very well be endless, but one fact about him is clearly etched. He didn't marry for love.

In 1911 it was time to find another wife, and Sickert probably premeditated this decision far less than his crimes.

His courtship was a blitz attack focused on one of his young art students described by biographer Robert Emmons as lovely with a "swan neck." She apparently suffered great misgivings, and jilted Sickert at the altar. "Marriage off. Too sore to come," he says in a telegram to Ethel Sands and Nan Hudson. Instantly he turned his attention to another one of his art students, Christine Drummond Angus, the daughter of John Angus, a Scottish leather merchant who was sure Sickert was after his money.

But that wasn't the only need in the fifty-one-year-old artist's life. He had no one to support him financially, no one to take care of his every want and whim. Christine was eighteen years younger and someone he could easily dominate. Intelligent and pretty with a childlike figure, she was a competent artist capable of museum-quality embroidery. But she was sickly and rather lame, having spent much of her life suffering from neuritis and chilblains, an inflammation of the nerves that causes painful itching and swelling.

She didn't know her art instructor personally when he decided they should marry. They had never socialized outside the classroom when he began overwhelming her with telegrams and letters. The unexpected and excessive attention from him made her ill, and her family sent her away to rest in Chagford, Devon. Sickert wasn't invited to join her. But he showed up anyway and got on the train, riding with her the entire way. Against her father's wishes they were engaged within days.

Mr. Angus finally agreed to the marriage after learning that the penniless artist had suddenly sold a large portrait to an anonymous buyer. Perhaps Christine wasn't making such a bad decision after all. This was another Sickert machination, yet one more example of his being a poseur and a fraud. The anonymous buyer wasn't anonymous at all. She was Sickert's patron and dear friend Florence Pash, whom he'd known since 1890 when he began painting portraits of her. Like Ellen, she was an enabler, and if Jean Overton Fuller's stories are true then Florence Pash was an enabler of the worst kind. But then most if not all of Sickert's women covered for him.

Ms. Pash was a devotee. She was quite willing to help him out, and her buying a big painting in the summer of 1911 likely wasn't coincidental or unsolicited. "Marrying Saturday a certain Christine Angus," Sickert announces in another telegram to Nan Hudson and Ethel Sands on July 26, not even a month after the previous art student had broken up with him. Christine and Sickert were married at the Paddington Registry Office. They began spending much of their time in Dieppe. Then in 1914 at the beginning of World War I they returned to London, and artistically, these were productive years for him. He wrote numerous articles. His paintings began reflecting tension between couples that is enigmatic and powerful, and he became more famous. He painted his masterpiece *Ennui* and returned to the music halls, going to the New Bedford "every bloody night."

As Christine's health continued to cause inconveniences, he wrote manipulative letters to his helpful lady friends, exclaiming how pleased he was "to make one creature happier than she would otherwise have been."

Eleanor Sickert   Christine Sickert   Walter Richard Sickert

Left to right: Sickert's mother, Eleanor Sickert; Sickert's new wife, Christine Drummond Angus; and Walter Sickert. Photo circa 1911.

If only he could make more money. He needed two servants to take care of his sick wife. "I can't leave my work & I can't afford to take her away to the country." He wishes Nan Hudson would let Christine come and stay with her for a while.

Many of Sickert's artworks after the beginning of World War I explored the dynamics of power within couples, such as *The Bedroom* **(right)** and *Jack Ashore* **(left)**, etching dated 1923. *Jack Ashore*, by Walter Sickert; Harvard Art Museums / Fogg Museum, gift of Patricia Cornwell, 2009.90.52 / Imaging Department © President and Fellows of Harvard College.

After the war the Sickerts moved to France. In 1919 he took a fancy to a disused gendarmerie, or police station on Rue de Douvrend in Envermeu. Christine paid 31,000 francs for the run-down barracks with its upstairs jail cells that had been converted into small bedrooms on one side of the floor. It was his responsibility to fix up Maison Mouton, as he called it. He needed to get it ready for his young, infirm wife while she stayed in London to settle certain matters and ship their furniture across the Channel. Intermittently Christine's neuritis flared up. It was so severe at one point that she was awake "for 45 nights . . . with drugs and infections, and even when the acute pain is gone, one can hardly move."

Sickert did nothing to help her. He didn't take care of himself or do anything he promised. A photograph he sent to her showed he hadn't cleaned his shoes since she saw him last some four months earlier. Maison Mouton was "uninhabitable," she writes to her family. She fears he had spent "all the money I had reserved for the kitchen floor and sink." He had bought "a loggia overlooking the river," she says, "and a 15th century life-size carved and painted Christ," which was to "preside over our fortunes." In the late summer of 1920, Christine writes to Sickert, "Mon Petit—I suppose it is the last time I shall write letters at the window looking into Camden Road." She says it would be wonderful to see him again "but very strange."

Soon after, she arrived with the furniture to move into their new home in Envermeu, only to discover there was no lighting or running water. Inside the well was a dead cat that "had been drowned," and tubs were set out to gather rain. Lame and weak, she had to walk to the back of the garden, and along a flint path, and finally down steep stairs to get to the "earth closets," or outdoor toilet. Her family would indignantly remark after her death that it was "no wonder poor Christine gave up the ghost."

She hadn't been well during the summer she was in London, and in France she was taking a dramatic turn for the worse. On October 12, Sickert telegraphs her sister, Andrina Schweder, that Christine was sleeping a lot and dying painlessly. Her spinal fluid had tested positive for "Koch's tubercle bacillus," and he promises to wire again "when death takes place." He announces that Christine would be cremated in Rouen and buried in the small churchyard in Envermeu, and her sister and father set out immediately.

When they arrived at Maison Mouton the following day, they were greeted by a cheerful Sickert waving a handkerchief at them from a window. They were further taken aback when he met them at the door dressed in a black velvet jacket, his head shaved, his face very white as if he were wearing makeup. He was pleased to tell them that Christine was alive although barely. She was unconscious in one of the former jail cells on the second floor while Sickert stayed downstairs in the spacious master bedroom. It had the only big fireplace in the house. Andrina sat with Christine while their father visited with Sickert downstairs, and Angus would later recall that he was so entertained by the artist's stories and singing that he later felt guilty for enjoying himself. The doctor arrived and gave Christine an injection. Her family left, and she died, and Sickert got busy with his usual preoccupations and affairs. He sketched her dead body while it was still upstairs in bed, and sent for a caster to make a plaster cast of her head. Then he met with an agent interested in buying paintings.

There was much to take care of and of course Sickert could use a little help. He asked Angus if he would mind sending a telegram to *The Times* about Christine's death, then afterward was irritated that she was referred to as the "wife of Walter Sickert" and not the "wife of Walter Richard Sickert." His faithful female friends gathered about him just like they always did, and artist Thérèse Lessore moved in to take care of him during his time of grieving, which likely was as staged as everything else he did. His sentiments about his "dear departed," Angus bitterly writes, were completely insincere. He says that Sickert "lost no time getting his Thérèse," who would become his third wife.

By the early months of 1921, when Christine's ashes had been in her grave not even half a year, Sickert was writing obsequious, morose letters to his father-in-law. Sickert wanted his share of Christine's estate prior to the probate of her will. He needed money to afford the workmen who were continuing to fix up Maison Mouton. It was so "unpleasant" not to pay one's bills on time, and since Angus was on his way to South Africa, it would be a good idea to give Sickert an advance ensuring Christine's wishes were respected.

Sickert had other good uses for the £500 sent. He was one of the first people in Envermeu to own a motorcar, and he spent £60 building a garage with a deep brick mechanic's pit. It "will make my house a good motoring centre," he writes Angus. "Christine always had that idea." Sickert's many letters to Christine's family after her death were obviously self-serving and manipulative. Her siblings passed them around and found them "entertaining" as he began worrying about dying intestate. He instructed Mr. Bonus, the Angus family lawyer, to draft a will right away. Mr. Bonus lived up to his name. Sickert didn't have to pay legal fees.

Finally the seventy-year-old John Angus wrote the sixty-year-old Sickert that his relentless "anxiety" about dying "intestate, may be summarily dismissed, as surely it won't take Bonus years and years and years to draw up your will." Christine's estate was valued at about £18,000, and Sickert wanted his money. He used the excuse that all legal matters needed to be settled immediately lest he suddenly die, perhaps in a motoring accident.

Should the worst happen, he wished to be cremated "wherever convenient, and my ashes (without box or casket)" were to be poured into

Sickert married his third wife, the dark-haired artist Thérèse Lessore *(above left and below left)*, in 1926. She had moved in with him to take care of him while he was grieving for Christine.

Christine's grave. He generously added that everything she'd left him was to revert back "unconditionally" to her family. They eventually would get some of his personal belongings, including the infamous red neckerchief Marjorie Lilly wrote about. But there was no money. His promise was "completely bogus," according to a relative of Christine's.

Even when he was on his best behavior Sickert was unfeeling and manipulative, and he may not have been aware of how obvious it was. Or maybe he just didn't care. Some ten days after Christine's burial he described the sad affair as a grand occasion. The "entire village" showed up, and he greeted each one at the cemetery gate, he writes to her family. She was buried "just under a little wood which was our favorite walk." It had a "lovely view of the whole valley." He explained that as soon as the earth settled, he planned on buying a slab of marble or granite. He would have it carved with the dates of her birth and death. But he never did. For seventy years only her name and "made in Dieppe" were on her green marble headstone. Eventually her family added the dates.

When I first began researching this book I visited Maison Mouton, and its owner at the time, Marie Françoise Hinfray, proudly gave me a tour. The former gendarmerie where Sickert lived and Christine died was occupied by her family, who were undertakers, and Madame Hinfray told me that when her parents bought the house from Sickert, the walls were painted in very somber shades, all "dark and unhappy with low ceilings." The former police station was filled with abandoned paintings, and when the outhouse or latrine was dug up, workmen discovered rusted pieces of a small-caliber six-shot revolver dating back to the turn of the century. It wasn't the sort of gun used by the gendarmes.

I was taken into the master bedroom, where I was told Sickert used to keep the curtains open to the dark street and build such big fires that the neighbors could see in. Then I was shown the upstairs room where Christine died, a former jail cell with a small wood-burning stove, and I stood alone looking around, listening. If Sickert had been downstairs or out in the yard or garage during her final days, it was unlikely he could have heard her call him if the stove needed stoking or if she wanted a glass of water or was hungry. But maybe he didn't need to hear her. Maybe she couldn't make a sound. Morphine would have kept her floating in painless slumber.

There's no record of the "entire village" gathering at her funeral. It seems that most in the crowd were Sickert's people, as Ellen used to call them. Angus later remembered being "shocked" by his widower son-in-law's "sangfroid," his complete indifference. Christine's modest headstone was hard to find when I visited the old graveyard surrounded by a brick wall, and I saw no "little wood" or "favorite walk." From where I stood there was no "lovely view of the whole valley."

The day of Christine's funeral was blustery and cold, and the procession was late. Sickert didn't pour her ashes into her grave. He dug his hands inside the urn and flung them into the air, and the wind blew them into the faces of everyone there.

MY CODA TO
JACK THE RIPPER

MY FIRST EDITION of this investigative work, *Portrait of a Killer: Jack the Ripper—Case Closed*, was published by Putnam (US) and Little, Brown (UK) in 2002.

I had no idea at the time how far I was from finished, and I was wrong-headed to call the case closed. It never will be, and I might have run like hell had I known. It's rather stunning to realize I've continued living with the Ripper ever since we met, so to speak. Funny thing is it's not because I've wanted to—not hardly when I consider the distractions, frustrations and aspersions, not to mention the time and expense.

But it's been the right thing to do. My pursuit of the Ripper isn't a murder mystery, a thriller or some idle preoccupation or fanciful whim. It's all too easy to forget that the defenseless people I believe he targeted were destroyed for real. They suffered and died terrifying deaths, and it will always frustrate me when I hear the same old baseless theory that the Ripper killed only the prostitutes we hear about—*five and only five*. This is a false claim that no longer should be accepted, and it's an insult to those he savaged who aren't included on the list. I've always believed it's a basic human right to let the world know what happened to you. Every victim should be called by name. Every one of them should get to tell their story.

News stories and police reports at the time cite a victim count of at least seven by the early winter of 1888. Much later when retired police officials began publishing their memoirs the number of victims was whittled away, and the history of the Ripper was revised, diluted and redirected. The more the theories about him have relied on recycled information, the further from the truth we've gotten. Jack the Ripper was a violent psychopathic killer whose outrageous crimes were sexually driven. But it's much more comfortable to turn him into a top-hatted man in the fog. How much easier it would be to believe there were only five victims. How politically expedient to decide this Victorian monster struck swiftly and then was gone for good, and better yet was motivated by an almost noble motive.

The mundane truth is that after Mary Kelly was butchered in November of 1888, the police stopped counting. If they didn't attribute any additional acts of depraved violence to the Ripper then maybe London's frightened citizens could assume this brutish Hyde-like madman had vanished. How convenient to suppose he was locked up in an asylum or better yet dead. Without a doubt the Ripper was an embarrassment to the government, to the police and to Her Majesty.

His crimes made a farce of them and drew international attention to the appallingly impoverished conditions of the Great Metropolis. Writers such as Charles Dickens had done enough damage with their depictions of orphans, child laborers, vicious overseers, slumlords and rat-infested hovels. As Queen Victoria busied herself with the expansion of her empire, she didn't need to be plagued with what the sensationalized crimes might imply, and she had no tolerance for what she perceived as the blockheaded ineptitude on the part of the men in charge. But the truth is, the progressive modern-minded monarch herself couldn't have stopped the Ripper if she'd tried. Nobody could.

As mundane as it may seem to those with a taste for elaborate theories, most of what went wrong in the investigation was due to ignorance. Serial crimes and the offenders who commit them weren't viewed then as they are today, and the Ripper got better at his role. He became more skilled in the execution of his lustful and enraged violent acts, evolving rapidly as the body count climbed. It wasn't understood in those days that a killer's

Walter Sickert toward the end of his life; he died in 1942. He rented a succession of small art studios, or "bolt-holes," as he called them, which were usually dark and cluttered.

MO can change, that sexual murders often become increasingly violent. Certainly the Ripper's did, and I put his toll at a dozen, maybe as many as twenty or possibly more. But he didn't slaughter only prostitutes, and it's also not true that he struck exclusively in the East End slums or even just in London. He killed in multiple cities, and he quickly escalated to mutilation, dismemberment and possibly cannibalism. His victim selection included children, and he boasted about all of it in his written communications that for the most part were ignored.

Many of his victims will never be identified or linked to him. Their cases remain unsolved horrors that tore apart loved ones and falsely pinned crimes on innocent people. In some instances the accused were hanged. They likely weren't guilty of anything more than being peculiar, suspicious, uncouth, mentally impaired, "sexually insane" (homosexual) or simply in the wrong place at the wrong time. It's appalling that many witnesses were inebriated. They were in poorly lit parts of the slums. They didn't have their glasses on (assuming they could afford them).

Some of the men of interest in the Ripper's murders became such pariahs they couldn't leave their homes without the risk of being pursued by a mob. What caused the police to take notice of these hapless individuals to begin with? I've concluded that the Ripper himself had a lot to do with it. An aspect of this case I didn't realize early on is that his diabolical antics included more than just his very public taunts.

He enjoyed cooking up mayhem, uproars and other chaotic concoctions. He deliberately implicated certain individuals in homicides he in fact committed. He disrupted, damaged and ruined those who cared for him, thinking nothing of wrecking reputations, careers and relationships. What great fun until he got bored, and that happened a lot. Walter Sickert was emotionally barren. He constantly sought stimulation as he moved about his chilly, dark and lonely life.

It's difficult to envision Jack the Ripper as a working man, a husband or a human being for that matter.

We don't think of him as admired and emulated, as having peers, friends and family. It's very difficult to imagine him as the brilliant artist England continues to revere and calls its own. It's bizarre to consider that Jack the Ripper was awarded an honorary doctorate from Reading University. His art has hung in royal palaces. He's inspired biographies and has been honored with commemorative plaques on the sides of buildings he once inhabited. He gave painting lessons to Winston Churchill and painted his portrait.

By the time Sickert died in 1942 there were many books and films about his evil alias. I feel sure he read and watched anything related to the Ripper. In early 1927 when he was sixty-six he might have taken in Alfred Hitchcock's silent movie based on Marie Belloc Lowndes's book about the Ripper. As I've watched the film I've wondered what Sickert's reaction might have been. What cryptic comments might he have made to those around him? In one of his later paintings he depicts a murky former music hall that has been turned into a movie theater. Men sit with their backs to us in darkness; the screen is a silvery flicker.

We know for a fact that he read at least one police memoir that discussed the Ripper. Sickert mentioned it in a letter, and I have good reason to suspect that when he was old and becoming demented he bragged about the atrocities he'd committed. It's possible that by then—when he was a heavy drinker "in his dotage" as one close to him put it—the response was to shush him and send him off to bed. I doubt anyone believed him. It's likely his unseemly stories were swept under the rug.

There's no statute of limitations on homicide although in this instance there isn't anyone left to bring to justice. Except me. I've continued to interrogate myself ever since my conclusions became public. What did I miss the first time? What mistakes did I make? What might I say or do differently? What if I was wrong? I don't believe I am. After more than fifteen years of additional analyses and discoveries I can say with confidence that what propelled the Ripper's violent impulses makes more sense with time.

I don't forgive the ruination and death he caused but I better understand why he was driven to it—as much as anyone can understand such a thing. I would go so far as to say that some of what the Ripper perpetrated upon others wasn't as horrific as what was done to him as a child. Think of

the surgeries he endured as a little boy in the 1860s. Think of how distant and cruel his mother and father could be. Such details offer insight into the many components that create the alchemy of a monster.

The Ripper's victims include himself. Whether it was seven or seventy people he slaughtered before his spree finally ended, he will always be that one additional casualty few people think about. Genetics aside, Walter Sickert didn't enter this world with the intention of leaving behind such carnage. I doubt he set out wanting to be the most infamous killer in history. I suspect he would have preferred to be known as an artistic master like Degas, Turner and of course Whistler, the master Sickert admired, resented and despised.

I've been asked if I would like to meet Walter Sickert were that possible. Absolutely. I would travel back in time for that. I'd put him through a metal detector and I wouldn't turn my back on him. But I fear I might have liked him or at least found him charming. He could be devastatingly attractive, entertaining and charismatic. People were eager to be in his circle—even as he exploited, belittled, mocked and betrayed them. Sickert was a baffling chameleon. He was witty. He was fascinating and flamboyant. He was too brilliant and wily to be caught.

But was he really the most notorious serial killer of all time? I'll let you deliberate and decide. Do so cautiously and with the respect that these violent deaths deserve. To loosely quote Chaucer, if you must eat with a fiend, use a long spoon.

Sickert often dressed flamboyantly, as he did for this posed portrait, wearing a checkered suit and gripping a bamboo walking stick.

HOW IT ALL BEGAN AND NEVER ENDED

 **ONE**

In late 2001, I was having dinner in New York City's Upper East Side and doing my best to appear composed and in a relaxed mood. The truth is I was unsettled, maybe as unsettled as I'd ever been about a commitment I'd made.

I don't remember much about that night, not even the restaurant where a group of us ate. I vaguely recall that Lesley Stahl told an intriguing story about her latest investigation for *60 Minutes*, and everyone at the table was talking politics and economics as Ground Zero continued to smolder. I was offering another writer encouragement, citing my usual empowerment spiels and do-what-you-love lines. But I didn't feel confident about my own career.

I was preoccupied with a project that I worried was going to derail my life, a good life, a privileged one I never in my wildest dreams believed I'd have when I was growing up not-so-well-off in the foothills of North Carolina. My heart felt squeezed, my stomach hollow while I made pleasantries and chatty observations. I felt overwhelmed and full of dread as I said good night to friends and left with my literary agent, Esther Newberg. On foot we headed toward our apartment buildings, just a street away from each other, and I had little to say. I was somber and distant on the dark sidewalk as we passed the usual suspects walking their dogs and the endless stream of loud people talking on cell phones. I barely noticed yellow cabs or horns as I began to imagine some thug trying to grab our briefcases or us . . .

I envisioned myself chasing him, diving for his ankles and knocking him to the ground. I'm five foot four and weigh 125 pounds, and I can run fast, and I'd show him, hell yes I would. I fantasized about what I would do if some psychopathic piece of garbage came up from behind us in the dark and suddenly . . .

"How's it going?" Esther asked.

"To tell you the truth . . . ," I began hesitantly because I rarely was honest with her about my feelings.

It wasn't my habit to admit to Esther or to my publisher at the time, Phyllis Grann, that I was ever uneasy or remotely insecure about what I was doing. I didn't want to let them know I was sorry about the contract I'd just signed. The two women were the big shots in my professional life and had faith in me. If I said I was investigating Jack the Ripper and believed I knew who he was, they didn't doubt me for a moment.

"I'm miserable," I confessed.

"You are?" Esther's stop-for-nothing stride hesitated for a moment on Lexington Avenue. "You're miserable? Really? Why?"

"I don't want to do this. I want to write my novels. I don't know how the hell . . . All I did was look at his paintings and his life and those letters, and one thing led to another . . ."

I explained to her that the Ripper investigation pulls you in like a black hole and then you can't get out. It turns you into antimatter, causes nonexistence, or words to that effect. Esther remained silent as I vented. I confessed that felt I was losing my life to Walter Sickert at a time when I was at the top of my game as an internationally successful crime novelist. He was stealing my charmed existence from me.

"I'm already exhausted by all this," I said to Esther. "And I've not even started writing yet."

TWO

The Ripper may be dead but he's not gone. From the first moment I began this work, I sensed an entity, a terrifically negative energy that when invoked causes strange aberrations of physics.

There were the electrical disturbances, the crazy computer malfunctions, the sudden floods, fog banks and wildfires. On one occasion, winds were so fierce we couldn't open the door of the jet that had just landed us in Cornwall, England, where the mysterious man in uniform examined our passports. As I've mentioned, the next day we were confronted by immigration police in London who claimed we'd entered the country illegally. There was no agent who'd greeted us in Cornwall, we were told. The police didn't know what on earth we were talking about.

The weirdness was never-ending. It usually manifested itself with a vengeance when something promising was imminent, such as the discovery of a nineteenth-century guest book signed and vandalized by "Jack the Ripper," or a critically important watermark or a positive presumptive test that indicated the possible presence of human blood on a Jack the Ripper letter. Doors opened and slammed, and windows flew up on their own. Footsteps sounded when no one was there. Lights flickered, alarms went off and computers malfunctioned. The autopilot on our jet quit while my team was flying over the Atlantic Ocean. Software and radios went haywire while I was flying my helicopter, and when I was sitting in Diane Sawyer's living room discussing the Ripper, a glass vase crashed to a floor as if a pair of angry hands had done it.

On one occasion an enormous "JR" appeared in the sand at the foot of my dock at a beachfront home where I was anonymous and in seclusion working on the first edition of the book. Other odd things happened, and I decided to relocate to a place more peaceful only to flee when the burglar alarm hammered as a door blew open and rain soaked through the walls of the office where I kept all my research. It turned out that the only transformer that blew on the island that night was the one right next to my house, and after that a military sonic boom cracked the swimming pool. Such odd and inexplicable phenomena were witnessed and experienced by other people. Some of them weren't eager to travel or stay with me anymore.

This has been going on for fifteen years now and the creepiness never ends. Recently, a newly acquired photograph of Sickert was hung inside my crime library, and no matter how many times the professional hanger straightened it, even resorting to putty, the photograph would be crooked again. I chronically find things I'm not looking for and lose other things I didn't move—such as research journals that contain important information written in my own hand. Notebooks, letters and other original documents vanish in thin air and then turn up in places that make no sense. It's like the curse of King Tut, the terrible misfortunes that allegedly befell those who first opened the tomb, and I admit I really don't like to think about such things.

But people have gotten sick and almost died. Their computers crash, telephones go kerflooey, boilers blow, water pipes burst, and there are odd accidents and mishaps, one bad thing right after another. My sister-in-law and archivist, Mary, has been talking about "bad juju" in this case from its inception. She's constantly plagued by technical failures and items seeming to vanish or relocate with no help from humans. When I decided to begin the rewrite of this book in 2012, her house was struck by lightning and caught on fire. From the very beginning, this project has had bad karma. The early morning when Esther and Phyllis were on the phone concluding the contract negotiations, the first plane flew into the World Trade Center. The deal was sealed on 9/11, and I didn't take it as a positive sign. But again, I tried not to think about it, and I'm not one who's easily spooked. If anything, it might be true that I don't know when to quit even if I desperately want to.

It surprises people when I confess that working this case has been grim and grueling. I've never been the obsessive Ripper crime buster that I'm reputed to be. I've never thought, *wow, how cool it would be if I solved the Jack the Ripper case*. It doesn't even feel like it was my idea. I've explained repeatedly over the years that it seems the Ripper picked me and not the other way around. For some reason I was meant to do this but I wasn't a willing recruit. That's the main reason I put off this massive revision for more than a decade. I honestly didn't want to do it.

"I don't want to write about *him*," I said to Esther as we walked back to our apartments that December night in 2001. "There's no joy in this. None."

"Well, you know," she said calmly, "you don't have to do it. I can get you out of it."

She could have but I could never have gotten myself out of it. I've been asked countless times if I regret writing this book. Do I wish I'd run as fast and far as I could in the opposite direction? My answer will always be the same. To not do it would feel wrong. It would feel cowardly. From almost the start I've believed I know the identity of the murderer, and I can't possibly look the other way.

"I'm suddenly in a position of judgment," I told Esther as we neared our buildings. "Every now and then this small voice asks me, *what if you're wrong?* I would never forgive myself for saying such a thing about somebody and then finding out I'm wrong."

"But you don't believe you're wrong . . ."

"No," I said. "Because I'm not."

THREE

It all started accidentally and without warning in May of 2001. I happened to be in London to promote the archaeological excavation of Jamestown when I was asked if I'd like to drop by New Scotland Yard for a tour.

"Not right now," I said. "I don't have time."

Even as I uttered those words I imagined how disappointed my readers might be. What would they think if they knew that sometimes I just don't feel like touring one more police department, laboratory, morgue, firing range, cemetery, penitentiary, crime scene, law-enforcement agency or anatomical museum? When I travel, especially abroad, often my key to the city is an invitation to visit its violent, sad sights.

In Buenos Aires I was given a proud tour of a crime museum that included a host of executed criminals' decapitated heads preserved inside glass boxes. Only the most notorious made it into this gruesome gallery, and they'd gotten what was coming to them, I supposed as they stared back at me with milky eyes. In the city of Salta in northwestern Argentina, I was shown five-hundred-year-old mummies of Inca children who had been buried alive. I can still see their forlorn faces. It was as if they knew what was happening when they were sacrificed to please the gods. Then there was the time in London when I was given VIP treatment in a plague pit where one could scarcely move in the mud without stepping on human bones.

In Rome I was invited to meet a forensic pathologist who had embalmed a pope. Not so long ago I was invited back to Jamestown to see the skull of a fourteen-year-old girl cannibalized by starving colonists in 1609. I can't drop by Knoxville, Tennessee, without being asked if I want to take a spin through the Body Farm, where bodies donated to science lie about in various states of undress and rot. A crime scene investigator's idea of a gift to me was a maggot in a vial of formalin, and then there are the offers of where to take me to lunch as bits of organs and innards are dropped into a plastic bucket under the autopsy table.

I worked in the Office of the Chief Medical Examiner in Richmond, Virginia, for six years, programming computers, compiling statistical analyses and helping out in the morgue. I scribed for the forensic pathologists, weighed organs, wrote down trajectories and the sizes of wounds, inventoried the prescription drugs of suicide victims who wouldn't take their antidepressants, and helped strip the bodies of fully rigorous people who rigidly resisted our removing their clothes. I labeled test tubes, wiped up blood and saw, touched, smelled and even tasted death, because the stench of it clings to the back of the throat.

I don't forget the faces or the details of people who are killed. I've seen so many. I couldn't possibly count how many and wish I could fill a huge room with them before their deaths happened. I would beg them to lock their doors or install an alarm system—or at least get a dog—or not park there or stay away from drugs or go see a psychiatrist or don't get so damn drunk that you drop your house key in the snow and freeze to death. I feel mournful when I envision the dented aerosol can of Brut deodorant in the pocket of the teenage boy who decided to show off by standing up in the back of a pickup truck at the exact moment his rowdy friends drove it under a bridge. I can't comprehend the randomness of a man handed a metal-tipped umbrella as he got off a plane in a thunderstorm. I still see the singed hair of his temple and the burn on the bottom of his foot from lightning. I remember he was headed home to his young wife and kids.

My intense curiosity about violence hardened long ago into a suit of clinical armor that's so heavy sometimes I can barely walk after visits with the dead. It seems they want my energy and desperately try to suck it out of me as they lie in their own blood on the street or the floor or on top of a stainless steel table. The dead stay dead and I stay drained. Murder isn't a mystery and it's my mission to fight it with my pen. So it would have been a betrayal of what I am and an insult to New Scotland Yard and every law enforcer everywhere for me to be too tired or busy the day I was told a private tour could be arranged.

"That's very kind of Scotland Yard," I replied. "I've never been there."

FOUR

The next morning, I met with Deputy Assistant Commissioner John Grieve, now retired but still the most respected investigator in Great Britain as far as I'm concerned.

As fate would have it he's an expert on Jack the Ripper's crimes and we began to talk about them in his office. I confessed that the notorious Victorian killer interested me mildly but I'd never read a book about him. I knew nothing about his homicides. I wasn't even aware that the victims were prostitutes or how they died, I admitted. Then I asked a few questions. Perhaps I could use New Scotland Yard in my next Scarpetta thriller, I suggested. If so I would need to know factual details about the Ripper cases. Perhaps Scarpetta would have fresh forensic insights about them.

John Grieve offered to take me on a tour of the Ripper crime scenes— what was left of them after more than a hundred years. I cancelled a trip

Author Patricia Cornwell *(left)* meets with Deputy Assistant Commissioner John Grieve of Scotland Yard *(right)* in London in 2001. Grieve, now retired, is also a Ripper expert.

to Ireland to spend the rainy, cold morning of May 4, 2001, with Grieve and Detective Inspector Howard Gosling. We walked about Whitechapel and Spitalfields, and on to Mitre Square, and then to what was formerly known as Miller's Court, where Ripper victim Mary Kelly was flayed to the bone. For hours Grieve went into great detail about the women who were slaughtered, and finally I asked him about the suspects. He dismissed the usual ones as "bull" but did say he "would want to talk to [Montague] Druitt," a young barrister who coached cricket at a boys' school until he was suddenly fired in the fall of 1888. While he was alive, Druitt wasn't a suspect in the Ripper's murders. He had to commit suicide to earn that distinction.

In November or early December he was fired from the school where he coached cricket. He left a note saying he feared he would turn out like his mentally ill mother, and he tucked rocks into the pockets of his overcoat and drowned himself in the Thames. "[He was] sexually insane—alleged by his family," John Grieve told me at the end of the tour when we were getting a bite to eat at the Charles Dickens Coffee House on Wellington Street. "Truth may never be known, may be in the bottom of the Thames . . ."

Then he had a suggestion for me. "There's one other interesting chap you might want to check out as long as you're going to look into it. An artist named Walter Sickert. He painted some murder pictures. In one of them in particular a clothed man is sitting on the edge of a bed with the body of the nude prostitute he just murdered. It's called *The Camden Town Murder*. I've always wondered about him."

FIVE

Walter Sickert was connected with Jack the Ripper long before I appeared on the scene. I'm not the first one to think of him. But I'm the first to investigate him the same way we would a suspect today.

He was never a person of interest at the time of the Ripper's crimes, at least as far as anybody seems to know. Other than in the peculiar anecdotes recorded by those who knew Sickert, he wasn't connected with the Ripper. This changed in August of 1973 when Joseph Gorman went public about Sickert's alleged involvement in the Royal Conspiracy. Three years later in 1976, Stephen Knight published *Jack the Ripper: The Final Solution*. In 1990, Jean Overton Fuller published her investigation into Sickert as Jack the Ripper, and the escalation continued.

In December 1993, the *Daily Express* published an article claiming that Sickert's handwriting had been linked to Ripper letters: "Compelling new evidence suggests that Jack the Ripper was a famous and respected society painter. A top graphologist claims to have matched up handwriting samples by artist Walter Sickert and the killer." Soon enough the art world began to take an uncomfortable look at the *roi*, or "king," as he was called by his devotees, and in 1996, a book by Sickert art expert Anna Robins created a flurry of news stories linking his art to violence. Dr. Robins stated in a interview that Walter Sickert was obsessed with the Ripper murders and with "perversion and mutilation."

Not familiar with what had preceded me, I began looking into all this and got an uneasy feeling instantly when I opened a book of Sickert art. The first plate I saw was an 1887 painting of the well-known Victorian performer Ada Lundberg at the Marylebone Music Hall. She's supposed to be singing. To me it looks as if she's screaming while menacing men in the audience leer at her.

I'm sure there are sound artistic explanations for all of Sickert's works. But what I see is morbidity, violence and a hatred of women. I find much of his art disturbing. During the early years of this investigation I acquired more than one hundred of his prints, sketches and paintings. I hung some of them in my house in Greenwich, Connecticut, and quickly discovered that I didn't enjoy the company I was keeping. A Sickert self-portrait seemed to reveal an inner malignancy. A portrait of his third wife, Thérèse Lessore, hinted of ribs gleaming through the reddish fabric of her dress. In *Putana a Casa*, a prostitute is seated in a chair, and red paint dripping from underneath her skirt to the floor was reminiscent of blood. None of these stayed on my walls for long.

From the beginning of my research on Sickert and the Ripper, I began to see unsettling parallels. Some of his art bears a chilling resemblance

A 1903–1904 self-portrait by the artist hints at his darker side. Self Portrait, by Walter Sickert, Harvard Art Museums / Fogg Museum, gift of Patricia Cornwell, 2009.90.33 / Imaging Department © President and Fellows of Harvard College.

to mortuary and scene photographs of Ripper victims. I noticed murky images of clothed men reflected in mirrors inside gloomy bedrooms where nude women sit on iron bedsteads. I saw a diabolically creative mind, and I saw evil as I began adding layer after layer of circumstantial and physical evidence. In 2002, some fifteen months after my first meeting with John Grieve, I sat down with him and presented the case.

"What would you do had you known all this and been the detective back then?" I asked him. "Tell me the honest truth."

He told me he would immediately put Sickert under surveillance in an effort to discover "where his bolt-holes were, and if we found any we would get search warrants. If we didn't get any more evidence than what we've now got," he summarized as we drank coffee in an East End Indian restaurant, "we'd be happy to put the case before the crown prosecutor."

SIX

I found out the hard way that it wasn't a popular position for me to take when I decided to depict a respected British artist as a serial killer. The rumblings of the earthquake began early on.

John Lessore, a nephew of Sickert's third wife, wrote to me soon after the publicity about my investigation began. He seemed to feel that I had interviewed him under false pretenses in the summer of 2001—since he didn't seem aware at the time that I was linking Sickert with Jack the Ripper. I no doubt added insult to injury in my January 7, 2002, response to him:

> *I would hope, John, that if you or yours have any Sickert personal items which could be significant that you would consider helping rather than condemning what I am doing. But I understand your feelings and sincerely regret hurting yours. If you feel deceived, I am sorry, but I did try to tell you I thought your uncle was a bad man.*

I assumed Lessore's reaction would be the exception rather than the rule but that wasn't to be the case. When my book was released in the winter of 2002 and I headed to the UK for the publicity tour, I was baffled to hear reports from FBI friends that "the Ripperologists are lying in wait for you." Apparently this was based on postings on the Internet, and I thought it all ridiculous, not quite sure who these Ripperologists were. I joked that their threat brought to mind Klingons in formation ready to fire upon the USS *Enterprise*. Fire away my critics did, and my book tour in the UK was pretty damn awful. Afterward I described it to my publicists as "a ten-day deposition." I was attacked and probably didn't handle it very well. In hindsight I was just as guilty of assumptions and prejudices as the Ripperologists were. I completely dismissed their theories as fanciful and meritless, and they did mine.

This was made quite clear when Ripper expert Keith Skinner reached out with a personal letter. It was dated October 6, 2006, although I didn't get it until many months later as he'd sent it to Richmond where I hadn't lived for six years. How on earth it ever found its way to me I have no idea, and as best I know, Keith Skinner's was the first direct communication I'd ever gotten from a Ripperologist. He pulled no punches about what he thought, and was quite blunt in his opinion that I was "wrong" not to have "met or spoken" to Jean Overton Fuller. I also should have talked to the late Joseph Gorman, Skinner said.

It was true I'd never made a concerted effort to talk to either of these people. But I had my reasons based on experience. After communications with Ms. Fuller in 2002, I decided not to meet with her or include her in the documentary I was filming for the series on BBC. I was especially wary of Joseph. He was one of the biggest sources of information that led to the Royal Conspiracy, which had always struck me as utter nonsense. I decided to avoid him completely when I called him once and he answered his phone, "Royal Palace." I instantly hung up and didn't try again.

I remember reading Keith Skinner's letter in Concord, Massachusetts, where I lived at the time, and saying to my partner, Staci, "I'm not sure what to do about this. The last thing I want is to tangle with Ripperologists." But I did some soul-searching. Maybe I did have mistakes in my book, I mused to her. Maybe I had overlooked certain people and details, and on

May 2, 2007, I informed Skinner by e-mail that I would meet with Jean Overton Fuller. I explained why I'd avoided doing so while I was filming the documentary and also finishing the first edition of my book:

> *I would be happy to meet [her] with you as I think her information (although "hearsay") is fascinating. That was my wish, to quote her rendition of it as it comes directly from her vs. her book. As I recall, she wouldn't allow me to do that without going into her "theory" as opposed to mine, and added to that, she had to see the MS and approve what I wrote about her and what she said.*

SEVEN

Sickert was known to act out murder and mock real cases of it. He was witnessed stepping into a killer's character while he painted, and such antics likely were viewed by those who knew him as nothing more than the unpredictable artist's typical flair for drama.

If anyone in Sickert's close circle of friends and artists suspected his obsession with violence might have manifested itself in actual acts of it, no one did anything about it while he was alive, it seems. Some descendants of people who knew him well are still protecting him, if you ask me. During the reworking of this book, certain estates in control of copyrights denied me permission to quote from the documents or include related photographs. This is the explanation for much of the paraphrasing in this work. It was the only way for me to include information that I consider critical to the case.

Other people didn't want me to use their names or the names of their businesses, or they've engaged in passive-aggressive manipulations to make it appear they were willing to answer questions truthfully when in fact they weren't. For example, not so long ago while I was in London doing Ripper-related research, it would seem that a Sickert art historian I've never talked to or met sent a spy to show up on my tour. If I had questions I could pass

The author applied modern science and worked with experts to shed light on the Ripper murders.

them on to this venerable expert, the spy volunteered, and then proceeded to follow me from room to room when I wouldn't take her up on the offer. I suppose for a prominent Sickert art historian to send in a messenger uninvited and unannounced is the same thing as being cooperative—or at least one could then make the claim of having been cooperative when it really isn't true. Politics, machinations, and at the end of the day those who might have something valuable to add to the story of Sickert haven't been forthcoming or even honest. Quite the opposite, and I continue to find all of this somewhat of a shock.

The documents I wasn't allowed to quote from aren't in someone's scrapbook or attic, for example. They're from collections donated to universities or government offices, ostensibly because the original owner or author wished to make his or her papers available for study. Maybe they are, but not for me. Then the rumors began that I singlehandedly destroyed the value of Sickert art by accusing him of being Jack the Ripper. Again, it's quite the opposite.

The price of his paintings, prints and sketches has soared since 2001. They sell quickly at auction for exorbitant prices, and I've also noticed a lot more works purportedly from him that probably are fakes. Recently while I was visiting Sickert's and Whistler's former dealer, the Fine Art Society on New Bond Street, I was shown two paintings by Sickert that the gallery had just gotten in. The asking price for one was a hundred fifty thousand pounds, and the other was a quarter of a million.

Truth is truth, and why are some people still afraid of it? I don't have a definitive answer but it stands to reason that it might be embarrassing if you're an art dealer, historian or biographer who claims to be a Sickert expert and yet you somehow missed the rather important detail that his artistic output might have been influenced if not inspired by the appallingly violent crimes he committed. It might be a bit of an oversight if not deceptive to fail to mention that there's good cause to suspect he lived the double life of a serial killer. Better to refuse to believe it and do what you can to make sure no one else does.

To this day the thought of Sickert as the Ripper makes a number of people extremely uncomfortable including his heirs, collectors, dealers and those who've made a name for themselves teaching about and studying him. It's as if to suggest such a thing is impolite, and maybe I'm exactly that, because in my world, manners and murder don't belong in the same conversation. The irony is that Sickert himself talked more openly about the Ripper than those who continue to protect him. He bragged, confabulated, spun wild tales and theories that clearly were inspired by whatever fed his sexually violent fantasies.

Why would he script such outrages? Was he a twisted joker who created the greatest horror show on earth that likely will endure for centuries more? Or was he a vicious killer whose savage acts were driven by malignant compulsions he couldn't control? No one can say with absolute certainty, and I don't think we'll ever know based on the extant evidence. But we might be much closer to having an idea about the real story, and that brings me back to my motive for taking on this case to begin with. It can best be summarized by a practical question I asked at the very start: "What if modern science was applied?"

I never imagined my efforts would be ridiculed and resented. With time and careful reexamination I admit I initially made minor errors in London geography, the spelling of names, some dates and a few minor facts. I was guilty of an anachronism or two, and yes, typos. Worst of all I fell into the trap of being a bit too adamant. That wasn't wise, and I won't make that same mistake again. People don't appreciate being told what to believe, especially if it's by an American crime novelist who probably came across as too sure of herself. Even so, the vitriol the first edition of my book inspired upon its initial release in the US and the UK was an ambush I didn't expect. I never saw it coming and I should have when John Grieve said to me in 2002, "You know you will be hated for this, Patricia."

I didn't believe him. Indeed I remember I laughed. But he wasn't wrong and it isn't funny.

EIGHT

As I make my case against Sickert, it's only fair I include the case against me.

Let me briefly reiterate and summarize the most vocal criticisms and accusations that have come to my attention over the past fifteen years:

CRITICISM: I supposedly ripped up a Walter Sickert canvas for no good reason.
FACT: I actually didn't rip one up for any reason.

But that hasn't stopped people from making angry comments about it publicly. "I can't believe she has done this," said art historian Richard Shone (*The Guardian*, December 8, 2001). "It all sounds monstrously stupid to me."

In a letter to the editor for *The Sunday Telegraph* on December 8, 2002, Bernard Dunstan wrote: "Patricia Cornwell says that she 'knows' that Walter Sickert was Jack the Ripper, and has cut up one of his pictures to help prove her point—oblivious, apparently, of the fact that he was perhaps the finest English artist of the last century. . . . I suppose Miss Cornwell has to be allowed her theories but I do hope she does not find it necessary to cut up any more paintings."

This act of vandalism in the name of science or otherwise never happened, and I've been saying this for years. But no one seems to listen. When the Sickert painting in question was transported from London to the Richmond, Virginia, crime labs in 2001, the dry-rotted canvas arrived with a large hole in it. An ABC crew was filming a show on this case, and apparently it was incorrectly assumed the damage to the painting was due to some sort of scientific extraction.

CRITICISM: Sickert couldn't have murdered anyone because he has an alibi. He was in France in the late summer and fall when the early Ripper crimes began.
FACT: This is patently untrue.

Sickert may have been in France often but he certainly wasn't away from London when every Ripper murder occurred. Sickert's own music hall sketches in pencil on small pieces of cheap notepaper place him in London's East End at music halls within days or even hours of at least three killings associated with the Ripper.

CRITICISM: The DNA testing done in this case proved to be worthless.
FACT: It might be more accurate to say that the analysis probably shouldn't have been done at all.

When forensic scientists swabbed Sickert and Ripper-related envelopes and stamps for the first time in 2001, we didn't know what we do now about the hazards of extracting mitochondrial DNA, much less nuclear DNA, from evidence that was inadequately stored and is extremely fragile. It's one thing to scrub a dirty bone or tooth and extract a clean DNA sample. It's quite another to rid old paper and cloth of contaminants.

As mitochondrial DNA expert Dr. Terry Melton summarized in 2012, "The Ripper and Sickert [documents] . . . had been handled multiple times by unknown individuals, each of whom likely left a skin cell or two on the surfaces. Confounding this was the actual age of the original handler's DNA, which would certainly be degraded and less recoverable than the highly intact modern DNA laid on the surfaces by modern handlers." Nonetheless I tried multiple rounds of DNA testing, and I've chosen not to exclude the original description of the analysis from the rewrite of my book.

It's an important part of the story, and I don't agree that the early results are completely irrelevant. They reflect what was found under the circumstances, and while certain matches we got might be significant, we'll never know for sure. As Dr. Melton explained in 2012, mitochondrial DNA analysis isn't reliable "unless biological materials [can] be washed and bleached to remove all contaminating modern DNA that had been introduced."

But some evidence including priceless documents can't be washed and bleached, and this is one of many reasons why I have grave doubts about a recent claim that DNA proves Jack the Ripper was a Polish immigrant named Aaron Kosminski. The origin of this genetic evidence is a large piece of blue silk material described as a "shawl" that purportedly was found with the mutilated body of Ripper victim Catherine Eddowes. The first insurmountable problem is that no such article of clothing or anything similar to this "shawl" is referenced in the original documentation about any of the Ripper's murders. There's no such detail listed in police reports, and a crime scene sketch made while the body was still at the scene doesn't show a shawl—certainly not one seven or eight feet long and made out of blue silk. (I've heard that it looks more like a decorative table runner than a shawl.)

I don't blame anyone for testing an item that maybe—just maybe—was associated with the Ripper case. But there doesn't seem to be a proven provenance of this segment of cloth, which has been handled by countless people over the years. I personally know of at least two individuals who tell me they examined it without wearing gloves. Who else did? Unless the DNA analysis withstands the peer review of forensic scientists, we really can't consider the results credible.

CRITICISM: The forensic analysis of documents in this case has no merit.
FACT: This is completely untrue and baseless.

From 2001 through 2007, I utilized top forensic scientists and art experts to examine the original letters and telegrams preserved at The National Archives and the London Metropolitan Archives. It was determined that quite a number of these rude, crude, violent communications appear to be written by the same intelligent, artistic individual. This person painted a letter with a brush in gorgeous calligraphy, sketched cartoons and wrote rhyming couplets. Under magnification, what appears to be a sketch of a Neanderthal is actually an intricate woodblock print. Then there are the paper and watermark matches made in comparisons of Sickert and Ripper letters. These results are statistically significant.

One reason detractors have hammered away at the forensic paper analysis is that expert Peter Bower didn't publish his findings. He has a good explanation for this that critics have failed to mention. In earlier years, Peter was hamstrung by copyright restrictions pertaining to Sickert art and documents, and publishing a journal article about forensic paper comparisons isn't possible if no images can be displayed. It's quite compelling to superimpose watermarks in Ripper and Sickert letters and see the results for oneself. In the instance of a fine stationery with a watermark, for example, five pieces of paper (three from Sickert correspondence, two from the Ripper) came from a paper run of only twenty-four possible sheets.

CRITICISM: The handwriting doesn't match.
FACT: Better to say that handwriting comparison has been unhelpful in this case.

Handwriting analysis isn't an exact science like trace evidence, DNA, fingerprints or toxicology. People can alter their handwriting, and there's ample evidence that the Ripper did. He even admitted it, boasting that he could write in "five hands," and Sickert's known handwriting is unusual and dramatically inconsistent. At times his penmanship is so wild and sloppy, it's almost impossible to decipher. It varies as much as the many ways he signed his name.

Close inspection of Ripper documents reveals oddities and contradictions that indicate some of the writing was deliberately disguised to look like the work of the illiterate or deranged. Misspellings in particular are a red flag. The language used is another. All of these details begin to form the profile of a violent, mocking, arrogant, cunning and intelligent creator even when the Ripper would have us believe he's a primitive brute.

CRITICISM: Sickert was a womanizer whose first wife divorced him for adultery. He had no sexual dysfunction. The surgeries he endured as a child were unrelated to his penis.
FACT: We honestly don't know anything about Sickert's sex life.

There's no absolute indication he ever fathered children, and we don't know if he really committed adultery or if that simply was the excuse his first

A Ripper letter brags, "you never caught me and you never will." More than 125 years later, this line remains all too true.

wife, Ellen, needed so that she could end the marriage legally. I've yet to find real evidence that he was adulterous, inappropriate or even flirtatious.

I'm still attempting to track down any extant medical records that might describe the exact nature of Sickert's problem. Maybe someone else will find them now but since the beginning of my work on this case I've been told those records no longer exist, and maybe they don't. But it wouldn't be surprising if his early surgeries left him with scar tissue and strictures that could have made it difficult or impossible to have an erection or engage in intercourse. Maybe he was able to function normally. I doubt we're ever going to know, and in the final analysis I don't believe it matters. The greatest damage done to him in those nightmarish operating theaters is what the gruesome experiences did to his psyche.

Jack the Ripper is uniquely baffling and overwhelming, and I predict that no matter what, he always will be. Without a doubt he's the most frustrating and sensationalized murderer in criminal history, and I hope he continues to hold that distinction. The world doesn't need to be revisited by a similar offender, certainly not a crueler or more cunning one who manages to turn human tragedy into a high drama that trivializes the real suffering he caused.

"I think you all are asleep in Scotland Yard," the Ripper complained. "You never caught me and you never will," he boasted.

He was right.

TIMELINE

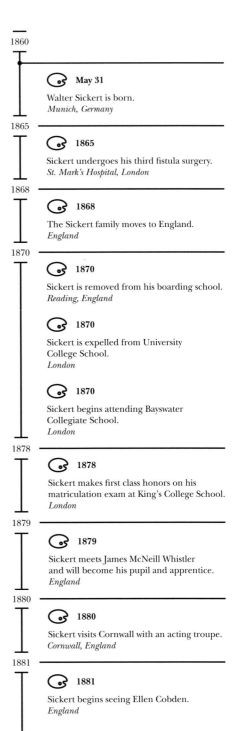

1860

May 31
Walter Sickert is born.
Munich, Germany

1865

1865
Sickert undergoes his third fistula surgery.
St. Mark's Hospital, London

1868

1868
The Sickert family moves to England.
England

1870

1870
Sickert is removed from his boarding school.
Reading, England

1870
Sickert is expelled from University College School.
London

1870
Sickert begins attending Bayswater Collegiate School.
London

1878

1878
Sickert makes first class honors on his matriculation exam at King's College School.
London

1879

1879
Sickert meets James McNeill Whistler and will become his pupil and apprentice.
England

1880

1880
Sickert visits Cornwall with an acting troupe.
Cornwall, England

1881

1881
Sickert begins seeing Ellen Cobden.
England

1881

Sickert enrolls in the Slade School of Fine Art.
London

1883

Autumn 1883 – March 1884

Sickert is in Cornwall.
Cornwall, England

1884

1885

June 10

Sickert marries Ellen Cobden.
Marylebone Registry Office, London

December

Sickert's father dies.

1888

April

Sickert exhibits his controversial painting Gatti's Hungerford Palace of Varieties—Second Turn of Katie Lawrence at the New English Art Club.
London

May/June

Sickert tries to arrange a meeting with George Lewis, attorney for the Duke of Clarence.

July 26

Sickert is at a London music hall.
London

July 30

Sickert is at a London music hall.
London

July 31

Sickert is at a London music hall.
London

August 1

Sickert is at a London music hall.
London

August 4

Sickert is at a London music hall.
London

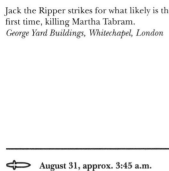 **August 7, 4:50 a.m.**

Jack the Ripper strikes for what likely is the first time, killing Martha Tabram.
George Yard Buildings, Whitechapel, London

 August 5

Sickert is at a London music hall.
London

 August 11

Sickert's mentor, James McNeill Whistler, marries Beatrice Godwin.
London

August 31, approx. 3:45 a.m.

Mary Ann Nichols found murdered.
Buck's Row, Whitechapel, London

 August 18

Inquest is held for the death of nine-year-old William Tillyer Rhodes.
Southport, England

September 8, approx. 6:00 a.m.

Annie Chapman found murdered.
29 Hanbury Street, Whitechapel, London

 September 11

Severed female arm found.
Along the Thames near Pimlico

September 17

Date of possibly the first Ripper letter where the name Jack the Ripper appears.

September 21–October 20

Ellen Sickert is in Ireland and writes that Sickert was in Normandy. She remains in Ireland throughout much of October.
Ireland/Normandy

September 22

Whistler is in France and writes a letter in which he seems to believe that the Sickerts are in London.

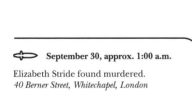 **September 30, approx. 1:00 a.m.**

Elizabeth Stride found murdered.
40 Berner Street, Whitechapel, London

 September 28

Sickert attends a performance at Collins's Music Hall.
Collins's Music Hall, London

September 30, approx. 1:44 a.m.

Catherine Eddowes found murdered.
Mitre Square, London

 October 2

Female torso found.
Scotland Yard's new headquarters

October 2

Date of a Ripper letter signed "Nemo."

 October 4

Sickert is at a London music hall.
London

October 4

Date of a Ripper letter sent to the City of London Police using stationery from the same batch Walter Sickert used.

 October 4

Date of a letter supposedly from a concerned citizen, which speculates "My theory of the crimes is that the criminal has been badly disfigured—possibly had his privy member destroyed—& he is now revenging himself on the sex by these atrocities."

 October 5

Date of a Ripper letter that says, "I like the work some more blood."

 October 5

Sickert attends a performance at Collins's Music Hall.
Collins's Music Hall, London

 October 8

Sickert attends a performance at Collins's Music Hall.
Collins's Music Hall, London

 October 16

George Lusk, head of the East End Vigilance Committee, receives a partial human kidney by post.
London

 October 29

Date of Jack the Ripper letter to Dr. Thomas Openshaw, written on A Pirie & Sons stationery.

 October 20

Ellen Sickert may have returned to London.
London

 October 31

Date of a Ripper letter that is sent using stationery from the same batch Walter Sickert used.

 November 2

Date of a Ripper letter that says, "I must have some more."

 November 9, approx. 10:45 a.m.

Mary Kelly found murdered.
No. 13 Miller's Court at 26 Dorset Street, Spitalfields, London

November 11

Date of a Ripper letter that says, "I have caught the pox and can't piss."

November 22

Date of a Ripper letter on A Pirie & Sons stationery.
London

November 22

Date of a Ripper letter on A Pirie & Sons stationery.
Manchester, England

November 26, approx. 6–7:00 p.m.

Eight-year-old Percy Knight Searle
found murdered
Havant, England

December 9

Date of a Ripper letter signed "Nemo."

December 20, 4:15 a.m.

Rose Mylett found murdered.
Clarke's Yard, Poplar Street, Whitechapel, London

December 29

Seven-year-old John Gill found murdered.
Bradford, Yorkshire

1889

January 22

Date of a Ripper letter signed "Nemo."

January 29

Date of a Ripper letter signed "Nemo."

February 16

Date of a Ripper letter signed "Nemo."

June

Unidentified dismembered female remains found.
London

July 17, approx. 1:00 a.m.

Alice McKenzie found murdered.
Castle Alley, Whitechapel, London

July 22

Date of receipt of a Ripper letter that depicts a
short knife and says, "Not a very big blade
but sharp."

August 6

Eight-year-old Caroline Winter found
murdered in Seaham Harbour.
Seaham Harbour, County Durham

September 30

Date of a Ripper letter depicting a truncated
knife blade and scalpel with the initials R
(possibly W) S on the blade.

September 10

Female torso found.
Pinchin Street, London

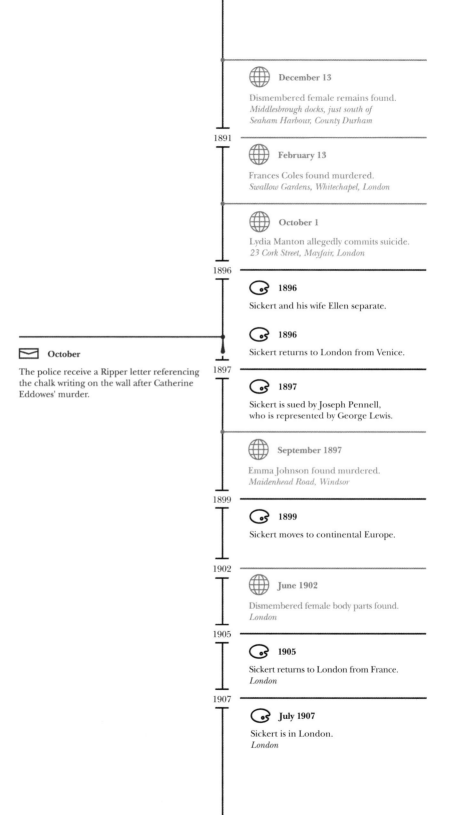

December 13

Dismembered female remains found.
*Middlesbrough docks, just south of
Seaham Harbour, County Durham*

1891

February 13

Frances Coles found murdered.
Swallow Gardens, Whitechapel, London

October 1

Lydia Manton allegedly commits suicide.
23 Cork Street, Mayfair, London

1896

1896

Sickert and his wife Ellen separate.

1896

Sickert returns to London from Venice.

October

The police receive a Ripper letter referencing
the chalk writing on the wall after Catherine
Eddowes' murder.

1897

1897

Sickert is sued by Joseph Pennell,
who is represented by George Lewis.

September 1897

Emma Johnson found murdered.
Maidenhead Road, Windsor

1899

1899

Sickert moves to continental Europe.

1902

June 1902

Dismembered female body parts found.
London

1905

1905

Sickert returns to London from France.
London

1907

July 1907

Sickert is in London.
London

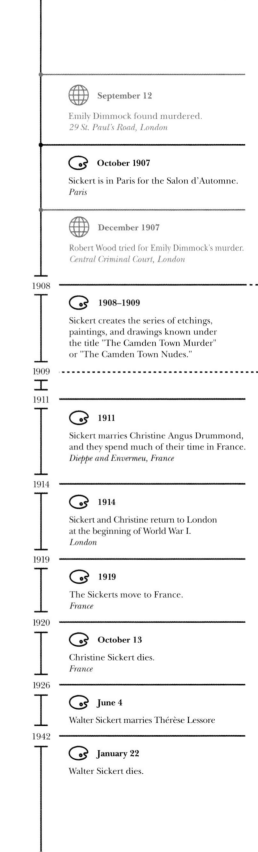

September 12

Emily Dimmock found murdered.
29 St. Paul's Road, London

October 1907

Sickert is in Paris for the Salon d'Automne.
Paris

December 1907

Robert Wood tried for Emily Dimmock's murder.
Central Criminal Court, London

1908

1908–1909

Sickert creates the series of etchings,
paintings, and drawings known under
the title "The Camden Town Murder"
or "The Camden Town Nudes."

1909

1911

1911

Sickert marries Christine Angus Drummond,
and they spend much of their time in France.
Dieppe and Envermeu, France

1914

1914

Sickert and Christine return to London
at the beginning of World War I.
London

1919

1919

The Sickerts move to France.
France

1920

October 13

Christine Sickert dies.
France

1926

June 4

Walter Sickert marries Thérèse Lessore

1942

January 22

Walter Sickert dies.

ACKNOWLEDGMENTS

Without the help of many people and archival and academic resources, I couldn't possibly have conducted this investigation or written the account of it. I couldn't have managed its revision, which has taken more than a dozen years.

There would be no story of Walter Sickert. There would be no resolution to the vicious crimes I believe he committed, had history not been preserved in a way that really is no longer possible. Almost gone are the days of letter writing and diary keeping, of people composing memoirs of those within their circle, and of police and others taking the time to record meticulous details of crime scenes, witness interviews and inquests. I couldn't have followed Sickert's century-old tracks had I not been aided by tenacious and courageous experts, many of whom at this writing are retired or employed elsewhere. A few have died or their companies or institutes no longer exist.

I am endlessly grateful to forensic paper expert Peter Bower, who unquestionably is responsible for the most important scientific evidence in this case. If anyone has caught Jack the Ripper, Peter has. My heartfelt thanks to historian Paul Begg and Ripper expert Keith Skinner, who have been such fearless sources and fact-checkers for this revision. I don't know what I would have done without my family, especially my archivist and sister-in-law, Mary Daniels, and my niece Hailey. They assisted me in putting this final work together by handling permissions, photographs and more details than I can count. Without them, this revision would not have been possible or at the very least would have taken another decade.

I remain indebted to the people of the former Virginia Institute of Forensic Science and Medicine, especially codirectors Dr. Paul Ferrara and Dr. Marcella Fierro and forensic scientists Lisa Schiermeier, Chuck

Pruitt and Wally Forst. Kevin McElfresh, Mitch Holland and the Bode Technology Group helped walk me through the complexity of mitochondrial DNA analyses, and more recently I have Dr. Terry Melton and Dr. Turi King to thank for their insights about the problems with contaminated samples in mitochondrial DNA analysis.

I remain grateful to researcher and former Sickert curator Vada Hart, art historian and Sickert expert Anna Robins, letterer Sally Bower, Harvard paper conservators Anne Driesse and Anne Kennett, forensic psychologist Dr. Louis Schlesinger, rare documents and antiquarian book researcher Joe Jameson, and Pom Harrington of Peter Harrington Antiquarian Books.

I thank artist John Lessore for his kind and gentle conversations and generosity, and I'm sorry that my exploration into this case and subsequent convictions would seem to have been painful and offensive to him and his family. I can understand why the Lessores would revere Walter Sickert and be proud to call him their own. Maybe someday they'll understand that what I've concluded is the truth as I know it. To not do so would seem cowardly and wrong of me.

I'm grateful to members of my relentless and patient former staff who facilitated my early work in every way possible, and demonstrated admirable talents and skills of their own: Irene Shulgin, Alex Shulgin, Sam Tamburin and Jonathan Daniels. I thank the late Jean Overton Fuller, and Edna Gorman and her children. How kind they were to open up their homes to me, and I regret not having met Joseph Gorman Sickert. I believe he's a man who deserves kindness and our respect. Despite it all, we don't know what's true or not and should keep an open mind.

I fear I can't remember everyone I have met along this grueling and often painful and depressing journey. I hope any person or institution I might have overlooked will be forgiving and understanding. But the list is long, and it's not possible for me to ascertain who is still working where. It doesn't matter. So many people helped me at some point along the way.

I couldn't have carried on without the following galleries, museums, archival sources and their staffs: Mario Aleppo, Michael Prata, Paul Johnson, Hugh Alexander, Kate Herst, Clea Relly and David Humphries of The National Archives, Kew; R. J. Childs, Peter Wilkinson and Timothy McCann at the West Sussex Record Office; Hugh Jaques at the Dorset

Record Office; Sue Newman at Christchurch Local History Society; Ashmolean Museum; Dr. Rosalind Moad at Cambridge University, King's College Modern Archives Centre; Professor Nigel Thorpe and Andrew Hale at Glasgow University Library, Special Collections.

Much gratitude to New Scotland Yard's Crime Museum for granting me entrance and allowing me to scan copies of original Mary Kelly and Emily Dimmock photographs. I thank Jenny Cooksey at Leeds Art Gallery; Sir Nicholas Serota, director, Tate; Robert Upstone, Adrian Glew and Julia Creed at the Tate Archive, London; Julian Treuherz at the Walker Art Gallery, Liverpool; Martin Banham of Islington Central Library, Islington Archives, London; Bibliothèque de L'Institut de France, Paris; James Sewell, Juliet Banks and Jessica Newton of the London Metropolitan Archives; University of Reading Department of Art; The Fine Art Society, London; St. Mark's Hospital; St. Bartholomew's Hospital; Julia Sheppard at the Wellcome Library for the History and Understanding of Medicine, London; Bodleian Library, Oxford University, MS English History; Jonathan Evans at the Royal London Hospital Museum; Dr. Stella Butler and John Hodgson at the University of Manchester, the John Rylands Library and Art History and Visual Studies Department; Howard Smith, Manchester City Galleries; Reese Griffith at the London Metropolitan Archives; Ray Seal and Steve Earl at Metropolitan Police Historical Museum; Metropolitan Police Archives; John Ross at the Metropolitan Police Crime Museum; Christine Penney of Birmingham University Information Services; Dr. Alice Prochaska at the British Library Manuscripts Collection; National Register of Archives for Scotland; Mark Pomeroy of the Royal Academy of Arts, London; Iain Maciver of the National Library of Scotland; Sussex University Library Special Collections; New York Public Library; British Library Newspapers; rare books, autographs and manuscripts dealers Clive Farahar and Sophie Dupre; Denison Beach of Harvard University's Houghton Library; Registrar Births, Deaths and Marriage Certificates, London; Aberdeen University Library, Special Libraries and Archives, King's College (business records of Alexander Pirie & Sons); House of Lords Record Office, London; National Registrar Family Records Centre; London Borough of Camden; Marylebone Registry Office.

I would have been quite helpless in all things French were it not for my former publisher Nina Salter, who mined the following sources: Professor Dominique Lecomte, director of the Paris Institute for Forensic Medicine; Records of Department of the Seine-Maritime; Archives of the French National Gendarmerie; Archives of the Central Police Station in Rouen; the archives of the Town Council, Rouen; the archives of the prefecture in Rouen; the Rouen Morgue; Reports of the Central Police in Rouen; Records of the Sectors of Dieppe, Neuchâtel and Rouen; Records of the French regional press; the National Archives in Paris; Appeal Courts 1895–1898; Dieppe Historical Collection; Appeal Courts of Paris and Rouen.

Of course, my respectful, humble thanks to New Scotland Yard's remarkable John D. Grieve; and to Detective Inspector Howard Gosling, Maggie Bird, Professor Betsy Stanko and Detective Sergeant David Field. I thank the people of the Home Office and the Metropolitan Police Service. You've never tried to obstruct justice no matter how cold the case.

My warmest gratitude to editor Charles Cornwell, and to Ben Schwartz. As always I'm grateful to my agent, Esther Newberg. I'm indebted to all the fine people who were so encouraging and helpful when this book began.

Most of all, I thank my partner, Staci, who has lived through more than a decade of this, and whose insights and guidance are always brilliant.

PATRICIA CORNWELL

APPENDIX

MITOCHONDRIAL DNA RESULTS

Note: Not all of these results are included in the text.

Division of Forensic Science *(Richmond)*

Sample No.	Description	mtDNA Sequence (see chapter 18 for more information)
8	Ripper letter to Dr. Thomas Openshaw adhesive beneath partial stamp on back of envelope (single donor) (very low-level mixture)	16294 C-T 73 A-G 263 A-G
6	Ripper letter to Dr. Thomas Openshaw perimeter swab from paper surrounding the back of the envelope flap* (mixture)	16292 C/T 16294 C/T 16304 C/T 73 A/G 150 C/T 152 T/C 195 T/C 199 T/C 203 G/A 204 T/C 250 T/C 263 A-G.
10	Sickert letter perimeter swab from paper surrounding envelope flap (mixture)	16294 C/T 16296 C/T 16304 C/T 16311 T/C 73 A-G 199 T/C 203 G/A 204 T/C 250 T/C 263 A-G
16	Ellen Cobden Sickert (mixture)	16294 T/C 16304 C/T 73 A/G 152 C/T
17	Ellen Cobden Sickert swab under envelope flap (mixture)	16294 T/C 16304 C/T 16311 T/C 73 A/G 152 C/T 263 A-G
22	Sickert swab under stamp (mixture)	16224 C/T 16294 C/T 16311 C/T 73 G/A 152 T/C 153 A/G 195 T/C 263 A-G
26	Sickert swab under stamp (mixture)	73 A-G 152 T-C 195 T-C 263 A-G

Sample No.	Description	mtDNA Sequence (see chapter 18 for more information)
33	Ripper envelope (single donor, poor data PS 2 & 3)	16223 C-T 16278 C-T 16294 C-T 16309 A-G 16390 G-A 73 A-G 195 T-C 263 A-G
34	Ripper letter with blood trails written in purple pencil (bloodstains) (single donor)	No Data PS 2 73 A-G 195 T-C 263 A-G
40	James McNeill Whistler envelope flap (single donor, poor data)	16311 T-C 93 A-G
108	Montague John Druitt envelope (single donor)	16223 C-T 16278 C-T 73 A-G 263 A-G
141	Ripper envelope (mixture)	16270 C/T 16294 C/T 16304 C/T 16362 T/C 73 A-G 150 C/T 195 T/C 263 A-G Several N's
143	Ripper envelope (mixture)	16271 T/C 16294 C/T 16304 T/C 16311 C/T 73 G/A 146 C/T 257 N 261 N 263 A-G
135	Ellen Cobden Sickert envelope	16294 C/T 16304 T/C 16354 T/C 73 G/A 263 A-G
138	Ripper envelope	16270 C/T 16271 T/C 16291 C/T 16294 C/T 16311 T/C 16327 C/T 73 A/G 150 C/T 195 T/C Several N's
113	Sickert envelope (mixture)	16294 T/C 16296 T/C 16311 T/C 73 G/A 146 C/T 152 C/T
118	Sickert envelope (mixture)	16294 C/T 16296 C/T 16304 T/C

BIBLIOGRAPHY

Abberline, Frederick. Metropolitan Police Service: Records of Police Pensioners. MEPO 21/21. [Pension details.] Records held at National Archives, Kew.

———. Inspector Abberline's press cutting book, Acc. No.: 373.88. Metropolitan Police Heritage Centre. [Private, unpublished diary kept by Frederick Abberline from 1878 to 1892.]

Ackroyd, Peter. *London: The Biography*. London: Chatto & Windus, 2000.

Adam, Hargrave L. *The Police Encyclopaedia*. Vol. 1. London: Blackfriars Publishing, n.d., ca. 1908.

Ainsworth, William Harrison. *The Tower of London*. London: Richard Bentley, 1840.

Albert Victor, Duke of Clarence. Letters to his barrister, George Lewis. December 17, 1890, and January 15, 1891. New York Public Library.

Aleph [pseud]. *London Scenes and London People*. London: British Library, Historical Print Editions, 1863.

Alexander Pirie & Sons Ltd., Paper Manufacturers, Aberdeen, Scotland. Records and papers. University of Aberdeen Historic Collections, Special Libraries and Archives.

Amber, Miles [Ellen Cobden Sickert]. *Wistons: A Story in Three Parts*. New York: Charles Scribner's Sons, 1902.

American Psychiatric Association. *Diagnostic and Statistical Manual of Mental Disorders*. 3rd ed. rev. Washington, DC: American Psychiatric Association, 1987.

Anderson, Sir Robert. *The Lighter Side of My Official Life*. London: Hodder and Stoughton, 1910.

Annotated scrapbook of newspaper articles [original owner unknown]. August 12–December 30, 1888. New York Public Library.

Apollo: A Journal of the Arts. "Sickert at the Leicester Galleries," March 1938.

Appia, P. L. *The Ambulance Surgeon*. Edinburgh: Adam and Charles Black, 1862.

Appleton, Douglas. *The Bloodhound Handbook*. London: Nicholson & Watson, 1960.

Aronson, Theo. *Prince Eddy and the Homosexual Underworld*. London: John Murray, 1994.

Artists of the Yellow Book & the Circle of Oscar Wilde. London: Clarendon Gallery, 1983.

Ashworth, Henry. *Recollections of Richard Cobden, M.P., and the Anti-Corn League*. London: Cassell, Petter, Galpin, n.d., ca. 1876.

Bacon, Francis. *Proficience of Learning, or the Partitions of Sciences*. Oxford: Rob Yound & Ed Forest, 1640.

Baedeker, Karl. *London and Its Environs*. London: Karl Baedeker, 1908.

Bailey, Roderick. "Jean Overton Fuller: Writer Whose Books Exposed Serious Failings in the SOE." *Guardian* (Manchester), May 18, 2009.

Baird, Henry Carey. *The Painters, Gilders and Varnishers Companion*. Philadelphia: Henry Carey Baird Industrial Publisher, 1875.

Baker, Richard Anthony. *British Music Hall: An Illustrated History*. Stroud, Gloucestershire: Sutton Publishing, 2005.

Barber, John. *The Camden Town Murder*. Oxford: Mandrake, 2006.

Baron, Wendy. *The Camden Town Group*. London: Scolar Press, 1979.

———. Letter to Julian Treuherz. October 12, 1980.

———. *Miss Ethel Sands and Her Circle*. London: Peter Owen, 1977.

———. *Perfect Moderns: A History of the Camden Town Group*. London: Ashgate, Aldershot, 2000.

———. "The Process of Invention. Interrelated or Interdependent: Sickert's Drawings and Paintings of Intimate Figure Subjects." In *Walter Sickert: The Camden Town Nudes*, by Wendy Baron (author), Lisa Tickner (author), and Barnaby Wright (author, editor). London: The Courtauld Gallery in association with Paul Holberton Publishing, 2007.

———. *Sickert*. London: Phaidon Press, 1973.

———. *Sickert Paintings and Drawings*. New Haven and London: Yale University Press, 2006.

Baron, Wendy, and Richard Shone. *Sickert: Paintings*. New Haven and London: Yale University Press, 1992.

Barrere, Albert, and Charles G. Leland. *A Dictionary of Slang, Jargon & Cant*. Vols. 1 and 2. Edinburgh: The Ballantyne Press, 1890.

Baughan, Rosa. *Character Indicated by Handwriting*, 2nd ed. London: L. Upcott Gill, 1893.

Baynes, C. R. *Hints on Medical Jurisprudence*. Madras: Messrs. Pharoah, 1854.

BBC News Magazine. "Was Dr. Crippen Innocent of His Wife's Murder?" July 29, 2010. www.BBC.co.uk/news/magazine-10802059.

Beamish, Richard. *The Psychonomy of the Hand*. London: Frederick Pitman, 1865.

Beerbohm, Max. Notebook, holograph. Max Beerbohm collection of papers, 1878–1964 [bulk 1909–1957]. The Henry W. and Albert A. Berg Collection of English and American Literature, New York Public Library. [Consists of preliminary notes for essays on the author's contemporaries, arranged alphabetically by the subject.]

Begg, Paul. *Jack the Ripper: The Definitive History*. London: Longman, 2004.

———. *Jack the Ripper: The Facts*. London: Robson Books, 2004.

Begg, Paul, Martin Fido and Keith Skinner. *The Complete Jack the Ripper A to Z*. London: John Blake, 2010.

Bell, Charles. *Illustrations of the Great Operations of Surgery*. London: Longman, Hurst, Rees, Orme, and Brown by A. and R. Spottiswoode, 1821.

Bell, Clive. *Old Friends*. London: Chatto & Windus, 1956.

Bell, Quentin. *Bad Art*. Chicago: University of Chicago Press, 1989.

———. *Some Memories of Sickert*. London: Chatto & Windus, n.d., ca. 1950.

———. *Victorian Artists*. London: Routledge and Kegan Paul, 1967.

Berkshire Chronicle (Reading, Berkshire). "Murder of a Woman Near Windsor," Saturday, September 25, 1897, 6.

Bertram, Anthony. *A Century of British Painting, 1851 to 1951*. London: Studio Publications, 1951.

———, ed. *Sickert*. World's Masters New Series. London: Studio Publications, 1955.

Besant, Annie. *An Autobiography*. London: T. Fisher Unwin, 1893.

Besant, Walter. *East London*. London: Chatto & Windus, 1912.

———. *Mediaeval London*. Vol. 1, *Historical and Social*. London: Adam and Charles Black, 1906.

Bettany, G. T. *Eminent Doctors: Their Lives and Their Work*, 2nd ed. London: John Hogg, Patterson Row, 1885.

Bingham, Madeleine. *Henry Irving and the Victorian Theatre: The Early Doors*. London: George Allen & Unwin, 1978.

Bird, Maggie, Inspecting Officer of the Records Management Branch of Scotland Yard. Interview. March 4, 2002.

Blair, R. J. R. "Neurocognitive Models of Aggression, the Antisocial Personality Disorders, and Psychopathy." *Journal of Neurology, Neurosurgery and Psychiatry* 71, no. 6 (December 2001): 727–731. doi:10.1136/jnnp.71.6.727.

Blake, P. Y., J. H. Pincus and C. Buckner. "Neurologic Abnormalities in Murderers." *Neurology*, September 1995.

Blanche, Jacques-Émile. *More Portraits of a Lifetime: 1918–1938.* London: J. M. Dent & Sons, 1939.

———. *Portraits of a Lifetime.* New York: Coward-McCann, 1938.

———. Walter Sickert correspondence, document numbers 128, 132, 134, 136, 137, 138, 139, 148–155, 164, 168, 169, 171, 179, 180, 183–86, 288–289. MS 4831(f.108, f.109, f.114, f.115) and MS 6282/III/(154–181). Paris: Bibliothèque de L'Institut de France.

Booth, Charles. *Life and Labour of the People of London.* London: MacMillan, 1902.

Booth, General William. *In Darkest England and the Way Out.* London: International Headquarters of the Salvation Army, 1890.

Borough of St Pancras Register of Electors 1907–1908 Ward 5, Number 3 Polling District, Marylebone. Holborn Library.

Bower, Peter. Preliminary report on the papers used by Walter Sickert and his wife for their correspondence and those of Ripper letters on papers with the same watermark; Sickert papers at the Getty; works on paper by Walter Sickert in the collection of Brighton Museum and Art Gallery; works on paper by Walter Sickert at the Fogg Museum, Harvard University, Cambridge, Massachusetts; Nemo letters at London Metropolitan Archives; London Metropolitan Archives JTR Documents; The National Archives JTR Documents; notes on Sickert letters at the Getty Museum, Los Angeles, California, and Glasgow University, Glasgow; *Brookleigh Fine* watermark; clarification of the paper evidence; works on paper by Walter Sickert at the Yale Center for British Art, New Haven, Connecticut; Whitechapel Murders newspaper reports 1888–1889; book of press cuttings relating to Jack the Ripper and other murders; the papers used by Eleanor Sickert for her letters to Penelope Muller, née Noakes, and other documents; two works on paper at the Birmingham Museum and Art Gallery; study of one piece of artwork at Bonhams, London. Patricia Cornwell Collection, 2002–2009.

———. *Turner's Later Papers: A Study of the Manufacture, Selection and Use of His Drawing Papers, 1820–1851.* London: Tate Gallery Publishing, Oak Knoll Press, 1999.

Bradshaw. *Bradshaw's August 1887 Railway Guide.* Newton Abbott, UK: David & Charles, 1968.

Brady, Jack. Letter to Walter Sickert. May 5, 1929. Joseph Sickert Collection. Collection held by the family of Joseph Sickert.

Brimblecombe, Peter. *The Big Smoke.* London and New York: Methuen, 1987.

Bromberg, Ruth. *Walter Sickert: Prints: A Catalogue Raisonné.* New Haven and London: Yale University Press, 2000.

———. *Walter Sickert: Prints, Paul Mellon Centre Studies in British Art.* New Haven and London: Yale University Press, 2000.

Brouardel, Paul, and Lucas Benham. *Death and Sudden Death,* 2nd ed. New York: William Wood, 1897.

Brough, Edwin. *The Bloodhound and Its Use in Tracking Criminals.* London: Illustrated "Kennell News," n.d., ca. early 1900s.

Brower, M. C., and B. H. Price. "Neuropsychiatry of Frontal Lobe Dysfunction in Violent and Criminal Behaviour: A Critical Review." *Journal of Neurology, Neurosurgery and Psychiatry* 71, no. 6 (December 2001): 720–726. doi:10.1136/jnnp.71.6.720.

Browne, Douglas G., and E. V. Tullett. *The Scalpel of Scotland Yard: The Life of Sir Bernard Spilsbury.* New York: E. P. Dutton, 1952.

Browse, Lillian. *Sickert.* London: Faber and Faber, 1943. [When I purchased this book, I was pleasantly surprised to discover that the previous owner was Dorothy Sayers.]

———. *Sickert.* London: Rupert Hart-Davis, 1960.

Buchanan, Williams. "Bloodhounds." *The Times* (London). October 9, 1888.

Burrage, E. Harcourt. "Jack." In *Five works from the Penny Dreadful Library Series*. England, n.d., ca. nineteenth century.

Burrard, Gerald. *The Identification of Firearms and Forensic Ballistics*, rev. ed. London: Herbert Jenkins, 1951.

Byrnes, Thomas. *Professional Criminals of America*. New York: Cassell, 1886.

Carter, E. C. *Notes on Whitechapel*. London: Cassell, n.d., ca. early 1900s.

Casanova, Jacques. *The Memoirs*. Privately printed, 1894.

Casanova, John N. *Physiology and Medical Jurisprudence*. London: Headland, 1865.

Casper, Johann Ludwig. *A Handbook of the Practice of Forensic Medicine: Based upon Personal Experience*. Vol. 1. London: The New Sydenham Society, 1861.

———. *A Handbook of the Practice of Forensic Medicine: Based upon Personal Experience*. Vol. 3. London: The New Sydenham Society, 1864.

Cassell's Saturday Journal (London). February 15, 1890, and May 28, 1892.

Cecil of Chelwood [E. A. R. Gascoyne-Cecil], P. Ahlefeldt-Laurvig and C. Brudenell-Bruce. *Queen Alexandra: A Pictorial Biography 1844–1925*. London: A. Melrose, 1925.

Centenary Exhibition of Etchings & Drawings by W. R. Sickert. London: Thomas Agnew & Sons, March 15–April 14, 1960.

Chambers, E. *Cyclopaedia: Of a Universal Dictionary of Arts and Sciences*, 5th ed. Vols. 1 and 2. London: D. Midwinter, 1741.

The Cheerful Warbler, or Juvenile Song Book. York, England: printed and sold by James Kendrew, Colliergate, n.d., ca. 1820. [Children's chapbook.]

Chicago (IL) Daily Inter-Ocean. October 6, 1891. [Reference to *The Star* article regarding Lydia Manton.]

Chitty, Joseph. *A Practical Treatise on Medical Jurisprudence*. London: Longman, Brown, Green and Longman, 1834.

Christchurch Times (Dorset). "Montague Druitt." Obituary. January 12, 1889.

Christison, Robert. *A Treatise on Poison*. Edinburgh: Adam & Charles Black, Northbridge, 1829.

Cobden, Ellen Millicent. Last Will and Testament, 1914. https://probatesearch.service.gov.uk/#wills.

———. Letter to her father, Richard Cobden. July 30, 1860. Cobden Papers, #38E. West Sussex Record Office.

———. *A Portrait, Richard Cobden-Sanderson, 17 Thavies Inn, 1920*. Islington: Woods & Sons. [One of fifty copies printed for private circulation.]

Cobden, Ellen, and Richard Brook Cobden. Letters. n.d., ca. late 1840s. Ref. Add Ms 6036. Cobden Papers. West Sussex Record Office.

Cobden-Sanderson, Thomas James. *The Journals 1879–1922*. London: Macmillan, 1926.

Colquhoun, Patrick. *A Treatise on the Commerce and Police of the River Thames*. London: H. Baldwin & Son, 1800.

———. *A Treatise on the Police of London*. Philadelphia: Printed for Benjamin Davies by Henry Sweitern, 1798.

———. *Duties of a Constable*. London: W. Bulmer, 1803.

Connett, Maureen. *Walter Sickert and the Camden Town Group*. London: David & Charles, 1992.

Cook, Andrew. *Prince Eddy: The King Britain Never Had*. Stroud, Gloucestershire: Tempus Publishing, 2006.

Cooper, Alfred. *Diseases of the Rectum and Anus*. London: J. & A. Churchill, 1892.

———. *A Practical Treatise on the Diseases of the Rectum*. London: H. K. Lewis, 1887.

Cooper, Thomas. *Tracts on Medical Jurisprudence*. Philadelphia: James Webster, 1819.

Corbett, David Peters. *Walter Sickert*. London: Tate Gallery Publishing, 2001.

Cormack, Sir John Rose. *Contributions to Pathology Therapeutics and Forensic Medicine*. London: J.

Churchill, 1844.

Cornishman (Cornwall), "Ghosts of Sickert and Whistler." March 10, 1949.

Cornwell, Patricia. Correspondence between Patricia Cornwell and Dr. Terry Melton, 2008–2012.

———. E-mail to Keith Skinner. May 24, 2007.

———. E-mail to Keith Skinner. October 10, 2007.

———. E-mail to Irene Shulgin, Keith Skinner copied in. November 25, 2007.

———. E-mail to Paul Begg. September 29, 2012.

———. Letter to John Lessore. January 7, 2002.

———. Letter to Keith Skinner. May 2, 2007.

———. Personal notebook recording details of conversation with John Lessore. July 6, 2001.

Cotran, Ramzi S., Vinay Kumar and Stanley Robbins. *Robbins Pathologic Basis of Disease*, 5th ed. Philadelphia: W. B. Saunders, 1994.

Cousins, Sheila [Ronald Matthews]. *To Beg I Am Ashamed.* New York: Vanguard Press, 1938.

Creswell, Julie, and Landon Thomas Jr. "The Talented Mr. Madoff." *New York Times*, January 24, 2009.

Criminal Trials in the English Courts 1559–1971. CRIM 10/98 364238. The National Archives. Kew.

Crook, Alice Elizabeth. Birth Certificate. April 18, 1885. General Register Office. District: Marylebone. Sub District: The Rectory of Marylebone. County of Middlesex.

Cruikshank, George. *Punch and Judy. Accompanied by the Dialogue of the Puppet-Show, an Account of Its Origin, and of Puppet-Plays in England.* London: S. Prowett, 1828.

Cullen, Thom. *Autumn of Terror.* London: Bodley Head, 1965.

Curling, T. B. *A Practical Treatise on the Diseases of the Testis, and of the Spermatic Cord and Scrotum.* London: Longman, Brown, Green and Longman, 1843.

The Daily Telegraph (London). September 1–28, October 1, 3, 4, 6 and 7 and November 13, 1888. April 21, 1969. March 13, 1990.

Dalziel, Gilbert, ed. *Ally Sloper's Half-Holiday.* London: Gilbert Dalziel, 1884–1891 (incomplete). Author's collection.

Darwin, Charles. *The Expression of the Emotions in Man and Animals.* London: John Murray, 1872.

David, Hugh. *The Fitzrovians.* London: Michael Joseph, 1988.

Defenders and Offenders. New York: D. Buckner, 1888.

DeForest, Peter R., R. E. Gaensslen and Henry C. Lee. *Forensic Science: An Introduction to Criminalistics.* New York: McGraw-Hill, 1983.

———. *The Notebooks.* Edited by Theodore Reff. Oxford: Clarendon Press, 1976.

Delafield, Francis. *A Handbook of Post-Mortem Examinations.* New York: W. Wood, 1904.

Derby Daily Telegraph. "Windsor Meeting." August 16, 1907.

Dilnot, George. *The Story of Scotland Yard.* New York: Houghton Mifflin, 1927.

DiMaio, Dominick J., and Vincent J. M. DiMaio. *Forensic Pathology.* New York: CRC Press, 1993.

Divorce case files (1858–1937). J 77/668/315, Divorce Court File: 315. Appellant: Ellen Millicent Ashburner Sickert. Respondent: Walter Richard Sickert. 1899. The National Archives, Kew.

Dobson, James. Letter to his wife. February 13, 1787. [The day before he was hanged before the Debtors Door of Newgate Prison.]

Dorries, Christopher. *Coroner's Courts: A Guide to Law and Practice.* New York: John Wiley & Sons, 1999.

Douglas, John, and Mark Olshaker, Mark. *The Anatomy of Motive.* New York: Scribner, 1999.

Douglas, John E., Ann W. Burgess, Allen G. Burgess and Robert Ressler. *Crime Classification Manual.* New York: Lexington Books, 1992.

Druitt, Montague. Papers. Christchurch Library, Dorset; Dorset Record Office; Greenwich Local

History Library; and Lwisham Local History Archives.

———. Papers. Christchurch Library, Dorset; Dorset Record Office; Greenwich Local History Library; and Lewisham Local History and Archives.

Dumas, Alexandre. *Celebrated Crimes.* Philadelphia: G. Barrie & Sons, 1895.

Dunstan, Bernard. "The Ripper Was Sick and Sickert Wasn't." *The Daily Telegraph* (London), December 8, 2002.

Eastern Mercury and Walthamstow Post (Waltham Forest, London). October 12, 1888, and February 12, August 6, September 10, 17 and 24, October 15 and December 17, 1889.

East London Advertiser. "The Mysterious Atrocity in Whitechapel." November 17, 1888.

Edsall, Nicholas C. *Richard Cobden, Independent Radical.* Cambridge, MA: Harvard University Press, 1986.

Edward VII. Letter to Professor Ihre (Prince Albert Victor's German tutor). July 12, 1884. New York Public Library.

———. Letters to George Lewis. November 17, 1890, and January 15, 1891. New York Public Library.

Edwards, Frederick. *The Ventilation of Dwelling Houses*, 2nd ed. London: Longmans, Green, 1881.

Ellis, George. *Illustrations of Dissections in a Series of Original Coloured Plates the Size of Life.* London: James Walton, 1867.

Ellis, Havelock. *The Criminal.* London: W. Scott, 1890.

Ellman, Richard. *Oscar Wilde.* London: Hamish Hamilton, 1988.

Emmett, George. *Sheet Anchor Jack.* London: Hogarth House, n.d., ca. 1885. [Chapter 6 includes the name "saucy Jack."]

Emmons, Robert. *The Life and Opinions of Walter Richard Sickert.* London: Faber and Faber, 1941.

Engels, Frederick. *The Condition of the Working Class in England in 1844.* London: William Reeves, 1888.

English Heritage. Sickert file: "Blue Plaque for Walter Sickert." Notice from the Greater London Council, Public Information Branch Press Office. November 29, 1974. No. 610. English Heritage National Office, Swindon, UK.

———. Sickert file: Undated letter from John Woodeson to John Phillips. Sickert addresses. English Heritage National Office, Swindon, UK.

Evans, Stewart P., and Keith Skinner. *Jack the Ripper: Letters from Hell.* Stroud, Gloucestershire: Sutton Publishing, 2001.

———. *Jack the Ripper: Scotland Yard Investigates.* Stroud, Gloucestershire: Sutton Publishing, 2006.

———. *Jack the Ripper and the Whitechapel Murders.* Richmond: Public Record Office, 2002.

———. *The Ultimate Jack the Ripper Sourcebook.* London: Constable & Robinson, 2000.

Evelyn, John. *Fumifugium, Or the Inconvenience of the Aer and Smoake of London Dissipated.* National Smoke Abatement Society, 1933. Reprint of 1661 edition.

Evening Post (Wellington, New Zealand). "The Chorus Girl's Suicide; Seamy Side of High Life." United Press Association. Vol. 42, no. 84, October 6, 1891, 2.

Evening Standard (London). "Horrible Discovery in Lambeth; Supposed Murder of a Woman." June 6, 1902.

———. "Sickert's Murder Picture." Monday, November 29, 1937, 6.

Exeter and Plymouth Gazette. "The Menu Case." August 26, 1907.

Fairclough, Melvyn. *The Ripper and the Royals.* London: Duckworth, 1991.

Fairholt, Frederick William. *Costumes in England*, 2nd ed. London: Chapman & Hall, 1860.

Fairstein, Linda A. *Sexual Violence.* New York: William Morrow, 1993.

Farr, Samuel. *Elements of Medical Jurisprudence.* London: J. Callow, 1814.

Ffrangcon-Davies, Gwen. Letters. Tate Archive, London.

Fielding, Henry. *An Enquiry into the Causes of the Late Increase of Robbers.* London: Printed for A. Millar, opposite to Katharine-Street, in the Strand, 1751.

Fisher, Kathleen. *Conversations with Sylvia: Sylvia Gosse, Painter, 1881–1968.* Edited by Eileen Vera Smith. London: Charles Skilton, 1975.

Fishman, William J. *East End 1888.* London: Duckworth, 1988.

———. *East End Jewish Radicals.* London: Duckworth, 1975.

———. *The Streets of East London.* London: Duckworth, 1985.

Fitzgerald, Percy. *Chronicles of Bow Street Police Office.* London: Chapman & Hall, 1888.

Fletcher, Anthony. *Gender, Sex and Subordination in England, 1500–1800.* New Haven and London: Yale University Press, 1995.

Foran, David R., Beth E. Wills, Brianne M. Kiley, Carrie B. Jackson and John H. Trestrail III. "The Conviction of Dr. Crippen: New Forensic Findings in a Century-Old Murder." *Journal of Forensic Sciences* 56, no. 1 (2011): 233–240. doi:10.1111/j.1556-4029.2010.01532.x.

Franklin, Benjamin. *Observations on the Causes and Cure of Smoky Chimneys.* London: reprinted for John Debrett, opposite Burlington-House, in Piccadilly; and J. Sewell, in Cornhill, 1787.

Fraser, Edward, and John Gibbons. *Soldier and Sailor Words and Phrases.* London: G. Routledge & Sons, 1925.

Friel, Lisa. Transcript of her summation for the prosecution in The People of the State of New York v. John Royster. Supreme Court of the State of New York, County of New York. March 6 and April 30, 1998.

Frith, Henry. *How to Read Character in Handwriting.* New York: Ward, Lock, Bowden, 1890.

Fuller, Jean Overton. *Driven to It.* Norwich, Norfolk: Michael Russell Publishing, 2007.

———. *Sickert and the Ripper Crimes: An Investigation into the Relationship Between the Whitechapel Murders of 1888 and the English Tonal Painter Walter Richard Sickert.* Oxford: Mandrake, 1990.

Furniss, Harold, ed. *Famous Crimes.* London: Harold Furniss, September–November, 1888.

Galton, Sir Francis. *Fingerprint Directories.* London: Macmillan, 1895.

———. *Inquiries into Human Faculty and Its Development.* London: Macmillan, 1883.

Garrett, Edmund H. *Victorian Songs.* Boston: Little, Brown, 1895.

George, Henry. *Progress and Poverty.* New York: D. Appleton, 1880.

Gilberth, Vernon J. *Practical Homicide Investigation*, 2nd ed. Boca Raton, FL: CRC Press, 1993.

Gillett, Paula. *The Victorian Painter's World.* Gloucester: Sutton, 1990.

Goldring, Douglas. *The Nineteen Twenties: A General Survey and Some Personal Memories.* Nicholson & Watson, 1945.

Goodwin, John C. *Insanity and the Criminal.* London: Hutchinson, 1923.

Gorman, Joseph. Copy of birth certificate, application number 6423A. October 1925. General Register Office, London. District: St. Pancras. Sub District: West St. Pancras in the County of London.

Granshaw, Lindsay. *St. Mark's Hospital, London: A Social History of a Specialist Hospital.* London: King Edward's Hospital Fund for London. 1985.

Gray, Henry. *Anatomy, descriptive and surgical.* London: Longmans, Green, 1872.

Grieve, John. E-mail to Patricia Cornwell. August 29, 2012.

Griffiths, Arthur. *Mysteries of Police Crimes.* London: Cassell, 1898.

———. *The World's Famous Prisons: An Account of the State of Prisons from the Earliest Times to the Present Day, with the History of Celebrated Cases.* London: The Grolier Society, 1905.

Grimm, Jacob, and Wilhelm Grimm. *German Popular Stories.* London: C. Baldwyn, 1823.

Guardian (Manchester). "Music Hall Mementos Go on Sale." Sickert cuttings. April 24, 1963. Islington Libraries.

Guerin, Marcel. *Degas Letters.* Oxford: Bruno Cassirer, 1947.

Guy, William Augustus, and David Ferrier. *Principles of Forensic Medicine*. London: Henry Renshaw, 1875.

Halliwell, James Orchard. *Popular Rhymes and Nursery Tales*. London: John Russell Smith, 1849.

Hamnett, Nina. *Laughing Torso*. London: Constable, 1921.

Hampshire Telegraph and Sussex Chronicle (Portsmouth, England). "The Doctor's Story." Saturday, December 1, 1888, 3.

Hampstead Artists' Council. *Camden Town Group. Hampstead Festival Exhibition Catalogue*, 1965.

Harris, Nick. *Famous Crimes*. Los Angeles: Arthur Vernon Agency, 1933.

Harrison, Michael. *Clarence: Was He Jack the Ripper?* New York: Drake, 1972.

Hassall, Christopher. *Edward Marsh: A Biography*. London: Longmans, Green, 1959.

Haydon, Benjamin Robert. *Autobiography of Benjamin Robert Haydon*. London: Oxford University Press, 1927.

Hemyng, Bracebridge. *Jack Harkaway and His Father at the Haunt of the Pirate*. London: Hogarth House, 1885.

Hey, Cicely. Papers. Islington Libraries.

Heywood, Thomas. *Gynaikeion: or, Nine Books of Various History Concerning Women; Inscribed by the Names of the Nine Muses*. London: Adam Islip, 1624.

Hill's Hotel guest book 1877–88. Lizard Point, Cornwall, England. New York Public Library.

Hinde, Wendy. *Richard Cobden: A Victorian Outsider*. New Haven and London: Yale University Press, 1987.

Hingston, Sandy. "The Psychopath Test." *Philadelphia Magazine*, June 28, 2012.

The History of a Little Boy Found Under a Haycock. York, England: printed and sold by J. Kendrew, Colliergate, n.d., ca. 1820. [Children's chapbook.]

The History of Little Tom Tucker. York, England: printed and sold by J. Kendrew, Colliergate, n.d., ca. 1820. [Children's chapbook.]

Holmes, Richard R. *Queen Victoria*. London and Paris: Boussod, Valadon, 1897.

Holroyd, Michael. *Augustus John*. London: William Heinemann, 1975.

Home Office Records. HO 144/220/A49301 through HO 144/221/A49301K. National Archives, Kew.

Hone, Joseph. *The Life of George Moore*. London: Victor Gollancz, 1936.

———. *The Life of Henry Tonks*. London: William Heinemann, 1939.

Hooke, Robert. *Micrographia: Or Some Physiological Descriptions of Minute Bodies Made by Magnifying Glasses. With Observation and Inquiries Thereupon*. London: Jo. Martyn and Ja. Allestry, Printers to the Royal Society, 1665.

Hooper, W. Eden, and Joseph Knight. *The Stage in the Year 1900*. London: Spottiswoode, 1901.

Hope, James. *Principles and Illustrations of Morbid Anatomy*. London: Whittaker, 1834.

House, Madeline, and Graham Storey, eds. *The Letters of Charles Dickens*. Vol. 2, 1840–41. Oxford: Clarendon Press, 1969.

Howard, John. *The State of the Prisons in England and Wales, with Preliminary Observations, and an Account of Some Foreign Prisons and Hospitals*. London: William Eyres, 1784.

Howard, Philip. "Enter Bill Sikes As Rescuer." *The Times* (London), April 21, 1969.

Howship, John. *Disease of the Lower Intestines, and Anus*. London: Longman, Hurst, Rees, Orme, and Brown, 1821.

Hudson, Nan. Letters. Tate Archive, London.

Huet, M. M. *Eva May, the Foundling or the Secret Dungeon*. New York: Garrett, 1853.

Hughes, Virginia. "Science in Court: Head Case." *Nature* 464 (March 2010): 340–342. doi:10.1038/464340a.

Hume, Joseph. [Five Tracts] *Retrospect of Philosophical, Mechanical, Chemical and Agricultural*

Discoveries. Vol. 5, *Mr. Hume's Method of Detecting Arsenic.* London: Printed for the Proprietors and sold by W. H. Wyatt, 1810.

Hunter, William. "On the Uncertainty of the Signs of Murder, in the Case of Bastard Children." *Medical Observations and Inquiries* 6 (1784): 266–290.

Huxam, John. *Observations on Air, and Epidemic Diseases.* London: J. Hinton, 1759.

Illustrated Police News: Law Courts and Weekly Record (London). "Another Windsor Tragedy." October 2, 1897, 10.

———. "Awful Discovery of a Woman's Remains in Lambeth." June 14, 1902, 3.

———. September–December, 1888.

Inbau, Fred E. *Lie Detection and Criminal Interrogation.* Baltimore: Williams & Wilkins, 1942.

International Society of Sculptors, Painters & Gravers. *Memorial Exhibition of the Works of the Late James McNeill Whistler. . . .* London: William Heinemann, 1905.

Irving, H. B. *Trial of Mrs. Maybrick.* Edinburgh and London: W. Hodge, 1927.

Irving, Henry. Private correspondence. New York Public Library. [Collection of letters that show the various cities where he and his company performed.]

Islington Libraries. *The Sickerts in Islington.* London: Islington Libraries, 1987.

———. *Walter Richard Sickert, 1860–1942: Catalogue of the Islington Libraries Sickert Collection.* London: Islington Libraries, 1970.

Jackson, Robert. *Coroner: The Biography of Sir Bentley Purchase.* London: Harrap, n.d., ca. 1963.

Jenner, Henry. *A Handbook of the Cornish Language.* London: D. Nutt, 1904.

Jervis, John. *A Practical Treatise on the Office and Duties of Coroners: With Forms and Precedents.* London: S. Sweet, W. Maxwell and Stevens & Norton, Law Booksellers and Publishers, 1854.

J.F.S. "The State Of Whitechapel." *The Times* (London), September 14, 1888.

John, Augustus. *Finishing Touches.* Edited by Daniel George. London: J. Cape, 1964.

Johnson, George. *Lectures on Bright's Disease.* London: Smith, Elder, 1873.

Johnson, Samuel. *A Dictionary of the English Language*, 2nd ed. Vols. 1 and 2. London: W. Strahan, 1756.

———. *A Dictionary of the English Language*, 10th ed. Vol. 2. London: F. & C. Rivington, 1810.

Kavanagh, Morgan. *Myths Traced to Their Primary Source Through Language.* London: T. C. Newby, 1856.

Kellogg, A. O. *Shakespeare's Delineations of Insanity, Imbecility and Suicide.* New York: Hurd and Houghton, 1856.

Kersey, John. *Dictionarium Anglo-Britannicum.* J. Wilde, London: 1708.

Kingsbury, Benjamin. *A Treatise on Razors. . . . ,* 2nd ed. London: W. Blackader, 1802.

Knapp, Andrew, and William Baldwin. *The Newgate Calendar.* London: J. Robins, 1824.

Knight, Stephen. *Jack the Ripper: The Final Solution.* London: Harrap, 1976.

———. "Why Sickert Denied Ripper Tale." *Sunday Times* (London), July 2, 1978.

Krafft-Ebing, Richard von. *Psychopathia Sexualis.* London: Staples Press, 1965. [English translation from 1886 German edition.]

Krill, John. *English Artists' Paper: Renaissance to Regency.* London: Winterthur Gallery and Oak Knoll Press, 2002.

Kuhne, Frederick. *The Finger Print Instructor.* New York: Munn & Company, 1916.

Lacassagne, Alexandre. *Vacher l'éventreur et les crimes sadiques.* Lyon: A. Storck, 1899.

Larson, J. A. *Single Fingerprint System.* New York: D. Appleton, 1924. [A bit of interesting trivia: On September 3, 1938, the author gave this book to a colleague and wrote, "With deepest appreciation in memory of hours spent in the search for truth." Under the inscription, Mr. Larson left his inked left thumbprint.]

Laski, Harold J., Sidney Webb and Beatrice Webb. *The Socialist Review*. London, n.d., ca. 1929, 17–20.

Lattes, Leone. *Individuality of the Blood: In Biology and in Clinical and Forensic Medicine*. Oxford: Oxford University Press, 1932. [I was fascinated to discover after purchasing this book that it was once owned by Dr. Bernard Spilsbury, and it would appear that certain key forensic passages were underlined by him. Spilsbury was perhaps the most famous forensic pathologist in England's history. He was called "the incomparable witness" and is believed to have performed more than 25,000 postmortem examinations in his career.]

Laughton, Bruce. *Philip Wilson Steer, 1860–1942*. Oxford: Clarendon Press, 1971.

Laurance, Jeremy. "Sickert obsessed with perversion." *The Times* (London), July 15, 1996.

Lavater, John Casper. *Essays on Physiognomy*. 3 vols. Bound in five. London: Printed for John Murray, H. Hunter and T. Holloway, 1792.

Laver, James. *Whistler*. London: Faber and Faber, 1930.

Layard, George Somes. *The Life and Letters of Charles Samuel Keene*. London: Sampson Low, Marston, 1892.

Lee, Celia. *Jean, Lady Hamilton, 1861–1941: A Soldier's Wife*. Privately published, 2001.

Leeson, Benjamin. *Lost London: The Memoirs of an East End Detective*. London: Stanley Paul, 1934.

Lellenberg, Jon, Daniel Stashower and Charles Foley. *Arthur Conan Doyle: A Life in Letters*. New York, Penguin Press, 2007.

Lessore, John. Conversation with Lessore at his studio in Peckham. Spring 2001.

Lilly, Marjorie. Last Will and Testament. The Principal Registry of the Family Division. Probate Department, London.

———. Letter to Stephen Knight. August 15, 1975. Stephen Knight Collection, c/o Keith Skinner, London.

———. *Sickert, the Painter and his Circle*. London: Paul Elek, 1971.

Linklater, Magnus. "Did Jack the Ripper Have Royal Blood?" *Sunday Times* (London), November 1, 1970.

Littlejohn, Henry Harvey. Manuscript notes for lectures on forensic science given at the Royal College of Physicians. Four autographed letters. n.d., ca. 1861–1927. University of Tennessee collection.

Llewellyn, Dr. Rees Ralph. Information regarding Dr. Llewellyn and fees charged by doctors called upon by coroners and police. Royal London Hospital Archives and medical directories at the Wellcome Library for the History and Understanding of Medicine.

Lloyd's Weekly London Newspaper. "Another East-End Mystery. Discovery of Human Remains." Sunday, December 13, 1889, front page.

———. "Suicide of a Ballet Girl. A Lord as a Witness." October 11, 1891.

Lombroso, Caesar, and William Ferrero. *The Female Offender*. London: Swan Sonnenschein, 1895.

London Antiquary, A [John Camden Hotten]. *Dictionary of Modern Slang, Cant, and Vulgar Words. . . .* Piccadilly, London: John Camden Hotten, 1860.

London, Jack. *The People of the Abyss*. New York: Macmillan, 1903.

Lowndes, Susan. *Diaries and Letters of Marie Belloc Lowndes, 1911–1947*. London: Chatto & Windus, 1971.

Luckes, Eva, and C. E. Matron. *The London Hospital, 1880–1919*. London Hospital League of Nurses, n.d.

MacDonald, Arthur. *Criminology*. London: Funk & Wagnalls, 1893.

MacGregor, George. *The History of Burke and Hare*. Glasgow: Thomas D. Morison, 1884.

MacKay, Charles. *Memoirs of Extraordinary Popular Delusions and the Madness of Crowds*. 3 vols. London: Richard Bentley, 1841.

Macnaghten, Melville. *Days of My Years*. London: Arnold, 1914.

————. Memorandum dated February 23, 1894. Scotland Yard.

Magnus, Philip. *King Edward the Seventh*. London: John Murray, 1964.

Male, George Edward. *Elements of Juridical or Forensic Medicine: For the Use of Medical Men, Coroners and Barristers*. London: E. Cox and Son, 1818.

Malthus, Thomas Robert. *An Essay on the Principle of Population, As It Affects the Future Improvement of Society*. London: J. Johnson, 1798.

Marsh, Arnold. *Smoke: The Problem of Coal and the Atmosphere*. London: Faber and Faber, 1947.

Martin, Theodore. *The Life of His Royal Highness the Prince Consort*. London: Smith, Elder, 1880.

Masters, R. E. L., and Edward Lea. *Perverse Crimes in History*. New York: Julian Press, 1963.

Matthews, John Hobson. *A History of the Parishes of Saint Ives, Leiant, Towednack and Zennor*. London: Elliot Stock, 1892.

Maugham, Lord. *The Tichborne Case*. London: Hodder & Stoughton, 1936.

Mayhew, Henry. *London Labour and the London Poor*. London: Griffin, Bohn, 1851.

————. *Mayhew's London edited by Peter Quennell*. London: Pilot Press, 1949.

Mead, Richard. *A Mechanical Account of Poisons*, 3rd ed. London: Printed for J. Brindley, 1745.

The Medical Standard. Chicago: G. P. Englehard, 1887.

Mellor, J. E. M. *Hints on the First Stages in the Training of a Bloodhound Puppy to Hunt Man*. Cambridge: privately published, 1934.

Membery, York. "Could Society Painter Have Been The Ripper?" *Daily Express* (London), December 31, 1993.

Menpes, Mortimer. *Whistler As I Knew Him*. London: Adam and Charles Black, 1904.

Metropolitan Police Historical Museum archives. London. [Details of police hand ambulances, buildings, salaries, uniforms and equipment.]

Metropolitan Police records: MEPO 2/22, MEPO 3/140–41, MEPO 3/182, MEPO 3/3153–57. The National Archives, Kew.

————. Metropolitan Police Crime Museum, London.

Metropolitan Police Whitechapel Murders Papers: Martha Tabram, MEPO 1/140 f.34–43, August 10–October 19, 1888. The National Archives, Kew.

Modjeska, Helena. *Memories and Impressions of Helena Modjeska: An Autobiography*. New York: Macmillan, 1910.

Moir, John Macrae, ed. *Capital Punishment*. London: Smith, Elder, 1865.

Moore, George. *Conversations in Edbury Street*. London: Wm. Heinemann, 1924.

Morley, John. *The Life of Richard Cobden*. 2 vols. London: Chapman and Hall, 1881.

Morning Leader (London). "Mystery of Camden Town Murder. Anonymous Postcard and a Chequered Past." September 14, 1907.

————. "The Summing Up. Most Remarkable Trial in the Annals of Crime." December 19, 1907.

Morton, Cavendish. *The Art of Theatrical Make-Up*. London: Adam and Charles Black, 1909.

Moylan, John. *Scotland Yard and the Metropolitan Police*. London: G. P. Putnam, 1929.

Munro, John. *Electricity and Its Uses*, 4th ed. London: Religious Tract Society, 1898.

The Murder of Harriet Lane. The Sensation Series. London: [Felix McGlennon], n.d., ca. late-nineteenth century. [Harriet Lane was murdered in 1875.]

Murphy, Edward. *Chloroform: Its Properties and Safety in Childbirth*. London: Walton and Maberly, 1855.

Murray, Harold. *Twixt Aldgate Pump and Poplar*. London: Epworth Press, 1935.

Nance, R. Morton. *An English–Cornish Dictionary*. Marazion, England: Printed for the Federation of Old Cornwall Societies by Worden, 1952.

Napley, Sir David. *The Camden Town Murder*. London: Weidenfeld and Nicolson, 1987.

Neil, Arthur Fowler. *Forty Years of Man Hunting*. London: Jarrolds, 1932.

New York Herald. "The Prince and the Chorus Girl. Albert Victor, Eldest Son of the Prince of Wales, Said to Be Implicated . . ." October 6, 1891.

Newall, Christopher. *The Grosvenor Gallery Exhibitions.* Cambridge: Cambridge University Press, 1995.

News of the World (London). September 15, 22, October 6, 13, 20, 27, November 3, 17 and December 1, 1907.

Nightingale, Florence. *Notes on Nursing.* London: Harrison, 1860.

Norman, Philip. *London Vanished & Vanishing.* London: Adam & Charles Black, 1905.

Norwich, John Julius, 2nd Viscount Norwich. Grandson of Dr. Alfred Cooper. Telephone interview. Spring 2001.

Odell, Robin. *Ripperology: A Study of the World's First Serial Killer and a Literary Phenomenon.* Kent, Ohio: Kent State University Press, 2006.

O'Donnell, Kevin. *The Jack the Ripper Whitechapel Murders.* London: Ten Bells Publishing, 1997. [Details regarding Johannis Palmer diary, page 40.]

Oliver, Thomas. *Diseases of Occupation.* London: Methuen, 1916.

O'Mahoney, B. M. E. *Newhaven-Dieppe, 1825–1980: The History of an Anglo-French Joint Venture.* Stowmarket, Suffolk: Cappella, 1981.

Ordronaux, John. *The Jurisprudence of Medicine.* London: T. & J. W. Johnson, 1869.

Osler, William. *Principles and Practices of Medicine.* New York: D. Appleton, 1892.

Oswald, H. R. *Memoirs of a London County Coroner.* London: S. Paul, 1936.

Pall Mall Gazette (London). September 3, 6, 7, 8, 10, 14, 21, 24, 25, 27, 28 and October 1 and 2, 1888.

Palmer, A. Smythe. *Folk Etymology.* London: George Bell & Sons, 1882.

Pankhurst, Christabel. *The Great Scourge and How to End It.* London: E. Pankhurst, 1913.

Parkin Gallery. "The Sickert women and the Sickert girls: Walter Sickert with Thérèse Lessore, Sylvia Gosse, Wendela Boreel, Marjorie Lilly [and] Christiana Cutter." Catalogue from Exhibition presented by Michael Parkin Fine Art Ltd. and the Maltzahn Gallery Ltd. 18th April to 18th May 1974.

Parsons, Usher. *Directions for Making Anatomical Preparations.* Philadelphia: Carey & Lea, 1831.

Pash, Florence [Mrs. Humphrey]. Letters from Walter Sickert to Florence Pash from edited transcript by Violet Overton Fuller. S/SFC/2/1/9/2. Islington Local History Centre.

Pash, Florence. Material in the Sickert Collection. Islington Libraries.

Paul, C. *ABC Simple Simon.* Bloomsbury, London, n.d., ca. 1840. [Children's chapbook.]

Pelham, Camden. *The Chronicles of Crime.* London: Printed for Thomas Tegg, 73 Cheapside; James Tegg, Sydney; S. A. Tegg, Hobart Town; R. Griffin, Glasgow, 1841.

Pennell, E. R., and J. Pennell. *The Life of James McNeill Whistler.* Vol. 2. London: William Heinemann, 1908.

———. *The Whistler Journal.* Philadelphia: J. B. Lippincott, 1921.

Pennell, Joseph. *The Adventures of an Illustrator.* Boston: Little, Brown & Co., 1925.

———. *Catalogue of the Etchings of Joseph Pennell.* Compiled by Louis A. Wuerth. Boston: Little, Brown, 1928.

Petroski, Henry. *The Pencil: A History of Design and Circumstance.* New York: Alfred Knopf, 2000.

Pickavance, Ronald. *Sickert: The Masters 86.* London: Knowledge Publications, Purnell & Sons, 1967. Originally published in Italy, 1963.

Pirie, Alex & Sons, Ltd. Samples of Ledger Papers and Printing Papers. Aberdeen. London: 1900. [Manufacturer's sample book, containing thirty-two papers with "weights, size, samples, watermarks &c."]

Pole, Thomas. *Anatomical Instructor, New Edition.* London: J. Calow and T. Underwood, 1813.

Police Review and Parade Gossip. "Double Duty." April 17, 1893, and August 18, 1905.

Poor Jack, the London Street Boy. London: St. George's Publishing Office, n.d., ca. late-nineteenth century.

Poor Law Commissioners. *Reports on the Employment of Women and Children in Agriculture.* London: W. Clowes and Sons, Stamford Street, 1843.

Poore, G. V. *London (Ancient and Modern). From a Sanitary and Medical Point of View.* London: Cassell, 1889.

Press Association. "The Suicide of a Chorus Girl." *Press* (Canterbury, New Zealand), October 5, 1891, Volume 48, Issue 7985, 5.

Pritchard, Eleanor. "The Daughters of Cobden Pt. 2." *West Sussex History Journal*, no. 26 (September 1983).

Prothero, Margaret. *The History of the Criminal Investigation Department at Scotland Yard.* London: Herbert Jenkins, 1931.

Punch, or the London Charivari. Vol. 95. London: Punch, 1888.

Ray, Isaac. *Insanity of King George III.* Utica, NY: Printed at the Asylum, 1855.

Rhind, Neil. Transcript of talk on November 21, 1988. Lewisham Local History Archives.

Ribot, Th. *Heredity.* London: Henry S. King, 1875.

Robins, Anna Gruetzner. E-mail to Patricia Cornwell. December 22, 2013.

———. *A Fragile Modernism: Whistler and His Impressionist Followers.* New Haven and London: Yale University Press for the Paul Mellon Centre for Studies in British Art, 2007.

———. Report on the hotel guest book, 2012. Patricia Cornwell Collection.

———. "Sickert 'Painter-in-Ordinary' to the Music Hall." In *Sickert Paintings*, edited by Wendy Baron and Richard Shone. New Haven and London: Yale University Press in association with the Royal Academy of Arts, London, 1992.

———. *Walter Sickert: The Complete Writings on Art.* Oxford: Oxford University Press, 2000.

———. *Walter Sickert: Drawings.* London: Scolar Press, 1996.

Rodwell, G. F., ed. *A Dictionary of Science.* London: E. Moxon, Son, 1871.

Rogers, Jean Scott. *Cobden and His Kate: The Story of a Marriage.* London: Historical Publications, 1990.

Rokitansky, Carl. *A Manual of Pathological Anatomy.* 4 vols. London: Sydenham Society, 1854.

Rothenstein, John. *The Artists of the 1890's.* London: George Routledge & Sons, 1928.

———. *Augustus John.* Oxford and London: Phaidon Press, 1946.

———. *Modern English Painters: Sickert to Smith.* London: Eyre & Spottiswoode, 1952.

Rothenstein, William. *Men and Memories.* Vols. 1–3. London: Faber and Faber, 1931–39.

———. *Twenty-Four Portraits, Second Series.* London: G. Allen & Unwin, 1931.

Rough and Ready Jack. Edwin J. Brett, n.d., ca. mid to late 1880s.

Rowell, George. *The Victorian Theatre: A Survey.* London: Geoffrey Cumberlege, Oxford University Press, 1956.

Royal Cornwall Gazette. Review of performance by Madame Modjeska as Juliet. August 19, 1880.

Rule, Ann. *The Stranger Beside Me.* W. W. Norton, New York. 1980.

Rumbelow, Donald. *The Complete Jack the Ripper.* London: Penguin, 2004.

Russell, Charles. Papers of Lord Charles Russell. Patricia Cornwell Collection, New York Public Library. [The collection includes news clippings regarding Florence Maybrick's marriage to James Maybrick, her trial for his murder and subsequent conviction, 1889–1904. Some clippings, added at a much later date, refer to the alleged James Maybrick–Jack the Ripper connection.]

Russell, John. *From Sickert to 1948.* London: Lund Humphries, 1948.

Ryder, Stephen P., ed. *Public Reactions to Jack the Ripper. Letters to the Editor: August–December 1888.* Madison, WI: Inklings Press, 2006.

Sabbatini, Renato M. E. "The Psychopath's Brain." *Brain & Mind Magazine*, September/November, 1998.

Sands, Ethel. Letters. Tate Archive, London.

Sanger, William W. *The History of Prostitution: Its Extent, Causes, and Effects Throughout the World. Report to the Board of Alms-House Governors of the City of New York.* New York: Harper & Brothers, 1859.

Schlesinger, Louis. *Sexual Murder: Catathymic and Compulsive Homicides.* Boca Raton, FL: CRC Press, 2004.

———. Telephone conversation. February 12, 2003.

Schweder, Andrina. Letter to Stephen Knight. October 20, 1976. Private collection.

Scott, Harold. *The Early Doors: Origins of the Music Hall.* London: Nicholson & Watson, 1946.

Sherson, Errol. *London's Lost Treasures of the Nineteenth Century.* London: J. Lane, 1925.

Sherwood, Jones & Co. *The Terrific Register; or, Record of Crimes, Judgments, Providences and Calamities.* London: Sherwood, Jones, and Hunter, 1825.

Shone, R. *Walter Sickert.* London: Guild Publishing, 1988.

Shuster, Seymour. "Jack the Ripper and Doctor-Identification." *International Journal of Psychiatry in Medicine* 6, no. 3 (1975): 385–402.

Sickert, 1860–1942. An Exhibition of Paintings and Drawings, a catalogue. London: Arts Council of Great Britain, 1964.

Sickert: A Lone Exhibition in Aid of the Artists' General Benevolent Institution. London: Fine Arts Society, 1973.

Sickert, Bernhard. *Whistler.* London: Duckworth & Co., n.d.

Sickert, Eleanor. Letter from Saint Valery en Caux to Mary Adams. August 19, 1888. AM/1023/1-2. Cornwall Records Office.

———. Seven signed letters to Penelope Muller. New York Public Library.

Sickert, Ellen Cobden, Jane Cobden Unwin, Richard Cobden Jr. and Richard Cobden. Cobden Papers. West Sussex County Library.

Sickert, Ellen Millicent Cobden. Letters. Ref. Cobden 965. West Sussex Record Office.

Sickert, Joseph. Collection of letters. Collection held by the family of Joseph Sickert.

Sickert, Walter. "The Aesthete and the Plain Man." *Art News*, May 5, 1910.

———. Bound volume of critical essays written by W. R. Sickert from 1908 to 1914, including an essay from the March 19, 1914, issue of *The New Age*, "A Stone Ginger," and an essay from the March 26, 1914, issue of *The New Age*, "On Swiftness." S/SFC/2/3/1/3. Sickert Collection, Islington Libraries, London.

———. Collected papers. Islington Libraries. [This collection of Walter Sickert's private papers includes some writings of his father, Oswald Sickert, and more than a hundred sketches on scrap-like paper that have no titles, dates or signatures. While one suspects that the sophistication of many of the drawings indicates they were done by Oswald, it is reasonable to attribute a number of the works to Walter, due to what appears to be a fledgling artist's early attempts at drawing in addition to a familiarity of style that is seen in his mature art. Sickert scholar Dr. Anna Gruetzner Robins, who looked at the sketches, verified that some of them were most likely done by Walter as a boy and possibly as late as 1880 or 1881 when he was in art school.]

———. Collection of Sickert sketches. University of Manchester, Art History and Visual Studies Department.

———. "Idealism." *Art News*, May 12, 1910.

———. "Impressionism." *The New Age*, June 30, 1910.

———. "The International Society." *The English Review*, May 1912.

———. Letter to Bram Stoker. February 1, 1887. Leeds University Brotherton Library, Department of Manuscripts and Special Collections.

———. Letter to Cicely Hey. n.d., ca. August 1923. Islington Libraries.

———. Letter to Jacques-Émile Blanche. 1906. Jacques-Émile Blanche–Walter Sickert Correspondence, Document Numbers 183–86. Bibliothèque de L'Institut de France, Paris.

———. Letter to Jacques-Émile Blanche. n.d., ca. 1906. Jacques-Émile Blanche–Walter Sickert Correspondence, Document Number 182. Bibliothèque de L'Institut de France, Paris.

———. Letter to unknown recipient; return address Frith's Studio, 15 Fitzroy Street. n.d., ca. 1915. New York Public Library.

———. Letters to D. C. Thomson. ca. 1890–1914. David Coral Thomson Papers, Research Institute, The Getty Center, Los Angeles, CA.

———. Letters and edited drafts of his published articles. New York Public Library.

———. Letters to James McNeill Whistler. May–June 1888. Manchester: Doc # 5340. University of Glasgow, History of Art. In *The Correspondence of James McNeill Whistler, 1855–1903*, edited by Margaret F. MacDonald, Patricia de Montfort and Nigel Thorp; including *The Correspondence of Anna McNeill Whistler, 1855–1880*, edited by Georgia Toutziari. Online edition, University of Glasgow. http://www.whistler.arts.gla.ac.uk/correspondence.

———. Letters to Miss Case. n.d. Add.50956 f.109. British Library. [Letters of Eminent Persons. Vol. 1. Letters, mainly to members of the Case and Stansfield families, collected by Miss E. S. Case.]

———. Letters to Sir William Eden. Special Collections Department, University of Birmingham Library, Birmingham, England.

———. Letters to Virginia Woolf. New York Public Library.

———. Letters to William Rothenstein. Papers of Sir William Rothenstein. BMS ENG 1148 [1367]. Houghton Library, Harvard University, Cambridge, MA.

———. "The Old Ladies of Etching-Needle Street." *The English Review*, January 1912.

———. *Patrol* [painting]. n.d., ca. 1921. Metropolitan Police Historical Collection, London.

———. "The Perfect Modern" (unpublished draft). *The New Age*. April 9, 1914.

———. "The Royal Academy." *The English Review*, July 1912.

———. Sketch with the caption "Boy Jos." 1926. Ref: British School: Box 3876. Witt Library Photographic Collection. Courtauld Institute of Art, London.

———. Sketches and paintings by. Oxford, Ashmolean Museum.

———. Sketches by. Brighton, Royal Pavilion and Museum, Fine Art Collection of the 20th Century.

———. Sketches by. Islington Central Library, Islington Archives, London.

———. Sketches by. Leeds Art Gallery.

———. Sketches by. Tate Archive, London.

———. Sketches by. University of Manchester, John Rylands Library and Art History and Visual Studies Department.

———. Sketches by. University of Reading Department of Art.

———. Sketches by. Walker Art Gallery, Liverpool.

———. "The Spirit of the Hive." *The New Age*, May 26, 1910.

———. "The Thickest Painters in London." *The New Age*, June 18, 1914.

Sims, George R., ed. *Living London*. London: Cassell, 1902.

Sinclair, Robert. *East London*. London: Robert Hale, 1950.

Sitwell, Osbert. *A Free House! Or the Artist as Craftsman, Being the Writings of Walter Richard Sickert*. London: Macmillan, 1947.

———. Letter to Sir William Rothenstein. Sir William Rothenstein correspondence and other papers, 1887–1957. MS Eng. 1148 (1381), Houghton Library, Harvard University, Cambridge,

MA.

———. *Noble Essences*. London: Macmillan, 1950.

———. *The People's Album of London Statues*. London: Duckworth, 1928.

Skinner, Keith. Letter to Patricia Cornwell. October 6, 2006.

The Slang Dictionary: Etymological, Historical, and Anecdotal. London: Chatto & Windus, n.d., ca. 1878.

Smith, Henry. *From Constable to Commissioner*. London: Chatto & Windus, 1910.

Smith, John Gordon. *The Claims of Forensic Medicine*. London: John Taylor, 1829.

———. *The Principles of Forensic Medicine*, 2nd ed. London: Thomas and George Underwood, 1824.

Smith, Thomas, and William J. Walsham. *A Manual of Operative Surgery on the Dead Body*. London: Longmans, Green, 1876.

Société du salon d'automne. *Catalogue des ouvrages de peinture, sculpture, dessin, gravure, architecture et art décoratif exposés au Grand Palais des Champs-Elysées du 1er au 22 Octobre 1907*. Paris: Compagnie française des Papiers-Monnaies, 1907.

Society for Photographing Relics of London. *Relics of Old London*. London, 1875.

South London Chronicle. "Terrible Lambeth Tragedy." Saturday, June 14, 1902, 8.

Spealight, Robert. *William Rothenstein*. London: Eyre & Spottiswoode, 1962.

Sphere (London). "Sir Henry Irving, An Appreciation." October 21, 1905.

Stage (London). "Death of Sir Henry Irving." October 19, 1905.

Stalking the Ripper. Omnibus. First broadcast October 30, 2002, on BBC Television. London: BBC, 2002.

Star (London). "In This Morning's Papers There Is a Story for the Lovers of the Sensational. We Print It . . ." Wednesday, September 12, 1888, 3.

Stevenson, Robert Louis. *The Strange Case of Dr. Jekyll and Mr. Hyde*. London: Longmans, Green, 1886.

Stewart-Killick, John. Collection of letters re: Penelope (Pennie) Muller. Author's collection.

St. John, Christopher, ed. *Ellen Terry and Bernard Shaw*. New York: Fountain Press, 1931.

St. Mark's Hospital. Interview with record keepers. 2001. [I was told that any old patients' records would be at St. Bartholomew's Hospital, and a check of the record books there revealed nothing prior to 1900.]

Stoker, Bram. *Personal Reminiscences of Henry Irving*. Vols. 1 and 2. London: William Heinemann, 1906.

Stowe, Harriet Beecher. "Sunny Memories of Foreign Lands." Volume 2, Chapter XXVII, n.d. Papers of Richard Cobden, Ref. Cobden 272, 1854. West Sussex Record Office. [Her essay on a breakfast with Richard Cobden.]

Stowell, Thomas. "Jack the Ripper—A Solution?" *The Criminologist* (November 1970).

St. Pancras Journal, ed. Frederick Sinclair, borough librarian. "He Painted Camden Town . . . Walter Richard Sickert." Vol. 3, no. 8 (January 1950): Article 12.

Sturgis, Matthew. *Walter Sickert: A Life*. London: Harper Collins, 2005. [Slightly revised paperback, 2011.]

Sugden, Philip. *The Complete History of Jack the Ripper*. London: Robinson, 1994.

The Surprising Adventures of Cinderella, or the Glass Slipper. York, England: printed and sold by J. Kendrew, Colliergate, n.d., ca. 1820. [Children's chapbook.]

Sutherland, W. D. *Blood Stains*. London: Baillière, Tindall and Cox, 1907.

Sutton, Denys. *James McNeill Whistler: Paintings, Etchings, Pastels and Watercolors*. London: Phaidon Press, 1966.

———. *Nocturne: The Art of James McNeill Whistler*. London: Country Life, 1963.

———. Papers of Denys M. Sutton (1917–91). Special Collections, Glasgow University Library,

Scotland.

————. *Walter Sickert: A Biography*. London: Michael Joseph, 1976.

Sutton, Henry G. *Lectures on Pathology*. London: J. & A. Churchill, 1891.

Swanwick, Helena [née Sickert]. Correspondence. Bodleian Library, Oxford University, MS English History.

————. *I Have Been Young*. London: Victor Gollancz, 1935.

————. Letter. n.d., ca. 1940. MSL/1976/5887. National Art Library, Victoria and Albert Museum.

Tallack, William. *Penological and Preventative Principles*. London: Wertheimer, Lea, 1889.

Tatlock, Cicely Hey. Last Will and Testament. The Principal Registry of the Family Division. Probate Department, London.

Taylor, Alfred Swaine. *The Principles and Practice of Medical Jurisprudence*. London: John Churchill & Sons, 1865.

Terry, Ellen. Letter to a Mr. Collier. March 24 [possibly early 1900s]. New York Public Library.

————. Private correspondence. New York Public Library. [Letters that show the various cities where she and Irving's theater company performed.]

————. *The Story of My Life*. London: Hutchinson, 1908. [Sickert's personal copy, fully annotated by him. Author's collection.]

Thomas, Dylan. *The Selected Writings*. New York: New Directions, 1946.

Thompson, Sir H. *Modern Cremation*. London: Smith, Elder, 1899.

Thompson, William. *Appeal of One Half the Human Race, Women, Against the Pretensions of the Other Half, Men*. London: Richard Taylor, 1825.

Thomson, Sir Basil. *The Story of Scotland Yard*. New York: Literary Guild, 1936.

Thornbury, Walter. *Old and New London*. Vols. 1–3. London: Cassell, Petter, Galpin, 1878.

Thorpe, James. *English Illustration: The Nineties*. London: Faber and Faber, 1966.

Thorwald, Jürgen. *The Century of the Detective*. New York: Harcourt, 1965.

The Times (London). Bound editions from 1888 to 1891. [These original newspapers exclude the Sunday editions, and were bound for me in fourteen volumes that I reviewed in their entirety for the years 1888–91.]

————. "Inquest on Miss Manton." October 6, 1891.

————. "London, Monday, November 14, 1887." November 14, 1887.

————. "Murder Near Windsor." September 21, 1897.

————. "The Photographic Salon." September 12, 1907.

————. September 12, 13, 14, 17 and 21, and October 1, 7, 8, 15, 16, 22, 23 and 29, 1907.

Titchener, Edward. *An Outline of Psychology*. Bristol, UK: Thoemmes Press; Tokyo, Japan: Maruzen, 1998. First published 1896 by Macmillan.

Traill, Thomas Stewart. *Outlines of a Course of Lectures on Medical Jurisprudence*. 2nd ed. Edinburgh: Adam and Charles Black, 1840.

Trent, J. *An Inquiry into the Effects of Light in Respiration*. Philadelphia: Way & Groff, 1800.

Treuherz, Julian. Letter to Wendy Baron. 1980. Manchester Art Gallery.

Treves, Sir Frederick. *The Elephant Man, and Other Reminiscences*. London: Cassell, 1923.

Trip, Tommy. *Giles Gingerbread, A Little Boy, Who Lived upon Learning*. York, England: printed and sold by J. Kendrew, Colliergate, n.d., ca. 1820. [Children's chapbook.]

Trotter, Thomas. *An Essay, Medical, Philosophical, on Drunkenness*. London: Longman, Hurst, Rees, and Orme, 1804.

Troyen, Aimee. *Sickert as Printmaker*. New Haven: Yale Center for British Art, 1979.

Tumblety, Francis. *The Indian Herb Doctor: Including His Experience in the Old Capitol Prison*. Cincinnati: published by the author, 1866.

Vasili, Count Paul. *World of London*. London: Sampson Low, Marston, Searle, & Rivington, 1885.

Virchow, Rudoff Ludwig Carl. *A Description and Explanation of the Method of Performing Post Mortem Examinations in the Dead House of the Berlin Charité Hospital.* London: Churchill, 1876.

Wade, John. *A Treatise on the Police and Crimes of the Metropolis.* London: Longman, Rees, Orme, Brown and Green, 1829.

Walford, Edward. *Old and New London.* Vols. 4–6. London: Cassell, Petter, Galpin, 1878.

Walker, Alexander. *Physiognomy Founded on Physiology.* London 1834.

Webb, Beatrice. *My Apprenticeship.* London: Longmans, Green, 1926.

Wedmore, Frederick. *Whistler and Others.* New York: Charles Scribner's Sons, 1906.

Weekly Dispatch (London). September 2, 9, 16, 23 and 30 and November 22, 1888.

Welch, Denton. *Sickert at St. Peter's.* London: Arts Council of Great Britain, 1981

Western Daily Press (Bristol, UK). "Funeral of Famous Artist." January 28, 1942.

Wheatley, H. B. *Reliques of Old London Suburbs North of the Thames, Drawn in lithography by T. R. Way.* London: George Bell and Sons, 1898.

Whistler, James McNeill. *Eden Versus Whistler: The Baronet & the Butterfly. A Valentine with a Verdict.* Paris: Louis-Henry May, 1899. [This particular volume was owned by one of Sickert's own circle, artist and writer William Rothenstein.]

———. *The Gentle Art of Making Enemies.* London: W. Heinemann, 1892.

———. *Mr. Whistler's Ten O'clock.* London: Chatto and Windus, 1888.

———. *Whistler on Art.* Manchester: Fyfield Books in association with the Centre for Whistler Studies, Glasgow University Library, 1994.

Whitechapel Murders files. London Metropolitan Archives. [These files include some three hundred letters, police reports and photos pertaining to the Ripper crimes.]

White, Charles. *Cases in Surgery.* London: Printed for W. Johnston, in Ludgate-Street, 1770.

Whitney, Daniel. *The Family Physician.* Penn Yan, NY: Printed by H. Gilbert, 1833.

Wilde, Oscar. *The Trial of Oscar Wilde. From the Shorthand Reports.* Paris: privately printed, 1906.

Wilder, Harris Hawthorne, and Bert Wentworth. *Personal Identification Methods for the Identification of Individuals Living or Dead.* Boston: R. G. Badger, 1918.

Wilson, A. N. *Victoria: A Life.* New York: Penguin Press, 2014.

Wilstach, Paul. *Richard Mansfield: The Man and the Actor.* New York: C. Scribner's Sons, 1908.

Wilton, George. *Fingerprints: History, Law and Romance.* London: W. Hodge, 1938.

Winslow, Forbes. *Youthful Eccentricity a Precursor of Crime.* New York: Funk & Wagnalls, 1895.

Winter, William. *Life and Art of Richard Mansfield, with Selections from His Letters.* 2 vols. New York: Moffat, Yard, 1910.

Wollstonecraft, Mary. *Equality for Women within the Law.* London: J. Johnson, 1792.

Woodruff, Douglas. *The Tichborne Claimant.* London: Hollis & Carter, 1957.

Woolf, Virginia. *Walter Sickert: A Conversation.* London: Hogarth Press, 1934.

Wray, J. Jackson. *Will It Lift? The Story of a London Fog.* London: James Nisbet, n.d. ca. 1900.

Wright, Barnaby, ed. *Walter Sickert: The Camden Town Nudes.* London: The Courtauld Gallery in association with Paul Holberton Publishing, 2007.

Wright, Joseph. *The English Dialect Dictionary.* London: Henry Frowde, 1898–1905.

Wright, Lewis. *A Popular Handbook to the Microscope.* London: Religious Tract Society, 1895.

W. R. Sickert: Drawings and Paintings, 1890–1942. Liverpool: Tate Gallery, 1989.

The Yellow Book: An Illustrated Quarterly. London: Elkin Mathews & John Lane, 1894–1897.

Yonge, Mary Charlotte. *The History of Sir Thomas Thumb.* London: T. Constable, 1856.

INDEX

IMAGE CREDITS

Title Page

Walter Richard Sickert *by Mrs. Florence Humphrey (nee Pash). Pastel. 54 x 46.5 cms [no date]. Islington Local History Centre.*

CHAPTER 1

p. 2: Portrait of Whistler, *Thomas Robert Way, 1895. Freer Gallery of Art, Smithsonian Institution, Washington, D.C.: Gift of Charles Lang Freer, F1901.188.*

p. 3: *M00981 © Tate, London 2015.*

p. 4: Walter Sickert (1860–1942), *sketching, 1885 (pen & ink on paper), Whistler, James Abbott McNeill (1834–1903), private collection. Photo © The Fine Art Society, London, UK; Bridgeman Images.*

p. 9: Record # 841/ PH 470. *Cobden Papers, West Sussex Record Office.*

p. 13: © The British Library Board, LOU.LON396. (The New Budget 4th June, 1895)

p. 14: CLA/048/CS/02/166. *London Metropolitan Archives, City of London.*

p. 15: MEPO 3/142 ff 396-7. *The National Archives, UK, and Patricia Cornwell Collection.*

CHAPTER 2

p. 18: *Evans Skinner Crime Archives.*

p. 27: *Fragmentary sketches, Walter Sickert (attributed) (1860–1942). Islington Local History Centre.*

CHAPTER 3

p. 38: *Patricia Cornwell Collection.*

p. 40: MEPO 3/140 ff 33. *The National Archives, UK, and Patricia Cornwell Collection.*

p. 41: HO144/221 #119 and #126. *The National Archives, UK.*

CHAPTER 4

p. 45: *M01620 © Tate, London 2015.*

p. 45: *3-1PB © Tate, London 2015.*

p. 48: *3-3PB © Tate, London 2015.*

p. 51: *3-11PB © Tate, London 2015.*

p. 52: *M00982 © Tate, London 2015.*

CHAPTER 5

p. 56: "Pot of Heads" *fragmentary sketch, Walter Sickert (attributed) (1860–1942). Islington Local History Centre.*

p. 57: *Fragmentary sketch. Walter Sickert (attributed) (1860–1942). Drawn when Sickert was a boy. Islington Local History Centre.*

p. 62: MEPO 3/142 ff 399. *The National Archives, UK, and Patricia Cornwell Collection.*

p. 63: MEPO 3/142 ff 517. *The National Archives, UK, and Patricia Cornwell Collection.*

p. 65: MEPO 3/142 ff 123. *The National Archives, UK, and Patricia Cornwell Collection.*

p. 66: MEPO 3/142 ff 7. *The National Archives, UK, and Patricia Cornwell Collection.*

CHAPTER 6

p. 72: SC/GL/NOB/C/047/0. *The London Metropolitan Archives, City of London.*

p. 75: MEPO 3/142 ff 339. *The National Archives, UK, and Patricia Cornwell Collection.*

p. 76: MEPO 3/142 ff 339 *(close). The National Archives, UK, and Patricia Cornwell Collection.*

p. 77: MEPO 3/142 ff 399. *The National Archives, UK, and Patricia Cornwell Collection.*

p. 80: *Metal and steel surgeon's kit, 16 parts, in black leather case, some instruments etched or stamped, "GMSD" and "1884." Patricia Cornwell Collection.*

CHAPTER 7

p. 84: Record #: 841/PH 406. *Cobden Papers, West Sussex Record Office.*

p. 89: Record #: 841/PH 452. *Cobden Papers, West Sussex Record Office.*

p. 93: R. Falkner & Co. photograph of Walter Sickert, age 24, © *Tate, London 2015.*

p. 95: *Photo courtesy of The Royal London Hospital Archives.*

CHAPTER 8

p. 100: *Evans Skinner Crime Archives.*

p. 102: Record #121870. *London Metropolitan Archives, City of London.*

p. 106: *Evans Skinner Crime Archives.*

p. 108: *Patricia Cornwell Collection.*

CHAPTER 9

p. 115: *Evans Skinner Crime Archives.*

p. 117: *Crown copyright and is reproduced with the permission of the Mayor's Office for Policing and Crime under delegated authority from the Controller of the HMSO.*

p. 120: *Patricia Cornwell Collection.*

CHAPTER 10

p. 129: *Patricia Cornwell Collection.*

p. 130: *Bull's-eye lantern, tin with glass, Hiatt & Co, Birmingham. Patricia Cornwell Collection.*

p. 131: *Evans Skinner Crime Archives.*

p. 132: SC/GL/PR/GP/006/k1237939. *London Metropolitan Archives, City of London.*

p. 134: *Walter Richard Sickert, English, 1860–1942.* The Passing Funeral, c. 1909, Graphite with red chalk on crème laid paper, 370 x 257mm (pencil border) 403 x 284mm (sheet), Restricted Gift of Mr. & Mrs. William O. Hunt. Image Number: 00084778-01, *Photography © The Art Institute of Chicago.*

CHAPTER 11

p. 136: MEPO 3/3155/1. *The National Archives, UK, and Patricia Cornwell Collection.*

p. 138 and 139: HO144/221 A49301C #138. *The National Archives, UK.*

p. 141: Ennui, *circa 1914. Walter Richard Sickert (1860–1942) © Tate, London 2015.*

p. 142: *Patricia Cornwell Collection; Manuscripts and Archives Division, The New York Public Library, Astor, Lenox and Tilden Foundations. Photo credit: Patricia Cornwell Collection.*

p. 145: *Acknowledgement to John Stewart-Killick. Patricia Cornwell Collection.*

p. 147: Walter Sickert in Highbury Place Studio, Islington, London, 1927–1934. *Islington Local History Centre.*

p. 150: Walter Sickert sketch of boy Jos, *dated 1925. British School Box 3876. Witt Photographic Library, Courtauld Institute of Art. Copyright Christie's Images.*

CHAPTER 12

p. 152: *Patricia Cornwell Collection.*

p. 153: Portrait of Florence Pash. Circa 1896-1897. *Walter Sickert (1860–1942).*

p. 156: Walter Richard Sickert *by Mrs. Florence Humphrey (nee Pash). Pastel. 54 x 46.5 cms [no date]. Islington Local History Centre.*

p. 158: Albert Victor, Prince, Duke of Clarence and Avondale, 1864–1892. *Patricia Cornwell Collection; Manuscripts and Archives Division, The New York Public Library, Astor, Lenox and Tilden Foundations.*

p. 161: Call Number T PHO A. *The New York Public Library for the Performing Arts. Billy Rose Theatre Division.*

CHAPTER 13

p. 169: MEPO 3/142 ff 496. *The National Archives, UK, and Patricia Cornwell Collection.*

CHAPTER 14

p. 172: Two Studies of a Venetian Woman's Head, *circa 1903. Walter Sickert (1860–1942). Current location and ownership unknown.*

p. 172: Nuit d'Ete, *circa 1906. Walter Sickert (1860–1942).*

p. 173: MEPO 3/3155/1. *The National Archives, UK, and Patricia Cornwell Collection.*

p. 174: MEPO 3/3155/3. *The National Archives, UK, and Patricia Cornwell Collection.*

p. 175: "Vacher l'Eventreur et les Crimes Sadiques" *by Alexandre Lacassagne. Photo credit: Patricia Cornwell Collection.*

p. 176: He Killed His Father in a Fight *(pencil on paper), Walter Richard Sickert (1860–1942). Whitworth Art Gallery, The University of Manchester, UK; Bridgeman Images.*

p. 176: MEPO 3/3155/4. *The National Archives, UK, and Patricia Cornwell Collection.*

p. 178: Patricia Cornwell and *Patrol* painting by Walter Sickert. *Painting is currently housed in the Metropolitan Police Historic Collection. Patricia Cornwell Collection.*

CHAPTER 15

p. 182: *Medical instrument box kit. J.H. Gemrig manufactured. 109 5th 8th St. Philadelphia, 17 pieces. Patricia Cornwell Collection.*

p. 184: MEPO 3/142 ff 234-5. *The National Archives, UK, and Patricia Cornwell Collection.*

p. 187: Portrait Sketch of Walter Sickert, 1895 *(oil on canvas). Whistler, James Abbott McNeill (1834–1903). Dublin City Gallery, The Hugh Lane, Ireland; Bridgeman Images.*

p. 189: London East End 1901. *The National Archives, UK, and Patricia Cornwell Collection.*

CHAPTER 16

p. 193: *Evans Skinner Crime Archives.*

p. 194: *Evans Skinner Crime Archives.*

p. 196: Acc. No. 373.88. *Metropolitan Police Heritage Centre and Patricia Cornwell Collection.*

p. 197: *Evans Skinner Crime Archives.*

p. 198: *Evans Skinner Crime Archives.*

p. 200: HO144/221 A49301C. *The National Archives, UK.*

p. 201: *Provided by Metropolitan Police Service and Patricia Cornwell Collection.*

p. 202: *Evans Skinner Crime Archives.*

p. 204: MEPO 3/142 ff 23f. *The National Archives, UK, and Patricia Cornwell Collection.*

CHAPTER 17

p. 211: MEPO 3/3155/2. *The National Archives, UK, and Patricia Cornwell Collection.*

p. 211: *Provided by Metropolitan Police Service and Patricia Cornwell Collection.*

p. 212: Papers of William Rothenstein. *MS ENG 1148 (1367) Houghton Library, Harvard University.*

p. 212: CLA/048/CS/02/224. *London Metropolitan Archives, City of London.*

p. 213: MEPO 3/142 ff 282. *The National Archives, UK, and Patricia Cornwell Collection.*

CHAPTER 18

p. 223: *Patricia Cornwell Collection.*

p. 227: *MEPO 3/3157. The National Archives, UK, and Patricia Cornwell Collection.*

p. 231: MEPO 3/3157. *The National Archives, UK, and Patricia Cornwell Collection.*

CHAPTER 19

p. 234 and 235: MEPO 3/142 ff 272-274. *The National Archives, UK, and Patricia Cornwell Collection.*

p. 237: (Top left) MEPO 3/142 ff 4. *The National Archives, UK, and Patricia Cornwell Collection.*

p. 237: (Top right) *Patricia Cornwell Collection.*

p. 237: (Center) MEPO 3/142 ff 339. *The National Archives, UK, and Patricia Cornwell Collection.*

p. 237: (Bottom) MEPO 3/142 ff 248–249. *The National Archives, UK, and Patricia Cornwell Collection.*

p. 238: MEPO 3/142 ff 175. *The National Archives, UK, and Patricia Cornwell Collection.*

p. 239: MEPO 3/142 ff 160. *The National Archives, UK, and Patricia Cornwell Collection.*

p. 240: MEPO 3/142 ff 76. *The National Archives, UK, and Patricia Cornwell Collection.*

p. 240: *Patricia Cornwell Collection.*

p. 242: MEPO 3/142 ff 272-274. *The National Archives, UK, and Patricia Cornwell Collection.*

p. 242: MEPO 3/142 ff 141. *The National Archives, UK, and Patricia Cornwell Collection.*

p. 243: MEPO 3/142 ff 480. *The National Archives, UK, and Patricia Cornwell Collection.*

p. 246: (Top) CLA/048/CS/02/380. *London Metropolitan Archives, City of London, and Patricia Cornwell Collection.*

p. 246: (Bottom) Papers of William Rothenstein. *MS ENG 1148 (1367) Houghton Library, Harvard University.*

p. 250: (Top) MEPO 3/142 ff508-509. *The National Archives, UK, and Patricia Cornwell Collection.*

p. 250: (Bottom) CLA/048/CS/02/380. *London Metropolitan Archives, City of London, and Patricia Cornwell Collection.*

p. 252: (Top) *British Library Board. Add MS 50956, f 109, and Patricia Cornwell Collection.*

p. 252: (Bottom left) *Courtesy of the Getty Research Institute, Los Angeles (910126), and Patricia Cornwell Collection.*

p. 252: (Bottom right) *Courtesy of the Getty Research Institute, Los Angeles (910126), and Patricia Cornwell Collection.*

p. 255: *Patricia Cornwell Collection.*

CHAPTER 20

p. 258: CLA/048/CS/02/395F. *London Metropolitan Archives, City of London, and Patricia Cornwell Collection.*

p. 260: MEPO 3/142 ff 95-96. *The National Archives, UK, and Patricia Cornwell Collection.*

p. 263: MS 7055 Folios 138 verso. *Bibliothèque de l'Institut de France, Paris, France © RMN-Grand Palais; Photo: Art Resource, NY.*

CHAPTER 21

p. 265: *Evans Skinner Crime Archives.*

p. 272: HO144-221 #138. *The National Archives, UK.*

p. 274: MEPO 3/141/184. *The National Archives, UK, and Patricia Cornwell Collection.*

CHAPTER 22

p. 279: (Top and bottom) FA101496. *Royal Pavilion and Museums, Brighton & Hove, and Patricia Cornwell Collection.*

p. 280: Painter in His Studio, 1907. *Walter Sickert. (Oil on canvas.) Art Gallery of Hamilton, Ontario; Gift of the Women's Committee, 1970.*

p. 287: HO 144 122 A49301. *The National Archives, UK, and Patricia Cornwell Collection.*

p. 289: HO 144 122 A49301. *The National Archives, UK, and Patricia Cornwell Collection.*

CHAPTER 23

p. 298: *Provided by Metropolitan Police Service and Patricia Cornwell Collection.*

p. 306: Sickert at Camden Road Studio. *Islington Local History Centre.*

CHAPTER 24

p. 310: *Evans Skinner Crime Archives.*

p. 317: *Provided by Metropolitan Police Service and Patricia Cornwell Collection.*

p. 318: *Photo courtesy of the Royal London Hospital Archives.*

p. 319: (Top left) Putana a Casa, *Walter Sickert, Harvard Art Museums/Fogg Museum, Gift of Patricia Cornwell, 2009.90.34; Imaging Department © President and Fellows of Harvard College.*

p. 319: (Top right) MEPO 3/3155 3. *The National Archives, UK, and Patricia Cornwell Collection.*

p. 319: (Bottom left) The Newspaper, *Walter Richard Sickert (1860–1942). Private Collection; Bridgeman Images.*

p. 319: (Bottom right) MEPO 3/3155 3. *The National Archives, UK, and Patricia Cornwell Collection.*

CHAPTER 25

p. 322: MEPO 3/142 ff 245. *The National Archives, UK, and Patricia Cornwell Collection.*

p. 323: MEPO 3/142 ff 104. *The National Archives, UK, and Patricia Cornwell Collection.*

p. 323: CLA/048/CS/02/392. *London Metropolitan Archives, City of London, and Patricia Cornwell Collection.*

p. 323: MEPO 3/142 ff 501. *The National Archives, UK, and Patricia Cornwell Collection.*

p. 326: The Fair, Dieppe, France, *circa 1902 (oil on canvas), Walter Richard Sickert (1860–1942) / © Rochdale Art Gallery, Lancashire, UK; Bridgeman Images.*

p. 330: Self-Portrait Wearing Glasses *(pen and ink with chalk on paper), Walter Richard Sickert (1860–1942). Ashmolean Museum, University of Oxford, UK; Bridgeman Images.*

p. 332: Death and the Maiden *(pencil, pen and ink on paper), Walter Richard Sickert (1860–1942). Whitworth Art Gallery, The University of Manchester, UK; Bridgeman Images.*

p. 333: Jack the Ripper's Bedroom, *circa 1906–07 (oil on canvas), Walter Richard Sickert (1860–1942). Manchester Art Gallery, UK; Bridgeman Images.*

CHAPTER 26

p. 336: *Patricia Cornwell Collection.*

p. 343: Record #967, *Cobden Papers, West Sussex Record Office.*

CHAPTER 27

p. 345: *Provided by the Metropolitan Police Service and Patricia Cornwell Collection.*

p. 347: *Patricia Cornwell Collection.*

p. 348: *The National Archives, UK, and Patricia Cornwell Collection.*

p. 353: (Top) *Bibliothèque de l'Institut de France, Paris, France, © RMN-Grand Palais, Photo: Art Resource, NY ART488827. Folio 169 recto.*

p. 353: (Bottom left) *Patricia Cornwell Collection; Manuscripts and Archives Division, The New York Public Library, Astor, Lenox and Tilden Foundations. Photo credit: Patricia Cornwell Collection.*

p. 353: (Bottom right) MEPO 3/142 ff 430. *The National Archives, UK, and Patricia Cornwell Collection.*

p. 355: MEPO 3/142 ff 458. *The National Archives, UK, and Patricia Cornwell Collection.*

CHAPTER 28

p. 360: *Patricia Cornwell Collection.*

p. 362: (Top) *Patricia Cornwell Collection; Manuscripts and Archives Division, The New York Public Library, Astor, Lenox and Tilden Foundations. Photo credit: Patricia Cornwell Collection.*

p. 362: (Bottom) MEPO 3/142 ff 193. *The National Archives, UK, and Patricia Cornwell Collection.*

p. 364: *Patricia Cornwell Collection; Manuscripts and Archives Division, The New York Public Library, Astor, Lenox and Tilden Foundations. Photo credit: Patricia Cornwell Collection.*

CHAPTER 29

p. 368: *Patricia Cornwell Collection.*

p. 369: (Top) *Patricia Cornwell Collection; Manuscripts and Archives Division, The New York Public Library, Astor, Lenox and Tilden Foundations. Photo credit: Patricia Cornwell Collection.*

p. 369: (Bottom) *Fragmentary sketch by Walter Sickert (attributed) (1860–1942). Islington Local History Centre.*

p. 373: (Top) MEPO 3/142 ff 544. *The National Archives, UK, and Patricia Cornwell Collection.*

p. 373: (Bottom left) *Patricia Cornwell Collection; Manuscripts and Archives Division, The New York Public Library, Astor, Lenox and Tilden Foundations. Photo credit: Patricia Cornwell Collection.*

p. 373: (Bottom right) MEPO 3/142 ff 515. *The National Archives, UK, and Patricia Cornwell Collection.*

p. 374: (Top) MEPO 3/142 ff 175. *The National Archives, UK, and Patricia Cornwell Collection.*

p. 374: (Bottom) *Patricia Cornwell Collection; Manuscripts and Archives Division, The New York Public Library, Astor, Lenox and Tilden Foundations. Photo credit: Patricia Cornwell Collection.*

p. 377: (Left) MEPO 3/142 ff 152. *The National Archives, UK, and Patricia Cornwell Collection.*

p. 377: (Right) Papers of William Rothenstein. *MS ENG 1148 (1367) Houghton Library, Harvard University.*

CHAPTER 30

p. 382: MEPO 3/142 ff 245. *The National Archives, UK, and Patricia Cornwell Collection.*

p. 386: MEPO 3/142 ff 307. *The National Archives, UK, and Patricia Cornwell Collection.*

p. 391: Walter Sickert with shaved head, *circa 1920s. Islington Local History Centre.*

p. 393: Max Beerbohm (colour litho). *Walter Richard Sickert (1860–1942). Private Collection. © Look and Learn, Peter Jackson Collection; Bridgeman Images.*

p. 397: The Servant of Abraham, *circa 1929. Walter Richard Sickert (1860–1929). © Tate, London 2015.*

CHAPTER 31

p. 400: *William Hartley Collection @ The Crime Museum, New Scotland Yard. © Metropolitan Police Service.*

p. 401: La Belle Gatee. The Camden Town Murder, *1908 (etching on laid paper), Walter Richard Sickert (1860–1942). Yale Center for British Art, Friends of British Art Fund; Bridgeman Images.*

p. 402: *Provided by Metropolitan Police Service and Patricia Cornwell Collection.*

p. 404: *Patricia Cornwell Collection.*

p. 405: Bathing at Sea in Dieppe, *circa 1920s. Islington Local History Centre.*

p. 408: Letter from Walter Sickert to Nan Hudson. *Date: unknown. Presented to Tate Archive by Colonel Christopher Sands in November 1991.*

p. 411: *Provided by the Metropolitan Police Service and Patricia Cornwell Collection.*

p. 417: The Camden Town Murder *or* What Shall We Do For the Rent?, *circa 1908-9 (oil on canvas), Walter Richard Sickert (1860–1942). Yale Center for British Art, Paul Mellon Fund, USA; Bridgeman Images*

p. 418: Ellen Melicent Cobden's Last Will and Testament. Date of death Sept 4, 1914. *Wills and Probate 1858–1996. The National Archives, UK. Contains public sector information licensed under the Open Government License v3.0.*

CHAPTER 32

p. 422: Sickert *by Jacques Emile Blanche, 1935. Islington Local History Centre.*

p. 423: Walter Sickert on chair with shaved head, *circa 1920s. Islington Local History Centre.*

p. 426: *Photo courtesy of the Royal London Hospital Archives.*

p. 432: MEPO 3/142 ff 93. *The National Archives, UK, and Patricia Cornwell Collection.*

CHAPTER 33

p. 436: *Evans Skinner Crime Archives.*

p. 442: *Patricia Cornwell Collection.*

CHAPTER 34

p. 449: "Vacher l'Eventreur et les Crimes Sadiques" *by Alexandre Lacassagne. Patricia Cornwell Collection.*

p. 451: MEPO 3/3155/4. *The National Archives, UK, and Patricia Cornwell Collection.*

p. 455: MEPO 3/140 ff 259A. *The National Archives, UK, and Patricia Cornwell Collection.*

CHAPTER 35

p. 461: Walter Sickert, Christine Angus Sickert, and Eleanor Sickert, *circa 1911.* © *Tate, London 2015.*

p. 462: (Left) Jack Ashore, *Walter Sickert. Harvard Art Museums/Fogg Museum, Gift of Patricia Cornwell, 2009.90.52. Imaging Department* © *President and Fellows of Harvard College.*

p. 462: (Right) The Bedroom, *Walter Richard Sickert (1860–1942). Roy Miles Fine Paintings; Bridgeman Images.*

p. 465: Walter Sickert with third wife, Thérèse Lessore, *circa 1930s. Islington Local History Centre.*

p. 465: (Bottom) Walter Sickert with third wife, Thérèse Lessore (left) and friend (unidentified), *Cyril How, circa 1920s. Islington Local History Centre.*

CODA

p. 471: Sickert in Studio at Highbury Place Studio, Islington, London, *circa 1927–1934. Islington Local History Centre.*

p. 474: Walter Sickert posing in tweed suit with bamboo walking cane, *Margaret Bentley Studio, London, circa 1920s. Islington Local History Centre.*

HOW IT ALL BEGAN

p. 484: *Patricia Cornwell Collection.*

p. 486: Self-Portrait, *Walter Sickert (1860–1942). Harvard Art Museums/Fogg Museum, Gift of Patricia Cornwell, 2009.90.33. Imaging Department* © *President and Fellows of Harvard College.*

p. 490: (Top and bottom) *Patricia Cornwell Collection.*

p. 497: MEPO 3/142 ff 234-5. *The National Archives, UK, and Patricia Cornwell Collection.*

ABOUT THE AUTHOR

Patricia Cornwell sold her first novel, *Postmortem*, while working as a computer analyst at the Office of the Chief Medical Examiner in Richmond, Virginia. *Postmortem* was the first bona fide forensic thriller. It paved the way for an explosion of entertainment featuring all things forensic across film, television and literature.

The transition to literary superstar was not easy. At her first signing, held during a lunch break from the morgue, Patricia sold no copies of *Postmortem* and fielded exactly one question—an elderly woman asked her where she could find the cookbooks.

Postmortem would go on to win the Edgar, Creasey, Anthony and Macavity awards as well as the French Prix du roman d'aventures—the first book ever to claim all these distinctions in a single year. To date, Cornwell's books have sold some 100 million copies in 36 languages in over 120 countries. She's authored twenty-nine *New York Times* bestsellers.

Patricia's novels center primarily on medical examiner Kay Scarpetta along with her tech-savvy niece, Lucy, and fellow investigator Pete Marino. Celebrating twenty-five years, these characters have grown into an international phenomenon, winning Cornwell the Sherlock Award for best detective created by an American author, the Gold Dagger Award, the RBA Thriller Award and the Medal of Chevalier of the Order of Arts and Letters for her contributions to literary and artistic development.

Patricia's literary career extends outside the realm of the Kay Scarpetta series—she's authored a definitive account of Jack the Ripper's identity, two cookbooks (*Food to Die For* and *Scarpetta's Winter Table*), a children's book (*Life's Little Fable*) and a biography of Ruth Graham. She's also developed two other series based on Win Garano, an upstart Boston detective, and Andy Brazil, an enterprising Charlotte reporter.

Though Cornwell now lives in Boston, she was born in Miami and grew up in Montreat, North Carolina. After earning her degree in English from Davidson College in 1979, she began working at the *Charlotte Observer*, taking whatever stories came her way and rapidly advancing from listing television programs to covering the police beat. Cornwell received widespread attention and praise for her series of articles on prostitution and crime in downtown Charlotte. From the *Charlotte Observer*, Cornwell moved to a job with the Office of the Chief Medical Examiner of Virginia—a post she would later bestow upon the fictional Kay Scarpetta. It was during these years that Patricia penned *Postmortem* and began submitting it to major publishing houses in New York, without initial success.

When not writing from her Boston home, Patricia tirelessly researches cutting-edge forensics to include in her work. She is currently researching drone technology as well as continuing her work in ballistics, explosives and firearms. Cornwell has also been learning about advanced trauma for the emergency responder through simulation technology, working with the Special Weapons and Tactics (SWAT) department, training in the VirTra Firearms Training Simulators as well as scuba diving in Bermuda.

Her interests extend outside the literary: Patricia cofounded the Conservation Scientist Chair at the Harvard University Art Museums. She appears as a forensic consultant on CNN and serves as a member of Harvard-affiliated McLean Hospital's National Council, where she advocates for psychiatric research. She's helped fund the ICU at Cornell's Hospital for Animals, the scientific study of a Confederate submarine, the archaeological excavation of Jamestown and a variety of law-enforcement charities. Patricia is also committed to funding scholarships and literacy programs. Her advice to aspiring authors: "Start writing. And don't take no for an answer."